Aspects
of Educational Technology
Volume XIV

Educational Technology
to the Year 2000

*Edited for the Association for Educational
and Training Technology by*
Roy Winterburn and Leo Evans

General Editor:
A J Trott *Bulmershe College*

**Kogan Page, London/Nichols Publishing
Company, New York**

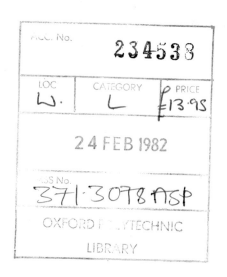
First published 1980
by Kogan Page Limited
120 Pentonville Road, London N1 9JN

Printed in Great Britain by
The Anchor Press Ltd and bound by
Wm Brendon & Son Ltd,
both of Tiptree, Essex

ISBN 0 85038 383 8

British Library Cataloguing in Publication Data
Aspects of Educational Technology

   Volume 14: Educational Technology to the Year 2000.
   I. Educational technology — Congresses
   I. Winterburn, Roy
   II. Evans, Leo
   III. Association for Educational and Training Technology
   371. 3'07'8 LBI028.3
   ISBN 0-85038-383-8

Published in the USA by Nichols Publishing Company
PO Box 96, New York, NY 10024

Contents

Editorial

The conference had as its theme the future of educational technology up until the end of the 20th century. As well as being of considerable significance to current practitioners in giving an overview of possible future developments, ETIC '80 can be regarded as being complementary to ETIC '79, which had reviewed the development and progress of educational technology up to that year.

The trend towards a greater number of practical contributions in workshop or demonstration form, which has been a noticeable feature of past conferences, continued at this one. The diversity of these workshops was encouraging, encompassing as it did the entire range of formal education, preparation for and the actuality of industry, and various other aspects such as health education. By their very nature, though, many workshops are not amenable to a report on paper, so that many which took place at ETIC '80 have not been fully described in this volume.

The co-operation and, particularly, the participation of industrial members of AETT had been actively encouraged before the conference, by holding colloquia at which were devised various categories of topic areas, and for which contributions were sought from persons other than those involved with formal education. This necessitated a rather broader interpretation of educational technology than usual. The principal positive results from this were the two panel sessions; one of these involved representatives from industrial management and the trade unions, while the second had contributions from members of the three branches of the armed forces.

This promotion of industrial training to balance the more usual formal educational emphasis of these conferences was reinforced by Dr Ashworth in his opening address statement that 'education might be considered as that which we can afford to provide, once we have got our training right.'

While both sessions were very successful in terms of liveliness of exchange, it was disappointing how few came to the industrial panel. All of its speakers advocated greater contact between education and industry, but this will depend as much, if not more, on interchange at the grassroots level on occasions such as this conference as on other levels.

This may be as much a problem of conference structure as of lack of interest. The matter of conference structure has been mentioned in previous editorials, but no totally satisfactory format has yet evolved. Parallel streams were designed again this year, but with fewer streams on the first and last days. Topics on one main subject area were kept in sequence in the same stream. This allowed both a wider range of subjects to be encompassed, and those interested in a particular subject to follow it through. A further factor of continuing significance is the refusal of many institutions to finance attendance at a conference unless presenting a paper. This may often preclude the very 'grassroots' practitioners who would gain most from attendance.

The main conference theme was considered by rather fewer contributors than we had hoped, though those who did address it provided significant inputs. There was a tendency by some others to describe where they had got to now, without thinking through to the appropriateness or applicability for the future. Nevertheless, their contributions were such as to be included in this account.

Despite the wide subject spectrum, levels of content and presentation seemed, with some exceptions, to have improved. With regard to content, neither the brief nor the extended abstract provides a reliable guide to the final paper, and neither exhortation nor example seems to improve some presenters! Perhaps the time has come for a full paper submission including media utilization prior to acceptance.

Inevitably, with such a wide range of subject matter, the decision as to which section should hold a particular paper is to some extent arbitrary: many papers could have been regarded as being equally relevant to more than one section heading. We have attempted to balance the content of sections, and to give an abstract at the beginning of most papers. At the end of this volume is a Table which shows papers linked together by common themes.

Leo Evans
Roy Winterburn
The City University, October 1980

Keynote Address

Dr J M Ashworth
Chief Scientist, Central Policy Review Staff

In speaking to the title I was given for this talk, I am very conscious of the perils of making any predictions about the future of educational technology, particularly as the crystal ball I have used does not give a clear picture: the sooner it has a display and print-out unit attached, the easier will talks such as this become.

The Association responsible for this conference includes in its title both education and training, thus drawing a distinction between them. Many have been the attempts made to define and distinguish one from the other, and perhaps you will permit me to make a contribution.

I would suggest that education might be considered as that which we can afford to provide once we have got our training right. We all recognize, I am sure, that a tremendous amount of learning takes place outside of formally established educational institutions. One does not have to be long in the company of children before one realizes how much they learn from television — now almost constantly available — and not always what their mentors might wish! Also, they learn informally subjects which until very recently have been regarded as the prerogative of the schoolroom. My own young children have learned to perform and understand a range of arithmetical operations by 'playing' with a calculator designed for such a purpose. This is made for a mass market, and as such can achieve the economics of scale and consequent lower cost than those produced specifically for schools.

The awareness of the effect of television is very widespread, particularly since Marshall McLuhan postulated the 'Electronic Village'. The use of satellites has made information available on a global basis, and I feel this is impressively illustrated by the use of a single source to transmit, via satellite, programmes to the entire Indian sub-continent.

In more industrially advanced countries, we are seeing the start of another development which will have a far-reaching effect: the combined use of telephone and television to give individually accessible information systems, such as PRESTEL in this country. Using these techniques, it is already possible in some US universities for students to pursue their studies, receive instruction, present course work and take tests, have marks, comment and correction — all without leaving their own room.

It is possible to extend this on a more open basis, so that we may not need to move from home in order to study at, for example, a distant university. Learning will become much more open, less formalized and potentially more readily available as a result of these innovations: translating the potential into reality is very dependent on the resources available.

Playing a vital role in these developments, computer technology is already producing changes in education and training. These will have a step function effect in the near future, as micro-circuiting and mass production bring the 'personal computer' from the realms of sci-fi to be as common, or more common, than hi-fi.

There can be no doubt that educational planners and practitioners will need to solve problems of a different nature and order from those which have faced them in the past decade. The world economic climate must inevitably affect the resources which can be made available.

Provided the enhanced communication and learning opportunities are used responsibly, great benefits may arise. There are considerable dangers, though, of producing tensions and possible conflict, particularly as the contrasts between resources and living standards in different countries become more widely known.

The brief which I was given was a difficult one. Changes and developments take place so rapidly that, whilst it is possible to hazard reasonable guesses over the coming decade, the following decade to the year 2000 is still more than misty. I am sure that the contributors of papers and workshops, and some of the demonstrations in the exhibition, will add to and extend the view that I have given. I express my appreciation of the invitation to deliver this opening address and hope that you have an illuminating and interesting conference.

Section 1:
Preparation and Training for Industry and the Services

1.1 The Higher Education/Industrial Training Interface: Panel Session

Ron Brown *National Computing Centre, Manchester*
John R Foster *National Organizer AUEW*
Brian T Lusher *Carreras Rothmans Ltd*
Frank Shaw *British Leyland Cars*
Sue Ward *(Chairman) Control Data Corporation, London*

Historical Perspective   *Brian T Lusher Carreras Rothmans Ltd*

The most cursory literature search reveals that the British have been preoccupied with the problems of education and training, particularly technical and professional, for at least the last century. A few quotations serve to illustrate this.

> The education which fits men to perform their duties in life is not to be got in school but in the counting-house and lawyer's office, in the shop or the factory.
>
> (The *Economist,* 1880)

The general tenor of comments at that time tends to be similar and reveals an already well-established prejudice against academic education as preparation for a career in industry and commerce. As, however, Britain's industrial lead (largely a result of a series of historical coincidences) diminished over the next half-century, increasing attention was paid to career preparation:

> Not a few censors have dilated upon the disadvantages from which young Englishmen suffer in industry and commerce owing to the superior preparation of their competitors in several countries of Continental Europe. These disadvantages are real.
>
> (Royal Commission on Secondary Education: *Report,* 1895)

The main disadvantages then, as now, were a general lack of technical knowledge and skills, poor use of languages other than English and a distinct lack of skill in managing people.

Ten years earlier, the Second Report of the Royal Commission on Technical Education had stated:

> Your commissioners cannot repeat too often that they have been impressed with the general intelligence and technical knowledge of the masters and managers of industrial establishments on the Continent.

Nearly a century later, the Plowden Report (1967) pointed out:

> Comparisons with other countries . . . (at a similar stage of economic development) . . .
> suggest we have not done well enough to provide the educational background necessary
> to support our economy, which needs fewer and fewer unskilled workers and increasing
> numbers of skilled and adaptable people.

Within that 100 years we had created in the UK a mass education system, with a
considerable number of layers and institutions. The technical college system, using
the syllabuses and systems of organizations like the City and Guilds of London
Institutions, has processed large numbers of people, mostly at the skilled craftsman
level. Most of this educative effort has tended to be locally based and narrowly
biased to a particular industry or craft. This was one reason why the Training
Services Agency in its report 'A Five Year Plan' in 1974 was forced to conclude:

> As it currently exists, the system has limited institutional means for aiding the mobility
> of labour between industries or between occupations, nor can it readily adjust to the
> decline of some industries and the rapid growth of others. Nationally accepted minimum
> standards of competence do not exist for certain important occupations that are found
> in many sectors of employment.

This was, of course, about the time that the then government, in an unexpected
and unscheduled diversion of effort, pushed the Manpower Services Commission
to spend most of its energies and resources on dealing with short-term schemes to
disguise, but not always to deal with, problems of rising unemployment. This
meant the MSC had difficulty in coping with its appointed task of long-term
planning for the nation's manpower needs.

There are so many reports in similar vein, both official and private, that it is
impossible to quote from them all.

The only optimistic report to be encountered is that of the Balfour Commission
on Industry and Trade in 1929 which concluded that it was: '. . . likely that the
numbers of men trained in the universities and larger technical colleges will not
only suffice for senior technical posts but will also extend to posts of lower grade.'

Less than 10 years later the re-armament programme revealed great shortages of
skilled technical people.

All the evidence suggests that we do not produce enough people with the proper
educational basis to pursue a career of excellence in technically based occupations.
This country lives by trade: more, it lives by trade in manufactured goods. In 1978,
of £42,000,000,000 of exports, £30,000,000,000 were manufactured goods. There
is no prospect of replacing earnings at this level by any other means. To sustain,
let alone develop and expand, this essential economic base means that manufacturing
industry needs a supply of the best people at every level.

There are a number of things we can do, if we wish. We have a lot of people in
manufacturing industries now. The model of the Open University has proved itself.
There must be a way of combining distance learning techniques with industry's
needs: although funds are short, it should be possible for us, jointly, in education
and industry to extend and improve the few schemes we currently have.

We can improve existing secondment arrangements between education and
industry, as well as industrial representation on syllabus bodies (such as BEC and
TEC).

Industry should spend more effort on evaluating the performance of their skilled
and highly educated entrants so as to obtain specific recommendations for
improvement in the education of those who follow. We can all, as citizens relying
in the last resorts on the UK's success economically, put more effort into
improving the social status of people working in industry.

A Personal View

There are many positive things we could do to improve the relationships between education, professional training and industry. Perhaps the Finniston proposals will achieve it for engineering.

However, I suspect that in the traditional British way, we will compromise, seek the middle way, not get too emotional about things, emphasize what a good country we live in, as 'we can fairly claim that in no other great industrial nation have (political and social changes) . . . been so consistent with the maintenance of . . . social and human values . . . this is why ours is a great country to live in. Our problem is to be efficient and yet remain "nice people".' (Sir Joseph Hunt, 1978).

If we do, we will go on being a contented nation declining gracefully in the West like all those who before us failed to see that the world had moved away.

Frank Shaw, British Leyland
The main theme of this conference is the interface between graduation and subsequent training in a profession, and it is apparent that training cannot be completely divorced from education. Before going on to comment on and make recommendations for a system of guidance from sixth-form, through the industrial stage, and in and beyond the university system, I wish briefly to mention primary education, as I regard this as being of prime importance as it should provide a foundation for all subsequent formal learning.

The educational system has tended to produce what one might term computerized robots, quite capable of operating advanced technological systems once they are set in motion, but quite incapable of understanding why they are doing so. For a long time, the illusion has existed that education for its own sake is commendable and proper, especially if it is free, and, that, the more education we have, the more prosperous and happy we will become as a nation. As a result of this, and against the wishes of both pupils and the majority of teachers, the school leaving age was raised. This resulted in an abnormal enlargement of sixth-form classes to the benefit of no one, and in the introduction of nursery schools, together with an elementary and primary system, which can never achieve the effectiveness of the first-class primary education of yesteryear.

It was the fault of the system and not of individuals that the highly qualified, dedicated teachers who were once found in the primary areas were moved to expanding higher school sectors. With them went an expertise with young people.

How is it possible for young people to grow up with a full awareness of the true values of human behaviour, and of their social responsibilities, if these are not demonstrated and instilled during the formative years, and developed throughout the whole training period?

On completion of schooling, the number of leavers with a burning desire to pursue the achievement of intellectual excellence does not match the increase to 60,000-70,000 university places each year. It is not reasonable that each year's school output can provide this number of applicants suited to this sort of academic pressure: the net result has been to lower the degree standard. The pressure exerted on unwilling young people to induce them to enter university means that many of these students do not then have the ability to meet up to industry's requirements. A degree obtained is not a job ensured.

Fortunately, there is a new awareness of the inadequacies of the current primary sector in education. Also, there are signs that the universities are improving their selection procedures and then caring more for their students and graduates. The quality of graduates coming into engineering improves each year, but we would like to see amongst them more female engineers — contrary to belief, gender is not significant for success in the engineering industry.

There is a long history of fairly unproductive dialogues between industry and universities, in which industry has tried to say what it wants to universities, and over the same period universities have tried to meet needs which they are unable to identify. The tendency to follow the latest 'ology' should be resisted. The role of universities is to build on a sound primary education and to teach people to think clearly and logically.

Graduates should then come to industry with a thorough understanding of the humanities and the fundamentals of whichever discipline they are following. Above all, they must have been trained and guided to use their brain which caused them to be selected initially. Their ability to see through a problem is the one major advantage which graduates should have over others. If industry will take a role in the selection and sponsoring of students, the universities can prepare students for their future industrial careers. It is up to industry then to train the resulting graduates to use their ability to good and effective purpose.

Having completed training, it should then be necessary to follow a well arranged career development route, which must include management training both within and outside the company. Although this is primarily a company responsibility, the institutions must take a prominent role by ensuring that all the previous preparation is not prejudiced by a tendency to get stuck in a limited field for too long. The institutions should also ensure that the means for a continuing updating of knowledge and skills is available.

To summarize, I believe that it is necessary to be educated well, particularly at the primary stage. Primary sectors should have improvements imposed upon them if necessary. Industrial experience should be given, with complete sponsoring, prior to university. At university, the student should be tutored with both depth and understanding: he should develop the ability to think well and effectively. Industry must then be prepared to train for the job, while the institutions should assist and guide career development and provide the means for continual updating of knowledge and skills. Through a monitored route to corporate membership, they must be the guardians of the entire education and training process, in order both to satisfy their requirements and to ensure that it is carried out correctly.

I believe that it is necessary to select better initially, and to check the selection at each subsequent stage — we may then see the results for which we crave. Human beings have changed less over the centuries than we are led to believe. It is not people who are at fault, it is the system. Only we who are interested will manage to change it for the better.

I think it is the duty of those of us who can do so to see that the training which modern youth is given will fit it better for the task ahead of it.

Ron Brown, National Computing Centre, Manchester
In my role of Manager in the Education and Training Liaison Division at NCC, I embrace an activity known as 'Schools/Industry Links'. My experiences in this area prompt me to ask how early in education should one pay any real attention to its relationship with industry? Certainly at secondary level there is the problem as to whether a given student is to be prepared for entry into industry or for tertiary education. This question could, and often does, provoke lengthy debate around — what is education — what is training — who does which and when? However, I will resist the temptation to tread that path in general terms and attempt to address a few fundamentals arising from associating my field (computing) with education and training and the theme of this conference, looking forward towards the year 2000.

As a starting point, consider the interface between education and the world of work. In this country, we have a serious and ever-worsening situation of unemployment, but at the same time serious shortages in a number of trades and professions. In simple terms we are playing a 'numbers game' very badly in so far as the education system is pushing out too many people of the wrong type at the wrong time in the wrong areas.

Now consider the computer and its proven, beneficial applications in planning, analyzing and forecasting. Consider also that it is rapidly becoming smaller, ever cheaper and therefore more readily available. Should it not therefore be extensively applied in improving our attempts to balance out this 'numbers game'?

On the one side, the 'world of work' should be able to make great improvements in planning and forecasting its manpower requirements. On the other, in the world of education the early application of aptitude testing and the timely input of industry's forecasts should produce more accurate correlation and greater ability to continually adjust to variables.

At the moment, in terms of curriculum/timetabling etc, it would appear that the system is extremely inflexible and incapable of rapid adjustment. There is continual acknowledgement of the need to incorporate new technology into the curriculum. This can be done (although it is a very slow process) when new technology is incorporated as a main subject, when it gains respectability with an examination at the end of the course. Unfortunately, the requirement is all too often an 'awareness for all' across the curriculum, which everybody acknowledges is absolutely essential (and impossible).

There is, of course, the immediate argument that you cannot put a quart into a pint pot when curriculum is so overloaded, nor take a quart out when related to insufficient teachers with the required expertise. This could initiate a number of arguments, one of which is a main theme of this whole session: should we not restrict schools to pure education and make training the total responsibility of industry? In its recent report, 'Employment and Technology', the TUC stressed this and also went on to state that: 'compulsory schooling should give young people a broad preparation for working life including preparing them to undertake subsequent vocational training'.

Relating computers to problems of overload and inadequate resources raises the question of whether one might do more in the application of computers to increase efficiency in the school system. There are two broad areas of application, namely:

1. administration and management (planning, organizing, scheduling etc);
2. educational technology (computer-assisted learning/instruction etc).

With reference to the latter, surveys have shown that appropriate use of individual instruction can bring about considerable compression in learning time (about 35 per cent). The image of the computer as a sophisticated turner of pages or, at most, a machine which can teach about itself (programming) or train staff in the operation of its systems, is about to be dispelled rapidly by the proliferation of inexpensive and powerful computer facilities. The computer in instructional mode can certainly achieve the compression claimed for individualized instruction and this can be exploited both in development of teachers and education of students. A further important facet of this is the wonderful opportunity for simulation and modelling made available by micro-computers. In many respect one can say this almost brings 'industry' into the classroom.

Obviously, there are many possibilities to be explored by way of applying computers in the education area in order to achieve greater efficiency and flexibility. Assuming that one achieved marked improvements and, using industrial terminology, the result is greater 'productivity', could one anticipate better pay for teachers? It is surely important to consider whether higher pay and more interesting techniques will encourage more of the right calibre of people into teaching rather than thinking along the lines that new methods and techniques will reduce the number of teachers required.

The present situation in teaching reflects the general situation in that it is a picture of unemployment, cut-backs and redundancies, coupled with an acute shortage of specialist teachers. In addition to the shortage in science and maths, I understand there is an acute shortage of foreign language teachers. As a result I read recently that modern European languages are amongst the dying subjects in schools. This seems a strange contradiction to the idea that the EEC should loom large in our world of tomorrow. The idea of exchange teacher schemes within the EEC to facilitate language teaching has apparently run into difficulties, one of the problems being that teachers' salaries are much lower here than on the Continent. Perhaps it is a little too much to anticipate the computer contributing towards improved pay and also facilitating the training of teachers to teach English as a foreign language.

Having briefly pursued the idea of the combination of education and computers being better able to prepare and supply people into the world of work, I suggest it is necessary to step back and take a look at the broad scenario within which one is playing.

An individual has supposedly 70 years of existence, and within this from the age of five years he has 10-15 years of formal education, then up to 45 years of working life. There are current and projected trends and, in some cases, forces distorting this framework. For instance, micro-technology is already producing effective, attractive and cheap teaching machines. To take one example, a machine costing about £30 to teach simple arithmetic might prove so fascinating to a child of three that at five years old (on entering school) he or she was already at the standard of a seven-year old. So, effective education is liable to start earlier and, of course, there are all sorts of reasons for delaying school-leaving.

In the 1980s, working life is liable to start later and finish earlier than in previous years and within it the actual time at work is liable to be ever shorter. It is also liable to be increasingly fragmented because, in addition to all the generally accepted reasons for change, it is anticipated that many people will be required to change trades and skills in mid-career. This will reflect the ever-rapidly advancing and changing technology. We have already experienced the tip of this iceberg in the requirement to train thousands of mid-career engineers in micro-technology. We were not prepared for this, and there is little evidence to suggest that we have analyzed the problem or implemented realistic solutions in an appropriate time-scale. I find it somewhat ironic that today one can readily hang a large question mark over industry's ability to handle its own training problems, whereas yesterday in this conference a speaker was reporting instances of large corporations (Mitchell, paper 11.3) operating their own accredited degree courses. Furthermore, he was questioning the effect of such corporations making their educational facilities generally available by operating in a similar fashion to the Open University.

As a final reference to the background life cycle, if all this power, control and flexibility is becoming available, do we need to continue with a system based on compulsory schooling taking place in the first 15-20 years on a continuous basis? This is particularly debatable against a background of speculation as to whether there will be a world of work in existence at all for most of us, let alone 45 years of it.

Whatever our views on that subject, there seems to be general agreement that new technology will have far-reaching effects which will be sufficient to raise the question of the need for national policies of control. Perhaps this can best be introduced by a simple diagram based on the two extremes of uncontrolled adoption and of prohibition.

Economic pressures, both national and international, will tend to force new technology into industry. Against new technology there are many forms of 'luddites'. At this conference there have been instances when educational technologists have tended to remark impatiently as to technology pushing its

Figure 1.

unwelcome inventions into education. There is also no lack of awareness concerning that paramount controller — money. Unfortunately this seems to be constantly and unacceptably restrictive.

In conclusion, I came into this micro-revolution little more than a year ago after spending most of the previous four years working in developing countries. As a result of this perhaps I am a little too sensitive concerning something that is popularly known as 'transfer of technology'. There have been situations that would have been better termed exploitation but not always just seller exploiting buyer — rather both exploiting the situation. Very often in the Middle East there are situations where money is not a controlling factor (in so far as it is not too restrictive) and the order of the day is 'massive', rather than 'appropriate', transfer of technology based on the philosophy that as there is so much to catch up on it is impossible to overload the situation. In reality, there can be so much of an overload that the result is not only no improvement but the achievement of chaos. I suggest it is pertinent here to consider how much a totally inappropriate transfer of technology contributed to the overthrow of what was, in part, an elitist bunch of technocrats by a disillusioned mass.

We in the UK have a sophisticated education and training system which appears to work in close association with a sophisticated industrial and commercial complex. It appears that way to the outsider, at any rate. There is also little doubt that we are on the threshold of revolutionary new technology. I strongly recommend that we make every effort to ensure that its transfer into education, as well as into industry and commerce, be very appropriate. The eventual consequences of either 'massive' or 'inadequate' transfer are, to my mind, unthinkable.

John R Foster, National Organizer of the AUEW

Most speakers during the course of this conference will have addressed the meeting as professionals in their subject. My attendance is as a full-time trade union official in a union (AUEW) having a membership of 1,250,000 in the engineering industry which employs approximately 3,250,000 workers in the United Kingdom.

As trade unionists we are as conscious, as are other sections of the community, of the tremendous contribution that education at all levels and industrial training have played in the life of our society.

But education in its fullest sense, and as practised in advanced societies, can be divisive. Learning and knowledge have provided status symbols and privilege for those best able to take advantage of their facilities. They reap a greater benefit from society in terms of income, standards and dignity — at the expense of the under-privileged and untaught.

Some will disagree with this assessment of the educational advances in our society, but they cannot disagree that the division (between the educated and uneducated) appears more so today than ever before. The world is divided between the North and the South in global terms, as set out in the 'Brandt' report, whose commissioners first met in Bonn in December 1977 and who adopted as terms of reference the problem I wish to address myself to today, which is:

To study the grave global issues arising from the economical and social disparities of the world community.

Most people recognize that there is a divided world. What may not also be recognized is that even in the most technologically advanced nations there is division. In addition, nobody can turn his face away from the emerging problems and demands of the third world which hungers for the benefits and privileges that an industrial society bestows upon some of its people.

New technology is accelerating in pace. At the same time there is mass unemployment. Even people in government circles in the UK acknowledge that the figures may reach 3,000,000, maybe 3,250,000 within the foreseeable future. These two facts may be coupled with far-reaching cuts at the very foundations of our society in education, health and housing which have a direct impact upon young people throughout the nation, with a greater emphasis in the very depressed industrial areas out of proportion to the rest of the country.

The Times on 27 March 1980 referred to an article in the 'Employment Gazette' based upon the Department of Employment's study which shows that youth unemployment is greatly enhanced in comparison to other unemployed groups in society when the economy enters a recession. This article submits that for every 1 per cent rise in total unemployment there will be a 1.7 per cent rise in unemployment amongst males under 20. The pattern is even more marked for women, with a 1 per cent rise in female unemployment leading to a 3 per cent rise in unemployment amongst women under 20. The reasons young people are particularly hard hit by the recession is that they start out with no jobs or are likely to try to change jobs frequently and they are thus particularly vulnerable to a decision by employers not to take on new workers.

What then has education in a society such as ours done to resolve that problem? It has been acknowledged that the present government considers that, as a result of unemployment and cut-backs, each individual will now battle harder in order to achieve a place, and this experience, while creating a leaner person, will help to make him healthier. Individual ability is the keystone to success; unfortunately it is always at the expense of some other individual. It is said that what is symptomatic of Britain's problems is 'The British Disease', that is: slow to learn, slow to accommodate advances in technology, reactionary and content to live upon an old colonial empire tradition.

These problems are not symptomatic of Britain alone. Low growth and inflation are root causes which are now international and which affect all societies, even the most advanced industrial nations.

Another factor to be taken into consideration is the now well-established transnational corporations or conglomerates which exert considerable influence on growth rate and manning levels. Such problems have a direct effect upon the benefits or application of education and training.

There are also the profits of leading banks, oil and chemical companies to be considered; while they have plans for further development we envisage significant difficulties in their maintaining their present standards and employment.

It is time to put the next question to those still in school and those seeking appointments to some occupation and needing further education. What purpose does this education serve? Is it for you, me, them or us? This question is very relevant to our argument about the future.

Collective Bargaining in all Factors

The trade union and labour movement has consistently focused upon the 'us' and 'we'. In the 20th, and well into the 21st century, the important issue must be as to how we can develop and extend the principle of the collective so that the individual is able to fit his individualism into the collective for the benefit of the collective.

The post-war years have seen the initiation and development of this theory of the collective; organized labour has projected in practical terms the manner in which the individual will become involved with the decision-making processes and actively participate in industrial democracy, both of which are central to collective bargaining. As trade unionists we argue that, as we have increased our understanding for the collective, educationalists must accept our view as to the manner in which education is developed and used. If our approach is not accepted, then there is a great danger that the backlash arising from an inability to be involved, coupled with being deprived and with being unemployed, will have a dramatic effect upon the type of society so far developed.

The Communicative Society

In coming to terms with this new society we have to consider the relevance of education and training on workers, with particular regard to microprocessors and robots.

The International Metal Workers Federation met in Vienna in October 1979, and considered submissions by Professor Tom Stonier from Bradford University who suggested that the technologically advanced sector of global society (that is, the West and other OECD countries) has moved into the communicative society characterized by the following features:

1. There is a high level of physical communications technology, including a high *per capita* ownership of television sets, radios, etc.
2. There is a large percentage of information operatives in the labour force, exceeding those working on farms and in factories.
3. The social and political manifestations of the first two features are:
   (i) An increase in democratization and consensus decision-making.
   (ii) An increasingly peaceful society both nationally and internationally.

Agreement for Change

Organized labour now poses to industry the need for technological agreements in order to negotiate and determine how and under what conditions control, knowledge, and change can take place. Implicit within these technological agreements will be education, training and retraining.

Change brings problems and a vital necessity for understanding the concept of change and its acceptability in such craft-based industries as engineering. It throws into question traditions and attitudes but also provides opportunities which require the trade unions to open up.

Within the engineering industry, and through the medium of the Engineering Industries Training Board, attempts have been made to come to grips with and to rectify the problem of change.

The industry put out for consultation, within an 'Information Paper', 49 proposals which included some vocational education in the latter years of full-time education to improve on mathematics and English, and a simple two-year apprenticeship to establish a basic skill status. The 49 proposals were put to over 2,000 representatives of industry, education and trade unions at conferences throughout the country over a period of some six months. The majority of these representatives were against the concept. The AUEW considered the concept's effect upon the traditions of craft apprenticeship and job opportunity and unanimously rejected the proposals.

This is the setting against which we approach training within the engineering industry.

Industrial Training

The present industrial training system in Great Britain is founded upon three central principles:

1. Training is the responsibility of employers.
2. There should exist bodies at national and industry/sectoral levels to monitor training performance in terms of quantity, quality and cost. These bodies should have instruments available to them to directly influence employers.
3. These national and sectoral agencies should be formally co-operative in nature, allowing trade unionists and educationalists as well as employers to have some say in how training is conducted.

This framework is unsatisfactory to trade unionists, although it is, of course, a vast improvement upon the position which pertained before the 1964 Industrial Training Act.

Imperfections in the System

INDUSTRIAL DEMOCRACY

AUEW (E) policy on industrial democracy underlines that it is the strategic extension of collective bargaining at the workplace (rather than workers on the board etc) which will give employees any real control over their working lives. At the present time training is a management prerogative, but just as other areas of prerogative (wages and conditions etc) have been eroded, so will management control over training. Training should, therefore, become as normal and natural a part of negotiation as bargaining over wages and conditions.

Training is assumed to improve both company performance and individual performance. It alters individuals' aspirations and perceptions. It offers the opportunity for career advancement, for example. Training can also bring about increased satisfaction from work, ie it affects personal development.

Training is, therefore, important both to the company *and* the individual. In both areas trade unions demand the opportunity to advance and defend their members' interests. Training, therefore, must become a legitimate area of collective bargaining.

Industrial Training Boards and the Manpower Services Commission

The present system of training through ITBs with the Manpower Services Commission is no longer a major impetus to training.

The system was set up because employers did not train, or trained badly despite it being agreed that training was, in itself, intuitively a 'good thing'. Employers have always cut corners in training, eg reduced intake of apprentices during depressions. We therefore need bodies to take a longer term view than the immediate commercial horizon. ITBs and the MSC do this, but their ability to influence employers has been severely weakened since the introduction of the Employment and Training Act, 1973.

A review of this Act (currently being undertaken by the MSC) should, we suggest, lead to:

(a) the readoption of national targets for the recruitment of craft and technical workers;
(b) the recognition of the high cost of initial training and, therefore, the provision of state support, ie collective funding;
(c) a higher levy than one per cent to bring about a real deterrent to non-training.

The Future of Industrial Training

At the present time, industrial training is suffering a twofold attack. This is in the form of:

(a) The government-induced contraction of the UK manufacturing base leading to immediate pressure on training programmes. Depending on whose forecast you read, national output will fall by three to five per cent this year and next recruitment at all levels of company intake will stop and a vast programme of redundancies will begin. Unemployment at 2,000,000 will be upon us soon. This is causing a backlash to appear among workers in depressed areas who say: 'Why co-operate over training or retraining? Why move house? Stay, fight and occupy the plant — that's positive.'

(b) The education sector cuts as part of the present government's programme of reducing public expenditure. (That is: £55,000,000 plus three per cent cuts in manpower costs in July 1979, £280,000,000 in November 1979.)

Cuts of this severity are bound to reduce the effectiveness of the education sector. Graduates and school leavers may, as a result, be less well educated and will be faced with fewer employment opportunities in the labour market.

In this sort of situation, philosophical questions about whether education should be responsive to the needs of industry tend to be forgotten. But this is an important question, particularly because the industrial society of the future is going to be based on high technology which may require rapid adaption to a new set of skills, and we submit that all sections must be involved in the decision-making procedures to ensure a positive future.

As a preliminary framework for that situation, it seems vital that school children should have some understanding of the world of work and industrial society. In particular, this could be best achieved by the interchange of personnel between the education sector and industry (including trade unionists).

At higher levels of education, courses should be based on more practical and problem-solving techniques rather than on the absorption of theoretical knowledge. This is a question of the *mix* between theory and practice *not* one rather than the other. The practical side of courses should be responsive to the needs of industry.

Finance

Industrial training depends on the level of funding. But how do you organize industrial training if:

(a) the manufacturing sector cuts back its training programme owing to poor economic performance? This would indicate a greater role for state-funded employment and training programmes; however,

(b) public sector provision is reduced because of poor national economic performance.

It is a vicious circle. To break into the circle public sector provision must be used as a pump priming device to initiate private sector development.

For example, training programmes for the unemployed must be expanded to allow career change and re-skilling. Without this provision a whole generation of graduates and school-leavers could find themselves in enforced idleness waiting for a new industrial revolution riding on the back of the microprocessor.

1.2 Innovation in Military Training: Panel Session

B J Hurn *RAEC (Ministry of Defence)*
B D Hilton *RAEC (Army School of Instructional Technology)*
M Easby *RAF (School of Education)*
B Drinkall *RN (Royal Navy School of Educational and Training Technology)*
N J Rushby *(Chairman) CEDAR Project, Imperial College*

Abstract: As an alternative to the 'future study' approach of predicting what should, and what will, happen in instructional technology over the next 20 years this paper takes a look at some past experiences to examine what happened and why, with the aim of helping us to plan effectively for the future. Usually we hear only about those projects which have been successful. This is unfortunate because we can learn as much, if not more, from projects which have failed or were only partially successful. In this paper we take a candid look at some of the recent innovations in military training — the Army, the Royal Air Force, and the Royal Navy.

Introduction

It can be argued that the prime function of the three armed forces of the United Kingdom in peacetime is to train for war. The majority of our resources (manpower, material and financial) are devoted to training and thereby maintaining the forces' state of readiness and morale. Furthermore, there is a very real need to search for new ideas and methods to maintain their professionalism and make training realistic and effective.

We in the armed forces have therefore had a number of opportunities to engage in innovation. We also have, in relative terms, a degree of flexibility, albeit within our financial constraints, because we are all part of an organization whose essence is training. As a result we spend considerable time and effort in attempting to keep abreast of developments in training technology. We must constantly strive to remain ahead of our rivals in the profession we practise, and search for any improvements we can make in our training to go towards the achievement of our overall goal.

The aim of this paper is to highlight some of the problems we have encountered in the Services when attempting to introduce innovation. These will be familiar to many readers and we only wish to reinforce them from our own experiences in training technology. But before we discuss work in the individual Services let us first look briefly at some fundamental problems that appear to be common to most situations when an attempt is made to implement new technology.

Firstly, there is the problem of organizational development. Innovation inevitably means change. Change in any one part of a training organization will sooner or later affect the entire organization, and so attention must be given to making innovation acceptable within the organization.

Cost is always a prime factor. The more costly a project turns out to be, the more apparent is the commitment to it. This in turn produces a dangerous situation and over-complimentary reports are the classic result. The more expensive it becomes, the more intent the policy-makers are on ensuring that it should be seen to succeed. Allied to problems of cost is what might be called the 'bandwagon syndrome'. That is: 'a project costs a lot, therefore it must be good. He's got it, we should have it!' This is an example of the fallacy that presupposes the training requirements of one organization are necessarily the same as those of another.

Innovation will very often incur a certain amount of R & D expenditure of funds and use of resources which are not always acceptable to either the financier or the ultimate user. The acceptability of possible failure in research and development is a difficult philosophy to put across but sometimes it is essential to prepare for the fact that it might not work first time and further development may be required.

Another prime requisite is continuity, particularly of personnel vitally involved in the project. This is, of course, an acute problem for all three Services where we seldom spend more than two or three years in any one appointment.

We have found that innovation is much more likely to succeed if the existing training system is soundly based — if, for example, it has proper training objectives based on a comprehensive job analysis. Innovation is very often the development of a new system of thinking about the training problem, rather than the introduction of new hardware.

Innovation is usually more successful when it arises as a result of a locally perceived need rather than by an imposition from a higher authority. Equally, as change is not always popular, there is a need for the right spirit to prevail before innovation can take place. Here, we in the armed forces see a vital role for our training consultants who are usually associated with a training technology project at an early stage. We see the consultant's interpersonal and diagnostic skills as being of paramount importance in the development of a project. In the first phases he is often acting as a change agent and as a catalyst, whose aim is to help the organization establish exactly what its training problems are and to begin to formulate ways of overcoming them. While continuity is particularly important, both the project and the consultant must be aware of the dangers of the project becoming personality dependent.

Christopher Evans, when referring to the problems of introducing innovation, says:

> Human inertia may be the most significant inhibiting force of all. Getting a novel technique or working strategy introduced into any large organization takes much longer than one expected it to, because of inertia in all its multifarious forms. It can vary from simple, dumb resistance and heel-dragging, to laziness, inefficiency or muddle, and has very powerful braking effects. But even the most entrenched inertia can be rendered ineffective when the innovative forces have sufficient strength (Evans, 1979).

Innovation in Army Training

The introduction of the Systems Approach to training in the Army has meant considerable change in a very well-established organization. There has been much expression of the feeling that we know how to do it because we have always done it — experience predominates. The intervention of training technologists as change agents has been resisted in a number of ways.

Objective Training

One of the first systematic attempts to design objective training in the army was carried out on clerks' training. A careful and detailed job analysis resulted in a redesigned self-paced course, leaning heavily on programmed learning. Large sums of money were saved, and criterion tests showed that the agreed training objectives were being met by the new system. However, this change was not always welcome, or understood. Users were surprised to get their trainees back early; the Army expects a six-week course to last that long and self-paced courses puzzled them.

Secondly, the careful design of the course, and its accurate testing produced many A-grade passes rather than the more usual spread of A to E. In fact over 80 per cent of students were graded A, a tribute to the effectiveness of the design.

The result of this, however, was that A-grade men were regarded as high flyers, as they always had been, and were given the most difficult tasks regardless of whether their training had prepared them. Their relative failure was then blamed on the programmed course and it was discredited.

Computer-Based Training

In our attempts to introduce ADP in training we co-operated with the National Development Programme in Computer Assisted Learning and helped in the development of the ICI CAMOL system (Rushby *et al*, 1976). This was trialled in a major training establishment which needed control of students on a complex of courses. A training technologist was put in to lead the project and eventually a mini-computer and a modified form of CAMOL was introduced. The change affected a team of examiners (quality controllers) and gave them time to supervise students rather than driving a complex testing and recording system. The trouble arose in this project with a change in its leadership. The training technologist, his job done, handed over to a unit project manager who was an ADP trained man but was not himself a trained or experienced trainer. Management changes to the computer system and the use of the facility for other non-training tasks began to degrade its service to the trainers and they reverted to their 'quicker' manual system. It appears that the fault here lay in three areas:

1. Lack of top management commitment to ensure the system was properly used.
2. Lack of training expertise on the part of specialist ADP management.
3. Lack of training of the quality controller in support of trainers so that they reverted to the more familiar (comfortable) clerical control of training.

Closed Circuit Television (CCTV)

Closed circuit television has been in use in the Army for some 12 years. Its introduction was interesting in that it tended to rely upon a band of enthusiasts, both in a central facility and in various training units. Despite the attempts of the central facility to encourage the proper use of TV, it was often seen as a sort of photographic record of normal training lectures and demonstrations to be played to larger overflow audiences or at later sessions. No real attempt was made to set up specially for TV. In several units extensive piped TV was installed with a studio or distribution point, resulting in very inflexible systems with frequent breakdowns. In CCTV, too, there was the idea that a 'show' must be made — half-hour programmes with music, credits, and production gimmicks to display artistic production. This led to attempts at documentary films on video-tape intended to stand alone as instructional packages.

This, we are glad to say, has changed. By dint of persuasion, demonstration and training we have encouraged the unique use of TV, for example to provide instant replay of skills, of military exercises, micro-teaching and, in particular, the production of video-tapes to be used as part of instruction supported by the instructor or other media — rather than as a *magnum opus*. In this case, at first the medium was not understood. It took time to settle and find its most effective role in training.

This role dictates that television should be no different from any other visual aid or piece of equipment in the classroom. We must overcome the monetary reluctance which encourages us towards high utilization of expensive facilities. Given this attitude we can distinguish three kinds of video presentation:

(a) The snapshot which is created locally to show real action to the trainee. An example would be to demonstrate the tying of knots, which is much easier to understand through the eye of a camera looking over the expert's shoulder than from in front.

(b) The home movies which make no pretensions to being 20-minute training sagas, and are of less than award winning quality, yet are successful in the classroom.

(c) The training epic, traditionally produced on celluloid but now available in video format. This makes them easier to use with small groups in undarkened rooms (we understand that soldiers, sailors and airmen do strange things in darkened classrooms — like sleep!). The days of the training cinema have ended and most new training schools do not have cinemas.

Problems

Time is a problem in innovation because of our funding and procurement system. Whenever any equipment is required it must be bid for in the autumn of, say, 1979 for consideration in spring of 1980, to be put into costings for the 1981-82 financial year. Add to this the system of Army postings which moves us every two or three years, and you will see that the instigator of a new idea can be gone before the wherewithal to implement it has been provided. We try to help by setting up pools of likely equipment, CCTV, micros, projectors etc, and we keep some of the current year's money in hand to meet the essential or brilliant ideas. But herein is delay, during which innovation goes off the boil.

We are convinced that innovation is highly dependent on people. It is necessary to convince top management, have an enthusiast and give him support particularly in his attempt to explain the innovation to those affected, provide resources, but above all apply a Systems Approach to the innovation. Define objectives to meet an identified requirement, select methods to meet that requirement, try out the innovation and validate and evaluate what you have done.

Finally, although it may offend the purists, we have to accept that face validity of innovation may help its initial acceptance. It needs to look good, feel good and perhaps, say in the case of simulation, look a bit more 'real' than transfer of training really demands. In our terms it must have a martial flavour and even perhaps have an element of fun. If this is the price, we will pay it to get acceptance of change.

Effective Training in the RAF

Effective training is the cornerstone of the RAF's ability to carry out its tasks in peace and war. Naturally, much of our training is carried out in the air, but since our inception in 1918 we have prided ourselves on the provision of management training as well as operational training. We believe in a progressive pattern of management training to equip our officers for the many and varied management duties which they will be called upon to perform throughout their service careers. As needs change, then our training must have the flexibility to adapt to the changing requirements. Such was the situation in 1972, when it was recognized that there was a need to train our squadron leaders, our first echelon of top management, in the skills, knowledge and attitudes they would require for command and staff appointments appropriate to their rank.

The Selective Studies Centre

The solution to this training problem envisaged an entirely new residential course of one month's duration to be held at the Royal Air Force Staff College at Bracknell. The training strategy of the new course included an individual learning centre — called the Selective Studies Centre which soon became known by its initials as the SSC. In this section we will present our solutions to some of the problems encountered in the organization, implementation and development of this innovation — an innovation which relied on a high degree of training technology.

The Centre enables students to study in their own time without a tutor, and yet to enjoy some of the benefits of individual tuition. Here, they can refresh their knowledge, extend their appreciation of defence matters and identify and remedy their weaknesses in the fundamental staff skills without sacrificing course time and instructor effort. The Centre offers two additional advantages. First, it can house, in pre-recorded form, presentations and lectures by recognized authorities who would find it difficult to commit themselves to a monthly speaking engagement. Secondly, the resources of the Centre are available for all staff college students and the directing staff.

A centre where students learn independently and in their own time demands both an environment conducive to study and equipment which the students can operate with confidence. Situated in the College library, the surroundings of the Centre are fully in keeping with the high standard of the College tutorial accommodation. The Centre itself comprises 12 learning positions, or carrells, arranged to facilitate individual study. Initially, the College installed a wide variety of teaching machines at a cost of £8,000. This cost has quickly amortized since 300 students use the facility each year. Later, during the development of the SSC the students and tutors selected two items of equipment which offered greatest value, the video-cassette recorder and the combined tape and slide presentation. Both of these can be used in such a way as to allow the student to interact with the training materials.

An Innovative Strategy

So much for the description. Readers would be excused if they thought that the scheme was simple and effective enough to succeed on its own merits. However, our experience in the Air Force is that this would be a dangerous assumption. We have seen other innovations, such as 'management by objectives' lose much of their momentum and so we were determined that the introduction of the SSC would not be a final act — we would provide continuous support. We were also conscious that there is not necessarily an orderly process of introduction from research through development to use. In this case, these are *not* discrete steps and much overlap must take place. Few, if any, innovations will be perfect first time and in our planning of change, allowance was made for the very necessary refining process, evidence of which is our concentration, after two years' use, on the most effective learning media — the video-tape and the tape/slide, accompanied by our rejection of other, less successful methods. If the process of innovation was simply about things, about hardware, or ideas, then the SSC would not need innovating. It would stand on its own merit. However, we see people being involved. We therefore adopted an innovation strategy which took account of the following factors (Rogers, 1962):

(a) Relative advantage
(b) Compatibility
(c) Divisibility

(d) Complexity
(e) Observability

The relative advantage of the SSC was the degree to which it was perceived as being somehow 'better' than traditional methods of individual study. The use of both audio and visual media provided more motivation for students than traditional methods, such as reading.

Compatibility is the degree to which an innovation is consistent with the students' existing values and past experience. Every effort was made by the design team to ensure that the environment, the hardware and the software were compatible with the views and values of the students. In particular, we were very conscious of the 'not invented here' syndrome. To overcome this, the design team were recognized as full members of the College tutorial staff so that all decisions were made 'in-house'.

Problems

The SSC was only *one* part of the overall training strategy of the new course, and as such it was possible for a student to adopt parts of the training as opposed to an all-or-none acceptance of the whole strategy. All the learning packages could be accepted on a whole or part basis. This we saw as the application of the divisibility principle. During the development of the SSC we fell foul of the principle of complexity. In the early days the provision of a range of electronic teaching machines and the plethora of different sorts of software was, to say the least, confusing. It was not long before the Centre was called the 'electronic playschool' and 'the supersonic cupboard'.

To ease this situation, we reduced the number of types of learning medium and made a rational effort to produce simple, unambiguous instructions for the use of the machines and the packages. Alas, senior executives, no matter what organization they belong to, will only resort to the instructions when all else fails!

The more visible the effects of an innovation are, the more general the acceptance of it will be. It is not sufficient to just demonstrate the benefits of an innovation — they must be seen to be applicable within the user's own situation. To avoid the comment: 'This is fine, but what's it got to do with me?', we made every effort to use software that had been produced in the College and that was clearly applicable to the students' situation. As explained above, the introduction of an innovation is not a final act, and we therefore provided time and effort to ensure the continued acceptance of the SSC as an effective method of learning.

To support our claim that the SSC provided our students with a better method of individual learning we evaluated the students' attitudes towards the Centre. Not only does the evaluation give indications of the success of the Centre; it also helps to prevent its devaluation. The less acceptable teaching machines were replaced as a result of our continuing validation.

Because of savings in tutor and syllabus time we had the resources to provide an instructor to be responsible for software development and a technician to maintain and service the hardware. Failure to provide this software and hardware maintenance would have resulted in unserviceability, which in turn could only breed distrust.

Diffusion of an innovation requires the innovation to be flexible. Students' needs may change over time and if we are able to reshape the innovation to meet their changing needs they will be more likely to continue using it effectively. An innovation must have a capability for continuing adaptation.

If an innovation is to succeed it must be built into the organizational structure. At Bracknell, the SSC was centrally located and left open 24 hours a day so that it became part of the everyday life of the College.

In looking back over the design and development of the SSC, I see that we had a golden opportunity to innovate — the concept of individual study was particularly sound and we were able to economize on time and resources by providing an individual learning centre. Some of the money saved was wisely used to provide the time and resources to evaluate the concept carefully — as a result, the new staff course, supported by the selective studies centre, has fulfilled its promise of being one of the most effective service courses ever devised. It is a true child of its time, retaining what it needs from well-tried traditional methods but applying the innovations of educational technology which can accelerate learning and make it more enjoyable.

A Naval Approach to Innovation

Underware

The very name 'educational technology' has, to many people, been an anathema for many years. It reflects the technological revolution of the 1960s when we finally got down to the business of beating our swords into ploughshares, and the education and training world entered an orgy of hardware procurement unparalleled since Roman times. There were CCTV, teaching machines, tape/slide devices, and 8mm loops (alas not of the contraceptive variety, otherwise the intended project would have ended where it began and we might have been spared some of the subsequent instructional technology disasters!). This hardware phase was followed fairly rapidly by a software phase, and programmed learning burst upon the scene as a placebo on which to feed these avid machines that we all now possessed. It seemed an eternity, although in fact it was only a few years, before we arrived at the underware stage as educational technologists developed philosophies which eventually generated software in accordance with sound educational principles and which in turn made demands upon the hardware; hardware which already existed or could now be developed to meet a properly defined need.

As an illustration we might note that the Navy is currently undertaking a study lasting about two years to develop such a philosophy for computer-based training, as a preliminary to setting up training projects which will use this medium.

Let us look at one example from training in the Royal Navy which illustrates the need to put the underware first, followed by the software and finally by the hardware.

A New Course

The poor recruiting in the 1960s presented problems of training organization because of the difficulties of building up traditional-sized classes of 15 or 20 trainees. This resulted in a loss of motivation among trainees waiting to be trained and some dismay and embarrassment to those trying to assemble full complements for ships putting to sea. At that time, although manpower was very short, we were in a position to introduce self-paced learning using teaching machines to overcome the organization problem, and so we set up a course on basic electronics using teaching machines. We shall not dwell overlong on that sad episode. We all know — now — the foolhardiness of supposing that total exposure to teaching machines over a period of days or weeks will lead to successful training.

This lesson having been learned, we decided to retain the advantages of individualized, self-paced learning and the concept of prestructural learning, but to vary the medium used. So we set about creating such a course, making very limited use of teaching machines, some programmed learning, lots of individualized laboratory experiments and a very small amount of tutoring. Time was pressing and so it was decided that parts of the course would be developed in parallel. Because at the time there was insufficient in-house expertise, the work was contracted out to a commercial company. The design was completed on time and the course was due to start.

Then word got around that in the Chief Petty Officers' mess, which was where the instructors were to be found, they were drawing straws for who should run the course — short straw losing and loser running the course. This was because they had heard, correctly, that the course was prestructured, self-running, and effectively automatic. What was their role in running the course? They saw themselves merely as monitors with their positions degraded; at the pinnacle of their professional careers as technicians they would be sitting in front of a class just making sure that the trainees did not wreck the equipment, worked reasonably hard, were tested and were passed to the next module.

Staff Development

Fortunately this was discovered in time for the start of the course to be put back two or three weeks while a one-day indoctrination course for the instructors was designed. This course caused the innovators to think about the whole philosophy of the prestructured learning situation and yielded many valuable lessons. The indoctrination course was intended to give the instructors-to-be some idea of the concepts and the theories behind the materials, and also to give them some idea of their own roles in that situation — roles as managers and tutors rather than mere monitors. The training course was ultimately successful and ran for several years, albeit with several problems.

Firstly, the 'not invented here' syndrome became apparent. No self-respecting naval officer would accept a course designed by a bunch of civilians, however expert they might be, and this bedevilled the course for the rest of its life. Secondly, there was a problem with the criterion-referenced assessment of the course which did not give a rank order of trainees' success. The Naval system wanted to award seniority on the basis of how well the trainee had done on the course and this information was not available. This was solved by awarding seniority on the basis of how quickly the trainee had completed the course. (It is interesting to note that a similar solution adopted by the US Army was less successful because the reward for completing their course quickly was that the trainees got to Vietnam that much earlier.)

However, the success of the course in overcoming the difficulties of small training groups now exposed a problem in the drafting system which was accustomed to large batches of trainees arriving from courses and could not cope with a continual flow. The waiting time had been transferred from the beginning of the course to the end, and this created problems of retentivity.

The course no longer runs in the above way but has reverted to a classroom based format. This is not as a result of deficiencies in the software — indeed, much of the material used in the classroom was created for the self-paced course. We suggest that the main reason why the course failed was because it was not executed within an overall training concept — an underware. Since that time, all three services have developed an underware known as the systems approach to training, and it is through that approach that we are able to implement new courses and techniques with a greater degree of success.

Conclusion

The experiences described in this paper provide a number of keys for successful innovation, not only in training but in education too. Some of these keys are:

☐ The development of the organization and its staff.
☐ The project plan must be right and fit in with the underware of instructional technology.
☐ There must be an understanding of, and strong commitment to, the innovation at all levels from the senior management to the most junior instructor.
☐ There should be staff development courses.
☐ The project should look for continuity in its key staff.
☐ The project should beware of personality dependence.
☐ Time factors should be considered very carefully.
☐ Bandwaggon tendencies should be avoided.

But, in our pursuit of guaranteed success, we should not forget the need for speculative projects. In many ways the hardware of educational technology is moving faster than the software and underware. For example, both microcomputers and video-discs exist and will soon be in use *before* we really understand how to use them effectively in our training. The only way to find out is to set up projects to evaluate their use in a variety of environments and in different ways. Not all these can be expected to be successful.

One challenge for instructional technology to the year 2000 is risk-taking and the acceptability of possible failure.

References

Evans, C (1979) *The Mighty Micro.* Victor Gollancz, London.
Rogers, E M (1962) *Diffusion of Innovation.* Freepress, Glencoe.
Rushby, N J, McMahon, H, Southwell, A and Philpott, A (1976) Computer-assisted management of learning: The CAMOL Project. In Clarke, J and Leedham, J (eds) *Aspects of Educational Technology* X. Kogan Page, London.

Acknowledgement

Crown Copyright: This paper is reproduced by permission of the Controller of Her Majesty's Stationery Office.

1.3 Eductional Technology Helps the Unemployed

J E Hills
Coventry Technical College

Abstract: A major side-effect of the Manpower Services Commission Youth Opportunities Programme has been the problem of staffing and staff training. A new course designed to provide instructor/supervisors with five basic areas of skill, and using a profile assessment based directly on the objectives, is described.

Introduction

1979 saw the introduction on a pilot basis of a new joint course by the City and Guilds of London Institute and the Manpower Services Commission. The course is intended to give support to those men and women working with the unemployed 16 to 19-year-olds who are taking part in schemes under the Youth Opportunities Programme.

Background

The unemployment figures for January 1980 showed that the number of school leavers without jobs was marginally smaller than a year ago. An age breakdown showed a broadly similar pattern for the under 18s as a whole, but the Department of Employment predicted that the general trend would be upwards. There is a strong tendency for youth employment to rise and fall with unemployment generally; the Department of Employment prediction has since proved to be correct, and the slight relief of the past year has been abruptly and emphatically ended.

However, it is estimated that the January 1980 figure for unemployed under-18s would be some 95,000 higher but for the Youth Opportunities Programme. The problem of the out-of-work school leaver and of the under-18s in general has been an ever-increasing one since 1975. On 1 April 1978 the Youth Opportunities Programme (YOP) was brought into operation by the Special Programmes Division (SPD) of the Manpower Services Commission (MSC). Estimated gross costs for the measures in the first year were £63,000,000.

The Youth Opportunities Programme offers unemployed young people of 16 to 18 years an integrated range of work preparation courses and work experience schemes. During the first year there were 162,000 entrants, divided almost equally between boys and girls. About 70 per cent were school leavers and some 90 per cent were aged 16 or 17.

About 75 per cent of all entrants had been registered as unemployed for six weeks or more and 15 per cent had been unemployed for six months or more. One major objective of YOP for 1978-79 was to ensure that no Easter or Summer school leaver who remained unemployed the following Easter should have been without the offer of a place on the programme. This undertaking was 99 per cent fulfilled.

Staffing the Measures

The various measures, whether sponsored privately or by a local authority, need staff to operate them. About 12,000 instructor/supervisors are currently involved within the YOP, many of them untrained in the techniques of instruction or supervision, and indeed a high proportion of them have experienced unemployment themselves. The MSC normally provide instructor training courses through their Instructor Training Colleges at Letchworth and Hillingdon. These establishments are unable to cope with such numbers and the diverse nature of the requirements of such personnel. The joint venture between the MSC and the City and Guilds of London Institute was proposed to help alleviate the situation. In April 1978 the CGLI put forward the following proposals:

> To devise a course and qualification for staff recruited under such programmes as the Youth Opportunities Programme and Unified Vocational Preparation, bearing in mind their various backgrounds and current training provision.

Pilot scheme proposals were prepared by the CGLI to fill an immediate need and in a shorter time than critical considerations would have permitted. Full consultation with the MSC had been established and maintained. It was the intention to use the pilot scheme proposals as a basis for the development of a definitive scheme for courses and assessment at a later stage.

The Pilot Course

The scheme for courses and related assessment is intended mainly for men and women employed as instructors/supervisors/responsible officers on such schemes as the Youth Opportunities Programme. The scheme has been devised on the assumption that the instructor/supervisor will pursue a course of study attached to an appropriate establishment of further education or other approved centre, for approximately 80 hours, and a similar amount of time in related on-the-job practice, including at least 10 hours which consists of supervised instruction.

Five basic areas of skill are provided for. These are: (i) instructional skills; (ii) communication skills; (iii) caring/guidance skills; (iv) evaluation skills; (v) job skills.

It is recommended that 60 per cent of the time available should be allocated to caring/guidance and instructional skills, and the balance of 40 per cent to the other three skills; within these two percentage areas different options may be applicable according to local requirements, provided that key objectives are fulfilled.

The Institute has endeavoured to produce a scheme aimed at taking into account the diverse backgrounds of the course participants, who could vary from newly qualified graduates or unemployed teachers to those recently working in a variety of occupations, perhaps now unemployed, and who were last involved in their own education/training several years ago.

The Institute has tried to avoid making the aims of the course so general as to be almost meaningless, and yet at the same time to avoid a degree of specificity that would inhibit flexibility within individual schemes. The scheme is aimed at giving those offering the course an opportunity to produce a programme having the greatest relevance to the needs of the instructor/supervisor in his locality. Emphasis should be directed towards integrated and participatory methods of teaching and learning. Although it may not be feasible, simulation of the instructor/supervisor's own working environment or a study of this environment is strongly recommended for appropriate parts of the course. The employer or immediate supervisor of the instructor/supervisor is seen to have an important role in helping to clarify the needs of the instructor/supervisor, and in providing the on-the-job opportunity referred to above. It is probable that any group of instructor/supervisors will have wide differences in their roles and organizations. This may require separate interpretations of the course aims and objectives.

Although it may not always be appropriate, the Institute hopes that formal class teaching will be kept to a minimum and that participatory and practical approaches will be adopted. The young people being trained by the instructor/supervisors may present problems unfamiliar to course tutors. For example, being unemployed and perhaps having other social problems, together with possibly insignificant qualifications for employment, may produce characteristics that must be taken into account when considering teaching/learning methods.

The pilot scheme was operated at 10 centres. It was well received and is expected to continue with full MSC support.

Method of Assessment

The nature of the course and the anticipated course participants suggest that it would be helpful to give course participants an achievement goal and, at the same time, minimize the possibility of failure. A profile assessment has been designed to

Objectives — By the end of the course the trainee instructor/supervisor should be able to:	Instructional Skills			Tutor's observations
	1	2	3	
1. Identify, select and demonstrate appropriate instruction methods and plan for instructing individuals and/or small groups.	Identification and selection is restricted in most cases — limited grasp of methods available.	Identification, selection and demonstration is correct in most cases — some lack of variety.	Identification, selection and demonstration is correct in all cases.	
2. Make effective use of available resources for updating his/her own knowledge, and preparing instructing/ learning materials.	Makes only partial use of available resources, and even then only in a limited way.	Makes use of easily available resources without seeking further afield.	Makes full and effective use of all resources for planning and preparation.	
3. Select and use appropriate resources, including audio-visual materials, effectively in a range of instructing/learning situations.	Uses learning aids and resources in a very limited way.	Makes use of available resources but has limited creativity.	Uses resources and aids to the fullest effect in an instructing/learning situation.	

Table 1. *Profile assessment for instructional skills*

meet this need; the part dealing with instructional skills is given as Table 1.

The profiles are based directly on the objectives written for the five main areas of the course. They are intended to be used mainly by the tutor and the instructor/supervisor together. The shaded part of the grid indicates the minimum acceptable standard. As each objective is assessed, a progress point can be shown on the profile to indicate the level of achievement and this level should be agreed by the tutor and the instructor/supervisor.

A record sheet, summarizing all the objective achievement levels, should be completed individually by the instructor/supervisor right at the start of the course in order to suggest the targets for each participant before the teaching/learning takes place. Subsequent movement of the assessed levels can be marked on the same sheet, and dated, to show progression. Most of the course objectives will be assessed over a period of time and achievement levels should be discussed with the instructor/supervisor as progress is made. The final entries on the profiles are intended to be used by the tutor to indicate the overall level of success or otherwise at the end of the course. Successful course completion would be indicated by each objective being realized to at least the minimum level as indicated. The profiles are the basis upon which the award is made.

Implications for the Trainer of Trainers

This course is intended to support a fast-growing area in further education. Many colleges now operate courses for young people within the scope of the Youth Opportunities Programme and these courses may be serviced by existing or new members of staff. The area of work demands empathy from lecturers and support from colleagues. This type of course is not another 'teacher training' course and may require a good deal of rethinking on the part of the trainer of trainers. Close co-operation will be required between course tutors, YOP scheme managers and local MSC personnel. The instructor/supervisors operate in an environment which is totally unlike that of a school or college; indeed it is expected to be similar to industry, commerce or the community. Assessment of attainment and progress will depend on a joint effort between course tutor (mainly during the observation periods), the scheme managers (who may be untrained), and MSC personnel who have to evaluate all such training programmes.

The tutorial staff/student ratio for this course appears to be most appropriate at 1 : 8, a figure which may be at variance with normal college ratios. Too few students makes for poor group interaction, while too many will cause isolation of some individuals and present problems during the supervision period.

Some of the students attending this course will display all the signs of the anxious student, and all the problems of the adult learner will be apparent. The only common factor among the students is that they all work with unemployed youth; otherwise their roles are as diverse as their backgrounds. Some will be purely job skill instructors, some will be supervisors of youngsters on work placements, and others will have a main responsibility for administration or counselling.

Course tutors may find that they have to spend disproportionate amounts of time on what may be regarded as a short course. Many of the methods and techniques used in teacher training courses are inappropriate for this course. Unsophisticated, student-centred learning is most appropriate but maintained at an uncommonly low level. All information passed to the students by whatever methods must be supported by a wide range of examples of how they may use it in their work.

Some Thoughts on the Use of Profile Assessment

Bearing in mind what has already been said above regarding the nature of the students on this course, and considering that there is an ever-increasing number of students at all levels for whom more formal assessment devices would be inappropriate, consider the following comments offered by Derek Rowntree (1977).

☐ Profiles can be used to spell out specific talents and abilities observed in a student.

☐ The dimensions of a student's work/attainment can be laid bare in great detail in a profile.

☐ By unravelling a uni-dimensional overall grade or rank, and showing rather how the student was evaluated in a number of component dimensions, the profile offers its recipients far more information on which to make their own overall evaluations. This type of profile based on semantic differentials will be a 'case history' or 'verbal profile' on individual students.

Reference

Rowntree, D (1977) *Assessing Students. How shall we know them?* Harper and Row, London.

1.4 Work Samples as Aids to Vocational Counselling

Donald C Moors *Nova Scotia Department of Education*
Kenneth L Ozman *Saint Mary's University*

Abstract: This paper describes a project which provided referred clients with the opportunity to simulate some job/production demands of various occupations. The results of this vocational evaluation service were used in subsequent counsellor-client meetings during which various training alternatives were discussed and occupational goals were established.

Introduction

Factors involved in the proper assessment and selection of candidates for training programmes tend to emphasize a two-fold process: the establishment of a career or occupational goal, and the development of a strategy through which the client is able to acquire the necessary training.

The means by which counsellors negotiate career goals and training strategies with a client tend to look towards a combination of five approaches. These include: (i) psychological tests, (ii) job analysis, (iii) work samples, (iv) situational assessments and (v) job tryouts. Of these five assessment approaches, work samples appear to encompass some of the most critical advantages of other approaches while avoiding other known major disadvantages.

The most obvious advantage of the work sample approach lies in the opportunity it offers to assess the client on the basis of the production of a job related product. In addition, work sample approaches provide the client with experiential evidence relative to some of the basic demands of the occupation to which the work sample is related. Thus the client not only demonstrates aptitude. Client interest may also be assessed.

It was anticipated that these two types of information would assist the employment counsellor in his efforts to determine for a client an occupational goal and training plan.

Description of Work Sample Stations

Following a review of the occupational exploration systems which emphasized a hands-on working sample approach, it was decided to purchase 20 commercially produced stations. These stations related to occupational/trade clusters such as electrical wiring; needle trades; sheet metal working; cosmetology; welding and brazing; and packing and materials handling.

Each of the stations is a self-contained unit and has available all of the tools and materials necessary for the client to perform the tasks required of the individual station programme. Audio-taped instructions are received by the client through a headphone set. The audio-tape is cued to a filmstrip projector apparatus. The client can control the speed of information presentation, thereby providing self-pacing assessment. Most station programmes require from two to three hours to complete.

Project Set-Up Activities

A process was initiated which provided information on the vocational evaluation system to potential referring counsellors. The briefing included:

- ☐ A one-day visit to the Vocational Evaluation Centre.
- ☐ Visits by one of the programme managers to the referring counsellors' offices throughout the province. During the visit a 10-minute video-tape, describing the system, was presented.
- ☐ Distribution to these counsellors of an information sheet with suggested referral guidelines.

Programmes

Clients were initially referred to the project for assessment by their employment-training counsellors. On the basis of a series of guidelines, clients were referred for a *specific assessment* (in which case the referring counsellor and client determined the stations on which the assessment would be conducted) or for an *overall assessment* (whereby the client and project staff determined the assessment stations to which the client would be exposed).

The results of a system-based picture interest inventory provided an indication of the client's initial interest in the occupational clusters to which the 20 stations related. Clients then began work on the programmes associated with their interests. Following the completion of the assessment programmes, clients were debriefed by staff and completed reports were sent to the referring counsellors. These reports included information on the client's performance levels, time requirements and ability to follow instructions.

Results

Throughout the section various types of data and the results of statistical analysis are presented. In many cases the size of the data base is large enough to permit tests of significance. In such instances, the results of a chi square (x^2) test are reported. In other cases, the size of the data base does not lend itself to statistical testing, and trends indicated suggest more cautious and therefore less confident projections.

Client Data and Station Use

An analysis of the data from the first 41 clients suggests that there was an equal distribution of males (22) and females (19) referred to the system ($x^2 < 1.0$). The male clients averaged 22.1 years of age with 19 clients (86.4 per cent) between the ages of 17 and 25. The average female client age was 26.9 years with 12 clients (63.1 per cent) between the ages of 18 and 25.

Of the initial 41 clients, 23 (or 56 per cent) were referred for assessments relative to specific occupations. A more comprehensive breakdown suggests that 5 of these 23 clients were referred for assessments on two stations; two clients were referred for assessments on three stations; and one client was referred for assessment on four stations. The remaining clients (15) were referred for an 'overall' assessment. Of these referrals, five clients completed programmes associated with two stations. Three clients completed assessments on three stations, eight clients completed assessments on four stations, and two clients completed assessments on five stations. These data are presented in Table 1.

		Number of stations completed during assessment				
Type of referral		1	2	3	4	5
Specific	N	15	5	2	1	—
	%°	65.2	86.9	95.7	100%	—
Overall	N	—	5	3	8	2
	%°		27.8%	44.4%	88.9%	100%
Total	N	15	10	5	9	2
	%°	36.6%	61%	73.2%	95.1%	100%

° cumulative percentages

Table 1. *Number/per cent° of stations completed by referral type*

The cumulative percentages in Table 1 suggest that the vast majority of future clients referred for specific assessments will particpate on three or fewer stations, and that very few of the clients (regardless of referral category) will require assessments on more than four stations.

Counsellor Questionnaire

A questionnaire was drawn up for distribution to counsellors who had referred clients to the vocational evaluation service.

Question 1
'Did the information contained in the report assist you in the occupational goal selection process with the client? If yes, how?'

Referring counsellors had sufficient information about their referred clients to answer this question in 37 instances. Of these, it was indicated that 35 (94.6 per cent) of the final reports contained information which assisted the counsellor in the occupational goal selection process with the client. In the other two cases the final report did not help in this. The differences between these two response categories is statistically significant (x^2 = 29.4, df = 1, p < .001).

Question 2
'Did the report provide you with information which you did not have prior to the referral? If yes, describe the type of information.'

A positive response to this question was obtained in 31 (83.8 per cent) of cases. The counsellors reported that no new information was provided in five instances (13.5 per cent) and in one case (2.7 per cent) the counsellor had an insufficient basis to make a judgement. The differences between positive and negative responses by the counsellors to this question is large enough to be statistically significant (x^2 18.8, df = 1, p< .001).

The data base relative to the number of referring counsellors does not allow for meaningful statistical analysis. However, if a larger sample were to reflect the trends it would indicate that a substantial number of referring counsellors gain access to new information about the majority of their clients as a result of system participation.

Question 3
'Did the report confirm information or conclusions which previously existed? If yes, which specific ones?'

This question gained positive responses in 32 (86.5 per cent) of instances. A 'no' response was reported in four (10.8 per cent) instances, while a counsellor reported an insufficient judgement basis in one instance. As in previous analyses, this difference in response levels is significant (x^2 = 21.8, df = 1, p < .001).

Again the data indicate that the high level of positive responses to this question is evenly distributed across referring counsellors.

Question 4
'In your opinion, did the experience of hands on activity assist the client during the subsequent counselling process?'

In 31 instances (83.8 per cent) counsellors confirmed this; in three instances (8.1 per cent) counsellors reported no assistance of this type to the client, while three client instances could not provide a basis for judgement.

The ratio of positive answers was not unevenly distributed among referring counsellors.

Question 5
'Overall, how would you rate the system as an assessment/information tool to a vocational counsellor? Highly useful/useful/of little use/of no use/neutral?'

It was expected that counsellors would not only take into account those benefits of the system which were mentioned in the previous four questions, but would also feel free to assess the system's potential in terms of other dimensions which they, as professionals, would define as relevant. Asked the question, the system was rated as 'highly useful' by counsellors as it applied to 18 (48.6 per cent) assessment situations. An additional 14 (37.8 per cent) of the assessment situations led to a rating of 'useful'. In no case did counsellors rate the system 'of little use' or 'of no use'.

In three (8.1 per cent) situations counsellors suggested that they would rate the effectiveness system as 'neutral' in terms of a specific assessment situation. In two cases the counsellor had insufficient information upon which to make a judgement.

In general, the responses to the questions indicate the system to be a highly useful assessment instrument for referring counsellors. Given continued attention to proper application guidelines through appropriate referrals, the system should continue to provide meaningful information to referring counsellors.

Client Questionnaire

A questionnaire was also drawn up for distribution to clients who had been referred to and who participated in the Vocational Evaluation Service.

Attempts were made to contact the initial 41 clients who participated in the project approximately two months following the completion of their assessment visits. Of these, 21 clients were contacted, and answered the questions. Responses were available from both clients and their counsellors in 18 (85.7 per cent) of these 21 situations. The responses were as follows:

Question 1
'Did the experience on the stations assist you in understanding more about various occupations (jobs)?'

All of the clients contacted indicated that the opportunity to complete the programme(s) assisted them in understanding more about various occupations.

Question 2
'Were you able to better discuss various occupational choices with your referring counsellor as a result of your experience of the unit?'

By far the majority of clients contacted (20 or 95.2 per cent) suggested that the assessment experience led to an increased ability to discuss various occupational choices during subsequent interviews with their referring counsellor. One of the clients reported that he '. . . didn't know' if this had occurred.

The counsellors suggested that 31, or 84 per cent, of their clients benefited in the subsequent counselling process from having had the 'hands on' experience (question 4 on the counsellor survey). Questions 1 and 2 of the client survey attempted to examine two dimensions on which this benefit could be noticed. Of the 18 clients who were contacted for the survey and who participated in further counselling sessions, 17 clients (94.4 per cent) were reported by their counsellor to have benefited from the 'hands on' activity. All of these 17 clients also reported that they learned more about various occupations as a result of system participation. Of these 17 clients, 16 reported that they were better able to discuss various occupations with their counsellors in subsequent interviews. Thus there was a high level of congruency between the benefits perceived as a result of system participation by both the counsellors and their clients. Specifically, it would appear that the hands on activity of the system provides information to a vast majority of the clients which benefits subsequent counsellor/client activities. This effect was perceived by the particular client with at least the same frequency as by counsellors.

Question 3
'How would you rate the service in terms of assisting your subsequent visits to Employment and Immigration (the referring agency)? Very helpful/helpful/ of little help/of no help at all/neutral?'

Of the 21 clients contacted, 13 (61.9 per cent) rated the service 'very helpful' in this respect. The remaining eight clients rated the service as 'helpful'. This final question provided clients with an open-ended opportunity to pass comment on all aspects of the service. Some comments offered included: 'It helped me nail down the electrician goal'; 'I didn't like the headphones'; '. . . very good for women . . . it increased my confidence'; 'I didn't know which of two areas I wanted before the test . . . it helped me zero in on welding'; 'It told me what I was best suited for'.

The nature of these comments emphasizes two important facts. First of all, clients were highly objective: some suggested that the programme was too fast (in certain frames) and that the use of headphones for an extensive period was distracting etc. Secondly, it was impossible to avoid noticing the enthusiasm of most of the referred clients concerning the benefits of the service. Clients regarded the event as an integral part of their career/training discussion sequence with employment and immigration counsellors. This speaks strongly for the use which referring counsellors are making of the service — in terms of the type (or needs) of the clients being referred, the information which they and their clients receive from the system, and the use of the information during subsequent counselling situations. It also emphasizes the integrated work or occupational, rather than test, characteristics of the system.

Future Plans

While this vocational evaluation system has continued to operate, additional interests have been identified. These include questions relating to the predictive nature of the system results *vis-à-vis* training programmes and an analysis of the reliability of the tasks required as they represent various occupations.

As the research associated with these questions is completed, further reports will be made available.

Workshop Report
1.5 The Work-Experience Project in Holland (AEL-Project)

Mia A Lezer and Wiel Veugelers
University of Amsterdam

Organizers' Account
Introduction

The practice of education has shown that when pupils are confronted with problems of society they want to discuss these problems within a single rather than within several discplines. At the same time they want experience rather than abstract information only.

The pupils can play a more active role in this learning process when they have their own experiences to learn from. This means that the initiative comes more from the pupils and less from the teachers. The teachers supervise the learning process of their pupils.

According to us an innovation in education must have the following characteristics:

☐ pupils should get experiences with the problems of society;
☐ these experiences should be the starting point of the learning process;
☐ problems of society should not be studied in different disciplines separately but jointly.

One of the central problems every pupil is confronted with, sooner or later, is the meaning of labour. For this reason the project 'work-experience-learning' has been started, that is: learning to get an insight into the meaning of labour and labour relations by means of one's own experiences.

The project started at the beginning of 1979 for 15- and 16-year-old pupils from all types of secondary school.

At this experimental stage, seven schools participate in the project, supervised by the Teacher Training Department and the Kohnstamm Institute (an institute for educational research), both of the University of Amsterdam.

Aims of the 'Work-Experience-Learning' Project

The central aim of the project is to gain a better view and knowledge of labour, so the pupils will be more conscious of the place and meaning of labour and labour processes in industry, commerce, civil service and society as a whole. The aims for the pupils are that:

☐ they must have a big influence on the content and organization of the learning process;
☐ part of this learning process is the gaining of experience about working and working situations. The pupils get these experiences by spending a week as a worker;
☐ they should learn to co-operate better.

For the content of the curriculum and the learning process, this means:

☐ the experiences of the pupils are the starting point of the learning process;
☐ the content is not determined by just one discipline but by the ideas and experiences the pupils have about work.

For the teachers this means:

☐ they should not in the first place transfer knowledge but they should supervise the learning process of the pupils;
☐ they have to co-operate with other teachers to realize an integrated approach to the concept of work;
☐ they have to indicate the connection of the project with their own discipline;
☐ they have to develop a system for assessment appropriate to this project.

Starting Points of the Process of Development

(a) The AEL-project is school-bounded. Each school gives concrete form to the project and is responsible for its realization.
(b) The AEL project causes a change in the school, particularly because it involves the teachers with society, takes the learning process out of the classroom and changes the relation between teachers and pupils.
(c) Every year each school makes a plan for the project. At the end of the year a new plan is constructed on the basis of the results of the evaluation.

(d) Because of the complexity of the changes, supervision of the change processes in the school and in the classroom is necessary. This is particularly important for the changes in the role of the pupil and in the role of the teacher as well as the realization and the assimilation of the work experience.

(e) To ensure the influence of the teachers on the development of the project, teachers participate in the committee that runs the project.

The Project in the School

The pupils themselves first contact the industry or institution of their choice. This is a part of the learning process. The teacher then makes definitive arrangements about the activities during the working week.

During the preparation period, the pupils decide on the items they plan to look for at their workplace, items such as atmosphere, working hours, conditions of employment, unemployment, work-consciousness, feelings about work, wages, economic position of the concern, women and immigrants. They prepare questions on these topics to ask fellow workers, or devise other means to get at the facts. By means of simulations they practice how to conduct a conversation.

During the period of gaining experience in the labour process they stay pupils and do not become employees; thus they do not receive a wage. They look, ask and inquire, while they follow a worker and help him with the execution of certain tasks. They also try to get a survey of the different departments of the concern.

The assimilation period after the working week consists mainly of four elements:

1. The pupils relate their experiences, ie whatever has impressed them deeply — mostly the atmosphere, communication, the way in which they were treated and their impressions about the professions they have seen.
2. Comparison of experiences and collected results to ensure the pupils think about the background and the causes of their experiences.
3. The working out of one aspect of work in small groups to try to explain the results they found.
4. The fixing and transferring of the results into a report, a simulation/game, a collage or a discussion. Besides this report about different items, all pupils make a full report about their own working week.

The project is running for the first time during the present school year. So far, we can make the following remarks:

☐ pupils are able to formulate the questions which they plan to investigate during the working week;

☐ about 70 per cent of the pupils find a workplace themselves. There is a tendency that the higher the level of the school, the fewer the workplaces in industry the pupils take;

☐ the working week gives the pupils a lot of experiences that they want to talk about with each other;

☐ the reports are extensive, but pupils often need a push from the teacher to find the underlying causes;

☐ 'work-experience-learning' is a learning technique that can be used for all pupils, and not only for under-achievers.

Problems Regarding the Learning Process

(a) Relating learning at the workplace and the learning in school.
(b) How to stimulate pupils to relate their personal experiences in the classroom.

(c) The co-operation of the pupils.

(d) The teachers must learn to supervise a process in which pupils have a major influence and in which it is not clear what the result will be.

Problems to Solve Regarding the Organization

☐ We can find a large number of workplaces, but we prefer a wider range of better quality places.

☐ The centralized final examination for every discipline promotes neither the co-operation between disciplines nor ways of learning other than the reproduction of knowledge.

☐ Often the schools are not equipped for project learning; the classrooms are small and there is hardly any audio-visual material.

☐ Too little time is available for discussions between the project teachers, and between them and the rest of the school.

Participant's Comments
J Pearson *City and Guilds of London Institute*

The workshop was attended by nine delegates. Wiel Veugelers described how the work experience project, with which he is involved, operates in Amsterdam. This system makes the student responsible for the first school-employer contact, gives him five weeks to organize an observation inventory for use during work experience, and allows an initial informal feedback prior to a more formal categorized report.

Workshop discussion concentrated on the merits and the problems of setting up work experience from schools. The benefits were:

(a) more informed choice of career (the headmaster in the group claimed that 90 per cent of his school's work experience students proceeded to jobs in the company 'tasted');

(b) broadening the curriculum (the appearance of employers and work-based assignments in schools);

(c) personal maturing and increased confidence of students. (Were the Dutch students less passive than the English, or did the Dutch work experience system stimulate their confidence more than the English?)

The following problems were aired:

(a) the minimum legal age for work experience;

(b) trade union complaints (one delegate had issued an instruction that work experience students were to be treated as apprentices);

(c) incentives for students — pocket money for attendance, 'plum' vacancies allocated to the students with the highest marks;

(d) work experience should be available to all levels of student (as in Amsterdam), not just the educationally disadvantaged;

(e) difficulties of transporting students from home/school to work experience;

(f) students should experience more than one type of work (but difficult to arrange);

(g) how to evaluate success;

(h) insurance of students at work: the need to check that a company has third party visitor insurance; only large local education authorities issue a letter of insurance cover intent to firms.

Dr Lezer and Mr Veugelers are anxious to collect the experience of others and information on this subject. They can be contacted at The Teacher Training Department, University of Amsterdam, Prinsengracht 227, Amsterdam.

1.6 Future Development of In-Company Training Packages

E T Brueck and S T McKay
Construction Industry Training Board

Organizers' Account

This was a workshop intended to explore likely future trends and design characteristics of training packages designed for in-company use.

Mode

Participants were introduced to, and discussed briefly, the main themes of the conference likely to influence design of learning materials in the future:
(i) introduction of sophisticated hardware; (ii) trend towards individualized learning; (iii) trend towards package learning; (iv) introduction of flexible and open learning environments; (v) trend towards learning in smaller groups.

A short presentation was made of the opportunities and difficulties experienced by the Construction Industry Training Board in the development and implementation of a variety of training packages for in-company use.

Participants were asked to complete a short questionnaire giving them the opportunity to express their views on which factors they considered to be most likely to influence the design of in-company training packages in the 1980s. The results of the questionnaire were, in order of priority, as follows:

    (a) Self-Instruction
    (b) Distance learning techniques
    (c) Group learning techniques
    (d) Self-Directed learning
    (e) Computer-Assisted instruction
    (f) Video
    (g) Achievement measurement
    (h) Tape/slide
    (i) Company learning resource centres
    (j) Action learning techniques

Participants broke up into syndicates to discuss in detail the design of in-company training packages in the light of future developments and with particular reference to opportunities and problems for the company using packages, the trainee learning from packages and the designer developing packages.

Participants then joined in a final plenary session to discuss the problems and opportunities identified by the syndicates.

Summary of Conclusions

In general it was felt that the trend towards packaged training materials would become even stronger in the future. This development reflected to a certain extent an underlying shift in industrial training towards more extensive in-company training activities. Training packages enabled trainers and managers to carry out training at source, making it more job-related and cost-effective.

Future developments and trends in training technology, as earlier identified, would provide a further impetus to this type of training. New hardware and more open learning environments would encourage greater individualization and flexibility and, in particular, more effective tuition on in-company training courses.

However, the new trends and developments would not necessarily solve many of the problems currently associated with the development and implementation of training packages. Indeed many of the problems may become more complex as a result. Opportunities offered by training packages, such as reaching a large number of trainees in particular target populations, and setting uniform standards, must be seen against the background of limitations imposed by the type of material and subject matter. The problem of identifying and determining entry levels will become even more acute within more open learning systems, particularly with regard to the role of the trainer.

Although training packages provide the manager and trainer with greater control of their particular training activities at their place of work, often eliminating the need for 'subject specialists', the provider of training packages must decide whether to develop company specific materials or use a more generalized approach. The question of compatibility will remain a difficult problem to solve.

A reduction in the workload of the company trainer is often quoted as a reason for using training packages, but adoption to company-specific areas of skill and knowledge may prove equally time-consuming and costly. In particular, acquisition of the new hardware may well not be cost-effective in the forseeable future, especially for the smaller company.

Training packages, particularly if applied within a more flexible and open learning environment, demand different skills from the trainer. Very rarely are trainers trained in the use of new educational technology techniques. This lack of training may well be the reason for resistance of trainers toward new learning techniques. A major attitude change will be required if the implementation of new techniques is to be a success.

Training which uses training packages quite often demands implementation outside the formal course-running framework. New developments will make it even more urgent that trainees are allocated sufficient time at their place of work to learn, and that a systematic internal support and resource system is available to the trainees. At the same time, trainees must continue to be motivated to make use of the opportunities offered by the more flexible system. Reward systems, whether financial or psychological, must be built into learning systems.

Firms and trainers experience great difficulties in identifying suitable training packages and must be provided with assistance by a suitable external organization, whether nationally or on an industry basis. They must have guidance in the choice of the new hardware and must be assured of the standard of the material they purchase. There may be a role for an external institution to co-ordinate these functions and help users to share development costs.

Finally, designers of training packages must try and get as much evaluation feedback as possible from the learners and users of their material, and there should be a continuous dialogue between the designer and trainees, at least at the early stages of preparation of new training packages.

Participant's Comments
J R S Bulford *Agricultural Training Board*

There were 10 delegates present. The group was asked to consider opportunities, problems or limiting factors which would face companies' trainers and trainees in using packages and designers in developing packages in the future.

The opportunities were seen to be the chance to further increase the performance, and job satisfaction, of workers by providing standardized and well-constructed material covering both technical aspects of skills and knowledge related to work and also spreading into areas related to aspects of everyday life and even leisure pursuits. The potential offered by ever-developing technology, such as tele-conferencing, would need to be constantly explored, as would the potential of an increasing target population. The need for designers to produce material which was flexible and adaptable, and capable of being used by inexperienced trainers, was also highlighted.

Some of the problems and limitations would continue to be the need for material to be idiot-proof, specific and yet capable of reaching a broad market, and being able to ensure proper use by adequate tutorial and managerial support. It was evident that only certain staff could benefit from such material and the whole question of establishing the entry level of the target population remains complex. It was felt that overcoming initial resistance and inertia in the use of packages was important, and in this respect more managements would have to consider setting aside specific training time for the use of packages and the possibility of some form of 'carrot' for successful completion. The need for adequate feedback from the target population of the package to the original designer was ever-important.

Turning to techniques, the group felt that the application of self-instruction and distance learning techniques would have most influence on package design in the future, although the possibilities of group learning techniques were felt to have great potential. The use of the computer and video and slide/tape equipment were seen as areas for further development.

Views were expressed that there was need for some type of co-ordinating forum for producers of material which might help also to assess potential markets.

Section 2: Teaching-Learning Techniques and Strategies – I

2.1 Educational Technology in the Affective Zone: Is it Possible?

Cynthia Stoane
University of Dundee

Abstract: This paper explains an attempt to apply educational technology to the design of a multi-media instructional package for use with 10- and 11-year-old children. Terminal objectives cover areas in both the cognitive and the affective zones. Illuminative evaluation has been used to assess application of knowledge gained and changes in attitude.

Introduction

This paper explains an attempt to apply educational technology to the design of a multi-media instructional package, to be used with 10- and 11-year-old children visiting Fife Folk Museum in Scotland. The package has been successfully used with a number of pilot groups, achieving its objectives and, perhaps more importantly, proving to be an enjoyable and effective experience for both teachers and pupils.

Specific objectives were in the cognitive zone but the terminal objectives also covered areas of the affective zone.(Figure 1.)

The aims of the package were that children would show an awareness of the work of museums, an appreciation of the need for restoration and preservation and a developing interest in researching their historical heritage (Stenhouse, 1967).

The aims have been translated into worthwhile behavioural objectives, and illuminative evaluation has been used to assess application of knowledge gained and changes in attitude (Henderson *et al*, 1966; Simonson, 1977; Zimbardo, 1970).

It has been said that:

> a weak spot in the systems technology is its inability to deal with the question 'Which objectives are most worthwhile?'. Emphasis is usually on the question 'Have the objectives been achieved?' instead of 'What has been achieved?'. (Rowntree, 1979.)

The package has attempted to allow pupils to display creativity, originality and a willingness to explore (Scriven, 1967; Stake, 1967; Schools Council, 1975).

Background

Experience as a teacher had shown that children — even those interested in learning — could visit a museum with its plethora of exhibits, look at so much and yet see and remember practically nothing. This can be soul-destroying and worrying for both parents and teachers.

Children like to know where they are going; they have to know exactly what to look for when they get there, as well as what to do once they have found it. In this respect they are no different from the rest of the human race. We all like to

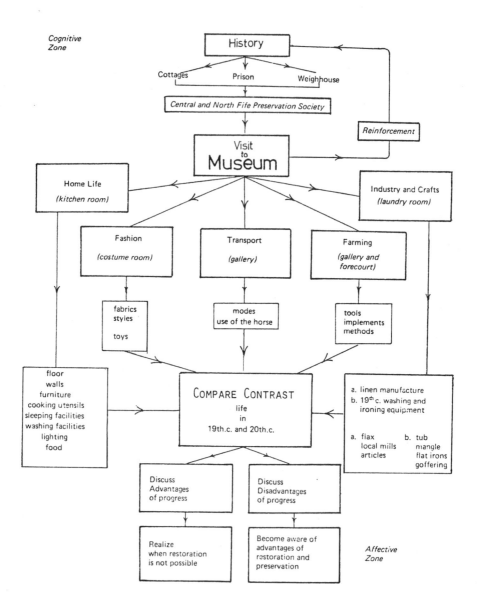

Figure 1. *Topic description*

		An Instructional Visit to Ceres Folk Museum Tape/Slide One Script	Instruction for Operator change slide at 'bleep'
No.	Visual	Sound	Instruction
Focus 1	Gramophone (drawing)	F/I Music .... F/O Music That was a song popular in late Victorian times and it makes a suitable introduction to the program you are about to see.	Focus Slide 1 Switch on tape
			change slide
2	A visit to Ceres Folk Museum **Title Slide**	This tape/slide presentation will help to prepare you for your visit to Ceres Folk Museum and show you what to look for when you get there.	
			change slide
3	Figures stepping from book	A folk museum is a place where you can see what life was like, in a bygone age. As if you'd turned back the pages of a history book, you will be able to see how people lived, worked and played a hundred or so years ago.	
			change slide
4	General view of Ceres showing Ceres burn superimposed Ceres	Perhaps you live and go to school in a village or perhaps in a town in Fife. Ceres is a village in Fife, quite a large village clustered along the banks of the Ceres burn, as you can see in this picture.	
			change slide
5	Copy of etching of Craighall Castle	Craighall Castle, a large and very old country house once stood nearby. Now demolished, Craighall Castle has however played a very important part over the centuries in the life of Ceres.	
			change slide
6	Archbishop Sharp's Bridge	When you arrive at Ceres you will leave the present and 20th century transport behind in the car park and walk over this bridge, one of the oldest things in the village — Archbishop Sharp's Bridge, which crosses the Ceres Burn. There is now also a modern bridge for today's traffic, but the old bridge is the one which would carry the traffic of another age to the true village centre.	
			change slide
7	Archbishop crossing bridge in coach	The bridge was built in the 17th century on the old main road to St. Andrews but there would have been a bridge of some description even before then.. It was named after Archbishop Sharp who met his death nearby in the year 1679. — The Archbishop was travelling from Edinburgh to St. Andrews. He crossed the Forth by boat to Largo, stopped overnight at Kennoway and then continued towards Ceres where he crossed this very bridge before stopping to smoke a pipe probably outside the Inn. — Little did he know that nine horsemen — Covenanters who had plotted to get rid of the Archbishop — lay in wait for him on lonely Magus Moor, beyond Ceres. He was murdered cruelly on the Moor, not many miles from his destination.	

Figure 2. *Part of script for tape/slide*

read up about a place before we go (for example in guides), we enjoy the satisfaction of recognizing places we have read about, and all this helps us to remember more about our experiences.

Design of the Package

The package, therefore, was designed to do just that – to let children know exactly where they were going, to set the scene, interest and motivate them and then instruct them on what to look for.

How was this Accomplished?

The first part of the multi-media package took the form of a tape/slide programme, shown in the classroom on the day of the visit to the museum. The programme was introduced with suitable music (HMV) and visuals to set the mood. The historic scene was also set, giving suitable backing and stories.(Figure 2.)

Preparation of Materials

Visuals were created in a variety of ways. Copies from books (Fenton, 1966) or old postcards, compared with present-day shots, gave children a before-and-after idea of the actual museum buildings (18th- and 19th-century cottages). What could have been rather dull, meaningless exhibits (laundry and kitchen utensils etc) were brought to life by historical reconstruction, using live models dressed in authentic costume and by the use of exhibits to reset the scene.

As a result of this 'scene setting', immediately the children stepped off the bus they recognized scenes and objects from the programme, such as the old 17th-century bridge which they walked over first (they had seen this bridge on slide and heard an exciting story connected with it); pantiles (the origin of which had been explained to them); and so on. Already they felt 'at home'. They recognized things, knew where they were going and there developed a 'we like this package because we get the answers correct' attitude – even though the answers had been carefully fed to them in the programme!

The children had been given simple ground plans of the museum (marking objects to be found) and response sheets for use at the museum. These were secured on clipboards. The printed materials were processed by offset litho so that the quality was good – not always possible for all schools but definitely helpful.(Figure 3.)

The response sheets were designed with as much variety as possible in the type of question and skills required to answer the questions. Many worksheets fail because all they seem to require of the children is to draw everything they see and many children cannot draw! The worksheets were well illustrated and the children were told that they could make additional drawings if they wished. Many did.

Back at school a second tape/slide programme was presented, giving the answers to the questions on the response sheets (reinforcement) and further back-up information. For example, the children had been told to identify an old biscuit cutter. They were now told that it was in fact a cutter used in a bakery worked in Victorian times. They were shown photographs of the inside of the bakery as it now is, with the ovens still in use and biscuits being made today using a cutter similar to the one identified in the museum.

The package also includes a workbook with follow-up activities based directly on the objectives of the programme and also a more specific short answer test designed for the less able reader.

This is a list describing Margaret Adams' 1980s style kitchen —

Floor covered in *Vinyl.*
Walls painted in *Vymura* paint.
Table and **Worktops** of *Formica.*
Stools covered in *Plastic* cushions.
Blind at window in *P.V.C.*
Cooker/Electric — surface *enamelled.*
Refrigerator/Electric.
Washing Machine/Electric.
Kitchen Sink in *stainless steel.*
Wash Up Basin in *Plastic.*
Equipment in *Plastic.*
Lightshade in *Plastic.*
Light/Electric.

Make a similar list for the kitchen you see in this room — 1850s style kitchen —

Floor _____

Walls _____

Table _____

Stools/Chairs _____

Blind/Curtains _____

Cooker _____

Refrigerator/Washing Machine ? ? ? _____

Sink _____

Basin _____

Equipment e.g. **bowls** _____
            spoons _____
            plates _____

Light _____

Lightshade _____

Figure 3. *Example from pupils' response sheet*

This is an example of what educational technologists can do for schools. For the unimaginative or busy teacher the work of the programme, the visit and the workbook to be used after the visit, all make a complete unit. But because of the open-endedness of the package, creative teachers can inject their own personalities into the work of follow-up projects, using the resource materials provided.

Assessment

It would have been inappropriate to assess the children by their ability to regurgitate lists and facts (although this is definitely the easiest way to test knowledge!) but knowledge of facts is only a small part of a much greater whole − of an attitude towards history and heritage, an appreciation of things of the past, an understanding of the need for preservation and restoration and an ability to compare the life of the past with the life of today. The assessment used therefore tested whether the children, as a result of the package and museum visit, had increased their ability and desire to observe and could describe the lives of the people who lived in the period studied − and even whether they could imagine themselves living the lives of those people.(Figure 4.)

Illuminative Assessment

Illuminative assessment played a large part in the evaluation of the attitudes of the pupils and teachers.

After the programme, most of the children showed a keen awareness of the work of museums. From answers in the follow-up workbooks it was obvious that they had gained an appreciation of the need for restoration and preservation.

Further favourable points worth mentioning are:

1. All the children (even the normally disinterested) were motivated and interested.
2. All children completed response sheets and pre- and post-tests with enthusiasm.
3. All children participated in question and discussion sessions.
4. Many children asked about the location of other museums.
5. Many children who did not normally attempt to write essays were sufficiently inspired to do so.
6. Teachers were delighted to have work prepared for them and were impressed with the interest and enthusiasm shown by the children.
7. Teachers commented that the work brought to light children's inability to read and answer questions accurately. Modern methods of teaching and assessment do not seem to reveal this inability. It is an interesting paradox that a project such as this in the affective zone can also affect attitudes to work and reveal inabilities.
8. Many individual projects developed as a direct result of the programme and its follow-up work.

Evaluation

What has been Achieved?

Far more than might be apparent from the limitations of even the worthwhile behavioural objectives. Given a list of materials used to furnish and equip the modern kitchen, the pupil may well be able to compare this with the 19th-century kitchen visited and list the furnishings and equipment used there. However, if the pupil writes about a day in the life of the inhabitants of that kitchen, designs a

4.   Read the following which is a part of Margaret Adams' Diary for 20th February, 1980 –
        Monday

        8.00 hrs   Got up – switched on water heater for bath

        8.05 hrs   Made breakfast : tinned grapefruit, cereal, coffee
                      and toast

        8.20 hrs   Took bath then dressed and made up

        8.30 hrs   Vacuumed floor
                      Tidied bed

        8.38 hrs   Programmed oven for evening meal

        8.40 hrs   Left house

        8.45 hrs   Caught usual bus for work _____

Pretend that you are a person living in the year 1880

*Now write your diary for 20th February, 1880 starting at the time you got up and finishing
when you went to bed. You can be a* man, woman *or* child.

Use the information you learned at the museum and during the two Tape/Slide Presentations.

                                                                                (10 marks)

5.   An old house built in **1760** stands in your town or village. It is no longer
                                lived in and is badly in need of repair. The local council has made it clear
                                that they want to demolish the house to make room for a car park and
                                picnic area. A group of people from your town (or village) have complained
                                because they feel that the old building ought to be **preserved**. A meeting
                                has been called to discuss the matter.

What is your opinion?

Write down what you think should happen and why?

                                                                                (5 marks)

Figure 4. *Samples from workbook used as assessment
instrument during validation*

classroom 'museum' to exhibit collections, and visits other museums in search of more knowledge, then creativity, originality and a willingness to explore will have been displayed.

If the pupil can discuss the benefits of progress on the one hand and appreciate the advantages of preservation on the other, we have come a long way from reciting that the Battle of Bannockburn took place in 1314 towards an appreciation of things of the past, an attitude towards history and heritage, and an understanding of past life and people.

It is hoped that the work of this programme has shown that educational technology has a great deal to offer in the affective zone.

References

Fenton, A (1966) (National Museum of Antiquities) *Scottish Country Life.* John Donald Publishers Ltd, Edinburgh.

Henderson, M E, Morris, L L and Fitzgibbon, C T (1966) *How to Measure Attitudes.* Sage, Beverly Hills, California.

Rowntree, D (1979) From educational technology to educational development. In Page, G T and Whitlock, Q (eds) *Aspects of Educational Technology* **XIII.** Kogan Page, London.

Schools Council, The (1975) *Curriculum Evaluation: the State of the Art.* Macmillan, London.

Scriven, M (1967) The methodology of evaluation. In Stake, R E (ed) *Perspectives of Curriculum Evaluation.* American Educational Research Association. Rand McNally, Chicago.

Simonson, M R (1977) Attitude change and achievement: dissonance theory in education. *Journal of Educational Research,* **70,** 3, pp 163-9.

Stake, R E (ed) (1967) *Perspectives of Curriculum Evaluation.* Monograph series on curriculum evaluation No 1. American Educational Research Association. Rand McNally, Chicago.

Stenhouse, L (1967) *Culture and Education.* Nelson, London.

Zimbardo, P and Ebbeson, E (1970) *Influencing Attitudes and Changing Behaviour.* Addison-Wesley, Reading, Massachusetts.

Acknowledgements

Mrs M Mercer, Curator of Fife Folk Museum and the Museum staff for their invaluable help and support. Mr A M Stewart, Dr B Rumble, Mrs E Johnson and the staff of Dundee College of Technology for their advice and for making available the resources of the Audio Visual and Reprographics Unit at the College for production of materials. Music used in the programme was taken from HMV acoustics records and from the BBC Sound Effects records.

2.2 Why Do We not Teach Students to Solve Problems?

G D Moss
University College, Cardiff

Abstract: Problem-solving is a high order skill, but one which is seldom taught and rarely assessed in higher education. Problem-solving is considered from several aspects: the nature of problems and their possible classification, the strategies which can be employed in solving problems, and the strategies that might be employed in teaching students to solve problems.

It is probably worth beginning by giving a definition of what I mean by 'problem-solving'. I am concerned in this paper to consider the skills of problem-solving as they relate to the solution of 'problems of consequence' as distinguished from relatively simple mathematical or computational problems, regarded by Gorman (1974) as pseudo problems. Gorman identifies a problem of consequence as one to which the answer or method of reaching the answer is not immediately apparent either to the student or the teacher. In other words, I am concerned with cognitive skills which would feature at the upper end of the Bloom (1956) hierarchy.

I firmly believe that the real problems facing society, as we move into the 1980s, are true problems of consequence. They involve issues such as industrial relations, environmental planning, policy formulation, diagnostic techniques, design techniques etc. Certainly some of these are areas which have already been identified as needing attention from the educational viewpoint, and around the world various specialist groups have recently reported development work in these areas. Engel, *et al* (1979) and Norman, *et al* (1977) have contributed to the growing literature on clinical problem-solving, while Angrist, *et al* (1979) and Moss, *et al* (1980) have written on problem-solving in relation to policy formulation.

However it is clear that, from an examination of recent literature, problem-solving as a specific skill, and more importantly as an investigation of the techniques which can be employed in developing such skills in students, receives far less attention than, say, developments in self-instructional teaching strategies. While there are notable publications on the efforts of educational psychologists to devise measures of problem-solving ability (eg Thorsland *et al*, 1974) very few have tried to relate this to classroom methods, Mahan (1970) being the notable exception in science education.

Furthermore, it is evident from various critical studies which have been made on examination questions, particularly at the tertiary level (Thompson, 1979; Beard, 1973) that very little attempt is made to assess the higher cognitive skills, the bulk of the overall assessment weighting falling on lower order descriptive accounts.

So we have a situation in which education in general appears to be ill-equipped in terms of technical know-how, to develop the skills in students which are acknowledged as being needed by society.

I have recently been able to spend some time examining the problems in teaching the skills of problem-solving to a large undergraduate class, and this is reported in detail elsewhere (Moss, *et al*, 1980). The difficulties encountered were not all obvious difficulties. What we were attempting to do was to encourage 100 first-year undergraduates in the School of Modern Asian Studies at Griffith University, Queensland, to tackle the following problem:

Australia's strategic, political and economic future lies with Asia and Australia should re-orient its policies accordingly. Present arguments for and against this and devise a coherent set of policies appropriate to your viewpoint.

This we did by dividing the class into four groups of 25 and organizing a series of workshops at which students could tackle the problem using a five-stage model:

1. Re-examine the problem and analyze it into researchable components.
2. Analyze each component into individual research tasks.
3. Assess and evaluate findings and formulate hypotheses.
4. Co-ordinate hypotheses into overall policy statement.
5. Evaluate the proposed policies.

Some of the more interesting points we came across in our study were as follows:

1. The students were extremely highly motivated and each spent many hours of non-formal time in solving the problem.
2. Students claimed to have learned more about the subject matter in this relevant way than via their formal courses.
3. Student ideas reflected their own idealistic values and the solutions were quite different from those that the staff felt should have been developed.
4. Student leaders in tutor-free groups are essential as managers.
5. Tutors are reluctant to release control of a group and frequently operate in a censorious, editorial way within a group.
6. Many workshop sessions operated tutor-free at the specific request of the students. These were as successful as tutor-led groups.
7. Problem analysis strategies became more sophisticated as the workshops progressed.

We were trying to identify a feasible method of operating large-scale classes for the solution of problems of consequence. In doing this we realized that there are problems which need to be overcome both before and during these classes. Thus:

1. Have preparatory sessions on group dynamics, problem analysis, problem-solving, synthetic skills (eg creativity).
2. Reduce tutor numbers to 1 : 25. Have tutors act as managers and troubleshooters.
3. Introduce a schedule of events.
4. Ensure adequate current resources (literature, staff, A/V etc).
5. Introduce a small group review of exercise and solutions.

This was an attempt to formalize the experience into a checklist of do's and don'ts, of advantages and disadvantages, with the intention of formulating a teaching strategy for the development of problem-solving skills.

It seems to me that, if educational technology is to remain a credible and genuine source of innovation and development over the next decade, then more developmental work of this nature will have to form a strong element of developments in educational technology in general.

References

Angrist, S S and Stewman, S (1979) Problem-solving for public policy: learning by doing. *Policy Analysis*, 5, 1, pp 97-117.
Beard, R (1973) Objectives in tertiary science education. *Aims, Methods and Assessment in Advanced Science Education.* Heyden, London.
Bloom, B S (1956) *Taxonomy of Educational Objectives, Handbook I: Cognitive Domain.* McKay, New York.
Engel, C E and Clarke, R M (1979) Medical education with a difference. *Programmed Learning and Educational Technology*, 16, 1, pp 70-87.

Gorman, R M (1974) *The Psychology of Classroom Learning: An Inductive Approach.* Merrill, Columbus, Ohio.

Mahan, L A (1970) Which extreme variant of the problem-solving method of teaching should be more characteristic of the many teacher variations of problem-solving teaching? *Science Education,* **54,** 4, pp 309-16.

Moss, G D and MacMillen, D (1980) A strategy for developing problem-solving skills in large undergraduate classes. *Studies in Higher Education,* 5, 2, pp 161-71.

Norman, G R, Barrows, H, Feightner, J and Neufeld, V R (1977) Measuring the outcome of clinical problem-solving. *Proceedings of the 16th Annual Conference on Research in Medical Education,* pp 311-16. Washington, DC.

Thompson, N (1979) The assessment of candidates for degrees in physics. *Studies in Higher Education,* 4, 2, pp 169-80.

Thorsland, M T and Novak, J D (1974) The identification and significance of intuitive and analytical problem-solving approaches among college physics students. *Science Education,* 58, 2, pp 245-65.

2.3 Educating for Justified Uncertainty

P Lefrere, J Dowie and P Whalley
The Open University

Abstract: Many studies have shown pronounced differences in people's ability to recognize when they are uncertain, to accept that being uncertain can be warranted, and to quantify their uncertainty. The inability to recognize, accept and express uncertainty, if widespread, will be important factors determining the effectiveness of teaching materials intended to prepare children or adults for change, especially if the direction of the change and its effect on the individual are themselves uncertain.

You may be certain there is a book called *Alice in Wonderland* and that it mentions a 'Mad Hatter'; that there is another book called *Alice Through the Looking-Glass;* that Sherlock Holmes remarked, 'Elementary, my dear Watson'; and that in the Bible story of Adam and Eve an apple is mentioned. In all five cases you are wrong. The first book cited was originally *Alice's Adventures in Wonderland* and it refers only to the 'Hatter', never to the 'Mad Hatter'. The other Alice book is *Through the Looking-Glass.* The Holmes passage runs: 'Excellent', said I; 'Elementary', said he. Finally, no apple is mentioned in the Book of Genesis. (Richard Asher, quoted in Hill, 1973, p 123).

Certainty about trivial matters such as these, or about weightier ones, may be justified or unjustified. Similarly, uncertainty may be warranted or not. In crude matrix form we have four possibilities:

(1) justified certainty	(2) unjustified certainty
(3) justified uncertainty	(4) unjustified uncertainty

It is not much of a distortion of our present educational system to say that, with rare exceptions, its curricula are dominated by cells 1 and 2, with occasional leavenings of cell 4 –(we refuse to identify the subject(s) in the last case). This leaves, in our view, one cell that, for justified uncertainty, is sadly neglected. If this were not so, we would believe those who point out the 'gambles' (probabilistic choices) involved in complex societal decisions would be less often resented for the anxiety they provoke. The implicit (or even explicit) call is frequently for educationalists to produce the 'one-armed' scientist, the one who does not respond 'on the one hand the evidence is so, but on the other hand . . .'

Why should we reject such calls, and strive towards educating for justified uncertainty? The question is clearly loaded and rhetorical: because uncertainty is always there, an essential element of the human condition.

> The decisions we make, the conclusions we reach and the explanations we offer are usually based on beliefs concerning the probability of uncertain events such as the result of an experiment, the outcome of a surgical operation or the future value of an investment (Tversky, 1974).

The significance of such sentiments will be apparent to anyone concerned with educating children, or adults, for tomorrow rather than yesterday. Tomorrow's world will need a greater acceptance of the likelihood of change, an acceptance which we believe can be fostered by a wider introduction to and dissemination of the notion of justified uncertainty.

The direction of change is indicated in a curriculum project of the 1960s and 1970s, developed at Stanford University, California, for elementary (primary or first) school students (Sieber *et al*, 1970). The curriculum developers took great pains to formally train and encourage students to recognize and distinguish between *un*warranted certainty and warranted *un*certainty. According to those researchers, the technique they used (teaching people to recognize the reasons why something may be unknown and why uncertainty may be warranted) had dramatic effects.

> The children . . . (were able) to defend themselves against children and adults who urged them to change their behaviour or adopt beliefs without thinking . . . (they) began to realize that teachers are not omniscient . . . (used) this new skill . . . (at home and with) friends outside the school . . . (and not just 'good' students but) children who had previously been withdrawn, bored . . . seemed particularly excited and enthusiastic after . . . the training. (Sieber *et al*, 1976.)

We do not know whether work such as Sieber's has been drawn to the attention of those drawing up British curricula for the remainder of the century, but we consider it unlikely that the high-sounding phrases mooted by politicians in discussion documents — for example 'to help pupils acquire knowledge and skills relevant to adult life and employment in a fast-changing world (Carlisle and Edwards, 1980) — will result in British school children of the 1980s even being prepared for changes which are already happening in California. (Not that California is always a good reference point, but we are 68 per cent sure that they are not always wrong over there!)

Our own attempts to do something 'relevant to adult life' are represented by the introduction of a new Open University course, U201 'Risk', first presented by Dowie in 1980. That course explores the idea of justified uncertainty, and since we are presenting it to students who are already adults we introduce them to material which may help them overcome, or at least better appreciate, the problems they already encounter. For example, we consider the use of stereotyped approaches to problem-solving, much discussed (in terms of cognitive and motivational origins) in the growing literature on behavioural decision theory; we each have our preferred heuristics, or mental strategies, which — although usually effective and economical of thinking time — can easily lead to systematic and predictable errors. Detailed reviews of such heuristics (and the biases in the estimates to which they lead) can be found elsewhere (eg Slovic *et al*, 1977), but listed below are a few of these of particular relevance here:

1. misperceptions of randomness;
2. overvaluation of data from small samples;
3. neglect of 'base-rate' (statistical) information when making predictions;
4. unwarranted confidence in one's knowledge: the 'certainty illusion', encouraged by many curricula;
5. desire for redundant information;
6. 'anchoring' bias;
7. 'availability' bias;
8. 'hindsight' bias.

Greater awareness of such factors may go considerably towards overcoming the finding that 'many, many adults unfortunately are already deeply involved in a social and emotional context where uncertainty is simply unacceptable' (Sieber, 1980).

This is, of course, the context we are in danger of operating in at the Open University. We therefore provide in our course a number of optional assignments (called 'Probers' in OU jargon) as a basis for discussing the concept of justified uncertainty and for investigating ways of making it operational for those who wish to do so.

While students may find tackling them improves their probabilistic thinking processes, our main purpose in introducing them is to produce a broad educational experience. They do, however, acquire specific acquaintance with some of the key questions raised in the literature, such as those below (after Fallon, 1976).

> Are most people capable of expressing their state of information about certain events or quantities in probabilistic terms?
>
> Are there any general biases or heuristics that individuals exhibit when asked to assess their uncertainty in these terms that distort their assessments?
>
> Can such biases, if they exist, be corrected or improved?

Perhaps (probably?) as a result of conventional curricula, the answer to the first question seems to be 'Generally, no'. Even professional statisticians and other mathematicians apparently display in their behaviour misconceptions of probabilistic processes often thought to be limited to naive subjects. For example, one study of the statistical intuitions of:

experienced research psychologists . . . revealed a lingering belief in what may be called the 'law of small numbers' according to which even small samples are highly representative of the populations from which they are drawn (quoted in Tversky, 1974).

The estimation of probabilities is certainly a complex task, particularly (as in our course) when the Prober questions range over such wide issues as politics, economics, sport and safety. This concern with real life may, however, have the benefit that students tackle the task more seriously than in other studies reported in the literature. While we do use the Prober exercises for assessment purposes this is only because assessment, however educationally detrimental, is a required part of our courses; conventional multiple-choice assignments, whilst more familiar, are of dubious worth. As our introduction to Probers for Risk students says:

The ordinary multiple-choice questions that you may have encountered in earlier courses (or life in general) ask you only to indicate the alternative you believe to be the correct answer. You may be certain that one of the alternatives provided is the correct answer, or you may be more or less uncertain about which is correct (overall uncertainty can, of course, include certainty that a particular alternative is not the correct answer). That sort of question has limited usefulness, but it doesn't allow you to convey how uncertain you are about the answer and as between the various alternatives. Indeed, it really implies that you ought to be certain and, when you are not, forces you to be overcertain in your response. It follows that it doesn't tell us about your uncertainty, so there is less feedback about our teaching and your learning . . .

The appropriate method we believe to be one that asks you to express your degree of belief about each of the alternatives provided in a question being the correct answer. Given that, in the questions we set, only one of the alternatives can be the correct answer and one of them must be the correct answer, your degrees of belief must constitute probabilities in the sense of adding up to 100 per cent (Dowie, 1980).

Each of the several sets of Probers for the course consists of 54 items. One-third of the items are two-alternative, one-third three-alternative and one-third four-alternative. This variation is intended to make the point that one's uncertainty will be partly a function of the number of alternatives presented. Typically, each Prober also contains some questions which are course-related (based on course material), some which are general knowledge ('quiz' items) and some of which deal with future events (five-week forecast periods).

First reports indicate that most students find Probers both challenging and enjoyable, thinking of them more in terms of providing an experience of coming to terms with one's uncertainty than in terms of a number-producing exercise. We have certainly emphasized in the course material that reasoning about the alternatives, rather than simply generating numbers, is what is needed.

The 'reward system' associated with any element of a curriculum, for example the extent to which students are encouraged to be curious (Sharroch, 1980) or to challenge their educators must have a pronounced effect on the credibility of the aspirations of the curriculum developers. In our particular case, we have chosen to 'mark' the Prober questions using a scoring system which 'rewards honesty', in the sense that only by reproducing his honest degrees of belief can a student maximize his expected score (Shuford and Brown, 1975). Those 'degrees of belief' must be translated into probability figures for each alternative offered. The student receives a score which is a transformation of the logarithm of the probability assigned to the correct alternative.

The realism of a student's assignments of probability may be 'externally calibrated' by noting what the actual outcome was for a given judgement, and by keeping a tally of the proportion of events that actually occur among those to which he assigns the probability. Specifically, XX per cent of the outcomes assigned a (subjective) probability of .XX should actually occur (Lichtenstein et al, 1977). For a person who is well-calibrated, 70 per cent of the outcomes for which he says 'my (subjective) probability is that there is a .7 chance of this happening' should turn out to be actual outcomes. Those interested in the technical details of such schemes, and their potential for computerization, can pursue this matter elsewhere (eg Dirkswager, 1975).

Our approach in our course is deliberately atheoretical as far as the precise nature of probabilistic thinking processes is concerned. We are not concerned to sell any particular brand or model of it, merely to put the product in general on the menu. Our feedback is therefore as 'raw' as possible — each student's responses are tabulated rather than processed., and we leave to individuals the task of relating their individual responses to those of the whole student population, shown in a (regression-based) 'external calibration' line.

'Justified uncertainty' exercises, such as Probers, are only possible where 'objective' answers exist; we define objective as 'very high inter-subjective consensus among relevant people'. This should be a clear indication that the Prober element of 'Risk' is complemented (indeed dominated) by concern for the rest of the course material, and student essays, to emphasize their epistemological probability! We would only wish to see them used in a (school or university) curriculum which addressed the notion of 'justification' alongside that of uncertainty. But, on the other hand, we would see little advantage in a curriculum which completely failed to address these issues in their quantitative — as distinct from qualitative — form, for that seems to be the opposite danger to the imbalance existing in most other curricula.

References

Carlisle, M and Edwards, N (1980) *A Framework for the School Curriculum.* Department of Education and Science (Welsh Office).

Dirkswager, A (1975) Computer-based testing with automatic scoring based on subjective probabilities. In Lecarme, O and Lewis, R (eds) *Computers in Education.* North-Holland.

Dowie, J (1980) *U201 Risk: Course Handbook.* Open University Press.

Fallon, R (1976) *Subjective Assessment of Uncertainty.* P-5581, The Rand Corporation.

Hill, E (1973) The art of accuracy. *Reader's Digest,* 103, pp 121-3.

Lichtenstein, S, Fischhoff, B and Phillips, L D (1977) Calibration of probabilities: the state of the art. In Jungermann, H and de Zeeuw, G (eds) *Decision-Making and Change in Human Affairs.* D Reidel.

Sharrock, W (1980) In defence of curiosity. *New Scientist,* 85, pp 1020-21.

Shuford, E and Brown, T A (1975) Elicitation of personal probabilities and their assessment. *Instructional Science,* 4, pp 137-88.

Sieber, J, Epstein, M and Petty, C (1970) The effectiveness of modelling and concept-learning procedures in teaching children to indicate uncertainty. *The Irish Journal of Education,* 4, 2, pp 90-106.

Sieber, J, Clark, R E, Smith, H M and Sanders, N (1976) *The Effects of Learning to be Uncertain on Children's Knowledge and Use of Drugs.* R D Memo 144, Stanford Center for Research and Development in Teaching.

Sieber, J (1980) Educating for uncertainty. *U201 Risk: Broadcast Notes (1).* Open University Press.

Slovic, P, Fischhoff, B and Lichtenstein, S (1977) Behavioral decision theory. *Annual Review of Psychology,* 28, pp 1-39.

Tversky, A (1974) Assessing uncertainty. *Journal of Royal Statistical Society, Series B,* 36, pp 148-59.

2.4 Educational Technology in Special Education

Cynthia Stoane
University of Dundee

Abstract: The methods and results of a project dealing with children who require special methods of education, appropriate to their individual requirements, are given. It was intended to determine whether the provision of an individualized learning system developed through an educational technology approach could help these children achieve maximum potential. A considerable improvement in learning abilities and in motivation was recorded.

Introduction

Can children who require special methods of education, appropriate to individual requirements, be helped to achieve maximum potential by the provision of an individualized learning system which has been developed through an educational technology approach?

This question formed the basis of a research project in special education. The project started in October 1976 when some preliminary work was carried out with a small group of children all with an IQ of below 55. Programmes were designed providing specific training which helped those children who had previously failed to learn to overcome some of their learning difficulties.

A considerable improvement in learning abilities and in motivation has been recorded. A systematic approach to curriculum development and the use of appropriate methods and media in instructional activities have been instrumental in bringing about this change.

Procedure and various uses of the programmes have been described in an instructional sequence for teachers so that the approach can be field tested with other similar groups.

Background to the Problem Area

Mental handicap is not a classification which produces a homogeneous group. Children whose IQ has been assessed as below 55 are grouped together. But far from being a like group, these children are as heterogeneous as any group of youngsters. Their abilities, disabilities and learning disorders are highly individual, as are all their needs, particularly those for learning.

If the Melville Report and the Warnock Report on Special Education, the two most significant reports of the last decade, are looked at, it is clear that there has been a slow movement towards recognition of the above statement.

The Melville Report and the subsequent Education (Mentally Handicapped Children) Act 1974 rejected the terms 'ineducable' and 'untrainable' and brought large numbers of mentally handicapped children into the educational system. It led to a definition of the aims and methods of education for children in Special Schools.

What Did 'Educable' Mean?

Children who had previously spent their days in occupational centres now went to school. And because they were in school it was felt that they must be educated.

What Does 'Educated' Mean?

What should they be taught? Arithmetic, reading, writing? Many teachers in special education are still asking this question.

The recent Warnock Report (1978) stated that the real question today is how to satisfy the particular educational needs of all children and stated that one in five of *all* children would at some time require special education.

This does not infer that one in five children is mentally handicapped, but merely that children in the normal streams of education may, for one reason or another (eg illness or a particular learning difficulty), at some time in their school career, require special educational help or individualized learning.

Perhaps the most important requirement for individualization is the availability of a wide variety of instructional materials and media from which to select in order to achieve any particular objective.

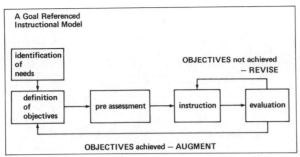

Figure 1.

The selection of the most appropriate methods and media after an analysis of objectives, strengths and weaknesses and individual requirements is the essence of an educational technology approach (see Figure 1). (Popham *et al*, 1971.)

Significance of the Problem

From the above observation then it would seem that children who require special methods of education, appropriate to their very individual requirements (Education [Scotland] Act, 1969) can be helped to achieve maximum potential by the provision of an individualized learning system (Duane, 1973) which has been developed sceptically and systematically through an educational technology approach (Rowntree, 1974). But there is very little available particularly in the realms of software and structured curriculum. Yet there is the potential for educational technology — for a systematic approach in Special Education (Cleary *et al*, 1976). Children in Special Education *are* special: they have special difficulties and they need special teachers, special methods and special resources (McConkey, 1974).

The difficulty of communicating the 'objective approach' to teachers and instructresses is often a barrier. Teachers are not inspired by the jargon or even the flow charts of the educational technologist. Practical demonstration and results cut more ice with those 'at the coal face' than esoteric theory. Years of valuable experience should not be sneered at. Teachers know a great deal about *who* they teach. Consideration of *what* they teach is of importance too (Is it appropriate? Is it clear what the child is expected to learn?) After having defined objectives or goals efficient decisions must be made about *how* goals can be achieved (Figure 2) and later, in the evaluation stage, consideration must be given to what has been achieved in addition to the question about whether or not the objectives have been achieved (Rowntree, 1979).

Design of Materials

The investigation started in October 1976, working with severely mentally handicapped children at a special school in Dundee. The school had previously been an occupational centre and the children had all been assessed as having an IQ below 55 (ie classified 'severely mentally handicapped' in Scotland, and ESN(S) in England and Wales [DES, 1975]).

Perceptual Development

Looking at the children's perception of the world, of themselves and of the objects round them became the first interest. What did they see when they looked at an

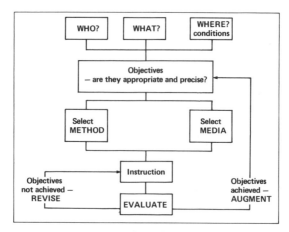

Figure 2.

object – a cup for example? Did it have meaning for them? And what did it mean?

It was found that many of the children had no difficulty with sight or sound. They were able to receive stimuli through sight and sound. But they had difficulty in integrating or processing the information received and responding to it meaningfully.

The truth is demonstrated in one of the old Chinese proverbs, expressed in this adaptation:

> *I hear and I forget;*
> *I hear and see and I remember;*
> *I do and I understand;*
> *I understand and I do.*
>
> Edgar Baker
> *adapted from old Chinese proverb.*

The children seemed to hear yet not *listen,* to look and yet not *see* and to do without *understanding.*

Problems Affecting Learning

It had been stated in the 1974 report that these children were capable of learning and yet they were failing in many cases to learn. It had taken four years for the question to emerge about how they could learn.

The problem seemed threefold:

1. There was no structure to their learning.
2. Any learning which took place was accidental, as if by chance.
3. Teaching or training was intuitive.

The problem identified a need – a need to find a way to focus, as it were, on learning. It was decided therefore that as early as possible the children required particular training in three ways to help them perceive; to give their everyday world first and their learning later some meaning:

1. They must receive stimuli through appropriate sensory channels.
2. They must receive help in processing information (the integration stage).
3. They must be encouraged to respond in order to consolidate what is perceived.

How Was This Done?

Training programmes were devised under the general title 'Listening-Seeing-Doing', a title which suggests the postulates underlying the design of the materials.

It was difficult working with 10 children, aged between six and 11 — mongols, autistic, spastic, partially blind and brain disordered children — all severely mentally handicapped and yet all grouped together, despite this multiplicity of handicap, in one room, with one instructress and a lot of patience. What was an educational technologist to do?

Designing the training programme was the first attempt. The series comprises nine taped programmes using wooden toys and a large number of support materials, including overhead projector transparencies, posters, board games and exercises. All materials are designed to help to overcome some of the difficulties of these children, in language development, body concept, number awareness, colour discrimination and spatial relationship.

Individualization of Learning

A frequent criticism of individualized learning is that programmes designed specifically for one child can never be used again and are therefore not cost-effective. This has certainly not been found to be the case in this investigation. Programmes or materials designed for one child have frequently been used again by other children with the same identified needs (Stoane *et al*, 1980).

Although some children offered resistance to headphones at first, difficulties were overcome. At no time was there any resistance to the use of tape recording. The children's instructress was at first very dubious about the acceptability of headphones and was therefore all the more impressed with the successful results.

Programmes have been designed so that they can be used with selected groups of children listening to the tapes, sitting at a table, with the wooden toys. However even greater success has been recorded using headphones (in series) so that a child is isolated and all extraneous noise is cut out. In this situation, it has been found that concentration has been increased and distractability decreased. The children make physical and verbal responses in a way that has amazed their instructresses and teachers.

An example can be taken from one of the programmes in the colour discrimination group. Based on the well-known rhyme 'Two little dickie birds' the objective is to differentiate between the colours yellow and blue. The programme was designed specifically for a child called Peter who in a class of other children seemed confused and able to achieve nothing. His needs seemed greater than his strengths but one strength was that he liked music; his weaknesses were inattention, inability to concentrate or focus attention and lack of speech with understanding. For example, he had 'picked up' the word blue which he used inappropriately.

Two wooden birds, one painted yellow and one blue, were made with holes in them so that they fit onto the child's fingers. There is also a wooden shoe because the birds 'Yellow' and 'Blue' sit on a shoe! The sound of birdsong introduces the taped programme. This intrigued Peter. His attention was gained using this stimulus. At first he resisted the headphones but soon accepted them in order to listen to the bird singing. The programme is short and requires the child to listen to instruction and, understanding it, make responses using the wooden birds. At the end of the programme the birdsong is heard again. Peter soon realized this and sat through the programme waiting for his 'reward'. The programme was used daily with him. He did not tire of it. Progress was slow, as can only be expected, but he did respond occasionally with correct actions. Most significantly, however, after three days he responded to the birdsong by saying the word 'bird'. This was a triumph. The next step was to associate the word 'bird' with the wooden simulation bird and ultimately with the real thing. A further progressive step was Peter's use of the word 'shoe', used in response to the wooden simulation and his own shoe.

As important as achievement of the specific objective was consideration about what else had been achieved.

Results

The use of the wooden simulations has proved motivational. The tape recorded instruction has stimulated the children. It has been stated (Morrison, 1977) that tape recorded instruction is obeyed more readily than direct instruction by mentally handicapped children. Certainly this was found to be the case in the investigation. Sound is focused and attention caught.

By using pairs of headphones in series with a child, a teacher or instructress can observe and assess a child's ability to make responses while working alone. Satisfied that he can do so, the teacher can leave the child to practise or repeat work. The pre-recorded tape has clear and precise instruction, eliminating ambiguity and confusion.

It must however be pointed out that in working with such a heterogeneous group success and achievement with the 10 children was at varying degrees and levels.

Generally, however, the programmes seem to have awakened an interest, stimulated and motivated the children; illuminatively evaluating it, it can be said that they used the language of the programmes, they 'talked' about the birds, looked for them outside, picked out colours like the birds in other objects and showed a slowly developing number awareness.

Testing

In order to validate the programmes, tests were devised, based on specific objectives for each programme. These printed testsheets now form an integral part of the programmes and can be used by teachers to test children's achievement of the objectives. What is meant, however, by achievement of objectives by the mentally handicapped child is rather different from achievement by the normal child. Judgement cannot be by normal standards.

The enabling objectives and how to administer both tests and programmes are explained in a teacher's book which accompanies the Listening-Seeing-Doing series.

Conclusion

This has been an attempt to make a contribution to methodology, to demonstrate how children in special education can be helped to overcome some of their learning difficulties and can be motivated and stimulated by the use of systematic methods and appropriate media. We have concluded that an individualized learning system can be developed using an educational technology approach.

In summing up what are the main features which have brought success, the following would be listed:

1. Design of materials has been structured.
2. Programmes are individualized to suit particular needs of children.
3. Appropriate media has been selected.
4. Materials have been proved acceptable with teachers/instructresses.
5. Materials are motivational.
6. Reinforcement is provided.

Educational technology — this rational problem-solving approach to education (Rowntree, 1974) — has its origins rather further back than is often imagined. Back in the 1940s, Ralph Tyler in advocating the use of objectives (Tyler, 1949) said that there are two screens in the educational process:

Screen One — The Philosophy of Education.
Should the objectives be taught?
Screen Two — The Psychology of Education
Can the objectives be taught?

Now, in the 1980s, two more screens could be added:

Screen Three — Technology *in* and *of* education
How can they be taught/learned?
Screen Four — Evaluation of Education
Have they been learned/taught?

References

Cleary, A, Mayes, T and Packham, D (1976) *Educational Technology — Implications for Early and Special Education.* John Wiley & Sons, London.

Department of Education and Science (1975) *The Discovery of Children requiring special education and the assessment of their needs.* Joint circular No 2/75 DES and No 21/75 Welsh Office.

Duane, J E (1973) *Individualized Instruction Programs and Materials.* Educational Technology Publications, New Jersey.

The Education (Scotland) Act (1969).

McConkey, R (1974) *The Nature of Research in the Education and Training of the Severely Mentally Handicapped.* Jordanhill College of Education, Glasgow.

The Melville Report (1974) HMSO.

Morrison, D (1977) Sounds familiar. *The Times Educational Supplement,* 19 October.

Popham, W J and Baker, E L (1970) *Systematic Instruction.* Prentice-Hall, Englewood Cliffs, New Jersey.

Rowntree, D (1974) *Educational Technology in Curriculum Development.* Kogan Page, London.

Rowntree, D (1979) Educational technology to educational development. In Page, G T and Whitlock, Q (eds) *Aspects of Educational Technology* **XIII.** Kogan Page, London.

Stoane, C, Dear, E and Learmonth, A (1980) *Two case studies showing successful examples of the application of educational technology to individualization of learning in Listening-Seeing-Doing.* Scottish Council for Educational Technology, Edinburgh.

Tyler, R (1949) *Basic Principles of Curriculum and Instruction.* University of Chicago Press, Chicago.

The Warnock Report on Special Education (1978). HMSO.

Acknowledgements

The author would like to thank Mr A M Stewart, Dundee College of Technology, for his help and support in the project. Also thanks are extended to the headteachers and staff of Coldside and Fairmuir Schools in Dundee, Scotland.

The materials described in this paper have been produced at Dundee College of Technology and will shortly be published by the Scottish Council for Educational Technology. The author is grateful to SCET for the financial support and assistance in the publishing and dissemination of the materials.

2.5 The Application of Technology to Aid the Investigation and Remediation of the Under-Achieving Child

Charles H Bedwell
Vision Consultant

Abstract: Probably the most serious aspect of educational under-achievement is reading difficulty. Reading and written expression in language is a basic skill and without it a child's academic progress is limited and under-achievement or even regression may occur. Causes, indications and remedial teaching techniques are dealt with.

Introduction

Probably the most serious aspect of educational under-achievement is reading difficulty. Reading and written expression in language is a basic skill and without it a child's academic progress is limited; he is likely to under-achieve and he may well regress. Unfortunately the proportion of children experiencing reading difficulty is considerable, and appears to be approximately 15 per cent to 20 per cent of children through to early secondary school years, and with a minority continuing until they leave school.

The Range of Reading Difficulty

Problems of reading difficulty range from the child with specific reading disability, often classified as dyslexic, to the child who, with sheer effort, maintains an average performance, though really under-achieving, with his difficulty possibly remaining unnoticed. There are many factors to be considered in relation to reading retardation, but when a child tries, and appears to have a degree of innate academic ability but is not achieving adequately, there should be technical reasons as to why he is not performing as adequately as he should. The problem appears particularly serious where a child has an above-average non-verbal intelligence for his age, but a much lower reading age. In other children, for example those who are educationally subnormal, the same factors might be involved from the perceptual point of view compared to the potentially bright child, but the lack of academic potential will then be a very significant factor in how far the child will be able to achieve.

Reading difficulty, and its effect on educational under-achievement, pose considerable problems to the child, teacher and parent, and educationalists in general. It leads to a feeling of inadequacy and frustration on the part of the child. Individual remedial teaching is expensive to provide, and availability tends to be limited by increasing pressure to reduce educational costs.

The Problem of Investigation

When a child is experiencing educational difficulty and under-achievement, the teacher and parents are in considerable difficulty in attempting to determine what are the likely factors involved. Educational psychological tests can, to a certain extent, point to certain areas of deficiency, but educationalists do not really have the technical facilities, and therefore expertise, in critically determining the likely cause of the child's problem. Unfortunately, the longer these problems of retardation are left, with the often unjustified hope that they will rectify themselves of their own accord, the more affected is the child, and helping him becomes more technically difficult and time-consuming.

If, therefore, better technical methods can be found of investigating the likely factors involved in reading difficulty, how any anomaly present can be treated and managed, and what is the most suitable technical approach to teaching to take with that child, remediation can be made more effective, less stressful to all concerned, and less time-consuming. If the problems can be detected and handled, at least by the time the child is seven to eight years old, remediation is usually much quicker, as the child has greater adaptability. However, if tackling the problem is left until secondary school age the difficulties in remediation increase.

Factors Involved in Reading Difficulties

Language

Language is a method of communication involving the use of a combination of sound codes that the child learns to understand by listening to his mother and those around him, and at the same time developing, through the power of speech, his ability to express himself vocally. Reading and writing is a further extension of visually coding a language so that it can be assimilated in reading and expressed in writing.

In the acquisition of language, the child therefore has to have the facility of being able to hear, discriminate and comprehend what is said to him without difficulty, so that he can readily recall from memory that certain combinations of sounds appear meaningful to him. When he learns to speak he subconsciously listens to himself at the same time so that he can compare how he speaks to those around him.

Aural Sequential Memory

Aural sequential memory is therefore important in the initial development of language ability. If a young child has had a history of catarrh, sinusitis, ear-ache, tonsils and/or adenoids, for example, his ability to discriminate sounds and hear himself speak may well have been affected. His initial build-up of language ability will therefore have probably suffered and he will either be hesitant at expressing himself verbally, or appear to have difficulty in using the right words. Later, these conditions may have cleared but the effect on his language ability may still be evident on careful probing. Though audiometric tests of hearing may be undertaken, they may not necessarily be sophisticated enough to detect some of the more complex aspects involved in aural discrimination, or that previous problems had existed.

Visual Sequential Memory

By the time the child is four or five years old he has usually been taught the early stages of reading. Some children learn to read almost automatically without difficulty whereas others, often in spite of trying hard, find reading achievement very difficult. Reading involves the perception of letters from their shape, and recognizing that certain letter combinations form words, which may be used to express language. When the child has learnt to write letter shapes and words he then learns to express himself in the written language. If a child is to recognize letters from their shapes, words from their letter combination and order, and certain aspects of grammatical construction, it is important each time he looks at letters and words that he sees them clearly without difficulty, so that an unconfused visual input can be sent to the brain. By this means he builds up a visual sequential memory, which is essential in assimilating language by reading, and expressing it in the written language. If a child has difficulty in obtaining an adequate visual sequential memory his reading achievement is likely to be poor, his writing ability reduced, and his spelling weak.

Additional Complicating Factors

Aural and visual sequential memory are essential in reading and written expression of language. In a minority of children with reading difficulty there appear to be factors which prevent related functioning of the brain centres controlling hearing, speech and sight; in some cases the causes may be congenital, and in others problems at birth.

Immaturity in development, and a poorly developed laterality and control, are quite common amongst children with more severe reading difficulty. In the case of ocular control, the development of this function is likely to be at the child's developmental age, not chronological age, thus further increasing his difficulties. Also there is likely to be the added problem of poor achievement, tending further to depress the child's feeling of immaturity.

There can also be innate differences in language ability and comprehension amongst individual children, eg because of early language deprivation.

Seeing and Reading

Commonly our vision is taken for granted, and a very simple concept taken of the eye and vision, rather like that of a camera. In the conventional investigation of vision the accent is on the ability to discriminate letters under fixed or static conditions of gaze, simple static tests on whether the eyes can maintain binocular alignment, and the correction of any significant refractive error. Where psychological testing is undertaken, attention is paid to visual motor skills and, for example, shape recognition, which becomes more relevant as the symbols used are more closely related to those involved in text.

Vision is much more complex than this simple concept, however, and involves using the eyes under dynamic or moving conditions, for example scanning along a line of text. Anomalies of behaviour and performance that can occur under dynamic viewing conditions are usually likely to remain unnoticed under simpler static methods of investigation.

Vision and Brain Laterality

The eyes are an extension of the brain, providing approximately 50 per cent of the neural input to the brain. Unlike the limbs, laterality and control of the eyes is far more complicated. The eyes are lined with a sensitive seeing layer, or retina, which is divided vertically into two halves about the fovea, or the centre of the retina, for maximum visual acuity. The left-hand halves of each retina are connected via the visual pathway to the left rear, or occipital region, of the brain, and the right-hand halves of the retinas to the right occipital region. Everything we see, therefore, on our right-hand side is imaged in the left-hand half of the brain, and everything we see on our left-hand side is imaged in the right-hand side of the brain. For a very small foveal area there appears to be some representation in both hemispheres. In reading, therefore, images of words are likely to fall on both retinal halves of both eyes, and therefore be transmitted to both cerebral hemispheres — a far more complex situation than that involving the limbs.

Binocular Vision

We are born with the facility of using two eyes together, but stable environmental adaptation is necessary if this function is to work adequately. In reading, therefore, it is necessary that the moving of the eyes together is finely co-ordinated. With stable co-ordination of the eyes, images of objects seen can then readily fall on the same corresponding retinal areas of both eyes. By this means we have the facility of being able to use both eyes together so that we can see singly. If this stable alignment of the eyes under dynamic conditions has not been achieved, images will be falling on different parts of the retina, sending a confused visual input to the brain. Visual mis-cueing, mistakes on reading, such as missing a line, mis-reading, and poor visual sequential memory can result. In general co-ordination of the eyes for near vision requires more effort than does looking into the distance. In some cases considerable effort and tension can be involved in using the eyes for close work, resulting in stress and possible discomfort, and making concentration for any appreciable period difficult for the child.

Research on Reading Difficulty in Junior Children

In an earlier research project the author (Bedwell, 1973) investigated an unselected class of eight-year-old children, taking a multi-disciplinary approach, and looking at approximately 100 factors which might be significant to reading difficulty. In subsequent research, classes of children of different age groups were examined, looking at what appeared to be the more significant factors in relation to reading difficulty.

In all cases, difficulty in dynamic control while reading, particularly when laterality was less well developed, appeared highly significant in relation to reading ability. It was noted that in general children with increased difficulty in ocular control tended to fidget much more while reading and writing, in an attempt to compensate for difficulties in ocular scanning control. Also various head postures, such as head on arm while writing, would be used to avoid binocular image embarrassment when binocular co-ordination was poor.

Of the eight-year-old children examined, it was found that there was a significant relationship between excessive head movement during reading, and unsettled eye control and poor visual fixation, in the poor readers. There was also a significant correlation between muscular stress (a narrow eyelid opening) and reading difficulty, and also signs of image confusion and reading difficulty.

Research with Senior Pupils

In a later research project (Bedwell, Grant and McKeown, 1980), a group of 40 13-year-old pupils at a secondary school were examined. Half of the pupils were retarded two years or more in reading and the other half were good readers and used as a control group. The pupils were assessed educationally; each group possessed a normal laterality distribution, and those with subsidiary handicaps, other than possible complex visual ones, were not included. It was found that there was little statistical significance of distance visual acuity to reading difficulty. When dynamic visual behaviour and ocular control were investigated while reading, however, difficulty and anomalies in ocular control and attempted postural compensation appeared highly significant in relation to reading difficulty.

Subsequent work has indicated that with many children, because the problems of ocular control for near vision are greater than for distance vision, reading was more fluent when enlarged text was displayed at a distance, compared to ordinary reading text at near. Many of the children with reading difficulty very readily suffered from early near visual fatigue, causing them to perform with less adequacy as they read down a selected test, indicating that their true reading ability was not necessarily being assessed adequately.

Remedial Teaching

Complex dynamic visual problems appear therefore to be very significant in relation to reading difficulty, though the adequate technical investigation of such children does require the use of specialized technology and expertise which the author has been developing. Recognition that a child might have contributory visual problems is the first step, however, towards aiding him.

The first aspect to remember is that the child with the type of visual problem described is liable to visual fatigue readily. With visual fatigue will come increased difficulty in ocular co-ordination, and therefore greater risk of confused visual input. Working in short periods will therefore help to reduce this fatigue in general and improve concentration.

The use of reasonably large and well-printed text will make discrimination easier. The teaching of pencil and pen holding and control, and the use of lined paper and a dense black hard-tipped nylon pen will again increase contrast against the paper, and aid the child in keeping along a line. A style of letter formation with upper and lower loops aids in a flowing form of continuous writing later.

Use should be made, where possible, of a combined phonetic approach to reading and spelling, so that sound can reinforce a visual perceptual system. As the visual span of fixation of most children is limited, breaking up words into smaller visual components aids visual discrimination.

Where possible the use of distance viewing techniques, eg spelling on a blackboard, projecting text from an episcope or slides, or the use of large-screened television monitors (an application with which the author is concerned) are an advantage as they reduce the risk of a confused visual input often resulting from near viewing. Particularly for the older child, who is more self-conscious, and where individual teaching help is limited, the author has been interested in the development of programmed learning methods of remedial teaching of English and maths, under the control of the teacher, rather as a language laboratory is used, so that the pupil will be able to undertake a certain amount of remedial work on his own.

Where parental help can be obtained, arranging for the child to dictate as though he was writing, spelling out any difficult words, initially to the parent who can write for him, and later into a tape recorder which can be replayed, can considerably improve English language expression without visual fatigue. This approach is particularly helpful in the evening when the child is tired, reserving additional reading and writing more for the weekend and during vacation, when he is likely to be less visually fatigued.

The author hopes that his taking a technical approach to the difficulty of educational under-achievement, to how problems might be investigated, and how to approach remedial teaching, will be of help to those concerned with the under-achieving child. He has found that by this means, when complex visual and ocular control anomalies have largely been contributing to reading difficulty and educational under-achievement, up to four times the usual expected rate of progress can be attained with the consequent saving of effort, time and frustration to all concerned.

References

Bedwell, C H (1973) The significance of visual ocular and postural anomalies in reading and writing. *The Road to Effective Reading*, pp 73-81, UKRA Conference. Ward Lock, London.

Bedwell, C H, Grant, R and McKeown, J F (1980) Visual and ocular control anomalies in relation to reading difficulty. *British Journal of Educational Psychology*, 50, pp 61-70.

Acknowledgements

The author would like to acknowledge, in addition to those mentioned, the help given by the Rank Benevolent Fund towards the cost of the development of the visual technology required for this work, and the interest and technical help given in the analysis and preparation of the data involved in this project by Mrs J Barnes.

2.6 Learning-to-Learn by Reading: Towards a Conversational Technology

Laurie F Thomas and Sheila Harri-Augstein
Brunel University

Abstract: Successfully submitting to being taught is not the same as learning how to explore one's own needs and purposes and make effective use of resources. Techniques have been developed for enabling learners to become more aware of, and to review and develop, the ways in which they learn, so as to enable them to take greater control of their learning. In this paper 'reading' is used as a vehicle for demonstrating both the learner-based philosophy and conversational methodology.

Introduction

Many of the advances in the technology of 'learning' emphasize the skills of the tutor as purveyor of knowledge. Programmed texts and computer-aided instruction take this one step further by embodying the method and content in the resource itself, thus dispensing with the tutor. Often this approach is seen as individualized learning, simply because the learner learns not to negotiate but to accept the purposes, methods and content offered. *But successfully submitting to being taught is not the same as learning how to explore one's own needs and purposes and make effective use of resources.*

Demands on self-organization in learning put considerable strain on most of us: professionals, teachers and students. We have been unprepared to learn for ourselves. In a series of projects based in educational institutions and in industry, techniques have been developed for enabling learners to become more aware of, review and develop, the ways in which they learn. Techniques which record the process can be used conversationally to mirror the process to learners in ways which enable them to take greater control of their learning.

Talk-back procedures have been researched and developed into a theory of learning conversations. The dimensions and content of this theory are described elsewhere (Thomas and Harri-Augstein, 1977; 1979).

In this paper 'reading' is used as a vehicle for demonstrating both the learner-based philosophy and conversational methodology. Two techniques, recording reading behaviour and the flow diagram for charting meanings in texts, are outlined in an attempt to demonstrate how conversational method can be recruited to enhance learning competence. Other learning skills such as discussion (in seminars), listening (in lectures), manual tasks (lab work), and thinking and feeling creatively (problem identification and solution) have also been investigated and an appropriate range of awareness-raising techniques and talk-back procedures have been developed. Many of these are computer-based.

Figure 1.

The Brunel Reading Recorder

One way of expressing what goes on during reading is that the structures of the words on the page provoke the reader into a search for stable meaning. The thoughts and feelings associated with this search take time. Therefore the patterns of time revealed in detailed records of reading behaviour can be used conversationally to infer the sequence of feelings and thoughts that accompanied it. But how can such detailed records be obtained? A series of prototypes led to the development of the Reading Recorder (see Figure 1).

It is a robust, easy-to-use machine which is commercially available on a limited basis. Developments in techniques for recording reading behaviour include a prototype mini recorder which works directly on to the pages of a book and various simple paper and pencil methods. In its variant forms the Reading Recorder is a tool specially designed to make the behavioural process of reading explicit.

> The text is printed on continuous stationery and is viewed through a window (represented by this rectangle). The size of the window can be varied to expose from 1 to 3 to 5 lines of text.

The movement of the continuous stationery is under the direct control of the reader. He or she turns a handle on the side of the recorder to move the text past the window, and the pen of a chart recorder incorporated in the machine produces a graphical record. Figure 2 shows a very simplified version of a record obtained on the Reading Recorder. This record shows the reading of a 400-line article in 20 minutes. We can see that the lines were not read at an even rate of $\frac{400}{20}$ ie 20 lines per minute. The first 100 lines were read in five minutes, ie at an average of 20 lines per minute, but then the reader spent five minutes not reading at all. Observations show that he sat thinking for three minutes and then made some notes. From the tenth minute to the fifteenth, he read more slowly from line 100 to line 150, ie $\frac{150 - 100}{5} = \frac{50}{5} = 10$ lines per minute. Then the reader speeded up and read from lines 150 to 250 in two minutes, ie 100 lines in two minutes at 50 lines per minute. At line 250, he stopped and then turned quickly back to line 150 and spent one minute making notes, not reading. He then scanned evenly and very quickly through from line 150 to line 400 in two minutes, ie at $\frac{250}{2}$ at 125 lines per minute.

Reflection upon this read record is the starting point of a conversational exchange between the reader and the tutor.

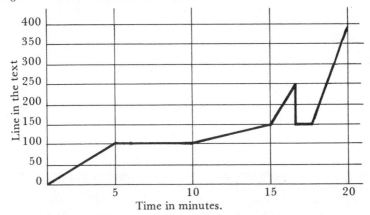

Figure 2. *Record obtained on the Reading Recorder*

1. What was in the first 100 lines that made the reader pause and think after reading them?
2. Why were lines 100 to 150 so difficult to read?
3. Why did he or she go back from line 250 to line 150?
4. Why was it then so easy to read through from line 150 to the end?

Conversational investigations may reveal that the first 100 lines were a simple introduction, the next 50 explained in detail the author's intentions; line 250 referred to an idea dealt with first in line 150; and the last 150 lines repeated the author's aims more elaborately. The tutor and reader can begin to infer quite a lot from the reader's behaviour, ie the read record.

The read record shows how time was spent. It shows changes in pace, hesitations, skipping, back-tracking, searching, and note-taking. Conversational interpretations of read records have led the authors to identify five types of 'read'. These are described in detail elsewhere (Thomas and Harri-Augstein, 1972; 1976; 1976 1978a).

These 'reads' are seldom observed in pure form, but usually each can be classified as one of five idealized types (see Figure 3). Actual records often contain

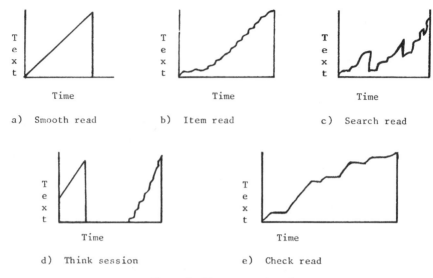

Figure 3. *Five types of read*

a mix of these, but nevertheless they serve to provide a common terminology for conversational exchange.

Read (a)   A fairly rapid more or less smooth continuous read from beginning to end.

Read (b)   A slow read from beginning to end, with detailed hesitations and possibly notes.

Read (c)   A read that shows considerable search backwards and forwards within the text.

Read (d)   An activity associated with 'thinking',note consultation, drafting sessions and so on during which specific parts of the text may be consulted briefly.

Read (e)   A fairly rapid read with few hesitations at selected parts of the text.

These basic read patterns combine in various ways to produce a more or less effective reading strategy. Conversational investigations have shown that this depends on the purpose, on the previous knowledge and skills of the reader, on the structure of the text, and on the personal criteria used by the reader for evaluating the outcome.

Talk-back Through Records of Reading Behaviour and Flow Diagrams of Texts

The reader is encouraged to go through each record and think himself or herself back into the frame of mind that he or she was in when the record was first produced. This is done by identifying on the record all significant events, ie hesitations, backtrackings, changes in pace, skipping forwards and searches. The reader is then encouraged to recall the original experience of reading and think carefully why at these points in the text a certain word, phrase, sentence, or idea led him or her to behave in a particular way.

We have found that behavioural records of reading can be recruited effectively to enable students to explore, review and develop their self-organized capacity to learn from print. When students embark on conversational investigations of their own reading they are seldom aware of the cognitive and affective processes which underlie their reading behaviour. By guiding learners into contact with their own processes, they become more aware of the existing state of their skills and attitudes towards reading and so bring these under review. An awareness of a wider range of skills and attitudes opens up alternatives which hitherto were non-existent. How is this achieved?

A read record used haphazardly in a 'talk-back' conversation does not allow a participant to achieve significant states of awareness. The tutor takes on a directive, guided, or facilitatory role, depending on the learner's ability to generate personal feedback. As this ability develops, the tutor offers greater freedom for the reader/learner to explore the consequences of relying on personal feedback. Gradually the learner acquires the perceptual skill to interpret his or her own records. The quality of the talk-back conversation depends on this sensitivity of the tutor to the information that the learner constructs from the read record.

When a record of the reader's behaviour is combined with a procedure for recording comprehension a more rigorous reconstruction and evaluation of the process of reading becomes possible. Having created an awareness of the personal process of reading by talk-back through the read record, a flow diagram technique is introduced into the conversation. In its basic form the technique contains four categories for describing the structure of a text.

1. *Text links.* Connections to other sections of text.
2. *Main theme.* The major ideas expounded by the author.
3. *Qualifications.* Statements which add to the main ideas but are of a lower order of importance, such as definitions, justifications, explanations and so on.
4. *Elaborations.* Reference to details such as dates, numbers, quantities, examples and so on.

These display a structure of meaning particularly suited for a general description of a text. A summary of the text is described in the meaning-flow within the main theme column. Other sets of categories more appropriate for a particular range of texts and for more specific reading purposes have also been developed.

Courses based on such conversational investigations of reading processes have led to significant changes in specific reading skills, general reading competence and academic performance (Thomas and Harri-Augstein, 1976).

The focus of the conversation is reflection and review of process. The tutor's function can be described as 'mirroring' the process to the learner. Mirroring leads to heightened awareness and this enables the learner to explore a personal language in which to think about and experiment with reading so that he or she moves towards greater competence. The authors have systematically analyzed conversational transactions and developed 'a science of learning conversations'. Different levels of discourse can be identified and within each level it has been found useful to identify a number of interwoven dialogues. It is beyond the scope of this paper to discuss this in greater detail but the concept of 'learning conversations' is described in a number of publications (Thomas and Harri-Augstein, 1976; 1977; 1978b; 1978c).

Looking to the Future

Conversational method embodies its own rigour and is based on the concept of *content-free heuristics*; articulating only the essential skeletal decision-making structure of the conversation. The content of the conversation is contributed by the participant. Thus, the heuristic offers a contentless form in which the participant may have an articulated learning conversation with himself or herself, with peers, or with a tutor or an expert. If the programmes continually analyze the learner's responses, the results can be used to provide a feedback commentary on the nature of the learning process being investigated. Interactive computer programmes and a wide variety of simple paper and pencil techniques have been developed at the Centre as conversational aids to learning how to learn. Microprocessor-based techniques for recording reading strategies, and for eliciting structures of meaning, are currently being further developed. Alongside these developments, a wider range of paper and pencil techniques which can be used independently by the learner are also being made available.

References

Thomas, L F and Harri-Augstein, E S (1972) An experimental approach to the study of reading as a learning skill. *Research in Education,* **8.** Manchester University Press.

Thomas, L F and Harri-Augstein, E S (1976) *The Self-Organized Learner and the Printed Word.* Centre for the Study of Human Learning. Brunel University (mimeo) and Final Report to SSRC on Techniques for the Further Development of Reading as a Learning Skill.

Thomas, L F and Harri-Augstein, E S (1977) Learning-to-learn: the personal construction and exchange of meaning. In Howe, M J A (ed) *Adult Learning: Psychological Research and Applications.* John Wiley, London.

Thomas, L F and Harri-Augstein, E S (1978a) The Kelly Repertory Grid as a vehicle for eliciting a personal taxonomy of reading purposes. *Journal of Research in Reading,* **1,** February. United Kingdom Reading Association, Leeds.

Thomas, L F and Harri-Augstein, E S (1978b) Learning conversations: a person-centred approach to self-organized learning. *British Journal of Guidance and Counselling,* **7,** 1 January. Hobsons Press, Cambridge. Careers Research and Advisory Centre Pub 4.

Thomas, L F and Harri-Augstein, E S (1978c) *The Art and Science of Getting a Degree.* Centre for the Study of Human Learning, Brunel University (mimeo).

Thomas, L F and Harri-Augstein, E S (1979) Self-organized learning and the relativity of knowing. In Bannister, D and Stringer, P (eds) *Constructs of Sociality and Individuality.* Academic Press, London.

Workshop Report
2.7 Learning-to-Learn by Reading

Sheila Harri-Augstein *Brunel University*
Roger Beard *Nene College*
Graham Crosby *Gomer County Junior School*

Organizers' Account

The theme of the workshop was the theory and practice of 'learning conversations'. Participants were introduced to 'awareness raising' techniques and talk-back procedures for the systematic exploration and review of reading skill and the development of a self-organizing capacity for learning. Teachers, industrial trainers and counsellors can only facilitate self-organized learning in others if they themselves have gained insights into personal learning processes. Opportunities were given to consider a personal 'process' model of reading-to-learn and to evaluate how a conversational technology can be applied to specific learning situations involving the printed media.

The Centre for the Study of Human Learning at Brunel University has 10 years' experience in the development of a technology for enhancing competence in reading-to-learn. Financed by SSRC, DES and Admiralty Research, active research has been carried out in schools, colleges of education, polytechnics, universities and in industrial training departments. Results show significant improvements in reading skill and academic performance.

The techniques and procedures include the following:

- ☐ Brunel Reading Recorder and associated paper and pencil techniques for recording reading strategies.
- ☐ The flow diagram technique for mapping the meaning in texts.
- ☐ Conversational Repertory Grid techniques and interactive computer programmes for explaining reading purposes.
- ☐ Heuristics for displaying structures of meaning or reading outcomes.
- ☐ Heuristics for structuring learning conversations with oneself or in groups.

Workshop activities included the development of an awareness of personal myths about reading; the recording to reading behaviour and the reconstruction of a reading-for-learning event; mapping meaning in a text by means of paper and pencil procedures; and the practice of 'learning conversations' based on records of learning behaviour and experience.

Sheila Harri-Augstein introduced the basic activities and commented on how these could be conducted on a one-to-one or small group basis. Classroom management of larger groups was also discussed. Roger Beard demonstrated how the Repertory Grid is used for evaluating progress in learning by reading. Graham Crosby offered activities which demonstrated how the techniques could be applied at all levels in a junior school. He commented on how reading-to-learn activities can transform the curriculum in ways which facilitate learning-to-learn.

Participant's Comments

Aled Rhys Wiliam, *University of Salford*

Some of the terms used in this workshop were not fully self-explanatory: the title, 'Learning-to-Learn by Reading', for example, required a lot of explanation and may have been interpreted by some to be an account of the way children acquire scholarly habits. Eventually, however, it became clear that the analysis of text was not only a worthwhile exercise in parsing but also a good way of developing critical faculties and judgement which are relevant to all learning. Similarly, the phrase 'learning conversations' did not immediately appear meaningful until it was explained as a kind of two-way traffic between the reader and the text.

Although it was clearly stated that the meta-language, rather than the content of reading, was the main concern of the exercise, some participants seemed to think it went no further than teaching children to gain fluency in reading. Perhaps the introduction should spell out more clearly the complexity and the variety of the skills we use when we read. More emphasis could be put on the various categories of reading: browsing, skimming, digesting, summarizing, abstracting, etc, and on the relationship between one's varying purposes in reading and the many different ways in which we use printed material.

Nevertheless, after making these criticisms I must say how valuable I found the workshop to be. I welcome very much the insistence on the importance of being aware of the different kinds of reading, and on the physical and mental processes that they involve. An objective record of one's own performance, therefore, is an indispensable tool for creating such awareness and I was impressed with the elegant simplicity of the Reading Recorder and even more so with the manual method of recording.

In the second half of the workshop, the use of the flow-chart in mapping meaning was well-exemplified and I was impressed with this method as a way of developing critical habits and personal judgement. The excitement for me was the realization that there can be some transference from the awareness of one's reading habits to an understanding of one's mental processes in general. From that it is a short step to realizing that, while one is aware of sensory information at several levels, one still has the ability to choose to concentrate attention on that input which is most relevant to the most immediate need. I found this workshop to be a stimulating exercise and the seminal ideas and techniques are most valuable tools in the development of educational technology.

Workshop Report

2.8 Construct, Reflect, Converse and Act

Laurie F Thomas and Sheila Harri-Augstein
Brunel University

Organizers' Account

The workshop offered participants experience in playing a series of Repertory Grid 'games'. The aim of these is to raise personal awareness and enhance the quality of conversational exchange. These games derive from interactive computer techniques, made available at the workshop.

Experience has enabled us to dispense with the computer by inventing a simple 'hand grid sorter'. The kit containing this can be used variously. 'Games' include:

1. *Perceive.* Exploring the perceptual basis of significant items of experience.
2. *Reflect.* Exploring the structure of personal meanings attributed to a system of experience.
3. *Exchange.* Exploring the underlying dynamics of understanding or misunderstanding and agreement or disagreement.
4. *Non-verbal.* Exploring tacit knowing without the disruptive influence of words.
5. *Converse.* A heuristic for increasing the probability of a creative encounter.
6. *Act.* Reconstructing behaviour as the test-bed of one's constructors of experience.
7. *Change.* Exploring the implications and causality of personally significant change over time.

Some BASIC computer programmes produced by the centre were made available for the 'games'. Participants were also given opportunities for practising paper and pencil procedures for analyzing grids and reflecting upon personal experience.

FOCUS

FOCUS is a method of grid analysis which uses a two-way hierarchical cluster analysis technique to re-order systematically the rows of constructs and columns of elements to produce a focused grid showing the least variation between adjacent constructs and adjacent elements. This is done with respect to the way in which the constructs order the elements, rather than the verbal labels given to the poles of the construct.

Input Specification

Number of grids. For each grid:

name or identification	number of elements
number of constructs	range of rating scale
matrix of raw grid responses	

Output Given

raw grid	element tree
construct matching scores	construct tree
list of reversed constructs	focused grid
element matching scores	

PEGASUS is an interactive programme to elicit a repertory grid. Initially six elements are chosen by the user with special attention to the purpose of eliciting the grid. The first four constructs are elicited using fixed triads and thereafter random or chosen triads are offered. Real-time data processing allows feedback about highly matched constructs and elements.

OPTIONS OFFERED ARE:
1. To add an element to split highly matched constructs.
2. To replace two highly matched constructs by one.
3. To add a construct to split highly matched elements.
4. To delete one or more element.
5. To delete one or more construct.
6. To add a construct without using a triad.
7. To add an element.
8. To change the level of feedback commentary.
9. To re-define the purpose for eliciting the grid.
10. To see the grid focused at stages during the run.

When the elicitation is completed a choice of printout of the analysis of the grid is given, together with the lists of elements and constructs.

PEGASUS-bank provides an 'expert' grid which the user does not at first see, but against which the elicited constructs are matched. Feedback is given not only on how the user's constructs match each other, but also how they relate to the 'expert' constructs. Finally the total grid is focused to show how the two sets of constructs are inter-related.

SOCIO-GRIDS analyze a set of repertory grids elicited from a group of people who share a set of elements. It focuses grids singly and in pairs, and produces a set of socionets showing the links within the group. A 'mode grid' of the most highly matched constructs is extracted and then focused. Each grid is focused with this mode grid and a measure of overlap of each with the mode is calculated.

Workshop Report
2.9 The Use of Filmstrips and Records and Computer-Aided Instruction

Robert E Burns and William I Davisson
University of Notre Dame, USA

Organizers' Account

Estimating how educational technology may develop over the next 20 years is perhaps best begun by reflecting upon what has happened in the past two decades. The enormous potential of television as an educational delivery system was widely perceived early in this period and much has been accomplished. Educational television networks are in place and some of our productions indeed have progressed far beyond the 'talking torsos' of sunrise semester. In general, however, the record of educational television is mixed. For many practical reasons the great expectations of the 1950s have not been fulfilled.

The history of computer technology during these same years has been similar. To be sure, educational computing has come of age. Networks for the exchange of programmes and data are being established and the development of hardware has been astounding. Moreover, many successful computer-assisted instruction projects (CAI) in a range of subject matters have given us a glimpse of what the general instructional potential of this technology may be. However, because most of our energies and resources have gone into hardware development, and into science and engineering education, the general instructional potential of CAI is a long way from realization. The development of CAI materials for the social sciences and humanities has proceeded slowly and dissemination of them has been limited.

Perhaps even more important for most teachers than the progress of either educational television or CAI has been the astonishing variety of electronic based hardware with obvious education applications produced and marketed since 1950. Though not developed primarily for educational institutions, carousels, overhead projectors, instant photography, sound-on-slide projectors, Super-8 cinematography, and copying machines have had a significant impact on them. Virtually all universities, colleges, and schools have educational media centres wherein such equipment is available to teachers with time and energy to devise ways of using it.

Finally, exhortations for teachers to introduce media segments in their courses have not been wanting. For several years, educational technology enthusiasts, some educational theorists, and no small number of equipment vendors have been preaching a gospel of media awareness to all who will listen. In this gospel, television, computer technology, and other electronic based hardware are represented as being instruments of a forthcoming instructional revolution. As most of us know, that instructional revolution has not yet occurred and the probability that it will in the near future is low. The reason why is fairly clear. Hardware development has proceeded much faster than software development. Quality instructional materials for use with available hardware are lacking. Most teachers must either develop their own materials or do without. Until we can choose from an inventory of materials in the same way that we are now able to choose from an array of equipment the much anticipated instructional revolution will be forever delayed. Hardware alone is not enough.

If the recent history of educational technology is any sort of guide for the future, then the next two decades should not be much different from the ones just past. Hardware developments will probably continue to outpace software production. For example, a wide range of inexpensive microprocessor systems are currently available but operational educational applications of microprocessors are few and instructional materials for use with them are rare. The entry of text editing/word processing systems into the educational market ought to challenge the imaginations of teachers of writing. The educational applications of this now expensive but extraordinary technology for the most part have not even been discussed. In fact, there is much about future developments in educational technology that needs discussion. The implications for education, as indeed for communications and society as a whole, of the ever-greater miniaturization of integrated circuits are profound. Within the next 10 years, since miniaturization tends to proceed at an exponential rate, computers will become so powerful, so portable, and so inexpensive that educational technologists and teachers will be hard pressed between now and then to find ways of exploiting this enormous potential. If hardware development has outstripped software production in years past, this problem will be greatly compounded in the future.

The thrust of the argument presented here thus far should be clear. The future of educational technology depends upon increasing the supply of quality instructional materials. One essential step toward that end is to find ways of multiplying the number of faculty and staff who are experienced in, and committed to, instructional materials. The fact that no generally recognized centre for training in this area exists in the United States is one indicator of the difficulty of this task. The skills required to write quality materials are not easily acquired. Transforming information taken from books and articles into formats which machines will accept and students will want to use is an exceedingly demanding, frustrating, and time-consuming task, which probably not more than one out of 10 faculty members are able to do well. The only effective way of learning is by doing, and there is a powerful reason why so few have undertaken this burden and why some who have taken it on have put it aside.

The reason is no more and no less than the attitude of academic faculty toward pedagogy. An interest in instructional materials development presupposes an interest in pedagogy; and traditionally, in most American universities such interests are valued lower than discipline-oriented research. Prestige, promotion, and pay raises go to those faculties who publish scholarly monographs and discipline-oriented articles in mainline journals and not to those who prepare multi-media classroom presentations or write CAI lessons. This is a condition of academic life which established departmental peer review processes makes difficult to change. However, difficult does not mean impossible, and as more faculties do this kind of work, and do it well, recognition will come. Old attitudes and the consequences that follow from them will change. One effective way of beginning such a change is to share knowledge and experience.

Film and Record Workshop

This workshop was just such an attempt to share such knowledge and experience by demonstrating how multi-media instructional materials can be integrated with readings and discussion in a traditional American history classroom.

The purpose of this workshop was to demonstrate how pictures and/or audio recordings can be combined with selected readings to develop an integrated set of discussion-oriented materials. Integration provides the key for the successful combination of pictures and/or recordings of historical dramatizations and of selections from socially significant music and song with assigned readings and class discussions. By pursuing a line of prepared sequenced questions, teachers can tie together audio-visual materials and readings with discussions to develop student analytical and inference-making skills, introduce new data, suggest and test hypotheses and illustrate concepts.

The specific historical subject matter explored in the workshop was chosen because of its applicability to such an integrated approach. In no case did the audio-visual materials function as supplements to the readings and discussions; they were, rather, an essential stimulus for successful discussion.

Two segments of the workshop dealt with American lifestyles. The first was concerned with the question of social class and lifestyle in three different 18th century American colonies. It explored these themes through the writings of a Massachusetts judge, a Virginia planter, and Benjamin Franklin, as well as through a filmstrip of paintings of five women of different social classes. The readings and filmstrip were then used to elicit student discussion on the variety of lifestyles in Colonial America. In the segment on America in the 1920s, readings and filmstrips were used to encourage student recognition of the frenetic search for pleasure, the political apathy, the intolerance, the hunger for heroes, and the rapid transformation of American life that characterized the Roaring Twenties.

The final segments of the workshop dealt with specific historical events. First, students read contemporary journalistic and personal accounts of the Boston Massacre and studied a map of the area where the incident occurred. Then they listened to a recording of an original playlet which dramatically illustrated the feverish emotional climate in which the incident occurred. Only then did students use these materials as a frame of reference for discussion of this incident and the other events that led to the American Revolution.

Finally, the segment on John Brown's raid raised questions about both slavery and the justice of taking the law into one's own hands. Students read contemporary accounts of the events before listening to a recording of John Brown's last speech. Only then did they attempt to analyze in discussion the meaning of John Brown's raid and the abolitionist movement.

CAI Workshop

The general instructional potential of CAI is great, but it is a long way from realization. Hardware development has proceeded much faster than software development. Quality instructional materials for use with available hardware are limited, but hardware is not enough.

Part of the difficulty stems from the fact that software materials are particularly lacking in the social sciences and humanities. As we have already mentioned, the development of CAI materials for the social sciences and humanities has proceeded slowly and dissemination of them has been limited. The problem is made worse by the fact that many social scientists and humanists are uncomfortable with, and sometimes threatened by, technology.

Hardware developments will probably continue to outpace software production over the next two decades. One essential step to improve this situation is to lessen the necessity of an individual teacher's possessing programming knowledge in order to create CAI materials successfully. Our CAI workshop was concerned with existing CAI materials which can be combined in such a way as to meet the individual teacher's needs. In addition, we explained how our new author language enables teachers unfamiliar with computer technology to create new materials and introduce them onto microprocessor CAI systems.

The purpose of this workshop was to demonstrate CAI materials for courses in the history of Western civilization, principles of economics and freshman composition courses. The CAI mode employed was the tutorial, which was pioneered by an instructional materials development group at the University of Notre Dame, USA. Tutorials consist of a lead, an action statement, four possible answer choices and four responses. The individual tutorials are combined into lessons and the lessons into inventories. Each of the subject areas had a large inventory of tutorials and review routines — approximately 600 for history, 200 for economics and 280 for English grammar and mechanics. Teachers construct daily or weekly CAI lessons by selecting from these inventories those tutorials and review routines which are appropriate to their individual instructional needs. Students access and run CAI lessons thus prepared over a data printing terminal and, upon completion of a lesson, have printed records of what they have done for future study.

Teachers can also create new materials with the CAI author language developed at Notre Dame. Use of this language requires only minimal programming skill and is designed to be used on a microprocessor. It is thus extremely accessible for teachers with limited equipment and/or minimal programming knowledge. Instructions for use of the language were distributed at the workshop.

Section 3:
Teaching-Learning Techniques and Strategies – II

3.1 The Potential Role of Games and Simulations in Science Education

H I Ellington, F Percival and E Addinall
Robert Gordon's Institute of Technology, Aberdeen

Abstract: The potential role of games, simulations and case studies in science education is examined in the context of two continuing trends: the developing shift from convergent teaching to divergent education, and the evolution from mass instruction through individualized learning to co-operative interactive group learning. Three areas in which simulation and gaming techniques are likely to prove particularly useful are identified.

Introduction

Games have been played for amusement for thousands of years, and simulation (in its broadest sense) has an equally long history. The application of simulation and gaming techniques to education and training is, however, a comparatively recent development. The first field in which such applications took place was military training; here, serious use of simulation and gaming began at the end of the 18th century, and the techniques have since been developed to an extremely high level of realism and sophistication (Tansey and Unwin, 1969). The next field in which important developments took place was business management training, where the use of gaming and simulation as a means of developing decision-making skills was first introduced in the mid-1950s and has since become extensively used at all levels from school to post-graduate and in-service training (Hart, 1978).

It was not until the early 1960s, however, that the use of games and simulations spread to secondary and tertiary education – first to teacher training and to the various social sciences (Duke, 1974) and eventually, during the 1970s, to the pure and applied sciences (Ellington *et al*, 1980). Such techniques have now started to make a significant contribution to science education, and the authors believe that this contribution will become progressively more important during the 1980s and 1990s. This is because an increase in the use of games, simulations and case studies in science education would be in full accord with two contemporary developments, namely the changing rationale underlying such education and the continuing evolution of didactic methods from mass communication through individualized learning to co-operative group learning.

The Changing Function and Methodology of Science Education

Function

Since its formalization in the latter part of the 19th century, science education has been essentially paradigm-based, its main function being the perpetuation of a scientific elite by producing 'licensed' research scientists who have received a thorough training in a particular subject area (Kuhn, 1962). Virtually the whole of science education at all levels was, until comparatively recently, designed with this overall aim in mind, the main function of school science being to prepare pupils for more advanced studies at university level, and the main function of university science being to prepare students for post-graduate research work eventually leading to the award of a PhD. As a result, science education has been systematic, cumulative and, in the main, introspective and uninspiring.

During the 1970s, however, an increasing number of people started to question this traditional concept of the role of science education (Reid, 1977; Ellington and Percival, 1977; Ziman, 1978; Lewis, 1978). They realised that there was a need to make science education much more relevant to the future lives of the great majority of our citizens. As a result, we can now see the beginnings of a progressive move away from convergent, content-orientated science teaching towards science *education* in the true sense of the word. As we shall see, gaming and simulation techniques are capable of making a major contribution to such developments.

Methodology

Traditionally, didactic methods have been both teacher-centred and authoritarian, with the student generally placed in the role of a relatively passive receiver of information and training (Burgess, 1977). During the last 25 years, however, the mainstream of educational research and development has moved away from such a methodology (Elton, 1977). First, during the late 1950s and 1960s there was a move towards student-centred, individualized learning — largely as a result of the influence of behaviourist psychologists such as Skinner. Then, during the late 1960s and 1970s, the influence of humanistic psychologists such as Rogers started a move towards co-operative learning based on group interaction, with the learners in what Elton describes as an *interdependent* role rather than a *dependent* role (as in teacher-centred mass instruction) or an *independent* role (as in individualized learning).

Since the widespread adoption of new techniques invariably lags behind the main research and development phase (Elton, 1977), it is only during the last few years that group learning has started to play a major part in our educational system. There is, however, a definite move towards the use of interactive techniques in an increasingly wide range of subject areas, and many commentators believe that such techniques will become progressively more important (Taylor, 1976; Elton, 1977; Teather, 1978). The authors believe that science education will follow this general trend and that games, simulations and interactive case studies will gradually be built into virtually all courses during the 1980s and 1990s.

How Games, Simulations and Case Studies Can be Used in Science Education

There appear to be three ways in which science-based games, simulations and case studies can be used in secondary and tertiary education, namely:

(a) as aids to the teaching of the basic content of science and engineering courses;

(b) for educating *through* science (using science-based exercises to cultivate useful skills and desirable attitudinal traits);

(c) for teaching *about* science and technology and their importance to modern society.

Teaching the Basic Content of Courses

Although games and simulations constitute an extremely powerful and versatile educational tool (Ellington and Percival, 1977), research findings indicate that they are no more effective than traditional methods in teaching the basic facts and principles of a subject (Wentworth and Lewis, 1973). Because of this, it is not advocated that they be used as a front-line teaching method, but rather in a complementary and supportive role. There are two main ways in which this can be done.

Firstly, they can be used for reinforcing basic facts and principles. This can be done by using games and simulations in place of some of the conventional worked examples that have traditionally been used to reinforce newly-acquired knowledge by making students demonstrate their understanding by applying it to a specific situation. Use of a few carefully selected games and simulations in such a role has the additional advantage of introducing variety into a course, and hence increasing student motivation. The types of exercise that are best suited to this form of use are fairly short games, simulation games and case studies of the sort that can be fitted into the curriculum without causing major disruptions. Examples are the various chemistry-based card games developed during the early 1970s (Megarry, 1975), the card and board games published by Longmans, and the interactive case studies developed by the Science Education Group at Glasgow University (Reid, 1979).

Secondly, they can be used as a supplement to, and in some cases, as a substitute for conventional experimental work. It is, however, simulations rather than games — and, in particular, computer-based simulations — that offer the most exciting possibilities in this area (Dowsey, 1977; Megarry, 1978). Here, the imminent prospect of cheap, highly versatile microcomputers becoming generally available in schools and colleges means that it will be possible to give pupils and students direct experience (through simulations) of a far wider range of experimental situations than has been feasible up to now, eg where a conventional experiment is extremely difficult or impossible for technical or economic reasons, where actual experimental work could be dangerous, or where a conventional experiment would take an unacceptably long time to complete.

Education 'Through' Science

A major theme of current thinking regarding the development of science education at both secondary and tertiary levels is the identification and achievement of the various 'desirable' skills, habits, attitudes and modes of thinking which the end products of that education should possess over and above purely factual knowledge (Ellington and Percival, 1977). Until recently the great majority of science courses have concentrated almost exclusively on the inculcation of cognitive and psychomotor skills in the vague hope that the various non-cognitive skills (eg decision-making, communication, problem-solving, library and interpersonal skills) and desirable attitudinal traits that are supposed to be a 'bonus' from a science education would somehow rub off on the students. There is, however, a strong case for making a conscious effort to foster their development, since even a professional scientist is unlikely to succeed in our complex and changing society purely on a basis of cognitive attainment.

Since traditional teaching methods have proved to be of dubious efficiency in achieving non-cognitive outcomes of the type described above, it is obvious that we will have to develop new methods that are specifically designed to achieve such outcomes (assuming, of course, that we accept the argument that they are educationally desirable). It is the contention of the authors that participative, science-based simulation/games and simulated case studies are capable of fulfilling this role (Ellington and Percival, 1977). If properly designed, these provide a means of educating 'through' science, ie of using a science-based exercise as a vehicle for achieving a wide range of educational objectives that go far beyond those that would normally be associated with its intrinsic scientific content. A large number of such exercises have been developed during the last few years, particularly by the authors and by the Science Education Group at Glasgow University (Ellington *et al*, 1980).

Teaching About Science and Technology

Since 1959, when C P Snow gave the now famous Reith Lecture in which he presented the doctrine of the 'two cultures' (Snow, 1959), there has been a growing realization of a number of fundamental deficiencies in our educational system — particularly in relation to science education. First, at an academic level, there is the undoubted dichotomy between scientists and technologists on the one hand, and non-scientists on the other. Second, at a more general level, there has been an almost complete failure to make our future citizens aware of the relevance of science to the real world and of the vital importance of science and technology to modern society (Lewis, 1978; Ziman, 1978).

During the last decade, however, a number of 'science in society'-type courses have been developed, first at tertiary level and, more recently, at secondary level (Boeker and Gibbons, 1978; Lewis, 1978). It is now generally accepted that games and simulations are capable of making a very significant contribution to courses of this type, and the authors believe that such exercises — particularly those with a multi-disciplinary basis — are ideally suited to such a role since they represent one of the most effective means at our disposal of demonstrating the roles of science and technology in modern society (Ellington *et al*, 1978).

One great advantage of exercises of this type is that they can be incorporated into both science and non-science courses. With the former, they can either be built into the main fabric of the course as supportive case studies, or can be made part of the associated studies element that is now becoming an integral part of most of our secondary and tertiary science courses. With the latter, they can again be made part of the general studies element of the course — possibly by 'watering down' or removing the 'hard science' content in order to convert them to a form that can be handled by people who lack a technical or mathematical background. Several of the exercises developed by the authors have been used successfully in this way (Millar, 1979; Ellington *et al*, 1980).

Conclusion

The gradual spread of gaming and simulation techniques to virtually all sectors of education has been one of the great success stories of educational technology during the last two decades. The authors believe that the next two decades will see an even greater expansion in the use of such techniques, and that one of the main growth areas will be science education. It is hoped that such a development will bring great benefits both to our educational system and to society at large.

References

Boeker, E and Gibbons, M (eds) (1978) *Science, Society and Education.* Free University, Amsterdam.

Burgess, T (1977) *Education After School.* Penguin Books, Harmondsworth.

Dowsey, M (1977) Computer simulation of laboratory experiments. In Megarry, J (ed) *Aspects of Simulation and Gaming.* Kogan Page, London.

Duke, R D (1974) *Gaming: The Future's Language.* Wiley, New York.

Ellington, H I, Addinall, E and Percival, F (1980) *Games, Simulations and Case Studies in Science Education.* Kogan Page, London.

Ellington, H I and Percival, F (1977) Educating 'through' science using multi-disciplinary games. *Programmed Learning and Educational Technology,* 14, 2, p 117.

Ellington, H I, Percival, F, Addinall, E and Smythe, M E (1978) Using simulations and case studies to teach the social relevance of science. In Boeker, E and Gibbons, M (eds) *Science, Society and Education.* Free University, Amsterdam.

Elton, L (1977) Educational technology – today and tomorrow. In Hills, P and Gibbot, J (eds) *Aspects of Educational Technology* XI. Kogan Page, London.

Hart, R T (1978) Simulation and gaming in management education and training. In McAleese, R (ed) *Perspectives on Academic Gaming and Simulation 3.* Kogan Page, London.

Kuhn, T S (1962) *The Structure of Scientific Revolutions.* University of Chicago Press, Chicago.

Lewis, J L (1978) Science in society. *Physics Education,* 13, 6, p 340

Megarry, J (1975) A review of science games – variations on a theme of rummy. *Simulations and Games,* 6, 4, p 423.

Megarry, J (1978) Retrospect and prospect. In McAleese, R (ed) *Perspectives on Academic Gaming and Simulation 3.* Kogan Page, London.

Millar, J W L (1979) The Power Station Game: a study. *Physics Education,* 14, 1, p 34.

Reid, N (1977) Simulations, games and case studies. *Education in Chemistry,* 13, 2, p 82.

Reid, N (1979) Simulation approaches in chemistry teaching: update. *Simulation/Games for Learning,* 9, 3, p 122.

Snow, C P (1959) *The Two Cultures and the Scientific Revolution.* Cambridge University Press.

Tansey, P J and Unwin, D (1969) *Simulation and Gaming in Education.* Methuen Educational, London.

Taylor, L C (1976) Educational materials: their development, supply, use and management. In *Materials for Learning and Teaching.* London Commonwealth Secretariat.

Teather, D C B (1978) Simulation and games. In Unwin, D and McAleese, R (eds) *Encyclopaedia of Educational Media Communications and Technology.* Macmillan, London.

Wentworth, D R and Lewis, D R (1973) A review of research on instructional games and simulations in social science education. *Social Education,* 432 (May).

Ziman, J (1978) Summary talk. In Boeker, E and Gibbons, M (eds) *Science, Society and Education.* Free University, Amsterdam.

3.2 How Real is Real? Simulation in Context

B Barnes
Birkbeck College, University of London

Abstract: The paper traces the development of 'Looking Glass Limited', a simulation of a complex business organization, and concentrates on attempts made to validate the simulation. There is a more general discussion of what has been learned in its development.

Introduction

This paper examines the issue of reality in relation to the design and testing of a large-scale simulation of a complex business organization. The simulation, called Looking Glass, was developed, primarily to research into leadership, by the Center for Creative Leadership in North Carolina over a three-year period. A team from Birkbeck College, as well as being part of the original development 'runs' in the United States, has participated in the programme over the last 18 months by translating the simulation into the UK environment and establishing the UK norms from which cross-cultural comparisons can be made. While potential uses of Looking Glass include research, training and assessment, the emphasis in this paper is on the training usage. The simulation in its UK form has been run with management groups from similar sectors of organizational life to the US sample.

When the issue of reality in the learning situation becomes pressing, an experiential rather than an information processing model of learning is used. This is because the acting comes before the understanding and the generalizing in the experiential model. The differences between these two models are perhaps synthesized in the work of Kolb (1979). The need for a link between the learning situation and reality is expressed in education, especially in the secondary and tertiary sectors, by the word 'relevance' and in training by the word 'fidelity'. A particular problem of simulation is that it is a *selection* of events from the real world, *designed* for a specific purpose and therefore it is naturally degrees removed from reality. The problem is further compounded, of course, when 'typical' rather than real events form the basis from which selection is made. Criteria for selection have been (i) positive — the learning objectives and the criticality of tasks for those objectives and the stage of learning; and (ii) negative — avoidance of expense and danger.

Simulators

Intensive research has been going on into simulators for the last 30 years. In spite of this the author found no examples of cross-referencing between what might be called the educational literature on simulation and the training literature on simulators, though there might be advantages in considering simulators and simulation as being of the same genre.

The main uses of simulators set out by Gagné (1962) are:

(a) Training,
(b) Assessment of Proficiency,
(c) Development of Operational Doctrine.

These functions may be re-interpreted in the wider sphere of simulation as education/training, assessment and research. Kincaid and Wheaton (1972) suggest that the fidelity of simulation consists of:

(a) *Equipment Fidelity* — the degree to which the simulator duplicates the appearance and feel of the operational equipment.
(b) *Environmental Fidelity* — the degree to which the sensory stimuli of the task situation are duplicated.
(c) *Psychological Fidelity* — the degree to which the trainee perceives the simulator as being a realistic duplicate of the operational equipment or task situation.

As reported in Miller (1974) a number of studies have examined the relationship between simulator cost, transfer of training and degree of fidelity. The results suggest that in designing a simulation for the training of experienced managers, the following characteristics would be important:

1. The simulation should be based on established task requirements.
2. It should have high task fidelity.
3. The environment should be represented as realistically as possible in terms of significant stimuli.

Looking Glass Limited

The Looking Glass simulation is a free simulation of a medium-sized glass manufacturing company. In each standardized run, 20 participants deal in a six-hour period with a variety of problems presented to them in the form of 'in trays'.

The participants are given the objective of running the company for a day and the controllers do not intervene. The controllers respond to requests for information by the participants from roles outside the 20 designated roles. Communication channels open to participants are telephone, memoranda and face-to-face meetings. No problems are posed to participants other than those in the 'in tray' at the beginning of the day. One decision only is required to be made during the course of the simulation: other than that, the play is free.

Looking Glass originated from a wish to study leadership and from a sense of dissatisfaction with the inconsistent results of the existing research. We know that the managerial task is mainly reactive, the work fragmented, the contacts varied, the main medium of communication oral; but the role in any generalizable sense is difficult to pin down. In such a context the attractions of a simulation, which can hold some of the variables constant, are obvious.

The Model

Given such difficulties, the decision to adopt an empirical model for the simulation rather than a theoretical model becomes understandable — such an orientation could enable the simulation to generate behaviour to generate theories rather than just to test a theory. However, that decision threw a greater burden on the authors to prove that the behaviour generated was indeed typical.

Organizational Type and Structure

The process of choosing a typical organization was essentially judgemental. The designers selected various criteria, and of the final choices, ship-building and glass, the latter satisfied the greater number of these criteria. This selection of type of technology, product and age helped determine the structure of Looking Glass, which is in three operating divisions. To help keep the number of participants to a minimum, four levels of hierarchy were chosen: (i) Chief executive, (ii) Managing directors of divisions (three); (iii) Directors of functional areas (three per division); and (iv) Factory managers (two to three per division).

Organizational Environment

The major elements of 'environment' were considered to be: the rate of change, the predictability of change and the rapidity of response required (hostility). Important components of environment were isolated as:

1. Legal/regulatory factors.
2. Boards of directors and shareholders.
3. Socio-economic factors — eg interest rates, political considerations etc.
4. Inputs — eg suppliers, raw materials, fuel and labour supply.

5. Throughputs — eg technological innovation, state of equipment, unions and labour mobility.
6. Outputs — eg customers (number, distribution reliability), competitors and markets.

These major elements of the environment determined the categorization of one division as facing a hostile and volatile environment (Advanced Products Division), one division as facing a stable environment (Commercial Glass Division), and the third as being a mixture of two environments (Industrial Glass Division).

Problem Clusters and Dimensions

Interviews were conducted with managers in glass industries and from these interviews about 200 events and problems were selected. Twelve activity clusters along the dimensions of managerial behaviour (Mintzberg, 1973) were generated to ensure that representative elements were included in the 'in tray' memoranda and, as a further check, the problems and events were examined for difficulty, magnitude and interdependence.

Some Results

Obviously, in a simulation designed to explore behaviour in organizations, the crucial question to be asked is whether the behaviours evoked by the simulation are both real and typical. To the extent that the behaviours are unreal or a-typical, the propositions and theories derived would be built on shaky foundations.

Reality is essentially personal and empirical in such a context. Although this simulation as an 'in tray' exercise avoids most of the pitfalls outlined in Gill (1979), reality is diminished to the extent that initially the problems are posed in a written rather than an oral medium. This, together with the restricted time span of the simulation, could discourage commitment from the participants. However, the adoption of the 'in tray' approach was essentially a compromise, trading off increased paper work against both a standardized input and background material to give some sense to the participants of a personal history and culture in the organization. If, to this extent, the past of Looking Glass as an organization can be represented, in no way can it have a future for individual participants. There could therefore be a tendency for participants to 'play for effect' rather than go for solid solutions, since the consequences of all the participants' actions are unlikely to rebound within the time span of the simulation. Our experience is that generally this does not happen — a high level of interest and energy is usually generated and sustained.

Space does not allow a detailed examination of all the measuring instruments used with Looking Glass. However, one instrument, activity sampling, is especially pertinent to the issue of the reality of the simulation. Activity sampling took place in all of the 10 runs of the simulation in the USA, and complete data are contained in McCall et al (1979). A summary of these data is given in Table 1.

The comparison baseline for this data, a measure of the typicality of behaviour, is derived from various previous studies of managerial work (eg Brewer and Tomlinson, 1963; Hinrichs, 1964; Horne and Lupton, 1965; etc). Because these studies varied in method, sample size, organizational type and levels of management, the unit of comparison is a range of means.

Activity Content

The results in general support the feedback we get from the participants — Looking

Activity	LGL range %	Comparison range %
What?		
Paper work	38 - 53	22 - 40
Telephone	5 - 17	5 - 17
Meetings	29 - 53	36 - 69
Other	2 - 4	2 - 19
Where?		
Own office	58 - 77	35 - 57
Other's office	7 - 28	3 - 26
Conference room	0 - 32	11 - 25
Other	1 - 4	5 - 38
With whom?		
Subordinates	20 - 47	26 - 37
Superiors	18 - 36	5 - 13
Colleagues	16 - 40	12
Fellow specialists	0 - 6	8

Table 1. *Time spent by Looking Glass managers on various activities*

Glass works: The table shows that managers in Looking Glass spend more time on paperwork, the same amount of time on the phone and rather less time in meetings than the referent groups. The greater amount of time spent on paperwork is not surprising, given the lack of familiarity of the participants with the company, the lack of secretarial support, the lack in many cases of 'live' subordinates and the fact that most of the initial information is in written form. A more detailed examination of the activity sampling data (McCall *et al*, 1979) against the time shows that the paperwork activity decreases from 54.9 per cent between 9.30 and 10.30 am to 35.3 per cent between 1.30 and 2.30 pm with corresponding increases in interactive behaviours such as meetings. Similarly, managing directors and directors of manufacturing (roles with both superiors and subordinates) lie more certainly within the comparison range than other roles without subordinates.

Activity Location

Participants spent more time at their desks than did the comparison group but about the same amount of time in the offices of others. They spent about the same amount of time with subordinates but more with superiors and colleagues. All these differences can be attributed to the simulation location or other artefacts such as lack of others to interact with, or the presence of factory managers in head office for a visit.

The Future

Developments in the USA

Our American colleagues will continue to use the simulation for the prime purpose for which it was designed: research. Their present intention is to examine the relationship between the degree of environmental uncertainty and those organizational characteristics which should correspond with it. Do effective organizations in uncertain environments have the characteristics of less structure, less hierarchy and less centralization? Does the reverse apply? A further direction of the US research is in developing Looking Glass as a managerial assessment device.

Developments in the UK

By April 1980 the last of the 10 norming runs of the UK version of Looking Glass was completed to add to the US data and provide a cross-cultural base to the norm data. In order to gain the co-operation of UK firms to participate in the generation of the norm data, we have offered in return a training day after each run. The experience gained in these training days has convinced us of the potential power of Looking Glass in the training mode, both for the training and development of managers and our own post-graduate students, most of whom themselves work in large organizations. With the latter group, Looking Glass has been used as an example of a simulation and as a framework for examining the theory and practice of the trainer as an interventionist. Training with the former group has consisted, so far, in a day's debriefing ending with the generation of individual learning agendas.

The main advantages of Looking Glass as a training stimulus spring from the accuracy with which it models the reality and complexity of behaviour in organizations: motivation, information flow, decision-making, conflict, group dynamics and leadership are all present, and 'live' as processes which can be 'unpacked' in a specific common context. We have plans for a training design which allows for a Looking Glass run, followed by a debriefing and the generation of individual learning agendas. Training sessions focusing on these agendas would be followed by a second run of Looking Glass with the participants adopting different roles in different divisions. Changes in behaviour and outcome between the first and second runs could be measured and analyzed.

Conclusions

The uniqueness of Looking Glass lies primarily in the fact that it is a 'free' simulation. It is free in the sense that the materials require a decision to be made on only one of the 200 problems embedded in the 'in trays': no additional problems are introduced by the controllers. It is free also in the sense that there are no game rules imposed by the simulation — though, of course, participants bring their own rules, the rules of their lives and their organizations. A second element of the simulation's uniqueness lies in the fidelity with which it represents organizational life. A third element is in the thoroughness with which the behavioural norms have been built up and related to previous research.

Experiential modes of learning necessarily concentrate attention on action and therefore on real world referents. However, some synthesis with the symbolic medium of the information processing models is necessary if maximum effectiveness in the learning process is required. Similarly, realism is not the only criterion of a simulation's effectiveness.

Simulator research has examined some of the relationships between fidelity and the stage of training, fidelity and the transfer of training. How the simulator was used, its place in the total programme and the attitude to it of the instructors have also been shown to be vital considerations. Researchers into simulators have typically grappled with the problem of fidelity by starting with the highest fidelity and then decreasing the degree of fidelity to establish a cost/learning-effectiveness cut-off point. Researchers into simulations and games have usually worked from low realism to high realism. We have suggested that the latter group could learn from the former.

Reality is messy and complex and is therefore not appropriate for all groups at all stages of learning. The answer to the question 'how real is real?', posed as the title of this paper, must therefore be 'very'.

References

Brewer, E and Tomlinson, J W E (1963) The manager's working day. *Journal of Industrial Economics,* 12.

Gagné, R M (1962) Simulators. In Glaser, R (1962) (ed) *Training Research and Education.* Wiley, New York.

Gill, R W T (1979) The in tray exercise as a measure of management potential. *Journal of Occupational Psychology,* 52, pp 185-97.

Hinrichs, J R (1964) Communications activity of industrial research personnel. *Personnel Psychology,* 17, pp 193-204.

Horne, J H and Lupton, T (1965) The work activities of middle managers. *Journal of Management Studies,* 2, pp 14-33.

Kincaid, R G and Wheaton, G R (1972) Training device design. In Van Cott, H P and Kincaid, R G (eds) *Human Engineering Guide to Equipment Design.* American Institute of Research, Washington.

Kolb, D A, Rubin, I M and McIntyre, J M (1979) *Organizational Psychology.* Prentice-Hall, Englewood Cliffs.

McCall, M W, Lomardo, M M and Rice, S S (1979) *Looking Glass Inc: Norm Tables.* Center for Creative Leadership, Greensboro, NC.

Miller, G G (1974) *Some Considerations in the Design and Utilization of Simulators for Technical Training.* Report AFHRL-TR 74-65. Air Force Human Resources Laboratory, Brooks AFB, Texas.

Mintzberg, H (1973) *The Nature of Managerial Work.* Harper and Row, New York.

3.3 Computer-Assisted Learning: Clinical Simulations for Nursing

Anna Taylor
CEGEP John Abbott College, Quebec

Abstract: This research project is involved with the design and development of computer simulations for nursing using the bilingual (English and French) NATAL-74 language facilities developed at the National Research Council of Canada. These simulations will provide a methodology for learning through the practice of intellectual skills and application of theory in specific clinical situations.

Introduction

This paper presents a research project being carried out during the 1979-80 academic year dealing with the design, implementation, and evaluation of computer simulations for nursing. Use of the NATAL-74 language facilities of the National Research Council Canada has begun via a DATAROUTE hardwired connection to their PDP10 computer in Ottawa. The study involves nursing students in the second year of their programme at John Abbott College. Students will complete simulated clinical experiences using a LEKTROMEDIA 304 terminal with a touch sensitive screen. The simulations are being designed around data collected from actual cases at the Montreal Children's Hospital. This approach seems to validate the computer-assisted learning activities with current clinical practice in the area of caring for children.

Origin

Since 1974, most of the 400 graduates from the John Abbott College nursing programme have been employed by several Montreal hospitals. One of these employers is the Montreal Children's Hospital where at present many of our graduates are employed in units such as school-aged medicine, infant surgery, orthopaedics, adolescent and infectious diseases. These graduates are expected to demonstrate the abilities of a beginning practitioner as outlined by the professional corporation (*L'Ordre des infirmieres et infirmièrs du Québec*) upon completion of their basic college nursing programme.

Graduates must be capable of making decisions while carrying out the nursing process for the children in their care as they begin their work role. Given these very concrete expectations of graduates, it becomes necessary for the college programme to produce practitioners who will be able to adjust with ease through an orientation programme to their beginning work. Given that (i) the number of clinical hours available within the three-year programme is only 990; (ii) the informal feedback from employers indicates the performance of recent graduates shows some cause for concern; and (iii) the trends in recent results of our graduates on National Nursing examinations has been on the decline (Taylor, 1978, 1978-79), it has become evident that additional methodologies should be designed and made available within the programme to facilitate student learning and the attainment of a performance nearer to the optimum prior to graduation.

Curriculum development has been a priority within our nursing programme recently and these efforts have received funding from the College Research and Development Committee. Now seems the appropriate time to become involved with the design and development of instructional methodologies which enhance learning. Computer simulation seems to provide the 'ultimate' alternative in intructional methodologies since it most closely approaches the clinical experience and yet provides the learner with a controlled environment for learning.

With the approval on 1 June 1979 for funding this project for 1979-80 through Quebec's Ministry of Education (*Programme de subvention à l'innovation pédagogique*), the author has been released from teaching activities to carry out the design, implementation and evaluation of computer simulation units validated with current clinical practice.

Project Design

The objective of the project is to develop computer simulation units for use by nursing students to improve their decision-making skills in terms of efficiency and accuracy. The research design includes diagnostic pre-testing, which has been completed. The experimental design involves a pre-test/post-test structure with a control group. Interest seems high from the selected sample who are students at present in the second year of the nursing programme at John Abbott College.

After an extensive search of the relevant literature and the investigation of techniques used in computer simulations (Scott *et al*, 1977) it appears that a five-point decision option format is appropriate in the design of items within the simulation. The five options will require the learners to make decisions about a range of actions or treatments in their order of importance, or relevance to the client case presented, based upon grading and comments defined by practitioner experts.

Robert Gagné has suggested that problem-solving requires the prerequisites of rules, concepts, discriminations and verbal associations, as well as stimulus-response connections (Gagné, 1970). With representative cases presented to the learner through computer simulation, an opportunity is provided for the learner to become the primary provider of care who then can incorporate previously learned connections, associations, discriminations, concepts and rules in a unique situation where error can occur without harm to actual clients. The learner can, indeed, practice his/her decision-making skills. This dynamic approach to learning will assist the learner to incorporate capabilities learned early in nursing courses and combine these with concepts acquired from other areas of his/her programmes, such as psychology, biology and pharmacology, as well as recall of other principles prerequisite to nursing in the fields of chemistry, physics and mathematics. Through simulated problem-solving, then, the learner recalls relevant rules and combines them to form a new complex rule which is the solution to the problem. This solution is discovered without the 'guidance' of the teacher. Computer simulation provides an optimal method for enabling this process in a protected environment.

Orientation to the use of computer terminals will be done with the sample using computer games, both on a DECWRITER II terminal linked to the Concordia University Cyber computer and the LEK 304 terminal linked to NRC's PDP10 computer.

During experimentation, participant responses will be recorded on hard copy so as to facilitate an analysis of the learning patterns within the sample. All testing results will remain confidential. Trends will be reported statistically after members of the sample have had the opportunity to review all units in a debriefing session with the author.

Discussion

The major constraints of the project have been (i) a cut-back in funding in October 1979 after the project was well under way; (ii) the lack of telephone lines during the month of January 1980, owing to changes at the college, and (iii) problems associated with the purchase of a LEKTROMEDIA 304 terminal.

It is hoped that through the vehicle of workshops, nursing educators will become familiar with this methodology and that it will provide a real resource to the nursing programmes of Quebec and across Canada as a vehicle for instruction through which the learners will be better prepared to make decisions in the clinical settings during their nursing programme as well as upon graduation as they assume their roles as nurses.

References

Gagné, R M (1970) *The Conditions of Learning,* 2nd edition, p 66. Holt, Rinehart and Winston, USA.

Scott, D B, Murray, T S and Cupples, R W (1977) *Decision-Making in Medicine Using Emergency Simulation and Case-Study Models.* University of Glasgow, Scotland.

Taylor, A (1978) *A Co-Relational Study Between College Nursing Grades and Grades Received on First Writing of Canadian Nurses' Association.* Testing Service Examinations for May 1977 Nursing Graduates of John Abbott College.

Taylor, A (1978-79) *Report of Committee of Examiners (Comité-des examinateurs - section anglaise).* Ordre des infirmieres et infirmiers du Quebec Rapport Annuel, pp 113-14.

3.4 Kent Mathematics Project in the Future

B Banks
West Kent Teachers' Centre, Tunbridge Wells

Abstract: After outlining the techniques and advantages of the Kent Mathematics Project, the paper goes on to consider possible developments in the near and distant future.

Description of KMP (Kent Mathematics Project)

General

KMP is a bank of mathematical learning material from which teachers extract a personalized course for each pupil. The material caters for mathematical concept development for children of all abilities between nine and 16 years, and ranges from material for the average nine-year-old in KMP level 1 to the highest grade at O-level in level 8. KMP is not a mathematics course but 'n' courses where 'n' is the number of pupils in a school. It can be used successfully for any known CSE or O-level mathematics examination syllabus and meets the individual requirements of each pupil in terms of ability and special interests. It also has a specially designed section for very slow learners who will not be capable of taking an examination.

The Operational System

In primary schools (seven to 11 years), teachers can gradually ease pupils into the scheme when the children have met the entry requirements for KMP level 1. Alternatively, they can follow the procedure of secondary schools receiving non-KMP pupils and administer the KMP entrance test. This is really a placement test to determine what KMP levels in number, geometry and general maths are most suitable for the pupil. In transfer from KMP primary schools, records of work are sent with the pupil, who continues his or her mathematical course with the same material.

Figure 1 shows the classroom system, which is operated in the following way:

A. THE MATRIX
This is a bundle of tasks recorded on a four by three rectangle (giving 12 cells) into which up to 11 workcard, booklet and tape numbers and titles are written out. The twelfth task is reserved for a Free Choice (see later). Between three and six matrices are usually completed each year.

B. HELP?
At any point during a task when the pupil runs into difficulty, the teacher is available to help.

C. TEACHER CHECK ON EACH TASK
Whenever a task is completed, it is checked off by the teacher.

D. OK?
Usually, this is merely a matter of initialling and dating or, if the pupil has not mastered the task, appropriate tutoring.

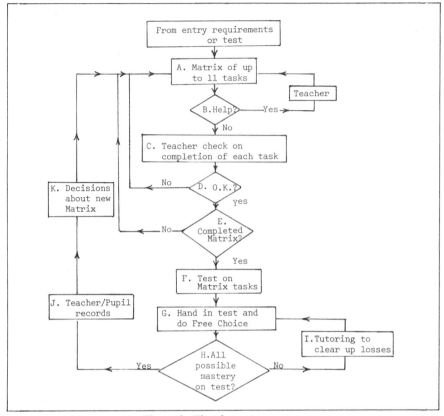

Figure 1. *The classroom system*

E. COMPLETED MATRIX?
Not all matrices contain 12 tasks. For slower and younger children, shorter term goals are established to reduce required retention time and ensure more frequent matrix testing.

F. TESTS ON TASKS
Test books for each level carry tests on all testable tasks. Pupils extract from the book the tests on tasks in their matrix.

G. HAND IN TEST AND DO FREE CHOICE
In order to keep the pupil busy whilst the test is being marked, remedial work or work on special interests of pupil and/or teacher is usually done.

H. ALL POSSIBLE MASTERY?
Most pupils obtain between 60 per cent and 90 per cent plus on their matrix tests. Below 60 per cent is a sign that the pupil is working on material too difficult; if the test mark is, say, 70 per cent, then the missing 30 per cent must be investigated and cleared up.

I. TUTORING
Appropriate action is taken to clear up the missing percentage.

J. TEACHER/PUPIL RECORDS

There are networks showing all tasks in each level. Copies of these networks are used as pupils' records and are marked up by the teacher and show which tasks have been completed.

K. DECISIONS ABOUT NEW TASKS

Taking into account the successes, weaknesses and special interests and requirements of the pupil, the teacher, usually in consultation with the pupil, selects tasks for the next matrix.

KMP Assessment Procedure

KMP material is organized into a structured framework of conceptual development. Hierarchically arranged, tasks develop a concept along a line of ascending difficulty and each task establishes entry behaviour for the next one. Thus, each task carries a level score which identifies mathematical ability when it is completed. The mean of a matrix of scores, suitably corrected from test results, can therefore be an objective assessment of mathematical ability. It is more objective than any one-off examination, having been evolved with a large population of pupils (about 35,000 in 1977-78).

KMP Material

Initially designed by a team of enthusiastic teachers from 10 experimental schools, the KMP material bank has been evolved through rigorous try-out for about 15 years.

Feedback about the material has shown that, in its published form, it has met a criterion of 80/80/80, that is, from experience of use in the classroom, 80 per cent of the teachers consider each published task to have been 80 per cent successful with 80 per cent of the pupils.

Advantages and Benefits

A summary of the main advantages and benefits from using the KMP learning model is:

(a) KMP learning is highly structured and based on successful mastery. Thus, whatever the ability of the pupil, his or her personal mathematics learning world is a successful one. (The difference between pupils is not what marks they can obtain on a rank ordering test or examination, but in the height of attainment in defined levels of achievement.)

(b) There are no problems in primary/secondary or middle/comprehensive transfer or, indeed, between any schools using KMP.

(c) There is no loss of vital learning if the child is absent.

(d) There is no serious interruption of work if the teacher is absent.

(e) Group constitution and group character do not affect individual success. Unpredicted advantages and benefits have been noted over the experimental period such as:

(f) High motivation, which is believed to come from the system, choice and design of material (which is in the form of workcards, booklets and tapes) and almost total absence of failure.

(g) Much improved teacher/pupil relationships as the teacher's function changes from an authoritarian role to that of diagnostician, guide and helper.

(h) Pupils show a much improved attitude to learning and the subject.

(i) Many unmathematical teachers, especially in the primary schools, have enjoyed a painless but effective in-service training and are now not only enthusiastic about the scheme but also the subject.

(j) Many a gifted child's mathematics learning career has been rescued from disastrous lack of suitable material and guidance.

(k) Many very slow learners have been given enough confidence on their special material to be transferred to the mainstream KMP scheme.

These main advantages of using KMP are in wide educational areas and are not specific to mathematics.

Near Future Developments

It seems that any change in secondary school education always assumes a lock-step teaching system with a group treated as a unit. Such a learning model is inefficient and inflexible. It requires specialist teaching and careful timetabling and is never suitable for all members of the group. The KMP learning model, as well as proving efficient for each individual pupil, also, surprisingly, makes many of the aforesaid changes obsolete.

For instance, one could argue the obsolescence of the present-day large comprehensive school. If we describe comprehensive education as that which caters for children of all abilities in all desired subjects, all that is required is a material-bank in each desired subject, plus a teacher who can guide, help and advise. Generally, such teachers are already available in secondary schools, so any secondary school, irrespective of size, could become a comprehensive school. The extreme of such an argument would be to re-open village and small urban all-age schools.

Schools are already suffering from a shortage of specialist teachers in some subjects. In mathematics, one can imagine the shortage becoming so desperate that a secondary school might be unable to offer a course in higher mathematics up to, say, A-level. With a material bank of higher mathematics, the specialist teacher could be peripatetic, visiting the school about once a week to administer the vital 'all possible mastery?' and 'tutoring to clear up losses' components and give help to other students who have run into difficulty on a task. These other students would have been working on another matrix task whilst shelving the difficult one.

Material bank learning would also solve the problem of the viable sixth-form. One would no longer need an enormous base to the school pyramid in order to obtain sufficient pupils at the tip to make sixth-form study viable. In all secondary schools there would no longer be the constraints of offering only restricted combinations of subjects because of specialist teacher or timetable difficulties. Schools could offer literally any desired subject, even a subject as rare in this country as Chinese language, provided there were available a Chinese language material bank and a peripatetic Chinese.

Distant Future Use

The KMP learning model is a joy to see being used in some of the Kent primary schools. The claim that secondary students 'go off in the third year' is not supported by the history of KMP, which shows that there is no significant difference in the attitude and work-rate of pupils throughout the whole of their secondary school career, whatever their age.

There is therefore no behavioural reason why secondary schools should not abolish the timetable, which is a serious constraint to learning with its change of lesson signal, and resurrect the Dalton Plan. With subject rooms or laboratories, each pupil could be given a weekly assignment of time to be spent on each subject and the choice of work at any time be conditional upon the availability of accommodation in the rooms. In KMP, what task is done at any particular time is conditional upon the availability of apparatus or equipment and there is no evidence in KMP history that unco-operative behaviour is a problem. A school multi-subject operational model would only be an extension of the KMP single-subject system.

One exciting prospect for 2000 AD would be the establishment of multi-subject material bank organizations which could cater for the needs of pupils of all abilities in all desired subjects. With a defined common core of compulsory subjects and freedom of choice of specialized subjects, without the constraints of a timetable, one could guarantee full development of each pupil's potential without time-wasting in subjects of proven unsuitability. Not only is the lock-step teaching model inefficient but a timetabled education cannot possibly be suitable for every pupil. Perhaps by 2000 AD a computer-assisted total education through personalized courses is also a likelihood.

One thing is certain. An application of an educational technology learning model to total education, even through to the highest levels of learning, will parallel the development of KMP and find unpredictable solutions to wide areas of educational problems. Education technology is essentially problem-solving in character.

3.5 The Hertfordshire Microcomputer Managed Mathematics Project

M H Aston and D A Walton
Hertfordshire County Council

Abstract: The philosophy and practice of a two-year computer-managed mathematics course, which is followed by all-ability secondary school first- and second-year classes, is described.

Introduction

The Hertfordshire Computer Managed Mathematics Project (HCMMP) originated from an investigation at Hatfield School, Hertfordshire, into the use of a computer-managed system within a first-year all-ability mathematics course. In 1972, money was injected into the scheme by the National Development Programme in Computer Aided Learning (NDPCAL) and by Hertfordshire County Council. Funding from the NDPCAL ceased with the end of the programme in 1977, by which time the HCMMP had established itself within the 12 development schools in Hertfordshire and three schools in the Inner London Education Authority. All these schools used a central computer facility.

In 1979, with the aid of funds from the Department of Industry, a version was made available for use on a microcomputer. This system was used by six pilot schools; two in Hertfordshire, three in the ILEA and one in Buckinghamshire.

The objectives of the Hertfordshire Computer Managed Mathematics Project were to produce a two-year computer-managed mathematics course to be followed by all-ability secondary school first- and second-year classes.

The Project

The project, with computer management, is seen as one possible solution to some of the management problems that arise from a teaching approach that has moved away from traditional 'chalk and talk' to a more individualized approach. By appropriate course design and structuring, and by computer marking and record-keeping, it has been possible to provide the correct work level for individual children and allow the teacher to play a tutorial role as demanded by an individual approach to mixed-ability mathematics teaching. The use of the computer ensures up-to-date marking for the pupils and keeps the teacher informed of general progress and particular difficulties. Course structuring has also been designed around the retention of a class identity (class lessons can occur *naturally* every two or three weeks) and a 'forced' frequent teacher/pupil interaction to mark certain worksheets and overcome problem areas.

Course Design

The course is worksheet-based and modular. A core of 25 modules have been published, aimed to cover years one and two (11 and 12 years old) of the English secondary school system. A number of other optional modules have been written.

The modules are topic-oriented and linear in progression. Although modules can stand alone, later modules build on the work done in the earlier ones but a more random progression can be followed.

In order to accommodate the wide range of ability, each child is allowed to work at his own pace and yet the mechanics of operating the course have been designed so that the whole class works on the same topic (module) together. Pupils are then allowed, through careful grading of the worksheets within a module, to progress to the limits of their ability, ensuring that as they do so they attain a satisfactory standard and body of knowledge. In addition, by retaining the class 'identity', teachers have the opportunity to teach the class as a whole and hence develop, through group activity, the more abstract and teacher-dependent variations which are so important in mathematics.

Module Profile

At the beginning of a module all the pupils in the class can be brought together to view a video-tape television programme (lasting approximately 15 minutes). The video programme aims to introduce the new section of work to the pupils in a light-hearted and entertaining way. In general, the teacher is recommended to follow the video with a 'chalk and talk' session, raising important points to be covered in the module and reinforcing ideas developed in the video programme.

A pre-test is used to determine at what point each pupil should join the module. Each of the pupils in the class will progress through the worksheets at his own pace. At the end of two or three weeks, when the teacher is satisfied that even the slowest pupil has achieved the central mathematical objectives, the class is brought together again and a new module is started.

General Project Philosophy

The project's philosophy has been formulated around the following major principles:

1. The course is designed for all-ability classes, and assumes that pupils have a reading age of at least nine years.

2. The course should prove a satisfactory foundation to subsequent mathematics courses in the later school years.
3. The course should be a balance of modern and traditional ideas.
4. The work should be structured to satisfy the logistics of computer assessment in so far as this does not conflict with educational demands.
5. The computer system should be flexible enough to allow the teacher to:
    (a) override its directions,
    (b) fall back on his own methods of assessment and direction should the technology break down.
6. That although the work is individualized, the 'group' identity of the class should not be destroyed.
7. Arithmetic is a necessary skill to be learnt and constantly practised.
8. During the development period the user of the project material (the teacher in the classroom) should be involved in as many of the decisions and development issues as possible.
9. The cost of the project, whilst largely an 'add-on' cost rather than a marginal cost, should be reasonable.

Module Structure

Each module, designed to last two or three weeks, is graded into levels of difficulty A, B, C, D and sometimes E:

A	Simple language, introductory concepts
B C	Main body of teaching material
D E	More challenging work for faster, more able pupils

It is expected that the more able children will by-pass, or progress quickly through, the early levels to the more demanding work on the C/D/E levels.

At each level there are up to four worksheets: M, T, X, S. All pupils do the M and T sheets; a pupil's result on the M sheet is used by the computer to schedule onto the X sheet or the S sheet, or directly to the next level.

All pupils do these sheets		Optional sheets, scheduled by the computer	
M	T	X	S
machine marked	teacher marked	remedial work (machine marked)	extra practice (machine marked)

In addition, each pupil receives a study-sheet with each module, which summarizes the main ideas in the module and acts as a quick reference point. Some teachers prefer to work through this sheet in class, although this is not the intention.

In general, all the worksheets in a level develop the same concepts at the same level of difficulty.

Because children are of differing abilities, the author defines a recommended cut-off point, usually in the C level, which in theory all children are expected to reach. Beyond this point no new ideas, central to the course, will be introduced. The work is more demanding for the more able pupils.

For each module, teachers are provided with a set of Teacher's Notes which outline the structure and aims of the module, the learning objectives, and equipment required, a synopsis of the video and, of course, the answers, including the computer answers.

Computer Involvement in HCMMP

A computer-managed learning package is available to service the worksheet-based course. The computer is involved in three ways:

1. To assess the pupil's work.
2. To schedule pupils from an M worksheet to an X or S worksheet.
3. To provide adequate feedback to the teacher on the pupil's achievement.

Assessment

All M, X and S sheets can be marked by the computer. To achieve this, a pupil codes his answers to a worksheet onto a specially prepared Optical Mark Recognized (OMR) card, which is subsequently processed by the computer. The pupil's answers are compared with a list of anticipated responses that have been built into the computer files, and the answers marked appropriately. Associated with each response in the computer file may be a comment that, particularly when a wrong answer has been received, can be fairly diagnostic or directive in nature. Hence, the marking that the pupil will receive on a portion of lineprinter paper will not only contain marking for each individual question and a score, but also helpful comments against any question that may have been answered incorrectly.

In general, pupils keep the computer output in their exercise books.

Scheduling

Routing occurs from each M sheet of each level. This scheduling is specified by the author of each module. Depending on what mark a pupil gets on the M sheet, he/she will be told to do the X sheet or S sheet, which is done after completing the T sheet.

Alternatively, the pupil may be allowed to proceed to the next level, after completing the T sheet.

Progress Reports

One of the most important requirements of an individualized scheme is related to record-keeping and 'keeping the teacher in touch' with day-to-day progress of the pupils. The HCMMP computer system, therefore, automatically produces a report detailing pupil attainment and progress. This register reports, on a daily basis, the details of the module currently being attempted by the class.

How Much does it Cost?

There are three kinds of costing: the transfer costs, the on-going costs and the hardware costs, all of which have to be taken into consideration.

The *transfer costs* (ie the sale price) to customers in the UK is related to the cost incurred by Hertfordshire County Council in transferring the HCMMP package. Sales policy is to issue a 'licence to use' to an institution and favours LEAs rather than individual school implementations. This covers software, data files, master of video programmes and all worksheet material.

The *ongoing costs* are not so easy to quantify. The terms of reference under which the NDP grant was given specified that computer-managed learning should be undertaken at 'reasonable cost'. Although the development grant was generous, the ongoing costs have always been looked at with great scrutiny. For this reason children receive only half a sheet of lineprinter output.

No one seems quite sure how 'reasonable' reasonable cost should be; it is fairly clear that for a school-based project 'reasonable' can only mean dirt cheap, and in the present economic climate it must be cheaper than this.

Apart from staffing, there are three broad headings under which costs may be reckoned:

1. CLASSROOM MATERIALS
Classroom materials include worksheets, games, study sheets, teachers' notes, etc. The cost of these depends in part on the cost of raw material and also on the cost of reprographic facilities. In Hertfordshire the worksheets are re-used and thus costs depend on how long the sheets survive classroom use.

2. TELEVISION PROGRAMMES
The cost of these includes the cost of video-tapes and also the costs of copying from master programmes. The overall cost of television in the project could not be defended, except that in Hertfordshire there is already a strong commitment to television, and studio and copying facilities and replay equipment in schools are already provided and well-used in other subject areas.

3. COMPUTER CONSUMABLES
Each time a pupil completes a computer-marked worksheet, he/she will use a mark sense card and half a sheet of lineprinter paper.

Other ongoing computer costs include lineprinter ribbons and service of hardware.

The *hardware costs* are available from the individual manufacturers/suppliers.

3.6 Possible Contributions of Mathematics Teaching for Technological and Social Education

P Boero and F Furinghetti
University of Genova
P Forcheri, E Lemut and M T Molfino
Mathematical Applications Laboratory of CNR Genova

Abstract: After reviewing the current organization of Italian secondary education, the authors explain the purpose and technique of their method for the better preparation of students for the social and technical aspects of life.

Introduction: Brief Review of the Present Italian Situation

Traditionally, education in Italian schools has always been essentially humanistic, but a reform in 1962 (at that time considered rather progressive) and the subsequent legislative revisions have introduced big changes in the Lower school sector, age 11-14 years.

Roughly speaking, the previous Lower Secondary school was of various types: professional, commercial, technical and, finally, humanistic and the curricula were very varied. The humanistic school (where Latin was taught) was the only one allowing admission to the University via the lyceum (Grammar school).

The reform has combined all these types of schools following the pattern of the English comprehensive school. The curriculum is rather interesting: Latin plays no part, and subjects like applied technical studies, elements of natural sciences, chemistry, and physics (an innovation for Italian pupils of this age) are taught.

Unfortunately, these changes have failed to influence the Upper Secondary school, and the situation for the 14- to 19-years-old pupils still conforms to the system which was initiated in the 1920s.

Brief Prospectus of the Italian School

1. *Elementare* (roughly equivalent to the English primary school): age 6-11.
2. *Secondaria Inferiore* (roughly equivalent to the English comprehensive school): age 11-14.
3. *Secondaria Superiore* (roughly equivalent to the English secondary school): age 14-19, which includes:

Licei (Grammar school)	{ *classico* (humanistic) *scientifico* (scientific) *linguistico* (foreign languages) *artistico* (artistic)
Istituti Tecnici (Technical school)	{ *nautico* (nautical) *industriali* (industrial) *commerciale* (commercial)
Istituti Professionali (Professional school)	{ *per l'industria* (for industry) *per il commercio* (for commerce)
Istituti Magistrali (Teachers' Training school)	{ for teachers in elementary school for teachers in infant school

As the political and historical situation has changed profoundly over the last 50 years, it is obvious that people operating in schools and involved in educational problems are waiting for a reform fitting schools to the present reality. Nothing official has been done to alleviate this problem and any innovations are the result of the goodwill of individuals or small groups.

In Italy about 10 groups of people are involved in research in mathematics teaching, all linked up with the University. We are working in one of these groups. Our aims are the following:

(a) proposals for new curricula,
(b) classroom experimentation carried out by teachers within the groups.

As far as mathematics is concerned, it is the initiatives in experimentation as part of the University research which are at present providing the most interesting stimulus. In fact, at the University at present it is possible to become a Doctor of Mathematics with specialization in teaching.

This fact has two important implications: university teachers involved in these types of course are interested in educational problems and the new generation of graduates is prepared more than before to meet the problems of the school.

Encouragement and support for our work comes from grants made by the Italian National Research Council which recognizes the activity of the research and experimental teaching groups.

Our Educational Principles and Objectives

Our aim is to give to present-day students the necessary instruments for interpreting reality from both the social and technical angle.

Perhaps, because of our profession as teachers or researchers in mathematics at University level, we recognize that science has a fundamental role to play in interpreting reality, and the alternative way of teaching mathematics which we have planned for Upper Secondary school stems from our belief in the important role this subject plays in our contemporary culture.

A Possible Alternative Way of Working in Schools

At present, mathematics is taught in schools as follows. A sequence of information is given; some it it is purely technical and some can be very interesting and informative. The motivations for the choice of the various topics learned are usually internal to mathematics and, overall, the subject is not taught as a coherent whole.

This way of teaching has many disadvantages, and consequently is frustrating for the majority of the students. It does not foster the attitude of mastering a subject (which has to be one of the aims of education, especially in the Upper Secondary school). Also, the students grasp only the purely technical or the purely formal side, and lose the cultural and formative aspect of mathematics.

In fact, mathematics is not only an intellectual training but it is also a useful instrument for understanding real life: this is the aspect we intend to emphasize as it seems to be very neglected in our schools at present.

We propose an alternative method, which consists of two phases:

1. We carefully choose a topic which seems interesting and reasonably workable (from both the educational and mathematical viewpoints).
2. We develop the chosen topic for some time (from one term to three years) in its technical mathematical, historical, social, etc aspects.

All the teaching staff have to take part in choosing the topic, as this is crucial to this type of project. The following elements may affect the choice:

(a) The time available for working on the topic.
(b) The pupils' ages.
(c) The social context in which one is operating.
(d) The type of school in which one is operating, and its curriculum.
(e) Real opportunities for teamwork among the teaching staff.
(f) The extra support supplied by the school (tools, books, projectors, pocket calculators, computers, laboratory, external experts in certain disciplines, etc)
(g) The pupils' preferences.
(h) The teachers' preferences.

As regards point (g), one can start with a questionnaire in order to investigate the classroom feeling, but our experience suggests that the interests of pupils aged 14 to 19 years are usually rather indeterminate, and are almost always influenced by the mass media.

The topic choice can be made in three different ways:

(a) It is possible to work out a problem internal to mathematics, starting from a basic knowledge until substantial results are achieved. This is the least significant choice, but sometimes the only possible one if the teacher is isolated or the environment is hostile to radical change.

(b) Another possible choice is a topic of interest (for various reasons) having evident implications for mathematics and also important links with social and humane disciplines, eg man and machines.

(c) Finally, a topic can be chosen simply because of its strong social and cultural interest.

Naturally, the choice of topic has to be made in such a way that it is possible to deal with the content (mathematical, in our case) organically so that it is possible to achieve real mathematical depth combined with mastery of the topic.

Below we give an example of a topic and the main features of its possible treatment in Upper Secondary school.

A Typical Topic – Demography

Since Malthus, the demographic problem has involved everybody who is concerned with social, political and ecological factors. It gets as much attention from the mass media as from scientists, because it is tied to:

1. Our concern about the shortage of energy and food resources.
2. Our concern about the imbalance in the demographic development in certain regions or entire countries.
3. Our concern about natural disasters (often not as accidental as we may think).
4. Analysis of the population boom after the Second World War.

It is useful to begin with geographical population studies in different countries and different environments. Following that, it is possible to begin investigating the connections between the previous data and (i) food consumption and malnutrition; (ii) *per capita* and national incomes; (iii) energy consumption; (iv) availability of raw materials; and (v) the animal populations – some examples of type of growth. At this point the students are ready to deal with: (vi) the demographic problem in history; and (vii) the connections between the demographic problem and economic, social and political problems (both past and present) and cultural development (literature, education, town planning, etc).

The pupils can then organize from a quantitative viewpoint: (i) calculation and comparison of birth and death rates; (ii) growth rates; (iii) population 'pyramid'; (iv) comparison of demography in various countries at different levels of industrialization; (v) population trends and stability; (vi) connections between population and energy consumption; and (vii) first example of growth models.

These calculations will involve pupils with the following mathematical techniques:

- ☐ tables, percentages, index numbers, arithmetic mean, median, mode, variance, etc;
- ☐ graphics, broken lines, confrontation of graphics;
- ☐ regression, exponentials, logarithms;
- ☐ deterministic and stochastic models (differential equations, graphical integration, etc);
- ☐ arithmetic, semi-logarithmic, log-log, etc papers.

Some Pedagogical and Educational Comments

From a pedagogical viewpoint, demography seems very suitable for pupils at the age in question. Psychologists consider the first interest of the child is his own person. This phase in the personality development is followed by an interest in nature and the connections between man and his environment. The last phase is a growing interest in the 'man/society' relationship.

In dealing with demography one can follow the same syllabus and choose which aspect one wants to emphasize. Starting from the aims of purely technical and scientific education, it is also possible to recover a part of the Italian humane method of education. In fact, we think this aspect may be interesting not only in Italy; in every country the possibility of recovering a certain balance between two different kinds of culture is an important aspect of education.

If the mathematics teacher cannot carry out the project with the co-operation of all the teaching staff, it is possible to deal with the topic at different depths by limiting oneself to the technological aspects only.

Incidentally, we maintain that it is possible to use the method outlined in this paper to deal not only with mathematics but with any subject.

Section 4:
The Use of Computers as Aids to Learning

4.1 Non-Literary Stylistics: Computer Help for the Student as Writer

E Clavering
University of Aston in Birmingham

Abstract: Stylistics lies at the heart of advanced language learning; appropriacy of utterance is the target. Linguistic stylistics is beginning to describe such appropriacy. The aim of the research described has been to make a simple computer analysis of language which will allow students to judge for themselves how closely their own efforts approximate to some defined target. The hypothesis is that the learner will find his own way to beat the target, and in so doing learn to write more complex and more appropriate texts. Progress is reported, and verification or otherwise of the hypothesis discussed.

Introduction

What might be called the Noddy stage of any new educational technology is marked by a strange marriage of advanced hardware and the most naive of software. Like early language laboratories (LL), early computer assisted-learning (CAL) suffered from a concept of 'teaching' rather more primitive than that of the most traditional of army instructors. True, it developed much faster than LL orthodoxy (which changed little over a dozen years), but the persistence in CAL of the most ancient of educational fallacies, that the teacher, or at one remove, his machine-substitute. somehow processes the truth and will in due course reveal it to his disciples, was demonstrated at ETIC 79 by Cooper and Lockwood's analysis of Open University use of the computer (Cooper and Lockwood, 1979) or the hope expressed by Alexander Romiszowski and Barbara Atherton that they had gone 'some way to answering that creativity and control are no longer neglected factors within SI programme design'. (Romiszowski and Atherton, 1979.) They gave as one example of 'limitation of design', as they euphemistically put it, a group instructional programme in literature. Language is an open-ended creative process: 'instruction', in either its appreciation or its production, is self-defeating. Yet, to be fair to educational reductionists, it must be admitted that they are neither more naive nor more unhelpful than many proponents of alleged 'creative writing' in the schools, who look on the production of a text much as Victorians did that of a child, a matter to which the spirit may or may not move us, but the less said about the details the better. Their pupils often come to university language courses much as the Victorian misses did to marriage — eager and hopeful, but short on co-operation.

Non-Literary Stylistics

My problem, in a use-orientated language department, is to get students to see why the careful avoidance of sin (seen as mechanical errors) does not result in the production of a French-like text — indeed is irrelevant to it — and then to understand what must be done to achieve one appropriate to given circumstances; that a business letter, for instance, does not just happen: in short, applied non-literary stylistics. The first step, of course, is to take samples of language appropriate as targets, and describe them quantitatively.

The quantitative analysis of language (as opposed to fine-honed syntactical enquiry) has seen two major forms of attack. The older is that of educationists in attempts to define age-group norms in language development, particularly in the field of reading. Often pragmatically reliable, because of the use of learner populations of impressive size, such research is linguistically so naive that even my students can understand it — a good example is the much-used Loban Scale (Berse, 1974). More recently, linguists using computer programmes of daunting complexity have examined certain language areas, usually highly specialized. At first they operated almost entirely at the lexical level (eg D E Ager's studies of specialized French vocabulary) but now they are advancing into the field of grammar (Moskovitch and Caplan, 1976) (see, eg, the programme used by M Boot at Utrecht [1976]).

In what is perhaps a weak English compromise, I have been looking at sizeable samples of language by using a form of linguistic analysis which is as simple as possible, this side naiveté, helped by a small computer programme, of an order suitable for a mini rather than a main frame, which merely takes the finger-ache out of totting up figures and looking up words in the dictionary. It is quite possible, and in the present state of over-use of Aston's computer, often quicker, to operate manually. A similarly simple research-teaching programme, EDIT (Davison, 1976) has been used in the USA by Ned Davison for literature. Actual analysis is done by the entrant, who for the computer flags, and makes machine-readable, the text (anathema, by the way, to serious computational linguists). The computer therefore does not 'know' the truth and, consequently, cannot be used to instruct the student by the obvious device of analyzing for him his attempts at writing, and marking them against a computer analysis of model texts.

The Future

We are approaching the stage where, at great expense, it will be possible for the computer to instruct the student. I hope it never comes to that. Because the computer cannot instruct; it can 'teach' in the proper sense of helping to learn. If a student can operate the system of analysis he can use the programme, but if so, he also possesses the tool necessary for examining the structure of his own and other people's writing for comparing and re-structuring. The computer becomes merely a try-your-strength machine. The teacher can say to the student: 'This piece of writing is unacceptably informal for the situation: look at your LD: it ought to be around 45 per cent in this situation — can you achieve that?' or 'Your FR is clearly zero: can you raise it to 30?'. In fact the most important area for practice and improvement is that of SC — Bogey for any given course can be stated, and 'style' becomes a quantified objective, like running a four-minute mile — the stop-watch can tell the runner only how near he is to his own target.

Computer-Help for the Student as Writer?

Does it work? Well, something has raised several students' writing to appropriate density and professional structure, but it would be both too early — few programmes have been run, partly because of computer overload problems — and too simplistic to give the credit to the computer. The student needed to be convinced that style was analyzable and that he himself could analyze and imitate it. The computer can play a role in gaining this conviction — once that is won, its use is far from essential. To some extent all educational technology is gimmicry justifiable by its power to challenge. Flashing lights and rattling coins are an irrational but effective invitation to gaming, and in one year TV microprocessor games have brought far more prople to the use of the VDU for SI, however frivolous, than years of educational technology.

Motivation in human activity is all: but it is complex. To play against Bogey keeps many a man fit: but the club professional offers a more exciting challenge. There are better motivators than computers. A colleague prepared a model answer for his students' written work. A busy and businesslike man, he used a dictaphone to record it, and as a result his supposedly written text had the lexical density of a formal lecture, not that of writing. To transform this donnish production into something more appropriately formal proved a better challenge than mere figures.

Conclusions

What conclusions can be drawn from this incomplete and regrettably anecdotal enquiry? Essentially that learning is a response to challenge, and challenge, to evoke response, must be precise, measurable — and somehow anthropomorphisized. Creativity is not 'taught' — a nonsense — but aroused in definable conditions. The most successful computer-aided teaching has been in chess, where human behaviour had been most nearly aligned on computer rules. In the field of language learning we shall do far more by teaching computers to play the linguistic games in which human culture is rich — 'capping quotations' is already well within even mini possibilities — than by repeating the behaviourist errors of the 'audio-lingual' courses of the late 'Language Teaching Revolution'. It is not an accident that programmes like EDIT and TEXTAN, designed originally for the great academic game of research, prove able to teach. But such games do not require the complexity and the cost of the mainframe. In language learning, what was always needed was ways of transforming the ill-named 'language laboratory' into a language gymnasium: perhaps now we should be thinking of exploiting microprocessors to turn it into a linguistic pin-table saloon.

References

Berse, P (1974) Criteria for the assessment of pupils' composition. *Educational Research*, 17, 1, November.

Boot, M (1976) Linguistic data structure. In Ager, D E, Knowles, F E and Smith, J (eds) *Advances in Computer-Aided Literary and Linguistic Research*. University of Aston in Birmingham.

Cooper, A and Lockwood, F (1979) The need, provision and use of a computer-assisted interactive tutorial system. In Page, G T and Whitlock, Q (eds) *Aspects of Educational Technology* XIII. Kogan Page, London.

Davison, N J (1976) Modular programs for individual literary researchers unfamiliar with computers. In Ager, D E, Knowles, F E and Smith, J (eds) *Advances in Computer-Aided Literary and Linguistic Research*. University of Aston in Birmingham.

Moskovitch, W and Caplan, R (1976) Distributive statistical technique in linguistic and literary research. In Ager, D E, Knowles, F E and Smith, J (eds) *Advances in Computer-Aided Literary and Linguistic Research*. University of Aston in Birmingham.

Romiszowski, A and Atherton, B (1979) Creativity and control: neglected factors within self-instruction programme design. In Page, G T and Whitlock, Q (eds) *Aspects of Educational Technology* XIII. Kogan Page, London.

4.2 Using Computer-Assisted Training to Learn How to Locate Faults

R Morris
Chemical and Allied Products Industry Training Board

A Logical Approach to Fault-Finding (LAFF)

The Chemical and Allied Products Industry Training Board has always been interested to discover how good fault-finders work. We know that they do it by 'experience' and 'intuition', but the question remains — are there some general fault-finding skills and concepts which can be translated to the less well-endowed?

For some five years we have been investigating this problem and developing the Logical Approach to Fault-Finding (LAFF) as just one possible solution to it. The first version of LAFF appeared as Section 10 of a CAP/ITB publications on the Training of Instrument Technicians and was taken up by the Technical Education Council as the basis of its fault-finding module.

The second version appeared as an information paper and formed the platform for a fairly large number of courses and seminars.

LAFF comprises a set of guidelines which we believe approximates to the thinking and strategy of a natural fault-finder. It is argued that it also provides a base from which others can learn.

Computer-Assisted Training in LAFF

The overriding factor in choosing to use computer-assisted training is that in certain areas we know of no other method which is likely to achieve the results we need. The reasons why we think it has this power are:

1. It allows infinite practice with immediate feedback of results. The computer programs can generate fault situations randomly and monitor the trainee's progress every step of the way. The training is therefore capable of being completely adaptive and is certainly dynamic.
2. It is non-judgemental. The trainee need not feel embarrassed about getting it wrong, nor does he feel the need to justify himself by making false claims about his search strategy.
3. It is patient, allowing trainees to proceed at their own pace and allowing constant and continuous repetition and practice.
4. It is firm. It can identify whether trainees are using the preferred approach and if they are not it can prevent them progressing until they do.
5. It is dynamic. No two situations need be the same. Thus, trainees must *understand* what they are doing. They cannot learn a set of rules and apply those, nor can they work 'from memory' on successive trials with the computer programs.
6. It can be used in private, for example during a spare half-hour on the night shift.

Phase 1

Phase 1 started in July 1979, and was (in theory) restricted to preparing specifications and documentation layouts. However, it soon became obvious that without programs it would be impossible to make any significant progress.

Phase 1 has concentrated on developing adaptive programs which allow trainees to discover the most efficient search strategy and which then allows them unlimited practice in this strategy.

Phase 2

Phsse 2 started in November/December 1979 and will:

1. Complete the work on search strategies to include:
   (a) the effects of probability,
   (b) the use of hierarchies (developing into a consideration of systems),
   (c) multiple faults.
2. Develop the remaining materials, when programmed learning text will be needed. This will probably be provided in manual form.
3. Produce similar materials for the symptom/fault matrix.
4. Provide 'keys' which will allow users to maintain student records.
5. Provide facilities which will allow the conceptual terms used within the package (eg fault 1, symptom 6, etc) to be replaced by specific equipment terminology.
6. Produce documentation, including some guidelines for others who may find themselves tackling similar problems through computer-assisted training.
7. Establish a comprehensive courseware design which will allow the computer-assisted training materials to be used effectively within a 'traditional' setting.

4.3 Cognitive Activities Related to Student Learning Through Computers

Gladys Marante
University of Surrey

Abstract: This is a study about some aspects of the process of student learning through computers. The main conclusions presented in the paper are, firstly, that there seems to be a connection between the cognitive activities the students are engaged in when working on a learning task and their perceived outcome, and secondly, that one could possibly promote the desirable cognitive activities through certain conditions in the task.

Introduction

Several studies have been carried out to investigate different aspects of the process of student learning. Most of these studies look at the process in terms of the input and output but some of them try to describe what happens during the process itself.

Only a few of these, however, attempt to describe the process of student learning at university level.

Marton and Säljö (1976) have characterized the differences in learning strategies in terms of deep and surface level processing. A collection of descriptions of the student's approach to a learning task refer, in the case of deep level processing, to whether student is thinking about the overall structure of the content. For surface level processing, the descriptions refer to whether the student only tries to memorize, or is focused upon the time factor and confronts the task rather passively.

Laurillard (1978a) developed a model that describes the relationship between some of the factors that influence student learning, such as learning style, learning strategy, the student's orientation, his response to the task, and the content of the teaching.

Learning through computers, and in particular through computer simulation packages, is discussed by, eg, Tawney (1976), Hinton (1978) and McKenzie (1978), who describe some of the aims and important features of graphical computer simulation programs. Simulations are said to provide motivation to the learner and to develop insights into the topic studied. Students' comments about the learning experience refer to 'getting a feel for it'. It is assumed that the student need not be concerned with the 'intimate details of the equations and rules controlling the simulation' (Tawney, 1976). This makes the simulation packages particularly valuable for topics which are mathematically complicated and for which it is difficult for the students to comprehend the full range of behaviour just from the mathematical formalism (Hinton, 1978).

When evaluating student learning in Computer-Assisted Learning (CAL), Laurillard (1978b and 1978c) describes a typology of CAL interactions, ie the interactions that take place at the computer terminal, for the particular situation of simulation packages. The categories of the typology are interpreting, experimenting and reasoning. Other descriptions refer to students' comments such as visualizing, gaining intuitive understanding, checking knowledge and understanding, and so on.

There is not much research done in the area of problem-solving with computers. Hinton (1978) affirms that problem-solving 'represents a higher level of activity than that of learning facts' and that 'it is often used to indicate a certain level of comprehension of the concepts, principles and facts that have been learnt'. This is so because the student must go beyond what he was taught, and look for a solution to a new situation. This condition is essential if the learning experience is to be named 'problem-solving'. Otherwise it should be considered just an application of a formula.

Peckham (1976) suggests that the computer is a tool that can be used by the student in his problem-solving. Thus, the solution of the problem could be expressed as an algorithm, ie the sequence of precisely defined steps by which the problem is solved. To solve a problem algorithmically requires not only a very clear understanding of the problem, true to all kinds of problem-solving, but a very precise statement of its step-by-step solution (Hinton, 1978), where this statement is expressed in a computer programming language. Thus, one advantage of the algorithmic approach is that it allows the teacher to detect the level of the student's understanding.

Another advantage of this approach is that the student could have an alternative approximate solution of problems for which an analytical solution is not feasible. Many research problems fall into this category (Harding, 1974). The student, not being distracted with the analytical feasibility of the solution, can concentrate his efforts in the formulation of the problem and the interpretation of the results.

In this study, I was mainly concerned with the kinds of cognitive activities the students were engaged in when working with simulation and problem-solving tasks, the characteristics the students perceived in the tasks that led them to particular cognitive activities and the connection between those cognitive activities and the students' perception of their outcome. If the student is to be considered as the active subject in the learning activity, then we have to recognize the importance of considering his perception of the experience.

Research Method

Learning through computers is a new way of learning. Therefore, it is necessary to describe it before attempting to explain it. Because of the descriptive nature of this study and the lack of an adequate theoretical framework for it, it seems appropriate to use an exploratory or illuminative approach in order to identify some of the factors that influence learning through computers and the possible relations between these factors.

The study was carried out with a group of 32 second-year students at the Department of Civil Engineering working with a simulation package and another group of six first-year students at the Physics Department, who had to write programs to solve some given problems. Both kinds of assignment were part of the students' academic work. The research techniques used for gathering the data were as follows.

Observations

The students were observed whilst working at the terminal and the interactions that took place between the terminal, student and tutor were manually recorded.

Interviews

The students were interviewed for 20-40 minutes, as soon as possible after the completion of the tasks. These interviews were rather open-ended and included questions about the students' aims, their expectations from the course and tutors, their perception of what was expected from them and also questions about the actual solving of the task, which parts were difficult and why and whether they made any reference back, etc. Additionally, I included a question designed to establish the students' understanding of what was done in the task. These interviews were transcribed verbatim and the protocols were used to elicit the categories.

Notes of the Students' Work

The students were asked to bring to the interview every piece of written work they had produced on the task, as well as a hard copy of the programs in the problem-solving situation. These notes served as an initial base for the interviews.

Analysis

The protocols from both groups of interviews, as well as the observation notes, were analyzed by looking for some aspects in which they could be categorized in terms of the cognitive activities they represented for the student. The results of this analysis are shown in the next section.

Results

As mentioned above, this study is an attempt to demonstrate, from the students' point of view, a connection between what they see in the task, how they perform in it, and what they feel they have learnt from it (see Figure 1).

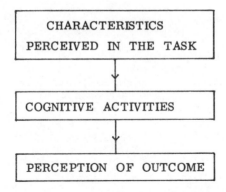

Figure 1. *Possible relation between characteristics perceived in the task, cognitive activities and perception of the outcome.*

Consequently, I shall present the results in such a way that this connection could be easily followed. Thus, the characteristics perceived in the tasks ranged from too easy and straightforward at the one extreme, to too difficult at the other, with different degrees of challenge in the intermediate situations. The students also give their reasons for such judgements.

The cognitive activities vary from 'none' to some of the ones described by Laurillard (1978b and 1978c) for simulations and, moreover, some other categories more directly related to problem-solving. Examples of these are: debugging, recognizing patterns and applying them to different situations, manipulation of information given, looking for a good approach in solving the problem and checking the solution systematically, step by step.

Accordingly, the perceived outcome varies from practically nothing or very poor in some cases, to new insights into the topic, different ways of looking at it, etc.

In order to illustrate more clearly this relationship, I shall present a few case studies of individual students working in particular tasks which are examples of actual combinations of categories within each of these three factors already mentioned.

Case Study 1

The simulation package included some questions supposed to check the knowledge of the concepts involved in it. Nevertheless, some of the students found the questions rather trivial as no previous knowledge of the topic was required to answer them. During the session at the terminal, these students were seen answering the questions very quickly, as they did not have to think about the answers. This fact was corroborated in the interview when they made comments of this sort:

'. . .I could tell the answers in the way they were worded though I could only guess **yes** or **no**. . .'

The students' perception of the learning outcome was that it was rather low. The comments about what they had learnt from the questions were of the following type:

'. . .you could go on pushing **yes** or **no** and go round and round and still didn't really know what was going on. . .nothing was being taught to us.'

These students perceived the task as a very easy one and engaged themselves on a surface level processing. Actually, the cognitive activities were at the level of trial and error.

Case Study 2

This is another student working with problem-solving. The case refers to one program he had to write in order to calculate the area of a triangle defined by three points given. It was required that the area should be expressed in terms of vectors, so the student had first to get the two vectors from the three points and then work out a formula to calculate the area of the triangle defined by these vectors.

It was not easy for this student to relate these concepts. Only after some suggestions and working on his own could he actually see it.

The student was trying to figure out how to express the area of the triangle in terms of a completely new situation for him.

> '. . .this is actually applying vectors, you're given a triangle. . .and you
> had then to relate it to vectors. . .this was an original piece of work in
> theory in working out how the area could be expressed in terms of vectors.'

As far as the actual outcome is concerned, the student was asked in the subsequent interview how he had managed to get the vectors from the co-ordinates and why the formula he had used could be applied in that case, and he was able to give a detailed derivation of the formula, starting from a triangle.

The solution of this problem required (i) manipulation of the information given, in obtaining the vectors from the co-ordinates, (ii) relation between known concepts, such as the area of a triangle, and (iii) application in a new situation, ie when the area is expressed in vectors. This student went through all these three stages and, although the concept of vector itself was not clearer, he had gained a different insight into it, because now he was able to look at it from the point of view of the possible applications of it.

Case Study 3

This case study illustrates how writing a program could help the student to clarify a concept, eg integration. This student had to write some programs on two methods of integration: by summation of rectangular areas and by the trapezium rule. This happened to be just before the students had actually covered the topic in lectures. This student found that writing the program had helped her a lot to understand the actual principles behind it.

> '. . .I think (programming) helps to a certain extent to the maths for
> something like integration. We were doing the sum steps in the computer,
> taking integrals and reducing it. That pretty well works on the basis or idea
> of integration and so you've got to use the basic principles for integration
> if you want to do the program for it. . .so, you have to understand exactly
> how to set about doing that and take into account all possible outcomes
> and everything. . .'

Concerning the outcome, the student referred not only to the clarification of the concept at that very moment but also that later on the lecture had been clarified as well.

So, by devising the step-by-step solution for a problem, the student was helped to understand the underlying concepts.

The whole idea of these case studies has been to illustrate that it is possible to promote cognitive activities which indicate a deep level processing by giving the students tasks which require systematic thinking and that enable them to show understanding. At no point do I wish to claim that the results shown here reflect generalities on learning through simulation packages and algorithmic problem-solving. The tasks themselves were a determinant factor on the students' degree of involvement. For example, if the students' guide of the simulation package referred to in Case Study 1 had been more open-ended, it would have prompted a higher degree of participation on the part of the student.

Conclusion

At present, the conditions for the use of computers in education are almost irresistible. Costs have decreased and software developments are such that learning computing is no longer so problematic to teachers or pupils. As these barriers have been surmounted, computers have become more widespread in education. But the question is: How should the computer be used?

In this paper we have seen examples of uses of computers that provided a good learning experience for the students, but also others which did not. So the use of the computer itself does not necessarily imply that learning is being promoted. The tasks to be performed in the computer should be carefully designed, as they seem to influence the students' cognitive activities and what the students learn depends largely on these activities. New situations and relations between known concepts should be aimed at as much as possible, as they appear to promote richer cognitive activities.

These aspects, however, make the task more complex; therefore, the students' background should be kept in mind before deciding on the level of difficulty of the task. An adequate degree of challenge in the assigned tasks would promote the cognitive activities which, in turn, would lead the student to a satisfactory perception of the outcome.

References

Harding, R (1974) Computer-aided teaching of applied mathematics. *International Journal of Mathematical Education in Science and Technology*, 5, pp 447-55.

Hinton, T (1978) Computer-assisted learning in Physics. *Computers and Education*, 2, pp 71-80.

Laurillard, D (1978a) *A Study of the Relationship between Some of the Cognitive and Contextual Factors in Student Learning*. Unpublished PhD thesis, University of Surrey.

Laurillard, D (1978b) Evaluation of student learning in CAL. *Computers and Education*, 2, pp 259-65.

Laurillard, D (1978c) In McKenzie, J, Elton, L and Lewis, R (eds) *Interactive Computer Graphics in Science Teaching*. Ellis Horwood, London.

McKenzie, J (1978) Interactive computers: graphics in undergraduate science. *Computers and Education*, 2, pp 25-48.

Marton, F and Säljö, R (1976) On qualitative differences in learning: — outcome and process. *British Journal of Educational Technology*, 46, pp 4-11.

Peckham, H (1976) Computers, confusion and complacency. *Computers and Education*, 1, 1, pp 39-45.

Tawney, D (1976) Simulation and modelling in science. *Computer-Assisted Learning Technical Report*, 11, p 13. Council for Educational Technology.

4.4 Applying Programmed Learning Techniques to Computer-Assisted Instruction (CAI), and the use of Computer-Managed Instruction (CMI)

H Butcher
Sales Training Officer, British Airways

Abstract: This paper describes how the disciplines of programmed learning form an essential basis for computer-assisted instruction, and how these principles are applied within the particular context of the British Airways computer system.

It concludes with an outline of the system of computer-managed instruction which is currently under development.

British Airways have highly sophisticated computer systems which are constantly being developed to perform more manual functions. These computer systems are marketed to other airlines and travel agents and earn British Airways much additional revenue.

To be able to use the various computer systems correctly, the training must be done quickly and efficiently with minimum costs. British Airways does this by using programmed learning techniques and applying them to CAI to provide self-teach courses on all aspects of the computer system.

Brief Description of the CAI System

To set the context of what follows, it is necessary to describe briefly the British Airways computer system.

There are about 4,000 Visual Display Units (VDUs) on the computer network. The CAI system operates on the same network, and the training is available on any of the 4,000 VDUs at any time that is convenient.

The CAI Library can be looked at in the same way as a library of loose-leaved books (groups in the CAI system), each with loose-leaved pages (frames), which can be freely inserted, extracted, copied and exchanged.

Currently, the Library capacity is 676 groups (or books), each of which contains up to a maximum of 126 frames (pages). Each frame is a display shown on any of the VDUs in worldwide use on the British Airways network.

A group is identified by two alpha characters, and a frame within a group by two alpha-numerics. Each frame therefore has a unique four-character identifier, for example:

ZADX,   ZAD2,   ZA45,   etc.

(The X against some of the groups shows they are not operational)

In July 1979, a new facility was introduced into the British Airways CAI system designed to help with the problem of testing. This shows how often each frame has been accessed, and how many errors have been made. An example is shown in Figure 1.

The group shown is the first group in the Library and tells how many times each separate course in the CAI library has been accessed in the nine-month period from July 1979 to March 1980.

The first frame ZA01 is the first frame displayed to a student when he/she accesses the CAI system. The count zeroes itself automatically when total 9,999 has been passed. It has done this four times since July 1979, which means the CAI system has been accessed 40,296 times.

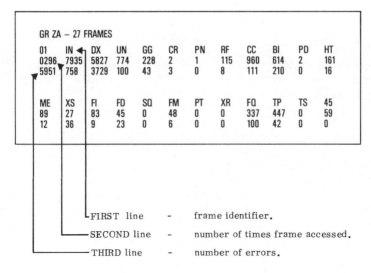

Figure 1.

Principles of Programmed Learning

In the broadest terms, programmed learning can be defined as self-teach, either in printed textual form or as displayed on a VDU in a CAI system, and, of course, as a mixture of both. As such, it has the advantage of being available to anyone anywhere at any time. Savings in costs are also very large and it is very flexible in its operation.

The disadvantages, however, are that it takes a lot of time and care to produce and *properly test* the training material. Because of this, another disadvantage of programmed learning is the difficulty of finding personnel to produce it.

Even at this late date we still hear assertions (sometimes called 'proof', 'demonstration' or 'experience') that programmed learning does not work. You might as well say bicycles do not work, or French cooking does not work. What is really being said by anyone making this assertion is that they do not have the skill or determination to apply the basic principles and do the job properly.

A CAI system which is properly designed can facilitate testing in a number of ways:

1. The system can keep and display a cumulative count for each frame of the number of error responses invoked by the students, and a frame can be amended if producing excessive error responses.
2. An amendment is made on line, once, to the single copy in the central computer only, and is then immediately available to all students.
3. It is possible to monitor student responses, response times, comments and observations.

So self-teach is not programmed learning unless it is properly tested. But that is not all; there are a number of other characteristics that define it, the first being the use of a:

> *stimulus* (question),
> *response* (answer), and
> *reinforcement* (pat on the back)

cycle to write the material. Programmed learning must be used for CAI, because you cannot display on a VDU any material that a student just reads.

The great benefit of CAI is that it lends itself readily to the well-balanced use of *stimulus-response*. Long stretches of beautifully written prose on a VDU look and are a misuse of the medium. But, more importantly, a student has to make some input into the system. It is obviously better if this is meaningfully related to the display than to ask him/her to make an input like 'next', 'page', or 'press transmit'.

Programmed learning also uses a second characteristic — the *demonstrate, prompt* and *release* cycle.

Demonstrate: shows *how* task is done with an explanation.
Prompt: gets student to perform task with some assistance.
Release: the student is asked to perform the task without assistance
(as he/she would in real life).

The system keeps a tally of the error responses, and at the end of the sequence this total is compared with a norm which has been pre-determined by the course author.

The advantages which the computer confers in presenting the *demonstrate, prompt* and *release* cycles are:

1. It can provide each individual student with exactly the amount of prompting he/she needs.
2. The feedback which the student will receive on his/her test performance *(release)* is both immediate and objective.

The third characteristic of programmed learning is that it is adaptive, that is, it tries as far as possible to stimulate a living dialogue between student and teacher in which the student's reactions determine the sequence of presentation and the amount of explanation, assistance and practice which he/she gets. This is an ideal which can never be completely achieved with self-teach material, but a CAI system comes closer to it than any other self-teach medium.

The students remain unaware that they are each following individualized courses and receiving more, or less, instruction according to their needs. Only CAI has the capacity to be adaptive in this way.

We define a *stimulus* as that part of a frame which asks a question to which the student must *respond* (answer). As a general rule, the more *stimuli* you can give the students the better, in order to increase the frequency of responses and therefore the amount of learning. To increase the frequency of responses without reducing our frames to triviality we exploit covert responding.

Covert responding can be defined as a response in a student's mind that cannot be seen or heard but which is induced by additional *stimuli* in the frame. The most common way in which this is done is by the use of mnemonics. So you introduce abbreviations like this:

1. British Airways (BA)
2. BA (British Airways)

For both, by covert responding, the student will associate British Airways with BA and from that moment will know what BA means when it is seen again. The covert *stimuli* and *response* usually relate to the overt, but they are not identical.

Figure 2 shows the use of covert responding in a very typical situation where a student is learning a code or an abbreviation.

Earlier, the easily adaptive characteristic of CAI was mentioned. But adaptability is important in another way when self-teach material is written. Wording must be very precise and clear. A common fault is being far too verbose. It is for this reason that thorough testing is essential to make sure the wording is clear to *all* students.

```
CORRECT – SOME FARES
ARE ONLY VALID FOR TRAVEL...   WEEKEND  (W)
                           OR  MIDWEEK  (X)  ...

...SO TYPE IN THE SINGLE CHARACTER THAT WILL SHOW A FARE IS FOR
WEEKEND TRAVEL ONLY...
```

Frame 1

W

Frame 2

```
RIGHT – W. FOR WEEKEND SHOWS A FARE IS FOR WEEKEND TRAVEL ONLY.

NOW TYPE IN THE SINGLE CHARACTER THAT SHOWS A FARE IS FOR
MIDWEEK TRAVEL ONLY...
```

Figure 2.

This kind of adaptability, as far as British Airways is concerned, exists within a framework of standardization and conventions. In an international corporation we are very aware that many of our students are not native English speakers, and we therefore pay particular attention to standardizing our vocabulary. Obviously, we avoid long words, but we also avoid stylistic variations. Figure 3 shows some examples of our policy in this area.

```
LOOK  - not - CONSIDER, OBSERVE, EXAMINE,  etc etc;

SHOWS
SHOW  - not - INDICATES, INDICATED
SHOWN

MUST  - not - ESSENTIAL, IMPERATIVE, NECESSARY

SURE  - not - CERTAIN, CONFIDENT, INFALLIBLE etc etc;

HAPPEN(S)  - not - OCCURS, EVENT etc etc;

NEARLY ALWAYS  - not - IN MOST CASES, IN MOST CIRCUMSTANCES etc etc;

CANNOT  - not - CANT

SHOULD NOT  - not - SHOULDNT etc;

WOULD NOT  - not - WOULDNT, WONT etc;

MUST NOT  - not - MUSTNT etc;
```

Figure   3.

Most of the lessons we have learnt over many years of applying programmed learning principles to CAI will be clear from what has already been said. But there are a few additional points worth noting:

1. The students show very little tendency to 'cheat', even on self-tests. The motivation to learn is much stronger than the motivation to 'beat the system'.
2. Students do not like to guess questions. They resent receiving an error response when the do not feel they have made an error.
3. Despite the impersonality of the computer terminal and the standardization of the vocabulary, it is still possible to put personality into a CAI programme.
4. The self-pacing aspect of self-teach material, and the independence it gives, is very much liked.
5. The slowest student will need one-third more time than the quickest.

Computer-Managed Instruction

The logical next step from CAI is to give the computer the chore of storing all the records of students' performance, and to programme it to make the decisions which can be made on the basis of that information.

Such a system of records and control is usually called Computer-Managed Instruction (CMI).

There is not enough space to fully cover the CMI facilities now being developed by British Airways, but the following is a brief outline of the aims:

1. Students must have both random and controlled access to the system.
2. If controlled, the student must have a sign-in and sign-out procedure.
3. As some 3,000 students need some form of control each year (on average), control must range from a minimum to a maximum amount of data to be stored and displayed when needed by the computer — maximum when any new course is being tested, and minimum when the course has been thoroughly tested and proven in practice.
4. Control parameters in 3. will be capable of adjustment by the course author as needed between minimum and maximum ranges.
5. Course codes to be used will automatically guide students through a course, or series of courses, according to student needs.
6. Access to student records at three levels:
   (a) Course author
   (b) Instructors or supervisors
   (c) Administration staff

These records will supply invaluable data automatically with a consequent saving of time and administration costs. As most of British Airways' functions are computerized, staff need constant training on carefully graduated courses.

Staff are not allowed to perform particular functions until they have successfully passed the appropriate course. The course records will quickly and easily tell whether this has been done. These facilities will also provide data by which 'managerial' decisions can be made.

Because of microelectronics, an expansion in the use of computers in industry and commerce is to be expected; by the next two decades they will be commonplace. These computers must be used efficiently, which means that training must be first-class.

If costs are to be reduced substantially and maximum flexibility achieved, the use of programmed learning in CAI must be implemented, particularly as CAI by its very nature lends itself readily to such techniques, and can be just as easily used to overcome most of the major disadvantages of programmed learning.

4.5 The Potential Role of Computer-Managed Instruction and Computer-Assisted Instruction in the Royal Navy: an Experimental Evaluation

J D S Moore, J A Hawrylack and M J Kitchin
Royal Naval School of Educational and Training Technology, Portsmouth

Abstract: In order to examine the potential for streamlining information creation, promulgation, modification and accessibility, a computer-based training project was started in 1978, using CMI and CAI. The paper discusses the results of these studies.

Introduction

The evaluation of computer-based training (CBT) in the Royal Navy began in 1978. A study of the naval systems approach to training had resulted in a major streamlining of documentation and design procedures. Further improvements in efficiency had therefore to be centred on the handling of training information, given that the information content had been firmly established. This led naturally to the possibility of using a computer, and in April 1978 the Royal Naval School of Educational and Training Technology (RNSETT) was given the CBT Project.

In addition to the objective of improving efficiency in the handling of training information, a need was seen to look at part-task simulation in order to compare CAI lessons with conventional, purpose-built simulators.

The objectives for the evaluation were therefore to:

1. Set up computer management of an existing high-throughput course and monitor the effects on trainee and staff performance.
2. Develop electronic documentation methods to set up a system for controlling the effectiveness and efficiency of course design and implementation procedures, as required in the RN six-part training documentation.
3. Design limited simulations, in order to assess their cost-effectiveness when compared with conventional simulators, for training operators and maintainers.

It was considered that the evaluation should involve real practical applications of a computer to training and that ease of programming was essential in that the personnel involved had not been trained in programming skills. At this time, the PLATO CBE System had just become available in the UK and a preliminary examination indicated it would be a suitable vehicle for the initial phase of the evaluation.

The PLATO System involves terminals linked to a central computer by telephone or dedicated line. It is dedicated to educational and training purposes. The terminals comprise a visual display unit and keyboard. The screen presents information to the user and can be programmed to accept touch responses. Displays can be printed and a marksense reader can be interfaced for entering data.

Bearing in mind the objectives of the evaluation and the features available on PLATO, the trial was organized into three separate areas — CMI, electronic documentation, and simulation. The CMI aspect entailed the computer management of an existing self-paced course; electronic documentation the development and application of a programme to handle course design and approval information; and simulation the construction of part-task operator trainers using the terminal touch facility.

CMI

A very important feature of a computer-based training system is a Computer-Managed Instruction (CMI) capability, which is a computerized method of testing, record-keeping and decision-making that assists the administration of classroom and individual learner management. A CMI system supports the instructional system by selecting and presenting tests, collecting and scoring test data, providing diagnostic feedback on student performance, and prescribing the use of various instructional resources. If its test administration and record-keeping functions are properly set up, CMI provides learners with the information they need to progress towards their training goals. The PLATO CMI structure is pre-programmed so as to allow questions, tests, marking criteria, learning prescriptions and general management procedures to be entered by non-programmers.

The course chosen for the CMI trial was the basic electro-technology module of the Mechanics Common Training (MCT) course at HMS Collingwood. This course is self-paced and, as such, student time on the course ranges from about two to four weeks, depending on the ability of the student. The BE course contains four modules, each of which is subdivided into sections and each section consists of a programmed text or procedure followed by a criterion test.

Trainees have to pass each criterion test before proceeding to the next section. At the end of each module there is a test which must be passed before a trainee is allowed to proceed to the next module. The final task of the trainee is to sit a test which is designed to ensure that he has retained adequate knowledge and skill for the BE course as a whole.

Three trials were conducted, with gaps between each trial for programming improvements. For the first trial only two modules were programmed, and control and experimental groups were used for the first and second trials. The results (Table 1) indicate that, on the whole, the CMI trainees took less time than the classes managed by an instructor. (The anomaly in the second trial was partially due to four trainees leaving; also to an inappropriate method of retention testing, which was re-programmed for the third trial).

An examination of mean module scores shows little real difference between the two groups, with results slightly favouring the control group. The mean scores for retention tests show a slight tendency in favour of the trial group.

During the first two trials, a record was kept of the time spent by the control group instructor in making tests (Table 2). The figures indicate, assuming an average marking time for an instructor of 57 minutes per trainee per course, that an average class of 22 trainees would take up approximately 20.9 hours of an instructor's time for assessment. By assuming a mean conventional course time of 12.7 weekdays (79.37 hours) and calculating instructor marking for a class of 22 students over that period, the amount of an instructor's time spent on assessment is approximately 30 per cent (based on 6.25 hours a day when the trainee is undergoing instruction).

		Number of trainees	Mean time working days (mins)	Mean module score (%)	Mean retention score (%)	failure rate (%)
First trial	Experimental	13	4.5*	92.3	84	0
	Control	12	6.5	94.9	84.5	0
Second trial	Experimental	7	12.4	93	88.5	0
	Control	13	11.5	96.2	86.8	0
Third trial	Experimental	15	10.9	91.2	91	0
	Comparison class	19	14.0	97.4	85.9	0

Table 1. *Results of PLATO CMI trials*
* *The structure of the CMI module during this trial covered only part of the course, ie the theory portion.*

		Number of trainees	Mean time spent marking (mins)	Total time spent marking (mins)
First trial	Experimental	13	0	0
	Control	12	57.5	690 (11.5 hrs)
Second trial	Experimental	7	0	0
	Control	13	56.7	737 (12.3 hrs)

Table 2. *Marking times of PLATO CMI trials*

Conclusions

On the whole, the CMI trials showed that it was possible to computer-manage a high-throughput course with no detriment to student performance and potentially useful savings in instructor and trainee time. Programming was simple and speedy. However, the full potential of CMI could not be realized due to the inability to generate and print a test for group off-line testing, which could be used to offset bulges in demand for terminal time, to set and mark tests for conventional group-paced courses, and to allow for an instructor's assessment of practical skills to be entered in student records.

Electronic Documentation

Naval training courses are documented and controlled by a six-part documentation system. This is a simple and efficient method but it has its limitations for controlling training because it relies on paperwork.

Effective monitoring and control of training can only be carried out if managers have easy and rapid access to reliable, comprehensive and up-to-date information. This could be done, and could achieve considerable savings in manpower and time, by computerizing some or all of the training documentation database.

A programme was developed to allow for electronic documentation, with the following features:

1. Any user with the appropriate level of access can instantly call up and inspect the documentation of any course in the database.
2. Data entered directly from a keyboard into any part of the database are entered once and are then available for all users and further data operations.
3. By using PLATO, features such as notes, term talk and monitor mode, designers and their desk officers can communicate quickly and easily and rapidly agree details of resources, objectives, etc.
4. Each user would be able to refer to a summary of the approval status of all courses of concern to him.
5. Security of documentation has been ensured by using each author's unique sign-on to allow rights of inspection and editing.
6. By linking to a wider information system, further benefits, eg automatic entry of data from sources such as course CMI files and course record files, could emerge.

The Storage Requirements

The PLATO system uses 10 character words, made up into files containing 2,240 words. Since Part 1 is a fairly complex document requiring much the same quantity of data for any course, it is reasonable to give a fixed amount of storage space to it. However, Parts 2 and 3 are simpler in format, but could contain widely varying amounts of data. It is obviously inefficient to dedicate space to all courses which would only be taken up by a few, so the programme allows the amount of file space allocated to each course to be varied.

Indications from the present stage of the programme are that it is entirely practicable to develop a computer programme which will store, and run the approval process of, Parts 1 to 3 of the naval training documentation system. Further, it is probable that this programme could be developed to undertake automatic training returns and course costing, centrally, updated as required, from the existing database.

Simulation

Much naval training is geared towards learning the skills and knowledge required to do practical tasks in the operation and maintenance of equipment and machinery. Trainees progress more quickly and more easily by actually performing practical tasks and procedures rather than by merely being taught how to perform them. A great deal of training resources are consequently directed towards training personnel in representations of operational equipment and environments such as simulators or mock-ups. Concentration on representing operational equipment closely means that training requirements become secondary or are overlooked, with the result that many simulators are not efficient learning devices.

Requirements of Simulator Training

The Trainee

The primary function of any training aid should be to promote effective learning, and the trainee's requirements should be paramount in the design of a simulator. Training should concentrate on building up the trainee's skills and knowledge progressively to the level at which he can be applied to operational equipment.

Part-Task Learning

Exposure to a high-fidelity, whole-job simulator can be very counter-productive for a trainee. A better strategy would be to concentrate on acquiring the constituent skills and knowledge in part-task simulators designed specifically for learning needs. After mastering these skills, the trainee will be able to make effective use of a whole-job simulator.

Control of Learning

Most existing simulators concentrate on presenting and processing information in as lifelike a way as possible, but like any other training strategy in a systematic approach to training, simulator learning requires monitoring and control of the process and the trainee.

In an area such as the acquisition of skills there are considerable advantages in individualized learning. To do this effectively implies pre-testing of skills, the assembly of an individual package to maximize the learning in deficient areas, and continuous assessment of learning and feedback to the trainee. This is particularly relevant to simulators which are generally very costly and need to be managed effectively.

Team Training

Much simulator training in the Royal Navy is geared to producing personnel capable of operating as members of a team. During training, each member develops skills and interacts with other team members who affect his development. After training, the team is often dispersed between several vessels. The individual has to develop his interactions with the new team. The trainee might well develop the appropriate skills more efficiently, and transfer these to the operational environment better, by interacting with a computer-generated team, which would be consistent, reliable, and produce correct responses.

Computer-Assisted Simulation

The above considerations in the training skills can often be met by using computers in both the management of simulations and as learning resources. As far as management is concerned, the principles of pre-testing of skills, learning prescriptions, automatic assessment and record-keeping apply equally to simulator training. Additionally, a computer-managed whole-task simulator could be run as a number of independent part-task simulators with independent control over speed and complexity, and an individual could perform as a member of a 'team' in which the actions of the other 'team members' are generated by the computer.

As a learning resource, a computer accessed by a terminal with a visual display unit (VDU) can provide effective simulation in many areas for which the degree of realism available is acceptable. This has considerable advantages since the simulation exists only in the form of software — there is no hardware to procure, update and maintain, and having finished the simulation the VDU is available for other purposes.

PLATO in Simulation

The use of PLATO as a learning resource has been investigated by the development of simulation lessons. The following areas were investigated as being important for a comprehensive use of PLATO or the other systems in this field:

1. The ability to represent an equipment panel or display, its controls, and the information presentation contained thereon.
2. The ability to allow trainee operation of the display and control of variables.
3. Computer-management of trainee skills.
4. Production of CAI lesson aimed at the development of specific skills as required by the CMI structure.
5. The development of team, inter-terminal simulation.
6. The capability of instructor monitoring and injection of stimuli.
7. Record-keeping facilities to aid in playback and debriefing purposes.

For the trial, two simulation lessons have been developed to represent typical training applications, a fleetwork trainer and setting up a communications receiver.

FLEETWORK TRAINER

The existing trainer is used to train up to 10 individuals or teams in fleetwork and voice procedures. A visual display is projected on to a large screen and is continuously updated, giving a moving display of ship dispositions. An instructor controls the development of the game, issues orders on voice circuits and controls the parameters of the display. He can also take over command of any vessel and communicate with individuals separately. Each student has a cubicle from which he can view the display and control his own ship's movement and voice circuits. Additional instructors tour the trainee positions to check on interpretation and procedure.

The PLATO simulation is necessarily limited to the visual aspects. The simulation centres around a display which shows ship dispositions and display parameters and has a number of touch-sensitive areas for student or instructor input; input is solely by touch and the use of the numeral keys on the keyboard. The simulation has the following features:

1. The ship positions are updated every 12-15 seconds to give a representation of continuous motion.
2. The student can control the following:
   (a) own ship's heading; changes may be made immediately or in an 'execute to follow' mode,
   (b) own ship's speed; changes being made as above,
   (c) the 'cleaning-up' of the display; this is necessary to remove the occasional spurious graphics and to replace areas of the graticule removed in the updating process.
3. The instructor has the following additional options:
   (a) any ship can be monitored so that student interpretation of, and action on, orders can be checked,
   (b) any ship can be controlled so that the instructor can override student heading and speed changes,
   (c) any ship may be moved to a new position as required to set up a new starting position,

(d) the centre of the display can be moved to a new location,

(e) true motion or relative motion with any ship as guide are available,

(f) scale can be varied (five or 25 miles range),

(g) exercise speed may be varied (X1 or X5),

(h) control of the clock; the game may be 'frozen' and re-started
     as desired,

(i) control of the initial positions on the display; this can be done
     by selecting ship types and defining positions and motions.
     Alternatively, a number of pre-set starting positions may be
     used.

4. In inter-terminal mode, up to nine students plus one instructor, each at
    a separate terminal, can run at any one time. All user displays are
    identical; changes of heading and speed made by each student are
    immediately evident on all displays.

5. The lesson can also be run as an individual lesson; by the addition
    of a pre-recorded sound channel synchronized to the display, students
    can individually develop and refine specific skills.

The Communications Receiver

The equipment is used to train operators in carrying out the correct procedure for
setting up a chain of equipments to receive a particular signal. The procedure
involves carrying out approximately 30 steps on a total of six different equipments.
The procedure varies depending on the type of signal. Only one trainee can
effectively operate the equipment at any one time, and his task has to be
continuously monitored by an instructor so as to identify any errors made.

The PLATO simulation involves a number of visual displays, each representing
one of the equipment used. The simulation has the following features:

1. The student or the instructor selects or defines the problem to be
    attempted.

2. The student selects the sequence in which equipments are set up.

3. The student sets up the equipment by 'operating' the various controls,
    touching the screen to indicate the control and the sense in which it
    is operated.

4. The display updates to give the correct response to a touch input.

5. The simulation can be run in either teaching or assessment mode.

In either mode, each student input is checked to ensure whether it is correct or not.
In assessment mode, errors are allowed to accumulate until completion of the test
and no feedback is given during the test. At the completion of the test, the errors
are used to give a score for the test, and are cross-referenced to task objectives to
give a breakdown of error distribution. By using a CMI student record file, CMI
data can thus be built up using this test. In student mode, at the completion of
each equipment stage the student is given feedback as to his performance and
asked to re-try until the procedure is correct before being allowed to proceed to
the next stage. Again, the six stages may be attempted only in the correct order.

In summary, the ability to represent an equipment panel or display, its controls,
and to present appropriate information, is generally adequately realistic.
Limitations are that:

1. The use of 512 x 512 dot mode display means that small graphics and
    text items can be difficult to read.

2. The 16 x 16 touch matrix limits the discrimination between adjacent
    touch inputs, although this is adequate for intput by finger touching.

3. The lack of colour places a limit on the complexity of information

presentation.
4. The slow write speed means that displays cannot be generated very quickly.

Advantages are that:

1. Trainees can operate the display by use of touch and number keys — no typing skill is required.
2. Student progress can be computer-managed.
3. A high level of inter-terminal simulation is possible and can be extended to students in the same lesson but having different displays and controls.
4. Students in an inter-terminal lesson can be monitored by an instructor via the system and instructor injection is easy.

The evaluation has shown that computer-based training techniques can advantageously be applied to both course design and management and to part-task simulation. Further work is under way to examine the problem in greater depth and to assess the potential of other CBT resources.

Acknowledgement

Crown Copyright: this paper is reproduced by permission of the Controller of Her Majesty's Stationery Office.

Workshop Report
4.6 An Experimental Evaluation of the Potential Role of CMI and CAI in the Royal Navy

J D S Moore, J A Hawrylack and M J Kitchin
Royal Naval School of Educational and Training Technology, Portsmouth

Organizers' Account

This computer-based training workshop dealt primarily with displaying on a CDL PLATO visual display unit (VDU) the results of trials on computer-managed instruction (CMI) and part-task simulation done by the Royal Navy. For the workshop the PLATO terminal was connected to the main CDL computer in Brussels via a GPO level 9 telephone line which operated without interruption during the workshop period.

The CMI aspect entailed the following displays:

— *course curriculum*, which was further broken down into the module and instructional unit levels and showed the specifics of the testing criteria and management procedures involved in each level.

— *individual student statistics,* which showed both a progressive and comprehensive record of the student's performance, including scores obtained for each module, and the management options available to each student.
— *group (class) statistics,* which included in both a graphical and tabular mode the following:
  (a) curriculum mastery
  (b) course progress summary
  (c) module progress summary
  (d) average module scores
  (e) average module durations.

To show the ease of enrolling a student into the curriculum and what he encounters with PLATO once he is signed on was accomplished by actually signing on one of the workshop participants as a student. Following PLATO directions, the participant then worked his way through part of the curriculum. His performance on a module and his input to group statistics were shown to all participants.

The part-task simulation of the workshop revolved around two displays — one dealing with a navigational radar display and the other with a communications receiver. It was pointed out that the former represented both radar screen and controls and the participants were shown how the simulation updated the screen picture regularly and allowed the trainees to manipulate display controls with the resultant action of controlling ships' course and speed. The simulation of the communications receiver showed a number of visual displays, each representing equipment that must be set up in a correct procedure to receive a particular signal. The participants were shown the results of inputting both the correct and the incorrect procedures. In both simulations, the versatility of the touch-sensitive screen proved to be a very interesting feature to the participants.

Acknowledgement

Crown Copyright: this paper is reproduced by permission of the Controller of Her Majesty's Stationery Office.

Section 5:
The Use of Computers –
Broader Aspects

5.1 Strategies for the Introduction of Computer-Based Learning

Nick Rushby
CEDAR Project, Imperial College, London

Abstract: The paper discusses a number of possible strategies used by CBL projects in various countries to overcome or circumvent problems facing them. Conclusions will be drawn as to ways in which CBL units can be set up to maximize their chances of success.

CBL Service Units

Following the period of growth of Computer-Based Learning (CBL) in the United Kingdom and continental Europe during the 1960s, three kinds of CBL projects can be distinguished:

- projects which aim to develop the use of CBL in a particular subject area, or in a limited range of subjects, within one department of an institution:
- co-operative projects which aim to share CBL materials and expertise in specific subjects between several institutions;
- institution-centred projects which aim to encourage and help the development of CBL in many subjects throughout an institution.

The first group is the strongest numerically and reflects the way in which CBL has grown as a result of individual enthusiasts in separate institutions. The effect of national funding programmes, such as those in the United Kingdom and in West Germany, has often been to consolidate the position of the department-based projects and to aggregate them into co-operative groups. In some cases, central co-ordinating units have been established, sometimes nationally funded, as with the French INRP group, and in other cases partly self-supporting, as with the various CBL package exchange organizations in the UK and the USA.

Partly as a consequence of the growth of CBL, and partly as a force for innovation in their own right, we now have a small number of projects which we can describe as CBL service units. They have varied ancestries; some are departmental, subject-based projects which have grown up and spread into other areas, while others, such as CEDAR at Imperial College, London were set up *ab initio* with an institution-wide brief.

This paper is concerned primarily with the strategies which these CBL service units might adopt to overcome some of the problems they face concerning their political base, credibility and limited resources. Lest it should be thought that this is just an academic exercise, let us be quite clear that the prospects for the survival of any educational technology unit over the next few years are bleak.

Problems of Location

Usually we have little or no choice as to where our service unit will be located because this has been dictated by history, the efforts of other individuals and the sources of funding for the unit. However, we might ask where, ideally, should a unit be located?

One obvious solution is that it should form part of a general educational development unit which also has responsibility for teaching methods, course development and audio-visual aids. Unfortunately, in many institutions the concept of educational development is limited to the use of audio-visual aids and there is then a danger that CBL will be perceived as just another kind of slide projector or video-recorder. As we know, CBL is, or can be, much more than this. Can we persuade others that it is really different?

When funding is limited, as it is in the United Kingdom at the present time, there is a strong temptation to cut back on activities that are *perceived* as inessential — like teaching methods units. Perhaps our service unit should seek a more secure base. Alternatively it can ally itself with its colleagues to argue that educational technology — in its widest sense — has a great deal to offer in time of financial stress.

We should note that the pressure for accountability and for real economies will force a change in the philosophy of educational technology in general and CBL in particular. During the 1970s the focus of efficiency and effectiveness was on improving the quality of learning and the quality of the graduate as the end product of the process (Crombag, 1978), even at the expense of a marginal increase in the costs of education. Now it seems that society may be prepared to accept a lower quality of learning if this means that we can reduce the costs of education.

If the project adopts a passive role, so that it is concerned only with obtaining existing materials, rather than with development, then it might be considered as a kind of library and be taken under the wing of the central library service. While this provides a safe, protective environment, it makes it difficult for the unit to contemplate taking any more active part in development.

In many instances, the initiative for CBL development arises from the service computer centre and the resulting unit is located in the centre itself. Although this should ensure that the unit is well provided with technical services, programming resources and a good interactive programming facility, it is likely to be weak in educational expertise and also to discourage some users by presenting a computing technology face to the outside world. Under these circumstances it seems best to try to hold the rest of the computer centre at arms' length and to identify with its educational users as closely as possible.

Projects based within a single department, but attempting to influence educational development on an institution-wide basis, almost invariably have problems of credibility in other departments. It may of course be forced upon a project which has started with a parochial role and is later extended to have a wider scope, but it is generally an unsatisfactory solution if it remains within that single department. However, one extension of this organization which has been suggested, is to distribute the project round a number of departments so that each one supports, and is supported by, one or two project staff who are specialists in that subject area but who owe a common allegiance to the CBL service unit.

Within the context of an individual project the location is essentially a local problem, requiring a local, institutional solution. Unfortunately, large changes, such as a complete reorganization of the unit and its base are usually difficult and so, if the rare opportunity of rethinking the organizational structure presents itself, all the possibilities should be examined with the utmost care. The final choice may pre-empt strategies and tactics in other areas.

Problems of Credibility

Credibility is a cyclic problem which besets a project trying to establish itself in the first few years of its existence or trying to develop into a new subject area. It is not only the CBL innovator who has to face problems of credibility in the eyes of his teaching colleagues; the situation is familiar to staff in most educational development units. It is, after all, the teachers themselves who have the experience of teaching their specific subject to their specific students. They are familiar with the difficulties and over the years they have developed approaches which seem to be effective. They can be understandably sceptical about anyone who offers an alternative computer-based approach claiming it to be better because it is individualized, provides deeper or different insights, or is cheaper. It is a cyclic problem because it is difficult to establish the credibility, both of the unit and of CBL as a viable teaching method, until CBL materials are being used effectively – but the introduction of the materials is problematic without that credibility. In the long term, credibility should come as project staff individually gain the confidence of their colleagues, as being conversant with an effective teaching medium and also acknowledging that teachers *do* know their subjects best. Co-operation and evolution are better strategies for educational innovation than revolution.

Notwithstanding this long-term view, there are some strategies that can be adopted to hasten the day of the revolution. Both in France and the Soviet Union, in-service courses on CBL have proved to be a key to teacher acceptability (Rushby, James and Anderson, 1978). It is to be hoped that similar courses will be developed in the UK under the aegis of the new government funding programme for microelectronics in schools and colleges (DES, 1980).

One effective technique has been to arrange demonstrations so that the teachers can play the student's role in working through CBL materials. Such role playing can only work well if the teacher can project himself into a learning situation, and this implies that the demonstration must be in his own subject area and at an appropriate level. If CBL is presented through games or trivial exercises, then it will be dismissed as irrelevant. So the CBL units must be able to draw on a range of good and credible packages for demonstration purposes. This fits in well with the innovative strategy of importing existing materials, described below. The project can respond to an identified learning problem by obtaining some computer-based materials which are likely to be of help, and organizing a demonstration for teaching staff. If they agree that CBL offers some possibilities, then the project imports the materials and assists the teachers to develop them. The credibility problem is circumvented because, after an initiative from the CBL unit, the teachers perceive themselves to be in control.

This approach is extended by at least one project which deliberately sets out to make it difficult, and therefore desirable, to become involved in a project with the CBL unit (Leiblum, 1979). A stringent selection procedure ensures both: that the unit takes on projects that are likely to succeed, and that there is a good supply of competitive projects.

Problems of Limited Resources

Perhaps the most obvious problem is that the resources available to the unit (indeed, available to education and training generally) are always limited.

Unfortunately, good quality CBL materials are expensive to develop and thus it is essential to find strategies which will make the best use of what is available and maximize the innovative effect. There are a number of possibilities.

The project can set up a number of small development teams consisting of teachers and project staff. The main burden of the development work is then carried out by the teachers themselves, supported by the project staff who have a specialist knowledge of CBL.

The scope of the development groups can be widened to include staff from other institutions with similar interests, with the aims of developing materials that can be used in several places and of sharing the development costs between the participants (Rushby, 1977). The main attraction is that this reduces the unit cost, but it is open to the criticism that in making the material more general it is likely to be diluted or made so complex that its effectiveness is reduced.

A third strategy is to draw upon the wealth of CBL material which already exists and is available at relatively low cost, particularly in the 'popular' subject areas such as mathematics, science and engineering. The project's resources can be focused on importing existing CBL materials, demonstrating their use in learning situations and helping teachers to develop the materials to meet their own specific needs. This strategy implies that the project should be able to provide a comprehensive information service on CBL literature and packages, and be able to give educational advice and support to the teachers. The advantage of this strategy is that it has a 'gain' in the engineering sense — the institution can actually get more out of the project in terms of teaching materials than it puts in as resources. However, although there are substantial advantages for the institution, it raises a number of questions at a national level. Clearly we still need development effort on new packages. Is academic satisfaction adequate motivation or should there be some centralized support at a national level? While the prices of existing packages are set by market forces, they are currently unrealistically low and provide little incentive to potential vendors who see no point in making the materials more generally available. Should there be a more commercial attitude to the exploitation of CBL courseware, or can we increase the academic rewards for producing good teaching materials?

Which Strategies?

This discussion has deliberately raised more questions than it has answered because, although there are a variety of possible strategies that might be adopted to overcome the problems of location, credibility and resources, there is no clear recipe for success. Generalized solutions are difficult to prescribe because institutions differ greatly and even within one institution there is unlikely to be a single ideal solution but instead, an ever-evolving compromise which appears to offer the best strategy — at the time.

References

Crombag, H (1978) On defining the quality of education. In Piper, D W (ed) *The Efficiency and Effectiveness of Teaching in Higher Education.* University of London Teaching Methods Unit, pp 68-85.

DES (1980) Microelectronics development programme for schools and colleges. Press notice.

Leiblum, M D (1979) Screening for CAL. *Computers and Education,* 3, pp 313-23.

Rushby, N J (1977) A consorted approach to educational software. *Computer Bulletin* Series 2, 14.

Rushby, N J, James, E B and Anderson, J S A (1978) A three-dimensional view of computer-based learning in continental Europe. *Programmed Learning and Educational Technology,* 15, 2, pp 152-61.

Acknowledgements

It is not possible to prepare a paper such as this without drawing on the contributions of many others, particularly from conversations and private communications. To all these, and particularly Mark Leiblum and Sinclair Goodlad, I owe my thanks.

5.2 The Economics of Computer-Assisted Instruction in UK Higher Education: Choices for the Year 2000

D W McCulloch
Ulster Polytechnic

Abstract: This paper attempts to show some of the complexities thrown up by a cost-conscious approach to CAI applications. The conclusion reached is that much more data are necessary before effective action can be taken.

The Reality of Software Exchange in the UK

The value of software exchange depends upon the homogeneity of educational objectives. There is not much evidence for or against homogeneity, though one pointer may be given by the TIPS experiment, run by Professor K G Lumsden and Dr A Scott of Heriot-Watt University. Fifteen institutions of higher education are running the same first-year economics course (with minor differences), using the same multiple-choice test questions, and setting the same examination at the end of the academic year. If this is typical, then software exchange offers much scope for improving facilities offered.

However, we cannot afford to assume that all the programs made available would be or ought to be run, given the different ranges of alternatives open to each institution, and given the cost of running each program in (academic and computer) staff hours and computer time. It is not determined, either, how extensive the difficulties of exchange are; the extent to which programs in use avoid non-standard facilities is the extent to which the UK program stock is freely available, that is, transferable without the expenditure of any resources beyond transport services. Finally, the scale of the resources necessary, even when conversion is needed, is also indeterminate; the FORTRAN program supplied as part of the TIPS project did need conversion at several of the institutions, but only one or two had to allocate more than one day of the programmer's time to complete the task.

Much more information will need to be gathered before a software exchange scheme can be realistically considered, and the problem is complicated by another available option, namely, the 'universal' CAI language. PLATO's TUTOR language (see Sherwood, 1977) and PMSL's MENTOR (CALNEWS, December, 1979) are two successive stages beyond BASIC; both have the facility for generating code from the user's simplified input, which takes the form of branches, texts and human responses.

The Costs of Computer-Assisted Instruction

The nub of the matter is our method for ranking programs — ie which are more valuable — how can this be done and how objective are the criteria? Though one should not underestimate the problems involved, this is not as difficult in principle as the educational evaluation of CAI (see Hawkins, 1979, for the best treatment of the issues involved). A variety of factors will need to be taken into account by the ranking process, and one can argue for the inclusion of the following:

- the number of students per run;
- the amount of student preparation before participating in the program run; it seems obvious that a batch-processed multiple-choice test marking program is worth more than an interactive instruction program;
- the fraction of available disc or core store space taken up by the program, etc.

Each institution will have to arrive at its own compromises, because of the diversity of their facilities and courses. The notion of opportunity cost applies to all, however, and this means, for example, that computer science projects also ought to be ranked by the criteria devised. No doubt they ought to have a degree of priority, but only up to a point, that point depending upon the importance of the CAI applications for students on other courses. Also, the different demands of all projects and programs on the various resources ought to be recognized — those requiring resources whose cost escalates rapidly as usage increases, eg because overtime payments become necessary, should be penalized accordingly.

Conclusion

Whatever choices are finally made, to determine the course of CAI over the next 20 years, there is a great lack of sound information to permit even crude assessments of opportunities and opportunity costs. Computers are not treated as a scarce resource often enough; if they were, every institution would have rigorous booking requirements for CAI and would have detailed criteria for acceptance. We cannot rely on the declining cost of hardware to facilitate the expansion of CAI in the future, mainly because the shortage of software and of resources for higher education will prevent such expansion. We need, now, to consider the choices carefully, and evaluate them consistently, if we are to make progress towards the second millenium.

References

CALNEWS (1979) December.
Hawkins, C A (1979) The performance and the promise of evaluation in computer-based learning. Computers and Education, 3, 4.
Sherwood, B A (1977) The TUTOR Language. Control Data Education Company, USA.

Acknowledgement

The author wishes to acknowledge the assistance of Dr A Scott of Heriot-Watt University, whose comments on a first draft were most helpful.

5.3 The Economical Production of Adaptable Learning Activity Packages for Computer/Video Based Education and Training

J W Brahan
National Research Council of Canada
G M Boyd
Concordia University

Abstract: For the economical generation of good courseware, the sharing and re-use of the best parts of different packages is needed. Structured computer languages such as NATAL provide a means of creating separable and re-combinable modular components.

Introduction

The development of any learning activity package can be characterized as a multi-stage activity. Starting with the opportunity or identification of the problem, a concept is formed which provides a solution. The concept is formulated in detail during the design phase which, in turn, is followed by the implementation of the design. Finally, the delivery phase sees the application of the solution to the original problem. At each stage in the development of the package, attributes can be assigned which include degree of definition, adaptability, investment and benefits which can be derived from the package at that particular point. The goals, which are not attainable at every stage, are high definition and adaptability, minimum investment and maximum benefits. Ideally, each of the stages would be independent of those which follow. Unfortunately, in practice the stages are not independent for a number of reasons but perhaps the most significant is the limitation imposed on the implementation of the design by the available technology and the influence that this has on the design and even the concept development. Thus, instead of the design providing the link from the concept to the general mode of presentation(computer terminal, video-tape, audio, etc), it is often a process whereby the concept is restricted by implementation considerations dictated by current technology.

Often, particularly in the case of computer-assisted learning (CAL) courseware development, there is tendency to link the design and implementation phase very closely, with the result that most, if not all, of the design information is embedded in the program code. The design is thus tied to a specific programming language, a particular display device, or even a specific computer. All of these may be obsolete within a few years' time, with the resulting loss of the courseware or the alternative of an expensive effort of distilling the design information from the program code so that it can be re-implemented. If courseware is to be developed in such a manner that it can survive changes in the technology, means must be found to increase the emphasis on the design phase.

There are two aspects to the solution. Through the use of a high-level programming language, design details can be represented in a format which is close to the design constructs and not hidden in constructs which are more closely related to the machine. The high-level language, in effect, transfers much of the implementation effort from the human to the machine by permitting the machine transformation of the design specification into machine-code. The second aspect of the solution involves providing the instructional designer with functional building blocks which can be assembled to form the required learning activity package.

The Modular Approach

One of the major difficulties in separating the design process from the implementation process is that most instructional designers do not have available the abstract schema necessary to produce courseware designs independent of the technology. Thus we find designs which incorporate limitations imposed by, for example, use of a teletypewriter as a display-response unit. The computer, however, offers the means of developing tools which, while still using a concrete design approach, raise the design process to the functional level so that it is not drowned in implementation details.

The process of instructional courseware development has an analogy in electronic equipment hardware development. In both cases, it is a question of applying some process to the available materials to produce the required result. Twenty years ago, electronic equipment was designed and produced using discrete components (resistors, capacitors, transistors, etc). The process required to convert these into the desired end product demanded complex design skills, a knowledge of individual component interconnection and interaction, as well as complex construction skills. Today, a large proportion of electronic equipment is produced using complex integrated circuit modules which greatly reduces the amount of processing required to design and produce the operational unit. Through the use of these integrated circuit modules the step from functional design to implementation has been greatly simplified. The same techniqus can be applied to the development of instructional software or courseware. Through the use of functional modules, courseware can be developed with a process which is much less costly, requires less detailed knowledge of the technology, and moves the focus from the technical details of the implementation to the instructional aspects of the design. Support of this modular approach to courseware design and implementation needs an adequate programming language to permit the design of the necessary modules and to permit them to be linked together in a straightforward manner as well as a standard format for describing the modules.

The NATAL Course-Authoring Language

NATAL (Brahan et al, 1980) is a high-level, procedure-oriented course-authoring language which has been designed to support a wide range of CAL applications. These include, among others, interactive tutorial, drill and practice, simulation, information retrieval, and management of non-computer-based instructional materials. The language incorporates a control structure which relates to the decision structures required for the design of effective instructional materials. Through this structure, materials are described at a level which is closer to the course author or designer than the machine. Thus, NATAL can be considered a vehicle for producing a detailed design as opposed to an implementation. The burden of converting the design to a form suitable for execution is thus transferred to the computer. NATAL also provides for a clear separation of logic and content. This separation of logic and content is further supported by a highly flexible file structure which provides for storage of course content as well as operating data gathered during the delivery phase.

The characteristics of NATAL promote the development of modular, structured programs. There is low binding between modules which allows individual modules to be considered as black boxes for which we know the input requirements, the function to be performed and the output supplied. The details of how the function is carried out within the module can be changed with no effect on other modules of the program. Thus, NATAL provides a powerful tool for the economical development of the modules on which a functional approach to courseware development can be based.

Within the NATAL language, there are four main elements: PROCEDURES, FUNCTIONS, FILES and UNITS. The first three of these are primarily concerned with control and data storage and are the basis for the modular structure discussed above. The UNIT is the element through which the user program communicates with the student and in it are found those special features which characterize NATAL as a CAL language. The display sub-language, embedded in the unit, provides a means of formatting information for the display screen with many of the details being handled automatically. At the time of delivery, the display sub-language commands are interpreted in accord with the characteristics of the particular terminal being used. It is possible, within functional limits, to design materials today which will run on terminals in the future which are yet to be developed, with no manual adjustment to the materials.

NATAL Applications

The NATAL system is currently operating in prototype form on a DECsystem-10 computer located at the National Research Council (NRC) laboratories in Ottawa. Work is under way at Honeywell Information Systems in Toronto on the development of an upgraded DECsystem-10 implementation as well as implementations on an IBM computer (the operating system is yet to be selected, but will be one of the 370 series) and the Honeywell Level-6 mini-computer. In addition, work is about to start on a single-user microcomputer implementation of the NATAL delivery system which will be fully compatible with the implementations on the larger machines. Modules which are developed using NATAL will be capable of being accessed on systems ranging from large time-sharing systems down to personal microcomputer-based units.

All testing, evaluation and applications of NATAL to date have been carried out using the NRC implementation. In addition to programme development under way within the laboratory, work is currently under way at eight centres from Montreal Quebec to Victoria, British Columbia which are linked to the NRC computer. Application areas extend from a course in punctuation at the University of Victoria to courses for aircraft maintenance technician training at Canadian Forces Base Trenton. As a result of these projects, NATAL has been shown to be effective in responding to the needs of the course author in a variety of applications.

The first NATAL project outside the laboratory was at the University of British Columbia. In this, a program was developed to provide drill and practice in addition, subtraction, multiplication and division of whole numbers and decimals. The program was divided into six modules with development of each module being assigned to a different student.

The second example also involves a drill and practice module. In this case the module was part of a program developed at the University of Calgary to teach basic arithmetic skills to the developmentally handicapped. This module has been used in several applications in addition to its original context. The significant factor, however, is not that these modules can be used in a number of applications, but that it requires negligible effort to move them from one context to another.

Computer-Generated Video-Tapes

The modular nature of the NATAL language has been particularly useful in an application which involves the generation of video-tapes through a computer program. This application also illustrates the different stages involved in the development of a learning activity package and shows that, if we keep the primary implementation close to the design stage, we have materials which can adapt to changes in requirements as well as changes in the technology.

The basic design of the video program is embodied in a script which exists in two forms. The first is the conventional written script and the second is a series of modules which make up a computer program. By executing the program with a video-recorder connected to the video display unit of the terminal, a TV program results. The audio track is generated through use of a random access audio unit which forms part of the multi-media terminal and is operated under control of the computer program.

When a video-tape is produced by conventional means, modifications usually require a certain expertise in video technology and access to rather expensive editing equipment. In the case of the computer-generated video-tape, a high degree of flexibility is achieved because the modular computer program can be modified with no demands for complex video or computer skills. To date, three video programs have been produced using this technique.

Types of Module to be Combined

From an instructional designer's point of view there are two general classes of module which may usefully be used as building blocks for new or different courseware: pedagogical modules which are procedures setting up certain strategies, and management modules which carry out assessment, or record-keeping, or dialogue flow control. At a lower level there are tactical modules of pedagogical sorts such as RULEG, or drill and practice, or instantiation modules. Similarly, there are management tactic modules providing menus, or help, or calculation, or glossary aids, or report generation procedures.

At the lowest level are display, presentation and response acceptance modules of various sorts. Animated graphics illustrations are often worth moving from one set of courseware to another. This is also true of some specialized touch, or voice input acceptance modules.

Summary

If progress is to be made in the economical generation of good courseware, we need to be able to share and re-use the best parts of each other's packages. For this to be possible, packages need to be structured into separable modules, and these should as far as possible be machine independent.

Educational technology provides a language for describing the functional elements in instructional sub-systems, and structured computer languages such as NATAL provide a means of realizing these functional entities (Boyd, 1971) as separable and re-combinable modular components.

References

Boyd, G M (1971) The appropriate levels of computer languages for the specification of instruction. In Peckham, D (ed) *Aspects of Educational Technology* V. Kogan Page, London.
Brahan, J W, Henneker, W H and Haldy, A M (1980) *NATAL-74: Concept to Reality*. Proceedings of the Third Canadian Symposium on Instructional Technology. February. Vancouver, BC.

5.4 Application of Educational Technology Methods to the Design and Retrieval of Information Data Bases

W J K Davies and M Needham
Hertfordshire County Programmed Learning Centre, St Albans

Introduction

AMOS, although cumbersome, showed that multi-facet indexing was feasible at local level but that the actual facet analysis for a given subject area was vital if any scheme was to be effective. Fortunately, after 1973, our attention was drawn to the existence of the QUERY information retrieval program that had been developed for use on the DEC 10 multiple-access computer at Hatfield Polytechnic.

QUERY is a computer program originally designed for the correlation of simple information data-bases with multiple facets. We are interested in local data-bases to handle comparatively small quantities of specialized information sources but to do this at a very detailed level. For this purpose QUERY appears quite acceptable.

As it was organized, QUERY appeared to have a number of disadvantages common to such programmes:

1. It was a sequential-search program which at the time meant that any file more than about 1,000 records long would take a barely acceptable length of time to search.
2. It required a computer of considerable power — which fortunately was available.
3. The actual inputting and outputting process was cumbersome because of the terminology involved and because of its rigidity — a single character error in a long query almost invariably required one to start again.

Nonetheless, it did seem that its nature was suited to multi-facet indexing.

Feasibility Study 1 — HEBE

At the time the Centre was involved in a small-scale CET project to try and find some way of providing an effective bibliography of educational technology information sources. The development of any complex knowledge tree was considerably hampered by the need to use identical or closely synonymous terms and the QUERY format gave promise of overcoming this problem. Hence, as a parallel exercise, a five-field tree was developed defining the *management of instructional* and/or *organizational processes* and/or *resources*.

From the beginning, HEBE was conceived as a complete retrieval system rather than just the search element, and the concept was tried out using a bank of some 200 entries covering all aspects of educational technology.

Feasibility Study 2 — IRAIS

Meanwhile, the Centre had completed work on multi-facet indexing its collection of some 626 remedial reading books which might have a wider usefulness in the county. The card index was sufficient for our own needs but was not easily replicable and was cumbersome. We decided, therefore, to see if the QUERY format would accommodate it, since many educational establishments in the county have access through computer terminals to the Dec 10 system at Hatfield Polytechnic.

We found that, in practice, the conversion was easy and we were able to use the experiment to carry out two developments:

1. To see what the problems were of including basic bibliographical data in any print-out.
2. To try constructing a thesaurus of topic headings as we went along rather than taking an existing one.

Where, then, have we got to? In terms of work, interest in more complex bases has been revived by two items:

1. The installation of a DEC 1091 at Hatfield which can provide much faster searches and thus allow upwards of 2,000 items per file, perhaps, without undue time-lag.
2. The development of a subsidiary program which allows information to be input as codes but 'expanded' within the program so that a user can interrogate it in plain language.

This has led us to look again at HEBE and to redefine its structure following:

(a) refinement of the main knowledge tree;
(b) a perceived need to see if the scope can be widened to include general educational sources in a professional library.

The revised HEBE structure gives us five main fields. Four comprise the main knowledge tree, being *management* of *educational processes* and *resources* with a total of over 100 available terms: the separate field nature of QUERY means that we have been able to build in the possibility of retrieval by quite a number of cliché or near-cliché phrases without risking false drops and also to allow for interrogation at widely differing levels of sophistication.

The fifth field is, in essence, a topic field to be developed and refined by users as they create a thesaurus of subject-area terms and is intended to extend HEBE's usefulness into the wider field of professional studies.

The whole data-base has thus, in the current Yuk speak term, been made more 'user friendly'. It has also been upgraded to include both a serial number giving reference to review data and also basic publication data for those who want a print-out. The design modifications are basically complete and the data are being compiled as this paper goes to press.

Conclusions

Work so far has tended to verify our original hypotheses that specialist data-bases or data files can be constructed which are both relevant to local use and also potentially transferable to other geographical areas, providing the contents are of common interest. It should be made clear that this does not imply a national data-base: it simply means that it can be used as a local resource anywhere if the information contained is of use in that locality.

5.5 Computer-Based Training: the Programmer's Problem

P. Messer
Leicester Polytechnic
Quentin Whitlock
Sheffield City Polytechnic

Abstract: A logical development from the spread of computer-based clerical procedures is the demand to develop training systems using the computer equipment that staff use in their day-to-day duties. This paper discusses the trainer's problems when faced with large-scale training of this nature. It is shown that the difficulties are not simply larger problems, but are problems of a different type.

Introduction

Since the development of commercial computers in the early 1950s the penetration of computer applications in both industry and commerce has continued to accelerate. Many areas of industry and commerce have only been developed due to the presence of the computer (eg the concept of the cashless society). In recent years a further complication (opportunity) has appeared — the microcomputer. This enables small businesses at very low cost to have computing power equivalent to standard machines of the early 1960s. Microcomputers have caused a very real revolution. For the first time they bring the computer physically into the office.

The idea of computer-based instruction is almost as old as computers. Some trainers view CBI with suspicion. Others view the computer as a boon. Their departments may even have been formed as a result of its introduction. In training, CBI has many advantages both economic and educational. These have previously been described in some detail.

In this paper we are concerned with the development of CBI training packages which contain a large element of training to use computer systems. Most of the points made are relevant to other large training systems, but training in the use of computer systems has special problems which lead to interesting situations. It has been pointed out that over 80 per cent of CBI in the UK business sector is in training for computer-related tasks.

The Training System

Computer-assisted learning languages already exist which make the writing of self-instructional material much easier than it would be in standard computer languages. Examples are IIS, MENTOR, TUTOR etc. One of the authors has also written a version of CET's STAF language which fits easily onto any 48K microcomputer with FORTRAN. This makes many of the large machine languages advantages available on quite small machines.

The Training Problem

Three aspects of the CBI training problem are considered here:

1. The size of the training scheme.
2. The staffing problems.

3. The influence of the computer system on the design of training materials.

Since the case under consideration involves a computer system deeply embedded in the clerical system, the third of these features is looked at most closely.

General Considerations

Size

The size of a training scheme is logically independent of the size of the computer on which it is implemented. Most training systems can be implemented on massive mainframes or microcomputers without many compromises in the quality of materials. So when size is considered it is reasonable to restrict it to the question of size of the training problem. Another difficulty met in this type of system is the lack of a specific sequence in which clerical tasks may require to be taught. That is, the main consideration is the complexity of the training task. In the case being considered here, the size of the training task is large — many clerical tasks to be trained for, with the possibility of many computer programs being used in the execution of the tasks. A typical situation to be considered is:

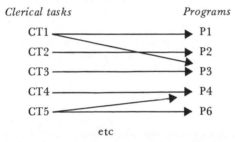

Clerical tasks   *Programs*

etc

Under normal conditions there will be more clerical tasks than programs with some programs used by many tasks (eg information units) and some relating to as few as one task (eg specific updating task).

Staff

The development of large packages must imply a lessening of the instructor-dependent element in the construction of the packages. This is because teams of staff are necessary to create the material, and since it cannot be guaranteed that the team will be constant it is important to use design techniques which are trainer-independent.

This is much easier to achieve if the following points are kept in mind:

1. The structure of the material developed should be relatively simple.
2. Documentation techniques should be standardized and should clearly lay out the design technique.
3. Prerequisites and objectives must be clearly laid out for each instructional sequence. This is not trivial, owing to the interacting nature of the clerical tasks.

Computer System

The computer system affects the development of training materials in two ways:

1. The facilities for the development of CBI materials.

2. The computer's impact on the system to be trained.

The second point is the key problem. Usually, the computer system has been integrated into the clerical system by the systems analysis group: the training department will not have had much say in its creation. Typically, there will be a number of programs the clerk can use to carry out the tasks, and the trainer's problem is to construct training sequences for these tasks. The situation will seldom be as simple as:

ONE PROGRAM   ONE TASK

For example, a computer program enabling a clerk to check the last payment on an account may be useful for two or three different tasks.

It is important not to train towards the idiosyncracies of the computer system. The trainer must keep in mind the objectives of the clerical task. In theory, the computer system has been designed to help the clerical tasks to be carried out, but the systems analysts have many conflicting demands on them when they are doing the planning. In the design of complex systems obscurities almost always appear, and since the man-computer interface involves difficult and unresolved problems, some of the worst mistakes are made in this area. But by far the most important element is the consideration that a computer system is not an unchanging entity. In fact, computer systems are much more prone to change than manual systems. Changes in information flow are made in the light of experience, errors are corrected and general tidying up is carried out. These changes are always a difficulty for the trainer, since it is important that the training department receives information on the changes well before they are implemented. For a computer-based training system the existence of continually changing requirements sets up new considerations from the normal situation in the early days of printed self-instruction.

The authors of the CBI material should try to design a system where the considerations are compatible, and this should be a highly conscious decision. It is perfectly possible to write individual training sequences each of which is perfectly good but which, taken together, do not satisfy the above criteria. They contain the seeds of disaster, and these particular hazards may be observable:

1. Staff changes, and loss of expertise making changes difficult.
2. Escalating maintenance costs as changes cause more and more 'patches' to be put into the system.
3. Documentation getting outdated and making changes even harder to make.

Consider the following simple example of three techniques for training CT3, from the program designer's viewpoint:

Sequence of information screen: (IS): IS1, IS2
Clerical tasks: (CT): CT1, CT2, CT3, CT4, CT5, CT6, *all using* IS1
eg CT3

| Receive Document | → | Use of IS1 | → | Complete Document | → | Use of Update Screen IS2 |

(a) *Develop a prescribed sequence of learning/do not develop IS1 as a separate unit*
Introduce each feature of IS1 as it appears in a clerical task and develop the material at that point.

(b) *Develop IS1*
   When IS1 is used in a clerical task, branch to IS1 training material
   if inadequate performance appears.
(c) *Develop an overview of IS1*
   An overview training program is developed and in addition detailed
   training material appears in the clerical task training program.

In our experience, method (c) is likely to be least successful. The initial design is
difficult, due to the problems of specifying exactly what goes where to the different
authors. Modifications to the material will be hard to carry out and in the long term
will almost certainly lead to a degradation in the quality of the training. This
method suffers from bad stability and localization problems.

Methods (a) and (b) are both possible, but for a program like IS1 used in six
different tasks it is better to adopt (b). The localization problems created in using
this technique can be minimized by pre-testing knowledge of IS1 before entering
CT3. The adoption of method (b) means that the structure of IS1 training material
has to be on a menu basis, with different parts of the material being available
when needed by separate training programs.

Method (a) will suffer from stability problems if the same material has to be
developed for more than one clerical task.

It is most important to realize that this discussion is solely about the
development of the material (and its structuring within the training package).
It is *not* about the material as the trainee sees it. In CBI these two viewpoints are
seldom distinguished but keeping them apart can solve many difficult technical
problems.

DOCUMENTATION
The documentation for the system should be simple and precise. Most of it should
be generated during the development phase as natural aids to the authors. As far
as possible the teaching material should be self-documenting. The teaching
program should contain statements of prerequisites and objectives as well as
detailed comments on the teaching sequences; such material is easily updated as
the program is updated. The structure of the material should be carefully
documented so that when changes are required the appropriate places for the
changes are easily located. An all-important feature is keeping the documentation
up-to-date. This is why the documentation is kept simple — if it is not, it will not
be kept up-to-date.

System Analysis and CBI

Consideration of CBI from the viewpoint of the systems analyst leads to interesting
conclusions. The development of self-instructional material involves a precise
analysis of the problems of the user of the analyst's system. Areas of difficulty for
the trainer correspond to areas of difficulty or failure for the analyst. Also, the
rigour of the analysis carried out by the trainer (eg problem, breakdown, S-R
analysis, rule set) corresponds to the rigour of the systems analysis carried out.
So it is reasonable to view the trainer's analysis as a clear statement of the user's
viewpoint. From this it is easy to see the possibility of co-operation between the
analyst and the trainer. When the trainer finds that clerical tasks need dense
teaching material (or exceptionally long linear sequences) to achieve the objectives
it is always worthwhile discussing the problems with the analyst. It may be that
technical problems have forced the analyst to his solution or the trainer may have
analysed the problem incorrectly, but it is more likely that some interface problem
that has escaped the analyst's notice will be revealed. Thus the analyst gets an
excellent source of feedback including the detailed statistics that can be obtained
from CBI.

In future, it may even be possible for the training department to be involved in the early stages of the analysis and develop the training material along with the system. In this way many user problems could be avoided before the system is complete. There is an indication that systems analysts are beginning to think in the same way.

Conclusions

There are four points of emphasis:

1. CBI is most likely to develop where computers are firmly embedded in the companies' day-to-day work. Thus CBI systems which contain a large element of computer training are very important.
2. The computer system must not be allowed to dominate the training task – the overall clerical task is the main objective.
3. Large CBI packages are subject to constant update and maintenance. It is essential that design procedures take this into account and that the system developed can stand the changes without degradation in performance.
4. The analysis carried out by the trainer makes him a natural ally of the systems analyst. In future this should lead to the development of CBI materials in parallel with the development of the computer system and be integrated with it.

Workshop Report
5.6 Authorship Technique in Computer-Based Instructional Programmes

Stuart Fisher *Barclaycard*
P Messer *Leicester Polytechnic*
Quentin Whitlock *Sheffield City Polytechnic*

Organizers' Account

This workshop was designed to enable participants to experiment in writing a learning sequence for presentation in computer-based form and to identify and discuss problems and opportunities confronting authors using this form of instruction.

Participants' sequences were subsequently presented via IBM's IIS language at the mainframe terminal or via the CALCHEM language STAF at a microcomputer.

Part 1
Introduction to the workshop and description of the project (20 minutes). Participants divided into four groups of five to six members to develop programs on a given task; there was the opportunity to inspect the organizers' version of another part of the given topic, identical sequences

being available on the micro and mainframe terminal.

Part 2
Groups inspected their own and other groups' versions at the terminals.
Groups compared notes, identified problem areas and inspected the
organizers' version.
Plenary review session.

Some groups found difficulty in getting started due to the complete unfamiliarity
of the topic given — a clerical task at Barclaycard.

Outcome

At the end of Part 1, six programmed sequences were produced, five of which were
converted to presentations at either the micro or the mainframe terminal.

The major point emerging in the discussion was that authors used to writing
printed self-instruct materials must prepare for a major readjustment to their
technique when they change to CAI programs.

In particular, these points must be borne in mind:

(a) That special consideration must be given to the use of illustrative
    material such as documents used in clerical tasks.
(b) That in systems like IIS, a programming methodology such as a
    mathematics Demonstrate-Prompt-Release model, which envisages a
    student response to every exercise or frame, is not easy to employ.
(c) That with larger scale clerical training operations, authors should
    aim to keep their material as economical as possible and not use
    CAI just because it is there.

Finally, it was noted that it was possible to produce identical presentations on the
micro and the mainframe terminal, given similar lead times.

Section 6:
Teacher Training
and Staff Development

6.1 The Technology of Teaching : Art or Science?

Nita Lougher
Goldsmiths' College, London

Abstract: Describes the evolution of a formal cybernetic model of teaching designed to help student teachers and teachers develop competence and confidence when teaching. The fundamental precept of the model is that teaching is communicating, and where learning does not occur there has been a failure in communication between teacher and learner.

Introduction

The technology of teaching I take to mean the application of knowledge and the design of systems to help teachers cope more successfully with the complexity of the teaching task. Over a period of 12 years we have designed, developed and used such a system. It is a closed loop communication system suitable for teaching in a wide range of teaching situations in schools and college.

The fundamental precept of the work is that teaching is communicating, and where learning does not occur it is usually because there has been a failure in communication between teacher and learner.

When I started to teach young children I regarded it as self-evident that in order to communicate with them I had to consider what they knew, think about what I wanted them to know, and arrange things so that they would share more and more of the knowledge available to myself and adults. To do this I had to use my imagination. I soon learned that children knew some things of which I was ignorant, that teaching was a reciprocal interaction. The extent of my ignorance has remained.

Students, when they come to college, are aware of the reciprocal relationship between teachers and learners. Over a period of five years, the question 'What is a good teacher?' put to students met with the same response — a good teacher must be able to communicate, and communication is a complex, two-way process.

As a sociologist I could draw on the findings of the founding fathers of sociology and many modern theorists to help students explore the communication process and its problems. The problem I had to solve was to help students teach children, to help them communicate successfully. Without knowledge and experience they were anxious and uncertain as to how to begin. It was my job to reduce that uncertainty by feeding in knowledge, and giving guidance as to how to proceed in the many and varied teaching situations they might meet in the schools.

What is Communication in the Context of Teaching?

The definition of 'communication' includes the idea of sharing, of the process of adjusting understandings and attitudes to arrive at common meaning. Our personal experience suggests that to achieve communication there must be some common aim and interest, a common curiosity or common problem. Teaching conceived as a system of communication is more than interaction; the teachers must have a goal and must intend to influence and change the capability and competence of those they teach. Teaching is interaction with a purpose, with the aims and objectives made explicit. The aims will reflect the philosophy of those who teach and, in the context of this paper, objectives will include sharing of knowledge, teaching of skills, influencing attitudes and values. It will be concerned with helping people to learn how to learn.

Because of my assertion that teaching is communicating, the most fruitful source of inspiration for tackling the problem of 'how to teach' is communication theory. It provides insights not only into teaching ordinary children but also children with special problems: the deaf, the blind and the physically and mentally handicapped. It is especially helpful in teaching in college. The idealized communication system has five components — source, transmitter, channel, receiver and destination — and in one form or another these five components are present in every kind of communication. In human communication such as teaching, the teacher is the source and the receiver is the learner. Where the learner's response to the message has no effect on the system, we have open loop systems. Where the source is able to modify the message on the basis of the response from the receiver, we have a closed loop system. This approach to teaching has much in common with that of the new science of cybernetics.

A central concept in the cybernetic approach is feedback control, through knowledge of results, both of error and success. There is growing agreement that the behavioural unit that best describes learning is the feedback loop.

It seems that more and more people who have devoted their attention to educational research agree on the importance of the concept 'feedback' and its usefulness in understanding human development and learning (eg Mayr, 1970). The idea of building, of constructing, of frameworks, scaffolding, of planning, of purpose, function and control and feedback are the important ideas in modern studies.

If teachers are to use the findings of so many experts who have studied human behaviour, then arrangements must be made to check that individuals make progress and learn successfully.

In my own teaching in schools, checking that children learned and keeping records of progress was a normal part of the job of teaching. So when I joined the staff of a college of education it seemed a realistic aim to try to achieve diagnostic teaching, to communicate this aim to the students and help them prepare their work carefully and evaluate their progress.

Problems to be Solved

The Diversity of Schools in Primary Education

Teachers had been trained at different times, and their teaching styles and the organization of schools ranged from the traditional class teaching to open plan classrooms and schools in which children had the choice of many activities (see, eg, Bennett, 1977). In the so-called progressive classroom, teachers and students had to plan and create an environment in which the children could learn, and keep a careful check on their activities and progress.

The Breadth of the Courses in Educational Studies

These included aspects of philosophy, sociology, child development and psychology. The assumption was that the student would be able to link the theory with the practice of teaching eventually. However, there was no evidence for this assumption. Many students did not expect to understand the theory of practice and it was not unusual for students to be told to forget theory when they were in schools.

The first innovation was a change in the way students kept accounts of their practical teaching in school. The need to consider the functions of the students' practical notebook was first introduced in 1969 (Lougher, 1969).

The change in format resulted from a decision, agreed with the students. Previously the account of students' experience of teaching in schools was written up as a detailed report of planning and a diary of events. To save time, it was decided that the planning and development should be written up in tabulated form, under headings and with diagrams. The headings directed attention to detail of organization, storage of resources, display of resources and children's work, the possible development of the work with children and the actual development that occurred. The actual development analyzed the communication process so that students should appreciate the links with their college courses. The result of this effort was a collection of what we called Flowplan-charts of actual teaching.

UNFORSEEN ADVANTAGES
In addition to clarifying the students' planning and organization, we had helped to clarify links with the college courses. But in addition we had produced most valuable learning aids. When future students discussed these Flowplans they had a far better understanding of the teaching tasks in school.

The second innovation was a schematic diagram of the task of reading. The next task to be analyzed as a problem was that of successful reading. With cues and guidance, useful summaries were constructed that took account of both function and structure and the knowledge essential for all readers. By analyzing the task of reading it could be demonstrated clearly that there was little point in advocating any one way of teaching reading. What was essential was to check that learners were secure in all the information that was needed to enable them to read successfully. This task analysis led to the problem of trying to understand the acquisition of language, and its many functions. 'Reading and writing' conceived as a communication system included the writer, the sender of the message, the message and the reader as the recipient.

This perspective led to some constructive and penetrating questions. What kind of written material would the young reader wish to receive and read? What kind of message would the young writer wish to send? How should it be received by the teacher? What is involved in listening to children read? This careful analysis drew attention to the possibility of overloading the young reader with too many unknown words and reduce his/her confidence by expecting him/her to remember too much too soon.

Evaluation

The only evaluation possible was that produced by the students. Their statements commented on the fact that they had found the effort of summarizing information both in the school practice notebook and the reading course a valuable aid to thinking and remembering. In their written evaluation they commented that the planning component of their practice notebook should be part of the work in college and part of the course for practical teaching. This would mean that they would go into schools with far more material prepared. Obviously they would need to adapt to the children and the schools, but students thought that being well prepared for a large number of topics would help them to be more flexible. The summary of the reading task was judged to be useful, not only as a guide to their teaching but also as a help when reading research into reading.

The Problem of Diversity in Secondary Teaching

The diversity of schools was just as much a problem for students preparing for secondary level teaching — types, sizes, split sites, streaming, spoken and written language difficulties, staffing problems — and in addition there was the problem of the number of pupils to be encountered. Students were expected to gain experience of teaching pupils of different ages, and this meant encountering anything from 100 to 500 pupils.

As someone concerned both with the theoretical courses and the support and supervision of students when they were teaching in schools, the task of preparation sometimes seemed impossible. Without a framework provided by a theory or model of communication it would have been even more difficult to give any constructive guidance.

The Innovation Extended to Secondary Teaching

The method of task analysis and the construction of summaries was just as useful when applied to secondary students. The need to plan carefully and organize resources and children was important whatever the ages of the children. In specialist teaching in secondary schools there could be more difficulties without thorough preparation. Some specialist teachers were more dependent on the precise use of language than others. The language of the teacher was, of course, related to the clarity of the plan, the objectives of the lesson. When the teacher intended that the children should use their imagination, the students had to think how this could be achieved and usually it was achieved by the choice of language. Discussion periods were difficult for students and considerable thought had to go into the questioning that could lead to fruitful discussion.

Improving the design of instructions, providing self-evaluation sheets and collecting examples of lessons and evaluation is undoubtedly helpful to students, but dealing with the problem of helping them to observe individuals and checking individual progress was another problem. All one could do was to draw their attention to the problem of assessment and testing, and to expect some notes on as many pupils as possible. It was possible for them to produce detailed accounts of the progress and problems of some individuals. Again, examples of such records of individuals were collected and discussed with student groups.

The Problem of the Course and the Work of Piaget

The worrying part of the students' course was the work of Piaget. He seemed to suggest that in order to think about teaching at the formal level we must be able to reflect on possibilities and make a selection that could be put to the test. We needed an explicit model of 'how to teach'. The guides to preparation and summaries of lessons represented a model of communicating and teaching, but how could this model be presented more clearly?

A Model of 'How to Teach?'

The answer to this question came from the work of my daugher in a special study written when she was following a Post-Graduate Certificate of Education course: from her reading on communication and her practical experience, she produced a

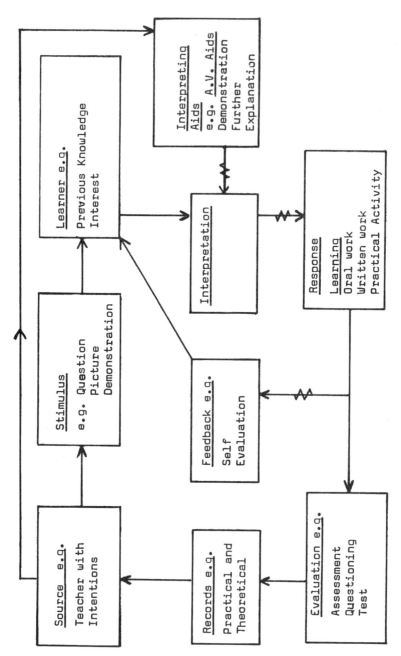

Figure 1. *Teacher-learner communication system (communication channel eg written, spoken, visual etc noise or interference eg audible noise, discomfort, poor organization)*

diagram that is proving to be a most helpful visual aid by presenting the essential components of the communication system in such a way that the components are seen to be related. (see Figure 1).

This model of the teacher-learner system was constructed as a response to the problem of teaching and understanding theory. It helps to illustrate the function of communication at different stages of the development of a lesson or teaching situation. It serves to clarify thinking on different aspects of the communication process. Courses in the use of instructional aids may introduce students to the nature and use of audio-visual aids, but the problem of using this knowledge is very difficult in practice. The model helps students and teachers to appreciate the many possibilities of different learning aids and their function in the development of the teaching process.

The Components of the System

THE TEACHER

The teacher must (i) have aims and objectives — to have thought through what is intended; (ii) provide suitable stimuli from different possibilities; (iii) select a suitable communication channel and provide effective interpretive aids. Adequate feedback must be established both to himself and also directly to the learner. The teacher must try to eliminate 'noise'. Each of these tasks may cause problems, and the simple communication model throws some light on the relationships between the problems.

THE STIMULUS

In a classical experiment a stimulus is selected by the experimenter. In teaching situations the teacher has to consider many possible stimuli and select to achieve the required response. The selection will depend on the age and existing knowledge of the learner. With young children the stimuli may be objects, pictures or play activities; with adults language will play an increasingly important part.

THE CHANNEL

The channel is the link between the source of the communication and the destination, and must accommodate different sensory inputs. In teaching young children to read, for example, the problem of redundancy in speech is recognized. The reduction of visual cues from body language and audial cues from stress and intonation must be taken into account when planning for young readers.

THE LEARNER

The learner is the recipient of the message and is the most important component of the system. Planning must take account of age, developmental stage and the existing knowledge of the learner. The different cognitive styles of the learner must also be considered. In addition, preparation must take into account what has to be learned.

The more difficult the problem the more the learner will be required to call on past learning of concepts and rules. Gagné's classification (Gagné, 1965) suggests that different kinds of learning require different approaches. For example, in teaching verbal chains such as counting, the alphabet and arithmetic tables, the spoken word will be the main communication channel and also the feedback channel in the form of the children's recitation. But when children learn the concepts of number and the concept of the alphabet, they will require very different kinds of experience and feedback devices.

INTERPRETIVE AIDS

Interpretive aids fall into a number of different categories according to the function they are intended to fulfil in the teaching system. In physical education and the performing arts, the aid to learning may be a demonstration by the teacher or student. In the visual arts, models, illustrations and language are all used to develop perception and extend thinking. Some subject areas are more dependent on visual representation than others, but in all teaching the selection of interpretive aids is part of the teaching process. Without the careful organization and appropriate dialogue, the intended discovery or interpretation will not be made.

FEEDBACK

The feedback process is a vital stage in the closed loop communication system. It ensures that the stimulus has been received and that the intentions of the teacher have been made clear, received and interpreted as planned. It is the means of preventing a cumulative build-up of misunderstanding.

NOISE

Noise in the communication system consists of all the external factors that prevent the learner taking in the message. These 'interference' factors will include audible noise, disinterest, physical discomfort, disturbance through inadequate organization of resources and the many distractions that are common in all institutions, especially schools. For one reason or another, whatever precautions are taken to eliminate noise the message will not usually be received the first time it is transmitted and the teacher will need to repeat it. To present the time concept in different ways and by using different communication channels, teaching is made interesting both to the teacher and the learner.

Conclusion

The development of a model to improve teaching continues. Students who have contributed to the work have looked at components of the model more carefully in special studies that are part of their course. Some have investigated teaching aids. Some have noted the language of the classroom and the different functions it serves. Some have studied the problem of noise or interference and ways of coping with it. Students who have studied special education have found the model of communication most helpful. A student who studied the use of Bliss symbols in helping a severely handicapped boy to communicate has produced a study that ought to be made available more generally. We are still learning, and there is no end to the development.

One of the findings that is most worrying is the resistance to what is a new and experimental approach. There is a strong dislike of tabulated summaries and diagrams. Perhaps this is a fact that ought to be considered very seriously. Not only do we need more people who are prepared to reflect on scientific approaches and the design process – we need to encourage observation, visual literacy, and imagination. Is educational technology the meeting place of art and science?

References

Bennett, N (1977) *Teaching Styles and Pupils' Progress*. Open Books.

Gagné, R (1965) *The Conditions of Learning*. Holt, Rinehart and Winston.

Lougher, N (1969) Teacher training and school practice journals. *Bulletin of the Institute of Education* (spring issue). University of London.

Mayr, O (1970) The origins of feedback control. *Scientific American*.

6.2 The Structure of Educational Technology Courses for Student Teachers in Further and Higher Education

C Bird
Garnett College of Education

Abstract: This paper attempts to consider the arguments for and against the substantial examination by all student teachers in further and higher education of computer-assisted methods of instruction. The conclusion is reached that learning about certain highly efficient uses should continue, but that at present certain other uses have little to offer.

The Background to the Problem

There are four colleges of education in the UK which train teachers for the colleges of further and higher education. The students on such courses are available for timetabling for roughly 1,000 hours (33 weeks of 30 hours), of which about 40 hours is spent on modules labelled 'educational technology'. In these modules, the student makes a survey of basic teaching practices arising out of the use of such as the chalkboard, handouts, duplicating processes, wallcharts, models and simulations, overhead projection, slides and filmstrips, cinefilm, sound and video recordings, broadcast and closed circuit television, programmed learning, packaged learning and resource centres. These are skills which current practising teachers use in their classrooms; it is therefore necessary that student teachers who will shortly enter such classrooms should be informed about these skills.

Preparation for Tomorrow

It is equally important to have an eye not only to what happens in classrooms today, but also to the possible needs of tomorrow. A general question can be posed: 'Is there any subject area now in embryo which could grow into a source of interest for the teacher in tomorrow's classroom?'

Some of the developments which might be considered are such as: (i) the extended use of simulators, (ii) the profferings of the video long-play record, (iii) a possible extension of CEEFAX, ORACLE and PRESTEL for educational purposes, (iv) the possible effects on teaching method of stereoscopic television, (v) above all, the computer. For the computer, some people contend, is revolutionizing society about us. An example of this contention comes from a meeting of the American Association for Educational Data Systems (1971) where one speaker said that 'we can't do without the computer in education.' He saw it as an integral part of today's educational system. Richard Hooper, the Director of the NDPCAL project, asserts: 'Computers in education are here to stay.' (1975). Another example comes from last year's APLET Conference: 'The potential for computer-based education is considerable.' (Bryce and Stewart, 1979).

The Problem

If the computer, then, is as important as the above suggests, it might well be asked whether it should now take its place with other classroom aids in the list of basic compulsory studies for student teachers.

An immediate reaction might be to say 'Why not?' and welcome the suggestion with an unqualified 'Yes'. But there is at least one very good reason why we should stop first to think carefully. Not all educationists applaud the results of the use of the computer in education. Indeed, some of them point to claims of success that are no more than hopes, expectations and speculations for the future. Computers are used in different areas of education, and seeming success or failure depends on which area is examined.

The Use of Computers in Education

There are at least five distinct uses of the computer in education today:

- (a) as a calculator;
- (b) as a word processor;
- (c) as a control device;
- (d) as a model;
- (e) in Computer-Managed Learning (CML) and Computer-Assisted Learning (CAL).

(a) *The computer as a calculator* is the application for which it was originally designed and in which it is extraordinarily efficient and thoroughly competent. All mathematicians and other users of mathematics find this use of the computer a great saver of time and effort.

(b) *The computer as a data-processing machine* is used in educational offices for, eg, the registration of students, accounting, storage of data, and in cataloguing in the library. In these areas, the computer has shown itself to be more efficient than (and has therefore taken over from and replaced) other competing office equipment.

(c) *The computer functions as a selector, as a simulator and as a control device* in laboratories, workshops, training areas and classrooms. It brings to these places a uniqueness and a novelty of experience of selected subject matter not formerly available.

(d) *The computer is used as a model* when students are being instructed in programming techniques and in computer science. It is ideal in this type of practice.

(e) *The computer is used in CML and CAL.*

The use of computers in areas (a) to (d) is accepted as fully justified and wholly commendable. However, when we look at CML and CAL, a very different situation is evident.

Shortcomings of CML and CAL

Adverse criticism of both CML and CAL comes from eminent authorities that should be both knowledgeable and capable of forming balanced opinions. For example, in the United States the Carnegie Commission on Higher Education reported: 'One of the greatest disappointments of the national effort to date is that for all the funds and efforts thus far expended on the advancement of educational technology, penetrations of new learning materials and media into higher education have thus far been shallow.' (1972). In the United Kingdom, J J Turnbull of the National Computing Centre writes that: 'It is also necessary to point out that high claims for CAI have often been followed by programmes which are little better than those of other forms of programmed learning and in which the principal difference is the cost of the medium.' (1974). Need I add that the cost of CAI is always the higher. Then there are educationists who doubt whether the long hours required for writing programmes are commensurate with the benefit to the students.

These criticisms seem to centre around two main contentions: (i) the programmes and tests possible with CML and CAL are shallow and sometimes trivial; (ii) teaching by computer is more expensive than teaching by other means of instruction.

COMPUTER-BASED LEARNING AND/OR TESTING IS SHALLOW

The contention that computer-based learning is shallow and sometimes trivial springs from the limitations of responses possible with the programmes available until now. The responses are of two types: (i) the insertion of a word/term, and (ii) the use of multiple-choice questions.

The insertion response is of the form where the student types an answer which the computer assesses. The assessment can allow not only for wrong answers but also for some mis-spellings. Two criticisms can be levelled: (i) the answers must be kept very simple — to a single word or to a phrase; (ii) it is normally too extensive a task to programme all possible wrong answers. If, on the other hand, the correct response only is programmed, then to all the incorrect responses that might be made can only be directed the instruction: 'Wrong, try again.' This is a somewhat bland admonishment for a student attempt that may be only a spelling mistake or a punctuation error from correctness. Indeed, the student's attempt can be a synonym of the correct answer, but it cannot be shown to be correct because the programming has not included such a synonym. In general, the insertion response has a limited application.

THE SHORTCOMINGS OF THE MULTIPLE-CHOICE QUESTION

The other form of response is the selection of an answer from a multiple-choice question: normally one in five provided answers is the correct answer. This mode of responding means that for every correct answer read, four incorrect answers are also read. Hence the time spent in reading is only 20 per cent informative. A second shortcoming is that the question becomes associated with incorrect answers and undesirable memory bonds may be formed. Thirdly, only *recognition* of a correct answer is required, ie *recall*. Fourthly, when compared to a dialogue that can take place between a tutor and his student, this is a very restricted means of testing. For when students are being tested, what is really being sought is an account of their experiences or of their thoughts expressed in sentences. However, once this expression consists of more than a word or a short phrase, then it is beyond the facility of the computer to make an evaluation. In other words, the capacity of the computer to evaluate a student's normal answer to a question is negligible when compared to the capacity of the student's tutor.

THE COST OF COMPUTER-BASED LEARNING

The second main criticism made against CML and CAL is that they are more expensive than learning in the traditional classroom. In 1975, UNCAL said of the cost of computer learning '. . .this voraciously expensive technology is still in its infancy and has already consumed vast sums in America and several fortunes here (in the UK). There is little to show for it.'

The largest CAL experiment in the UK so far has been that of the NDPCAL during 1973-78 on a budget of £2,500,000. The report of the financial evaluation states that insurmountable difficulties made exact costing impossible. However,

estimates are available for further and higher education and these vary from
£4 to over £20 per student terminal hour (Fielden and Pearson, 1978). The report
continues: '. . .the cheapest CAL project cost of £4 per student hour is more than
the upper end of the range of conventional teaching costs. . .' (ibid).

The lowest estimate for CAL that I found anywhere is that for PLATO IV in the
USA. With an output to 4,000 termianls, the cost per student terminal hour was
estimated at 34 cents, which is little different from the comparable traditional
classroom cost (Bitzer and Skaperdas, 1973). However, it should be noted that
this was only an estimate; the computer up to this estimate (1973) had never
seemingly had more than some 900 terminals connected.

There are other costing figures for CAL available and they all more or less tend
to the general conclusion that CAL is more costly than conventional classroom
teaching.

But some supporters of computer-based learning argue that, even though it is
more expensive than the traditional classroom, this does not mean that it is not
good value for money. They claim that outcomes of CAL are, for instance, added
educational value, enhanced understanding of concepts and other qualitative
products. It is further asserted that such factors cannot be measured but only be
appreciated as 'subjective value judgements.' The trouble with accepting this
statement is the paradox it creates. For it comes from the very people who at the
beginning of each computer program should be insisting on 'specified objectives in
behavioural terms'. In other words, different standards are being applied at the
end of the program from those which ought to obtain at the beginning.

Perhaps the wisest verdict about the cost of computer-based learning comes
from Fielden and Pearson, who say: '. . .no overall conclusions can be reached on
the value for money of CAL and CML . . . the probable range of unit costs is now
known but it is not possible to quantify the outcomes, nor even always to identify
them.' (1978).

Conclusions

The original question which we asked was: 'Is computer-based learning now so
important that all student teachers in further and higher education should be
informed of its present uses and future potentialities?'.

Three conclusions from the foregoing examination bear upon the question:
(a) the computer as: (i) a calculator, (ii) a data processor, (iii) a control/decision/
simulator device, and (iv) a model, is accepted as a totally effective and highly
proficient instrument; (b) in CAL and CML the limitations of the modes of
responding raise suspicions of 'superficiality' of subject matter; (c) the cost of
CAL and CML are always more than the cost of conventional classroom instruction.

Applying these conclusions to the starting question, we seem to arrive at an
answer which says that those students who are concerned with the computer in
its uses (i) to (iv) above, which are highly efficient uses, should continue to learn
about such uses. However, for the rest of the students (the other 90 per cent?),
CAL and CML seem to have little to offer at present. But it is important to keep
an open mind.

If a cheap microchip in the future causes computer costs to plummet, then we
would need to re-examine the costs of CAL and CML. If these costs approached
or fell below the costs of the traditional classroom instruction, it would be
necessary to re-appraise the above findings. The Editor of the DES publication
Trends in Education apparently thinks that this will happen. He writes of recent
developments in computers: '. . .within the next few years microcomputers in
educational institutions will be almost as common as typewriters.' (HMSO, 1978).

With this possibility in view, the need to improve the quality of education cannot be overstressed. A useful analogy comes from horology. The clock in the tower of Salisbury Cathedral dates from the 15th century. it was made entirely with *hand tools*. Nearby, in the museum, is another clock showing the same time; it is a product of the industrial revolution and was made on *machines minded by men.* Nor far away in the Woolworth store are wrist watches for sale. Wall pictures show how, in the making of the watches, bars of metal feed into a machine and finished parts appear at the other end. Not until the parts are fitted together to form the movement are they touched by hand for the first time. *Automation* is here.

It may well be that the computer will some time in the future become the automaton of the classroom. Certainly, anyone today can be forgiven for getting the impression that some of our classrooms are still back in the 15th century.

References

Association for Educational Data Systems (1971) Report of the 1971 Annual Meeting. Lubbock, Texas.

Bitzer, D and Skaperdas, D (1973) The design of an economically viable large-scale computer-based education system. *CERL Report X-5.* University of Urbana, Illinois.

Bryce, C F A and Stewart, A M (1979) The application of random access back projection in CAI. In Page, G T and Whitlock, Q (eds) *Aspects of Educational Technology* **XIII**. Kogan Page, London.

Carnegie Commission on Higher Education (1972) *The Fourth Revolution — a Report and Recommendations.* New York, McGraw Hill.

Fielden, J and Pearson, P K (1978) *The Cost of Learning with Computers.* Council for Educational Technology, London.

HMSO (1978) *Trends in Education.* Department of Education and Science, London.

NDPCAL (1975) *Two Years On.* Council for Educational Technology, London.

NDPCAL (1977) *Final Report of the Director.* Council for Educational Technology, London.

Turnbull, J J (1974) *The Computer in the Learning Environment.* National Computing Centre, Manchester.

6.3   Criteria for the Design of Educational Technology Courses

Bernard Alloway
Huddersfield Polytechnic

Abstract: A model of analytical design encompassing past, present and future design criteria in the field of educational technology is presented by means of a visual display matrix. Serial influences can be identified from this, together with how items influence each other across the visual display.

Introduction

The evolution of educational technology (node 1a) can be traced through a number of its functions, perhaps the most frequently recorded being the datal points for the emergence of hardware and software systems and their accompanying techniques. Thus, by diligently searching, the first appearances can be traced (in education and training) of film, visual aids, language laboratories, programmed learning, teaching machines and closed circuit television. The later techniques of simulations, games, micro-teaching and learning skills analysis have been followed by mainframe and micro-computer applications.

The adoption of such hardware, software and analysis systems by specific users has subsequently led to the organization of professional, trade union and resource centre groups. In some cases, substantial academic organizations have been sponsored and learned journals have emerged, capable of holding their own in the status-conscious world of educational publications. In 1967, with the formation of the National Council for Educational Technology, the Department of Education and Science did much to establish the position of educational technology in Britain, although considerable individual effort went into the early formation of professional groupings from both education and training — indeed, as this conference proves, this effort has continued throughout the past quarter of a century. These organizations receive varying publicity and approval amongst our non-educational technology colleagues, seemingly according to economic climate and the sense of educational wellbeing.

Certainly the areas of 'technology in education' are found to be popular in educational technology courses (node 1b), although many of those examined encompass a study of the 'technology of education' later in their curricula. This is especially so where a course leads to a broad educational qualification, or is aimed at educational technology organization and management. A further starting point for course design is to look at the priorities that led to the formation and the subsequent evolution of specific educational technology associations (node 1c), currently strong associations of practitioners exist in the United Kingdom covering programmed learning, games and simulations, educational television, photography, film, and educational and training technology.

Coupled with the evolutionary developments of both educational technology and its associations above, is the rather slow emergence of a theoretical basis for educational technology (node 1e). Obvious components (from the examination so far) include elements of behaviouralist psychology, sensory perception, alternative media learning strategies and the application of interaction analysis techniques. Much remains to be identified, categorized and argued if educational technology is to be seen as anything more than an equipment appendage to the serious business of education and training. This suggests that such theoretical analysis and reinforcement should form a substantial part of any future educational technology course that is to have credibility in the competitive academic world.

Finally, as a starting point the author would put considerable emphasis on the experiences of users of the CET Support Materials for Courses in Educational Technology (node 1e), for which project he was Implementation Fellow in 1973 and 1974. With over 200 institutions making use of these multi-media materials since they were published in 1973, experiential evidence of considerable value to future course designs has been assembled from many different types of institution, course level and subject specialism.

Potential Course Structures

It follows that there is a need to collect existing (and extinct) course data (node 2a) to identify previous design priorities. Ironically, some of the early courses in programmed learning, teaching machines, and feedback classrooms, reveal criteria which have surprising relevance for course design in computer-based learning routines with their need for multiple-choice and interactive-response techniques. However, techniques courses in a variety of media are but one aspect

	a	b	c	d	e
Starting points ⇧	1a Educational technology evolution	1b Sampled history of educational technology courses	1c Educational Technology Association evolution	1d Theoretical base and development	1e CET materials course leaders project
Potential course structures ⇧	2a Course data collection	2b Education and training client populations	2c Prescription v negotiation	2d Course combinations	2e Huddersfield Polytechnic course evolution
Attitudinal surveys ⇧	3a Element priorities and sequences	3b Pre-course and in-course	3c Re-course and post-course	3d Economic v technological interaction	3e Population ranges
Element analysis ⇧	4a Educational technology professional practitioners	4b Times, scales and patterns	4c Continuity v modularity	4d Intra- or extra-mural	4e Course environment
Rolling finishing points ⇧	5a Trends and movements	5b Regulating authorities	5c Course models	5d Assessment evaluation and validation	5e ? !

Figure 1. *Educational technology course design criteria: factor analysis matrix*

of course design. Others include resource generation, support for specific subject teaching, learning theory and practice, and curriculum development. Much depends upon demand (node 2b) and who wants what, where and when! Our concern is: how can we provide meaningful educational technology courses in the future for very diverse populations? Traditionally, in keeping with other subject specialisms, educational technology has generally been provided by prescribed courses. We may now, because of diversity of demand of study times available and of environmental alternatives in which educational technology courses will need to be held, have to offer an individually negotiated course for each individual's need (node 2c). The prospect for different course combinations (node 2d) are legion, different elements of educational technology itself have been successfully combined in several well-documented applications. But this adoption is gradually becoming widespread in other subject areas. Simulations and games are available covering roles and events in both real-world situations, ie management and ecology, and for purely theoretical subjects such as mathematics and philosophy. Video-taped case studies provide a normal method of learning in both education and training.

The author's experience at Huddersfield Polytechnic during the past five years has included (node 2e) course evolution which has identified 21 'modules' (see Figure 2). These are commonly requested by pre-service and in-service teacher training courses, by industrial training, clinical tutor and overseas courses at certificate, diploma and degree levels taken at the Educational Technology Centre.

Attitudinal Surveys

Initially, in 1975, it seemed important to identify (node 3a) educational technology priorities and sequences, ie to rank opinions from vocationally different populations and to establish the most valuable strategies for dealing with selected modules within a course design. This presumed that a total understanding of priorities was possible at the pre-design stage of a course (nodes 3b and 3c). Gradually the author has come to realize that the very nature of the technology of education must allow creative change at all stages of a course, through to almost the final session. Hence, while a pre-course determination of individual priorities, obtained by interview, application form and short essay, may be highly desirable, the opportunity for in-course/re-course changes of direction are essential if course members are to receive the maximum benefit related to developing demands and interests. Post-course questionnaires and observations, if conducted objectively, reveal that such changes of priority do frequently take place as also does the emergence of peer group loyalty, attitude and priority. This information seems to help course tutors to understand themselves and their biases as much as the hidden truths of their courses.

Of considerable significance during the five-year period (since working with CET) has been the diametrically opposed movements of economic constraints with technological advancements (node 3d). While wholesale restriction has plagued education and training, the electronics and electro-mechanical research and development organizations have designed some of the most sophisticated hardware ever to be available to the public at large.

Course design in education that does not stay up-to-date, with at least the theoretical knowledge of such developments, is highly vulnerable. Understandable contempt from industrialists and frustration from academic colleagues in other subject areas, stems from the fact that they now receive a continuous bombardment of information literature on new developments. Within the limits of expenditure, and certainly within the capacity of educational technologists, a continuing effort must be made to stay abreast of new information. An

Communication media	Design and production techniques	Systems analysis applications
Visual communication: graphical media Visual communication: projected media Audio communication: media and distribution Reprographics: duplication and copying Small-scale closed-circuit television Multi-media packages Educational broadcasting	Tape-slide production Ciné photography and cinematography Studio television production Simulations: roles and events Educational games Project design: management and evaluation Evaluational models: theoretical and practical	Skills analysis using educational technology Micro-teaching design and implementation Programmed learning and teaching machines Feedback classroom systems A critique of audio-visual systems Ergonomics in classroom, workshop and laboratory General systems applied using educational technology

Figure 2. *Educational technology module synopsis*

'information service' based on library skills should be available in support of any realistic course.

Survey information is also regularly necessary giving a clear indication of new sources of course members (node 3e). Traditional practitioners in primary, secondary and tertiary education, and commercial and industrial training, are now being partnered by staff from libraries, museums, information services, and local and national government organizations. Educational technology has relevance to their vocational demands: all have a need for the knowledge and skills of communication, media presentation and systematic methods of information analysis.

It would be both presumptious and churlish to set out to design educational technology courses for the future without consultation with educational technology practitioners (node 4a). Some quarter of a century of experience has been stored covering a wide range of communication and learning objectives, and the necessary strategies and tactics to achieve them.

Truly, things have now changed: apart from the economic/technological mis-match mentioned above, the structure of future courses (node 4b) is going to offer new opportunities in the way in which courses are put together (node 4c), where they are held (node 4d), what constitutes a meaningful career-related experience, and how courses will be certified.

The author's experience in organizing a selective module structure for a wide variety of courses (node 4e) points toward the relationship between content and environment. Traditionally our courses have been institution based; exciting experiments are now emerging where experience is mixed directly with study, and the classroom, home, TV studio, real or simulated environment forms the setting for learning by doing (a version of educational technology 'on-the-job' training – a technique known to industrial training for many years). How does one reach a satisfactory course design with so many factors interacting on each other? The rapid obsolescence of the technology in education and the continuingly deeper insights into human behaviour will be with us, one suspects, whatever the state of the economy.

Rolling Finishing Points

In the new science of 'futures' the aim is to achieve a rolling finishing point (node 5a), ie (as in surf riding) to reach a wave of development and to stay near the crest of activity at any point in time. The analogy has faults, of course, but the concept is fundamentally sound, bearing in mind the continuous information flow to which educational technologists are prone. Yet even in states of hyper-change, there are (node 5b) regulating authorities. Fortunately, guidelines are published for many of the new course structures, ie CNAA, BEC, TEC, CET, CGLI, as well as by institutions for their own forms of certification. These are very helpful in the design of courses, especially where submission for validation precedes permission to run the course (node 5c).

New prospects are continuously emerging for modes of assessment and evaluation (node 5d)., including by observed simulation, peer group, experiential journal, and computer interaction. With rolling finishing points, however, we may expect to see the emergence of up-dating revisions at much more frequent intervals for curricula, application and evaluation. Appropriate educational technology can demand no less.

References

AETT (1979) *Register of Members* (Corporate and Individual). Association for Educational and Training Technology.

CNAA (1978) *Guidance on the Validation of Courses which make Significant Use of Resource-Based Learning.* CNAA, London.

Course Leaders Manual (1973) *Support Materials for Courses in Educational Technology.* Council for Educational Technology.

Crosland, A (1967) First meeting of the National Council for Educational Technology. *The Times Educational Supplement,* 2 June.

Howarth, T (ed) (1977) *Guide to Careers in Education.* Nelson.

Howe, A (ed) (1980) *International Yearbook of Educational and Instructional Technology.* Kogan Page, London.

National Diploma in Educational Technology (1979) *Guidelines and Regulations for Prospective Providing Bodies.* Council for Educational Technology.

Tucker, R N (1979) *The Organization and Management of Educational Technology.* Croom Helm.

Visual Education (1980) Degrees and diplomas etc. (February.)

Wright, J W (ed) (1979) *Courses Leading to Qualifications in Educational Technology.* Council for Educational Technology.

6.4 Learning by Tram

Mia A Lezer
University of Amsterdam

Abstract: A project used by the Teacher Training Department of the University of Amsterdam. It intensively involves student teachers with a small group of secondary school pupils. It is a valuable learning experience for the student teachers.

Learning by Tram

Since the mid-1950s, teacher training for secondary school teachers in the Netherlands has been organized according to an academic statute. This gives the universities precious little time, and no means of rejecting unsuitable candidates, if they have attended the required minimum number of hours. This statute is, though, soon to be amended after which teacher training will take several months instead of 150 hours.

The learning by tram project is used by the teacher training department of the University of Amsterdam because:

☐ it takes only one day;
☐ it involves student teachers intensively with a small group of secondary school pupils;
☐ it gives them an idea of some of the skills needed for project teaching, something never experienced during their own school days;
☐ it is the kind of teaching we expect to be practised at most schools in the future;
☐ it greatly affects students.

In project teaching and learning, pupils go out of the classroom to collect facts from real life experiences. They then go back to libraries and the classroom to compare and digest their findings. Teachers of several disciplines have to co-operate to assist them.

In learning by tram, one student teacher goes with a group of about four secondary school pupils. They have a workbook full of information and problems – about economic, social and ecological aspects of life in the big city, public transport, and people's behaviour. Most of them relate in one way or another to the tram.

To solve these problems they have to work together, observe well, use their imagination, initiative, creativity and the three Rs. Problems vary from simple to very complicated, and are suitable for pupils aged from 11 to 15, from all kinds of secondary schools. The workbook is produced by the Amsterdam Public Transport Authority and is regularly revised. A workbook about national public transport is soon to be published.

Each group chooses its own itinerary through Amsterdam and the workbook. Their experiences are totally different, and it is a very forceful reminder that a class is not to be regarded as a group of clones.

The pupils start the day as an outing; it is necessary to get them to work. Our students have been instructed to make the day enjoyable, but to ensure that the work is completed. The coffee bar, park, station or, indeed, the tram, rather than the classroom, is the learning environment. They all return to our teacher training institute, where they compare findings and work them out on large sheets.

After this day out, student teachers report having learned a lot about the pupils:

☐ how they live and learn;
☐ what they like and dislike;
☐ how they should be treated in order to get them to work cheerfully.

We hope they will remember this for a long time.

6.5 Utilizing Educational Technology in Teacher Training: Preliminary Implications

Don M Beach
University of Texas at Arlington

Abstract: By using micro-teaching situations and video-taping those sessions, it is possible to focus on specific strengths and skills as well as weaknesses. The paper shows the value of such a procedure and provides descriptive data regarding the success of such a process with changes in trainee behaviour.

Educational Technology in Teacher Training

The training of professionals in a number of fields is aimed at providing training in a realistic setting. Through the use of technology, particularly the use of video-tape recording systems, it is possible to establish simulated situations and record trainee responses on tape for later analysis.

By using micro-teaching situations, where a student conducts a short lesson for a few students in a seven to 10-minute time period, it is possible to focus on specific skills and assess strengths as well as weaknesses. Data collected over a period of time can document professional growth of the individual and show the effect of instruction in terms of skills learned and mastered.

In the teacher education programme at the University of Texas at Arlington, senior students in the secondary (high school) certification programme have two opportunities to develop a micro-teach. The micro-teach consists of a 'class' of six members of the course. The teacher then teaches students within the college age group. The lesson is seven to 10 minutes long and focuses on four critical teaching skills: set induction (the ability to prepare a class for learning, to establish proper frames of reference), questioning skills, stimulus variation, and closure (the ability to bring the learning activity to a close).

At the end of the seven to 10-minute teach, the class completes an evaluation form. This form is also completed by the person who did the micro-teaching session, by the university instructor, and by an independent observer who sees nothing but the replaying of the tape and has not been involved in the total instructional process.

Therefore, at the end of one micro-teaching session the student who did the actual teach has four pieces of information: a self-evaluation, peer evaluation, instructor evaluation, and an outside observer evaluation. This critique is then processed and the person plans for the second micro-teach, using the information from the evaluation form. The teacher tries to improve in each of the categories from the first teach.

The data collected from these microteaching situations over the last three semesters shows that there is a significant increase in the teaching ability of the students when measured by the evaluation instrument and when given detailed scores of the first teach situation. Six classes have participated in the microteaching sessions. Half of each group was given detailed feedback on performances in the microteaching session and subsequent instruction and suggestions on how to correct the areas of concern. The other half of the group was allowed to view their video-tapes but was not given any detailed critique, only numerical ratings.

Preliminary findings would indicate that those students who received detailed critiques and instruction (three classes: 67 students) scored significantly higher the second time they did their microteach. Those students who received no detailed numerical ratings on their microteach evaluation forms and recieved no detailed remarks or subsequent instruction did not make significant gains in their second microteaching session. The scores of the students with detailed critiques of the microteaching episode showed significant gains in the second microteach at the 95 per cent confidence interval. The students who only received numerical ratings did not show a significant gain in scores on the second microteach session.

The use of the video-taping system makes the critiquing of sessions available for several persons. How those critiques are completed can make a significant difference in changes in trainee behaviour.

Workshop Report
6.6 Learning Materials for In-Service Training

Betty Hollinshead
Manchester Polytechnic

Organizer's Account

The theme of the ETIC Conference is 'Educational Technology to the year 200 AD'. This workshop looked at one small aspect of in-service training and made some suggestions of possible approaches in the next 10 years. Participants were asked to consider the following situation by working in a two-stage pyramid system and to discuss their suggested solutions in a plenary session.

1. A number of institutions have staff who are concerned to:
    (a) enhance their approach to teaching through lessons, demonstrations and practical work,
    (b) wish to introduce other approaches whilst recognizing the need for students to achieve a considerable number of objectives in a relatively limited time.

2. Those staff who are employed in institutions in Area A find it extremely difficult to obtain release for in-service work. The situation varies in Area B in that some staff are able to attend two days per term whilst others are limited to half a day or one day.

What in-service approach would you suggest to meet the perceived needs identified in 1. whilst, at the same time, taking into account the varying difficulties of staff release as stated in 2.?

Discussion in a plenary session from pyramiding highlighted the following points:

☐ Differing in-service approaches, such as: independent learning, distance learning; central institutional or teacher centre provision; interchange of providers with participants in colleges; courses to be mounted in 'free' time — Saturdays and between 4.00 pm and 7.00 pm; work through college-based staff development tutor.
☐ A need to know ability, knowledge and experience of recipients, as well as budget constraints.
☐ A need to achieve student, as well as staff, objectives.
☐ An assumption that motivation of recipients would be high.
☐ A possibility of staff who could be released on in-service developing self-study materials for those who cannot.

This discussion was then followed by some detail of the approach used in the CET 'Designs for Teaching' project which had at an early stage identified the aspects given in the simulation workshop exercise.

For this project, undertaken by the Staff Development Unit, Manchester Polytechnic, a systems approach was used to identify perceived further education lecturer needs, to determine resources and constraints, and finally to decide the appropriate strategy for project materials which were then used in a pilot study for evaluation, revision and implementation.

The systems approach to in-service work allows logical and organized response to immediate needs. It is one which will become more essential as rapid incorporation of radical technical innovation in the home and at work leads students to expect their teachers to make use of, and keep pace with, the modern developments they have already met in their commercial, industrial and domestic life.

This rapid change is occurring at a time when resources for in-service are likely to diminish. Already greater stringency makes it very difficult for some further education lecturers to obtain more than one day release for in-service work. Indeed, the initial survey carried out for the 'Designs for Teaching' project indicated that in some authorities no release is possible at all. However, it is encouraging to note that college-based in-service work is being supported in a number of colleges with a staff member designated as the 'Staff Development' tutor.

It therefore seems appropriate that in-service activities should be flexible enough to take into account not only the various professional needs of staff but also the various constraints of day release. In any consideration of patterns for future in-service, colleagues may wish to take into account the format used in the 'Designs for Teaching' materials of the Council for Educational Technology project.

The materials consist of workshop modules: (i) lessons and lectures; (ii) independent learning; (iii) practical work, demonstration or project; (iv) small group teaching; (v) team teaching.

Each of the modules is complete in itself, and is designed to take half a day, except Module B which requires a full day or two half-days. The structure therefore allows for varying in-service course length, from half a day to three days.

In addition, recognizing that contact time is limited, not every aspect of each teaching method is included. It should therefore be looked on as a sensitizing

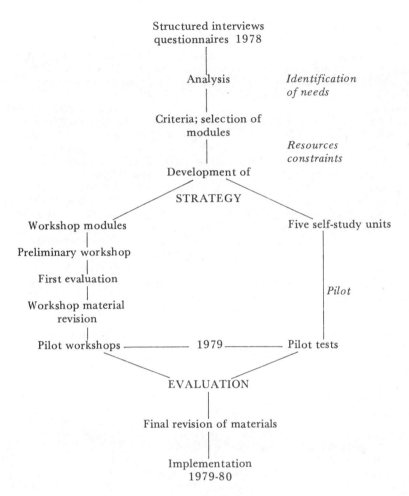

Structured interviews
questionnaires 1978

Analysis   *Identification
of needs*

Criteria; selection of
modules

                    *Resources
constraints*

Development of

STRATEGY

Workshop modules   Five self-study units

Preliminary workshop

First evaluation

Workshop material   *Pilot*
revision

Pilot workshops ———— 1979 ———— Pilot tests

EVALUATION

Final revision of materials

Implementation
1979-80

Figure 1.

exercise for further education college or local authority-based workshops with
the capacity to give more extended coverage. The materials are divided into an
organizer's manual as well as participants' materials, so that where appropriate,
the in-service organizers, who may either mount the workshop within a college or
of local authority level, have written material to assist in the effective organization,
clear presentation of content and maximum use of the modules.

Again, to overcome the time constraints and to reinforce workshop activities,
support material in the form of self-study units based on the workshop activities
and developing their respective themes a little further have also been produced.
The self-study units also stand alone as an alternative to the workshop materials
and already a number of further education lecturers have requested these, having
indicated that they were unable to attend workshop activities. This type of material
on its own may well have as great an impact and use as workshop activities, if not
more, and may be a necessary reinforcement tool to workshop activities where
long-term use is envisaged.

It is interesting to note that several colleagues who attended 'Designs for Teaching' workshops over a year ago have indicated that they are finding the self-study units, based on the workshop activities, of greater use now and state that they will continue to do so in the long term. Several colleagues said they welcomed self-study units, since these enabled them to pass the information on to other interested colleagues.

G B Shaw said: 'teach a man anything and he will never learn'. It is recognized that self-study units have the advantage of allowing students to work at their own pace, in their own way, as well as allowing them the opportunity of focusing on their chosen areas of study in any particular module. This applies just as much to learning materials for in-service training as to self-study units for students. Looking to the future, self-study units based on print and/or tape/slide, may well be replaced by computer-based packages. Squadron Leader Upham (1979) states that British Airways and Barclaycard, both of whom have on-line terminal systems, have claimed significant advantages in computer-based training. Upham indicates that 'the problems of skill transfer are removed, reduced training times are the norm, accommodation and travelling expenses are reduced . . . and training materials are more readily up-dated'. As inter-active systems increase, then other advantages such as immediate feedback, a check list on progress and increased motivation follow.

Learning materials based on individual needs, using methodology which reflects current and future technological developments, have a place in any in-service programme. Evidence from the 'Designs for Teaching' project indicates that lecturers not only see self-study materials as being of use in their own staff development in-service programmes, but anticipate that far more independent and distance learning will take place in their courses for students. However, such developments are not the panacea of all time and, as shown by the Open University, will still require the interaction and tutorial input of staff with student, and student with student. Will tele-conferencing and phono-viewing answer this need?

Finally, the 'Designs for Teaching' materials give an example of a 'flexible' in-service mode to meet a variety of needs:

- ☐ Workshop materials of organizer's pack and participants' materials for workshops to run centrally or in college.
- ☐ Workshops of varying lengths of half a day to three days.
- ☐ Self-study units to reinforce the workshops, or to stand on their own for those staff unable to obtain release.

It is within the context of self-study that developments in micro-electronics and related communication sciences may well extend in-service training for the individual lecturer.

Participant's Comments

Ken Adderley, *Brighton Polytechnic*

This problem-centred workshop used to good effect during the first 50 minutes the pyramid format popularized by Graham Gibbs of the Open University. Participants worked first in pairs then in fours and then in plenary. The last part of the workshop (30 minutes) was given over to an explanation of Betty Hollinshead's tried and tested solution to the problem set, a solution which had received the backing of the Council for Educational Technology.

The task presented to us was to devise a method of providing in-service training in teaching skills, which could accommodate a wide variation in 'release' time ranging from two days per term to zero.

The varied backgrounds of the participants and the open nature of the brief produced a variety of interpretations of the problem posed. Some directed their attention to induction course provision, some to the needs of experienced teachers and some, unsuccessfully, to the framework of their overseas environment (eg Australia, where differential treatment of staff release time is reputedly unknown).

All participants quickly recognized the economy of producing dual purpose materials for use either by individuals or by small groups, but went on to suggest various other strategies, eg:

☐ To appoint a staff development officer.
☐ To identify pockets of expertise in the locality.
☐ To get teachers who can be released to prepare materials for those who cannot be so released.
☐ To offer group sessions in the evening so that most teachers could attend.

The participants were well-motivated by the problem's realism and the pyramid format but tended to impose constraints based on their own experience. The notion of making a market research plan to identify the needs of teachers did not occur to us, nor did our discussion progress far enough for us to consider planning for limited field trials, revision, full implementation and evaluation.

These features were explained during the plenary, but could have been extracted from us to better effect by guided discussion (a workshop strategy which would have maintained the impetus gained in the first 50 minutes). This would then have formed an identifiable foundation on which to base Betty's explanation of the materials devised by CET/Manchester Polytechnic and now in use. What a pity these materials were not available for inspection during the session.

Reference

Upham, J A (1979) Computer-based training: thoughts on the way ahead. *RAF Education Bulletin,* 17 (autumn). RAF School of Education.

Section 7:
Informal Learning –
Systems and Learners

7.1 Open Systems for Open Colleges from 1980

Pat Noble
Garnett College of Education (Technical)

Abstract: After reviewing current flexible learning systems in post-compulsory education, some indication is given of the potential market for alternative learning systems in the light of likely social and economic changes. There will be a need for educational technologists to keep aware of curriculum developments to fulfil their consultancy role in further education.

Openness in College Instructional Systems

Openness as an attitude to the educational role of colleges can be identified in learning systems, approaches to staffing and use of other college resources. There is already evidence of openness in post-compulsory education in the universities, polytechnics and colleges of further education that is so extraordinarily diverse in levels of studies .. . . in modes of attendance . . . in students' ages . . . in course emphasis . . . and in types of college (DES, 1978).

Colleges have already proved quite enterprising in devising instructional systems. Over the next 20 years these may prove capable of bringing education to the post-16 age-group who are currently underrating it, dismissing it – or finding its barriers too great. Most courses are offered full- or part-time with lectures and formal classes for 10-30 students, but workshop techniques are extending beyond craft and laboratory skills into the fields of communication studies and numeracy (Sproule, 1974; Sands, 1977). Directed self-teaching, based in college libraries or departmental resource centres, uses both book and non-book materials (Negus, 1977; November, 1978; Sheridan, 1978).

Learning-on-demand and learning-by-appointment have also found a place ready for the 1980s. The sale of time and facilities in a learning centre using largely programmed materials has been extended to accommodate the administration of Flexistudy and adult literacy with their negotiable tutorial arrangements. With the help of outreach workers, colleges have shown an openness in staffing and location of courses. Learning-on-demand courses are described in Mackie (1975), Foster (1979) and Albrecht and Spencer (1976).

The Demand for Openness

Only 10 per cent of the 16-18 age group are attending full-time courses in colleges, and allowing for those remaining in school 60 per cent to 70 per cent remain unprovided for. Of young women in this age group, barely over seven per cent are given day release — and the level only reaches 30 per cent for young men. Instructional systems need to be devised for these inadequately trained adults, especially as between six per cent and nine per cent of this age group are already among the unemployed and are likely to remain so given modest skills, little experience and waning self-esteem. Some measures of open learning are found in recently devised courses of vocational preparation.

Over the next 20 years the two to five million unemployed in the UK and those seeking re-training will be a significant element in potential demand for access to resources at present allocated to colleges on behalf of their *enrolled* student body. Yet their demand may be for more casual, episodic access, for 'non-work' oriented opportunities to learn, for variants of what is now found in the programmes of community self-help groups, the public library service, university extra-mural departments, the WEA and post-experience courses from the Open University. Youthaid is studying this area of need for the Further Education Curriculum Review and Development Unit. Educational technologists will be exploring how learning systems can provide for those who need to substitute their own labour for that of expensive specialists in home maintenance, home management for the old, gardening and the micro-horticulture of the window-box . . . How far can we harness the new technologies and the most promising of the known learning systems to meet these far from trivial demands?

Meeting the Demand: Systems with Potential

Instructional systems include information transmission, learning activities, elements of diagnosis and counselling (from tutoring or computer-managed sub-systems), and concern for student motivation including knowledge of results and formal assessment.

Distance learning materials will surely continue to contribute to information transmission and to the provision of learning activities through self-teaching workbooks. These have extended well beyond the course-units of the Open University, as in the Polymaths course (Kellaway, 1978), post-experience courses for educational technologists and, under the aegis of the Technician Education Council, the vocational preparation of technicians (Coffey, 1978).

The part to be played by recorded sound is by no means yet fully exploited. Audio-tapes can carry instructional messages and tutorial support to wider audiences and there is considerable evidence that the self-teaching audio-tutorial is acceptable and effective over a range of age-groups, subject areas, academic levels and for a range of learning activities from reading-to-learn to practical work (Fisher and MacWhinney, 1976). Mackie (1977) specifically acknowledged the role of audio-commentary in bridging diagrammatic and practical work. As the audio-tutorial was enlisted for the laboratory in biology early on — and there is further evidence that students can master practical skills with self-teaching materials (Noble, Holt and Stacey, 1979) — then the use of laboratories-by-appointment becomes an extension of existing learning-by-appointment schemes. Even the post-experience development of the teaching profession can derive from predominantly sound broadcast materials; in the colleges, adult evening schools offer tutorials and discussion groups.

Local radio stations have found ways of putting people in touch with experts and educationalists; they collaborate to help with the intense revision for public examinations and the urgent search for college places. There may, however, be limits to the extent that students can be expected to take the initiative in tutorial relationships; not all learners are *ready* to use an open system.

Other presentation devices may help to meet the demand for open learning. Iterative, gaming devices demonstrate their acceptability in leisure centres; there is evidence that their overtly educational counterparts are equally acceptable – even without coin-in-the-slot control. Linked to VDUs, the instructional potential of such devices is perhaps more potent than mere display of banked information on living-room screens.

Students with a preference for distance learning may never need to attend at the providing institution. A most interesting model of an open (in the sense of responsive) course was reported by Baume and Hipwell of North East London Polytechnic (1977). Distance learning materials were prepared for use on location on oil rigs; these materials were then augmented by the comments of practitioners of the developing technology – the course was expanded by its members. For post-experience courses, this model may have much to recommend it, though it may pose problems for administrators.

The demand for openness in no way denies a student preference for social learning or need for tutorial support. Mature students can undoubtedly establish informal networks by telephone and can arrange meetings to prevent the isolation that can accompany home-based study. College architects, however, have rarely been able to provide informal meeting places in circulation areas; refectories and libraries can as rarely offer space for impromptu seminars!

Certainly in the early stages of any course of independent or home-based study, the learner is likely to need support to avoid 'discontinuance'. Even the chatty printout from a computer-managed system may not carry conviction. Devising and sustaining student support systems may prove the biggest challenge of open learning – and the one where educational technologists already engaged in staff development may be best placed to make contributions (Noble, 1979, 1980).

The Administration and Staffing of Open Learning

Where college management seeks to implement an open college philosophy, there will be administrative and staffing implications deriving from curriculum innovations.

Innovations in the form of new courses – basic education, pre-retirement, adult education – merely compete in understandable ways for resources. Openness that affects the timetabling of full-time and part-time students, that gives them discretion in pacing and location for their studies, begins to impinge on administrative procedures, on the designation of rooms as resource centres (additional to library provision), and on the use of facilities such as language laboratories and computer terminals previously seen as departmental territory. Openness that entails the enrolling of linked course students, the provision of learning-by-appointment facilities or the setting up of correspondence courses of directed private study (generating and marketing, learning materials by the course team) (Jones and Wylie, 1977), strains the current bases of educational accountancy. The individually responsive, outreaching system proposed by Farnes and his colleages (1975), involving institutional collaboration, has not been realized but collaborative systems are being attempted (Coffey, 1978; Hills, Lincoln and Turner, 1977). College collaboration with open courses offered by the broadcast media (Salkeld, 1975; Stringer, 1979) suggest considerable grounds for optimism, particularly if technological and copyright developments bring home-access to educational recordings. Explorations of teletext potential are equally encouraging (Anderson, 1980).

Most moves towards openness in educational provision seem to demand new skills from staff. Learning-on-demand enhances the tutorial role of academic staff at the expense of their information transmission role (in which they will have invested their professionalism); informal evidence from Flexistudy schemes, and self-teaching located in departmental resource centres, indicates that whilst the basis of staffing is voluntary, their job satisfaction can be enhanced. In 1977, however, Medland mentioned instructor boredom as a disadvantage of a course built on relatively tutor-proof materials. The burden of routine supervision can be overcome to some extent by home-based study, especially where new technologies lend themselves to take-away learning.

The availability of educational technologists within colleges appears to be growing, not least as a result of the post-experience courses. This process of staff development results in knowledge of open learning systems and of the design and management of resource-based learning being available to college decision-makers.

References

Albrecht, A and Spencer, D (1976) *Flexastudy.* Further Education Staff College: Coombe Lodge Information Bank No 1119.

Anderson, J S A (1980) Exploring teletext as a resource. *Programmed Learning and Educational Technology,* 17, 1, pp 27-35.

Baume, D and Hipwell, J (1977) Adaptable correspondence studies for offshore engineers — a course that learns. *Teaching at a Distance,* 9, pp 27-35.

Coffey, J (1978) *Development of an Open Learning System in Further Education.* Council for Educational Technology Working Paper 15, London.

Department of Education and Science (1978) *Report on Education,* 94, p 1.

Farnes, N, McCormick, R and Calder, J A (1975) A proposed system for mass continuing education. In Evans, L and Leedham, J (eds) *Aspects of Educational Technology* IX, pp 74-95. Kogan Page, London.

Fisher, K M and MacWhinney, B (1976) AV autotutorial instruction: a review of evaluative research. *A V Communication Review,* 24, 3, pp 229-61.

Foster, J (1979) Learning by appointment. *Educational Technology in the Community.* pp 55-6. Scottish Community Education Centre.

Hills, P J, Lincoln, L and Turner, L P (1977) *Evaluation of Tape-Slide Guides for Library Instruction.* British Library: Research and Development Report 5378HC.

Jones, L H and Wylie, A W (1977) A case for directed private study. *Education and Training,* pp 67-9. March.

Kellaway, F W (1978) Polymaths for the mature student. *The Times Educational Supplement,* p 27. 7 July.

Mackie, A (1975) Consumer-orientated programmed learning in adult education. In Evans, L F and Leedham, J (eds) *Aspects of Educational Technology* IX, pp 110-17. Kogan Page, London.

Mackie, A (1977) Appointment learning, the serial class and the emergent role of audio exposition. *Independent Learning Systems for Technicians,* pp 65-71. Society for Electronic and Radio Technicians.

Medland, K G (1977) Naval experience of free-running systems of training. *Independent Learning Systems for Technicians,* pp 53-8. Society for Electronic and Radio Technicians.

Negus, P (1977) Individual learning in economics. *The Social Science Teacher,* 7, 2, pp 1-6.

Noble, P (1979) Providing environments for resource-based learning in colleges of further education. In Page, G T and Whitlock, Q (eds) *Aspects of Educational Technology* XIII, pp 87-93. Kogan Page, London.

Noble, P (1980) *Resource-Based Learning in Post Compulsory Education.* Kogan Page, London.

Noble, W C, Holt, G and Stacey, L M (1979) Comparison of the efficacy of slide-tape and cine-loop as teaching aids for a microbiological technique. *Journal of Biological Education,* 13, 3, pp 204-6.

November, P J (1978) The tape-tutorial-document package. *Studies in Higher Education,* 3, 1, pp 91-5.

Salkeld, P E (1975) BBC living decisions in family and community. *Ideas Series 4,* 30. pp 230-6.

Sands, T (1977) The development of a mathematics workshop. *Continuing Education News,* 4, pp 4-5.

Sheridan, P (1978) A tape-lecture course in electro chemistry. *Education in Chemistry,* 15, 4, p 109.

Sproule, A (1974) Language for the working world. *The Times Educational Supplement,*
    p 28. 8 November.
Stringer, D (1979) *Make it Count.* IBA, London.

7.2   The Potential of Packaged Learning for Meeting Changing Demands for Education and Training

Clive Neville
The Council for Educational Technology for the United Kingdom

Abstract: The paper draws on experience gained from three recent CET activities to try to answer some of the questions that would be posed by any attempt to increase rapidly the provision of adult education and training through packaged learning.

During the 1980s the demand for retraining, professional updating and for vocational qualifications in the United Kingdom is likely to increase as the new technologies are introduced into industry and commerce. As patterns of employment change, demands for adult education and instruction to support leisure activities will also increase. There is likely, for demographic and economic reasons, to be a re-structuring of the educational system to make pre- and post-compulsory education less the responsibility of local schools than at present.

It is not the aim of this paper to defend these assertions but, assuming them to be reasonable, to assess the potential of one particular solution, the provision of education and training through packaged learning, to meet the problems that the changes outlined above would cause. The Council for Educational Technology, through three of its current activities, is gathering information which, within the limited contexts of the specific activities, provides indications of the weaknesses and strengths of the approach when applied to meeting large-scale needs in the framework of a decentralized system.

The problem generally stated is: can we provide adequate education or training when and where it is required by an individual? The three CET activities to be discussed are all concerned with providing in-service training to teachers or lecturers. These form a potentially large audience, but one for which the needs are seldom the same at any one time, and for which conventional methods of training (ie attendance at taught courses) are increasingly impractical.

The DOLMINSET project (Development of Learning Materials for the In-service Education of Teachers) was set up to test the assertion that a Local Education Authority (LEA) has the means to design, produce, administer and evaluate training packages for its own teachers (CET London, 1977). The second project (here referred to as the TEC associated project) was designed to explore the potential of in-house and in-service training workshops supported by centrally produced materials. The third project – RADLMATS (Resources for Authors of Distance Learning Materials) is less advanced, but aims to demonstrate that the skills of producing effective distance learning materials can themselves be learnt from such materials.

None of the projects is designed, or funded, as a rigorous piece of research. Nevertheless it is hoped that the findings so far will give indications as to what the answers might be to key questions which might be asked about any system for the provision of packaged learning. These questions are as follows:

1. How is the training need to be diagnosed?
2. Who should, could or might meet the need by providing packaged learning?
3. Are the necessary skills and resources available to that group?
4. What is the likely cost of producing the packages, and who will pay? (Can cost comparisons be made with other forms of provision of training?)
5. What information and dissemination methods are necessary to secure effective use of the packages?
6. What changes of role are implied by the change of training methods and are they acceptable to trainer, trainee and their employers?

There are, even in a largely decentralized system, occasions when centrally dictated changes determine a training need. Such was the case when the Technician Education Council decreed that course submissions made to them for validation should be expressed in behavioural objectives with correlative assessment schedules. Many staff in further education found themselves required to practice a technique for which they had had no training. Unfortunately, the TEC is not in a position to provide the training to meet the need it had created, and it was left to local institutions (notably the polytechnics), the four colleges of education (technical) and Coombe Lodge (the Further Education Staff College) to do what each could within its own resources. Only CET attempted a solution on a national scale, through the provision of a workshop pack for in-college training (CET, London). CET is not a central body for the monitoring and provision of in-service training generally and it only used the TEC created needs as an opportunity to test the potential of training materials.

It is difficult to point to any central body in the UK which could be said to have a brief to diagnose, and meet, or cause to be met, in-service training needs at a national level. The same could be said of most of the other training needs likely to arise in the near future, with the possible exceptions of the industrial training boards within their own terms. Lack of any central co-ordinating body is likely, therefore, to restrict considerably the ability of package learning to meet training needs.

When it comes to deciding who should produce the packages, the overwhelming factor appears to be the credibility the producer will have with the user. In a study undertaken by CET on the exchange of training materials between educational technology courses it has been found repeatedly that materials are bought by tutors because they know and respect the authors as authorities in educational technology. As part of DOLMINSET, in-service training materials produced outside of the pilot authorities have been tried and rejected, although all had been well received in the (basically similar) situations for which they were devised. The reasons given for rejection almost invariably indicate that some factor in the presentation could imply that the author comes from a situation different from that in which the user finds himself, and therefore lacks credibility. A highly structured and well-researched programme on questioning technique for teachers was rejected because of the middle-class accent and vocabulary of the children shown responding, rather than because the techniques shown were inapplicable.

It seems, then, that for packaged learning to be both economic in scale and acceptable to users, some compromise must be made. Production by a team or individuals too remote from the users' experience weakens the acceptability of the material. There are indications, also from DOLMINSET, and from the way the workshop materials produced by CET have been used, that this problem can to some extent be overcome by the mediation of the materials through a tutor, adviser or respected colleague. Moreover, the actual production by local teams of learning packages can in itself provide a powerful training experience for those involved, and this may justify what would otherwise appear to be an uneconomic scale of production and use.

Although the RADLMATS project has shown that effective training can be given in package writing, the 'respected authority' on the content of the training often does not possess the packaging skills, or access to the technical resources required, and most training packages are produced by a team combining the subject expert with programmers, and given access to technical facilities through the good offices of a commissioning agency. DOLMINSET experience has shown that this works well only if *all* parties concerned value the considerable commitment that must be made, and someone is given clear responsibility to co-ordinate the activity. That said, it is also clear that the necessary skills and resources can be mustered at all levels from national bodies, such as CET, to single educational institutions. The nature of the commitment is different, and CET, for example, has had to 'buy in' the expertise to design its TEC syllabus writers' pack and the 'Designs for Teaching' materials at a total cost of approximately £8,000. CET staff have acted only as co-ordinators between the designers, publishers and distributors. Conversely, within DOLMINSET schools are now producing packages for the in-service training of their own staff, and are using little more than encouragement from outside their own resources. However, the commitment of time the staff involved must make is enormous, and is at present in addition to their normal duties.

In short, at whatever level the preparation of packages is undertaken, the commitment of resources is considerable. The variable is the nature of the resources to be committed. It follows that if packaged learning is to make any sizeable contribution to meeting education and training needs, conscious decisions must be made at some level to divert resources to production, or to accept considerable add-on costs. No claim could be made from the CET project experience that packaged learning provides a cheaper alternative to conventional methods. It is different, not better, and so suited to solving different problems.

Comparative costing of training through packages with training by other methods is, to a certain extent, meaningless since it does not compare like with like except in the most superficial way. In addition, the package is seldom self-sufficient but is only one element in a training strategy. The DOLMINSET investigator has identified at least six different modes of use for packages in in-service training strategies and many more must exist. Nevertheless it is instructive to cost the production of a training package in terms which begin to allow comparisons with, say, taught courses, if only as a means to demonstrating the real cost of conventional training. It also serves as a device for highlighting the significance of value judgements when planning training. For example, a set of materials produced by one of the DOLMINSET authorities has been costed at £3,000 in real terms (that is, including the cost of the time of developers etc), and the cost of using the materials as intended is £1 per teacher/hour of training provided. The cost of providing similar training without the materials is £2.75 per teacher hour but there are no development costs. It would seem, therefore, that unless a great many teachers are to be trained (approximately 250 for six hours each) using the package, there will be no saving. In practice, the package is able to provide classroom observation on video-tape of the kind that could not be provided in reality to anywhere near 250 teachers, so that calculation of the 'break even point' becomes a matter of value judgements about how important that classroom observation is to the quality of the training provided.

Even so, once a commitment of the kind required to produce these materials *has* been made, it is obvious that irrespective of the quality of training, the greater the number of trainees trained the less the cost per trainee. It follows that the economic production and dissemination of packages will depend to an extent on the establishment of effective systems for information (about availability) and dissemination. There is at present no generally acceptable cataloguing service for many types of package (but see note after references), so that information is largely by word of mouth and chance encounter. Similarly, unless materials are commercially established they are often difficult to obtain. Many of the producers (eg LEAs or polytechnics) are not constituted as publishers and often find external demand for their materials an embarrassment. Newer methods of distribution, such as PRESTEL, optic fibre cable television, or even additional broadcasting channels may overcome some of the logistical and technical problems of distribution, but will raise new problems of payment and copyright. Poor information and distributory networks already inhibit the wide use of packages and perpetuate the cottage industry approach to production. Advisers, training officers and staff developers seem to be the key agents in obtaining effective use of packages within the present system of education and training. This is because, in effect, they control the extent and nature of the training available. It is not clear who the equivalent agents are in informal education. For advisers, training officers, etc, who have a training as well as an advisory function, the use of packaged training poses a threat to their perceived role. DOLMINSET has again shown that, even where an adviser has been involved in the production of a package, he finds it difficult to accept that it will operate effectively without his presence. Conversely, the difficulties experienced by the distance learner are now well understood, though not necessarily surmountable, and the least tractable of these are those which stem from a strong feeling that truly satisfactory learning results only from the kind of complex personal interaction between teacher and taught which is impossible to package. Certainly when the aim of the training has been primarily attitude change, didactic self-instructional material alone has not proved successful. It has, however, proved a useful component in a programme designed for self-help, problem-oriented groups providing the confidence to practise new techniques once the significance of these is recognized. The acceptability by trainees of packaged training appears from all three of the CET projects to depend almost entirely on the extent to which the materials relate to a need perceived by the trainee. If motivation is high, the difficulties and inconveniences of working from packages are surmounted, and even poorly constructed materials are welcomed and used with success, as has been shown by the earliest trial versions of the RADLMATS materials. Where the user is poorly motivated, the materials, of course, stand less chance of maintaining contact than other potentially more coercive forms of training. However, 'contact' does not necessarily imply effective training in either case.

The change of role for the material producer meets with varying degrees of acceptability. Where the producer had no previous access to his potential audience the issue is largely one of confidence to commit his 'teaching' abilities to programme form. From the projects' experience, there does not appear to be a strong correlation between being a good classroom teacher or trainer and being a good programmer. It is not surprising, therefore, that those who enjoy face-to-face teaching often find changing to package production unsatisfactory, even disorientating.

Present indications from employers (in this case the LEAs) are that they are less concerned with, or are unwilling to make judgements about, the relative quality of training provided by packages. As a strategy for getting more training done in the employee's time, rather than on release, packaged learning has distinct appeal to employers. If packaged learning is to become a widely used method of professional updating and upgrading, then the equivalent of 'release time' for that training will have to be negotiated between employers and employees.

So far, therefore, the CET projects appear to indicate that packaged learning has considerable potential to meet the new training needs, even for a decentralized education and training system, and that the resources and skills to provide the packages exist. However, for economic reasons, some central co-ordinating mechanism will be necessary. Whether such a mechanism is acceptable, and can be funded, is a matter on which at present the projects offer no evidence.

References

CET (1977) *The Generation and Use of Learning Materials for the In-service Education of Teachers – a Discussion Document.* London.
CET *TEC Syllabus Writers Workshop Materials* (available free from CET). London.

Note: Specialized catalogues exist. For example *The International Yearbook of Educational and Instructional Technology,* published by Kogan Page, contains a list of programmed materials on the market in the UK; The British Library publishes the *British Catalogue of Audio Visual Materials,* the first experimental edition 1979 comprising largely commercially available teaching resources; The British Universities' Film Council publishes *HELPIS* (Higher Education Learning Programmes Information Service), latest edition 1978, listing teaching materials for higher education.

7.3 The Design of Instructor's Notes in Package Training Materials

Mike Tyrrell and Rebecca Davies
The Institute of Chartered Accountants in England and Wales

Abstract: The Institute of Chartered Accountants has, since 1975, been developing a range of package training materials for qualified accountants and their staff, intended to provide all the materials needed to run a course. They were a response, during a period of rapid change in the accounting profession, to a demand for flexible and cost-effective training materials.

Introduction

A major development in accountancy has been the production of a comprehensive range of training material. This development reflects a substantial increase in training demand within the accountancy profession, and is a result of rapid changes in an accountant's work and professional firms' needs for comprehensive training programmes if they are to attract capable staff and students.

The Institute of Chartered Accounts in England and Wales, along with other accountancy bodies, found that only about 10 per cent of its total membership attended any of its conventional courses. This encouraged the development of package material within the Institute and the basis of this work is described elsewhere (Tyrrell, 1978). The present programme includes 27 titles and the volume of business is expanding, so that in 1980 the package sales turnover is likely to exceed £200,000.

Two ideas lay behind the package concept. First, the use of video enabled a good lecturer to be seen and heard all over the country without having to repeat his performance. Second, case studies and practical exercises which, to be successful, often take considerable development time, could be designed on a co-operative basis by accountants through the Institute. While this material could be used without guidance by experienced trainers, the likely number of inexperienced presenters suggested that careful guidance was necessary if packages were to be handled competently. This guidance was contained in a document called the 'Leader's Guide', which has subsequently evolved into the key document for any of the packages produced by the Institute, whether supported by video, audio or just print material alone.

The early Leader's Guides had followed the layout of conventional course synopses. However, as package courses became an important feature complementing Institute courses, efforts were made to secure outside consultancy help. This greatly improved the overall presentation of the material, but production delays and the small-sized runs meant that costs were high. Some users had reservations, particularly that excessively high standards of physical presentation might actually detract from the document's training value. With the development of a specialist section to deal with package courses in 1977, the opportunity was taken to design Leader's Guides internally.

Leader's Guide

A few sophisticated training departments want just the video films. These apart, users' reactions suggest that the Leader's Guide has become the crucial element of a package course and therefore its design is all-important. The production process itself reflects this importance in that the Leader's Guide is usually drafted first and everything else follows.

A few individuals have, however, insisted that the Leader's Guide is too elaborate. The impression is that these critics are experienced trainers who wish, for their own reasons, to make substantial changes to the packages.

The growing importance of the Leader's Guide, and the criticism of over-elaborateness, prompted a careful assessment of the approach. This assessment involved four questions:

1. Is there a clearly defined approach to the design of the Leader's Guide?
2. If so, what specific design principles are actually used in practice?
3. Do users feel that the current Leader's Guide approach meets the primary objectives of package courses: that of significantly reducing preparation time?
4. Are there specific changes to the present approach that users want to see?

Design Approach — Content

A package course should include all the material required to run the course. Too much material, however, will give the inexperienced presenter difficulties in

Year published	Number published	Video based	Word processed	Time and activity table	Detailed talk outlines	OHP slide style		Preliminary notes				Questions/ answers for leaders	Updating service
						effective visual	other	Video equipment	OHP slides	Case study	Audio tape		
		%	%	%	%	%	%	%	%	%	%	%	%
1975	2	100	–	–	50	–	100	100	50	50	–	–	–
1976	2*	100	–	–	50	–	100	100	100	50	–	–	–
1977	6	50	–	83	67	17	83	–	50	–	–	–	–
1978	8	–	25	100	88	75	25	–	100	63	17	–	63
1979	5	–	60	100	80	100	–	–	100	60	–	–	40
1980	2	–	100	100	100	100	–	–	100	50	–	50	100

Per cent expressed as per cent of number published in year.   * Practical Auditing modules (publication period 1976-1977) included under one publication date of 1976.

Table 1. *Analysis of Leader's Guide content*

selecting what he needs to use for his course. Thus the content selection of the Leader's Guide is likely to be crucial to the success of a package. Table 1 analyzes the content of Leader's Guides produced since 1975. This shows that the content has been increased in one or two areas, particularly in suggesting ways of mounting the course.

The first Leader's Guides were designed as instructions for the users of video-tapes. With the advent of non-video packages the Leader's Guide was enlarged to include detailed talk outlines usually with reproductions of the OHP slides.

Later additions were usually a result of difficulties identified at validations. The number of inexperienced presenters led us to expand the preliminary notes concerning the use of package materials.

Unfamiliarity with the effective use of OHP slides led to the re-introduction of notes on their use. This time, however, the emphasis was on the ideas behind the designs rather than the use of the hardware.

Controversial or difficult material may lead trainees to ask awkward questions which the leader cannot answer directly. Hence the introduction of the question and answers in 1980 for current cost-accounting.

Since the trainer needs to be sure that his course is up-to-date despite changes in legislation and advice, a formal updating service became an integral part of many packages. This service is easier to provide now because the Leader's Guide text of recent packages is maintained on a word processor. At any one time, a small number of Leader's Guides are printed. When major changes occur these are accommodated by changing the relevant pages on the word processor. One side-effect of introducing word processing has been the use of office litho machines rather than a professional printer. As the feel of the paper, but not the visual effect, is reduced in quality, users appear more prepared to annotate their copy when preparing to give the package.

Talk Outlines — Page Analysis

The original concept of a video package had been to encapsulate a lecture. Very rapidly it was realized that the expense of the medium and the boredom of talking heads required a stronger reason for video use. Such justification was found for practical auditing when it was necessary to take trainees 'out' of the classroom to see the work done on client premises. The video lectures were then replaced by talk outlines in the Leader's Guide, together with overhead projector slides. The production of non-video packages gave greater emphasis to the Leader's Guide, particularly the page layout for the talk outlines and the visual sequence of the OHP slides. The talk outlines were designed so that a presenter can use them as a prompt (but not a fully-written speech), while still giving all the relevant background.

The page layout of a recent Leader's Guide is illustrated in Figure 1. Providing all relevant material in lecture note form involves reconciling two very different objectives. For this reason, some trainers criticized the Leader's Guide as over-elaborate.

The page layout is designed by identifying the key points of the lecture. Devices such as bold dots are used to highlight these in roman type. Subsidiary material is in italics and this includes stage directions and notes on examples. These are deliberately worded so that individuals will not be tempted to read them aloud. Wherever a slide is shown, whether for the first time or otherwise, the relevant part of the slide is reproduced in the material. A photographic origination process ensures that the quarter-size reproductions in the Guide use the same artwork as the slide itself.

We assumed that the effectiveness of the layout depends on how easily a presenter can look down and pick up the key points or focus on slides or stage

Balance Sheet Presentation

Show top half of OHP slide no. 26 'Fixed Assets – Balance Sheet Presentation' and explain it using the notes below.

Ref. No. 423/IBF.

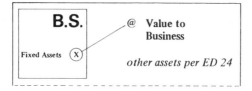

- fixed assets are to be stated at the value to the business

- other assets are to be stated as laid down in ED24

ED24
para 28

It is not suggested that you go into the detail of the valuation of other assets unless these are likely to be material in the context of accounts drawn up by the course participants.

Remove cover on OHP slide no. 26 to reveal:

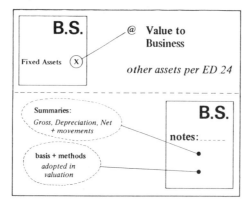

The details of fixed assets should be supported by summaries of those assets.

para 38a
and 43

Figure 1. *Example of Leader's Guide page layout.*

directions as appropriate. Had a distinctive design approach evolved? To assess this, the Leader's Guides were analyzed, using a 10 per cent random page sample. The number of breaks (new paragraphs or new lines) were counted, as were the number of changes (from roman to italic, italic to slide or any combination). An average figure (per page) was worked out for each Leader's Guide. The results of this analysis suggest that the 1979-80 Leader's Guides follow a consistent style which over time has moved towards a more varied page layout and a greater use of visual aids. While the pages have always been more broken up than conventional texts, variety has been introduced in the editorial design. This analysis may be used in future as a check on the effectiveness of a set of talk outlines.

Practical Work

An original intention of package material was that it would support a trainee in his day-to-day practical office work rather than his efforts to pass the professional examination of the Institute. This slant affected the choice of appropriate media whether print, audio, or video. If the real-life situation has a particular form, such as an invoice or a cheque, these are provided as facsimiles to the trainee. One package has specially collated mock cheque stubs to be cross-checked against a bank statement. If information were to be gathered through the spoken word, an audio-tape, giving either an interview or telephone conversation, is used to give the relevant detail to the trainee.

This choice of media is reflected in the course, and hence the Leader's Guide structure. Talk outlines are followed by discussion problems followed by suggested solutions and so on. This ensures that trainees receive appropriate reinforcement and motivation throughout the course. The laid-down sequence may well give an inexperienced presenter considerable psychological support, since each session is broken down into manageable proportions, each of which is carefully defined.

An analysis of the time and activity tables was undertaken to identify the extent of the support given by practical work. This analysis is shown in Table 2 identifying the CPE (Continuing Professional Education) packages intended for updating an accountant in a particular subject from those packages intended for basic instruction.

When the packages in each category are compared there is a reasonably consistent proportion of practical work. This is about 50 per cent for basic material and between 30 per cent and 40 per cent for CPE. Those with a lower proportion of practical work (particularly Practical Auditing 7 and Computers and Accounting) have not been as successful as we had hoped when compared with the potential market.

Users' Reactions

Seventy-six known package users representing all sections of our market except overseas were asked for their reactions to the present Leader's Guide format through a questionnaire. Forty questionnaires (53 per cent) were returned to the Institute and analyzed. The non-respondents were spread evenly between the various categories of user with a better response from smaller professional firms (63 per cent) and a poorer response from industry and commerce and educational institutions (both 38 per cent).

The reaction to the Leader's Guide format was a general preference for the present layout. Only once did less than half the respondents give a rating as either average or below average (1, 2 or 3, on a 1-5 rating scale) out of a possible 22 instances. This was the detail of the Course Leader's activities given in the time and activity table (45 per cent above average). Ignoring four other ratings on the

Practical work proportion	Basic*	CPE
Highest	71%	62%
60% and above	1	1
50% to 60%	4	–
40% to 50%	6	1
30% to 40%	1	3
20% to 30%	2	3
Under 20%	–	3
Lowest	20%	2%

* Practical Auditing 1-3 and 4-6 are assessed as single packages.

Table 2. *Package courses practical work analysis*

detail in a time and activity table there were only three other instances (out of 14) where less than 60 per cent of the respondents rated the approach above average. These were in answer to questions:

☐ How adequate do you consider the approach presently adopted
to OHP slides is?   *50%*
☐ How far do you find the statement of objectives aids you in
planning and assessing the success (or otherwise) of the
course content?   *55%*
☐ Do you consider that sufficient background information is
provided for the course case studies?   *55%*

Were these satisfied respondents basing their experience on a narrow range of package courses? Respondents were asked to say with which courses they were familiar. A total of 225 responses were given (a mean of 5.6 courses per respondent) with the most often-used guide being mentioned 20 times (nine per cent of the total responses and 50 per cent of the number of respondents). This suggests that the answers reflect the use of a wide range of our package material.

Users were asked to say whether the notes were too detailed, about right, or not detailed enough. Seventy-five per cent said that the introductory pages were about right, with exactly the same proportion saying the same for the talk outlines. However, only five per cent said that the talk outlines were too detailed, as against 15 per cent for the introductory pages.

Bearing in mind some of the general criticms described earlier, we asked for specific details about the presenter's background and the way in which the material was used. Only 23 per cent of the respondents had less than three years' training experience. Fifty-six per cent had lectured to audiences greater than 50 at some stage in their life. Since packages are intended to help inexperienced presenters this suggests considerable experience, although some of this could have been with Institute packages. However, many users spent less than 50 per cent of their time lecturing or presenting courses (some 72 per cent of respondents) and 36 per cent of respondents lectured only occasionally.

Respondents were asked how much longer than the allotted time for the course they spent in preparation. Forty-five per cent said either as long or twice as long, and a further 37 per cent said three times as long. Only three respondents reported spending more than four times and the maximum time given was seven times. In general, the presenter found familiarizing himself with the lecture outlines or the case study material took the most time. These results accord with the advice given to package users that preparation should take about three times as long as the lecture timings.

Respondents were asked to state a preference for possible changes to the present format. The only strong support for change was to provide the Leader's Guide in loose-leaf binders (85 per cent of respondents). There was some support for integrating the Student's Manuals with the Leader's Guides (44 per cent of respondents) but 49 per cent preferred separate supply as currently done.

Conclusions

The results of this review suggest three things. First, the design approach to the Leader's Guides has a consistent pattern which reflects the original purpose behind package material. Second, users feel that the Leader's Guides are neither too elaborate nor too brief, to support their presentations. Third, packages cut down preparation time to between two and three times the course length, which is significantly lower than the usual 15 to 40 times quoted for developing a course from scratch. Some individuals, however, may have a particular approach and this will add greatly to the preparation time.

The Future

The results of this assessment of the format suggest that the approach enables basic technical training to be conducted at a wide range of sites by inexperienced presenters while maintaining a high quality of training. The Institute is likely to maintain and develop where necessary this basic range of training packages using this present format in the immediate future.

Many other trainers in industry and commerce face a situation where large numbers of people require training or retraining. In some circles it has been felt that the use of packages by inexperienced presenters will undermine the professionalism and skill of a trainer. We feel that this view is misplaced. The potential for developing packages aimed at inexperienced presenters is far larger and far more effective than the present range of training aids which are used by the trainer for professional support. The development of packages will enhance the role of the training professional since he or she can, through developing material and monitoring its effectiveness, ensure that the quality of learning is maintained while vastly increasing the quantity.

Reference

Tyrrell, D M (1978) Design of package material for accountancy firms. In Brook, D and Race, P *Aspects of Educational Technology* **XII**, pp 126-31. Kogan Page, London.

7.4 Who's Continuing Education?

Adrian Kirkwood
The Open University

Abstract: If continuing education is to cater for the educational and social needs of a large proportion of the population, the various factors, particularly social and psychological, that may deter adults from becoming involved with continuing education activities must be overcome.

Introduction

In recent years it has been increasingly argued that education should be considered as a process continuing throughout life. At a time of unprecedented social, economic and technological change, 'continuing education', 'lifelong learning' and 'recurrent education' have become concepts that are shaping the future policies of many national education ministries. In Britain, it has been advocated that education after school should cease to be considered a minority activity and that, in future, opportunities for education in adult life should be wisely available to meet the changing needs of individuals in our society. The discussion paper 'Towards continuing education' (ACACE, 1979) proposes a distinction between 'initial' and 'continuing' phases of education. Whilst the initial phase comprises schooling and any higher education or training that follows after school without a break, continuing education should be considered to include all subsequent educational activities, whether they be full- or part-time, vocational or non-vocational.

There are clear indications that over the next 20 years the demands for post-school education will increase, and that the demand will not only change quantitatively but qualitatively as well. But even if the financial resources are made available to increase the educational provision for adults, it is important to consider *who* is going to be continuing their education in the year 2000. Other articles here illustrate many new possibilities for making education available to learners of all ages and in varying circumstances. However, if continuing education is to benefit more than just those people who have already done well in the education system, it must be recognized that extending opportunities for post-school education cannot merely be a matter of providing 'more of the same' — even if packaged or presented differently. If, by the end of this century, we are to see a fundamental change in the pattern of adult educational involvement, the nature of existing provision must be re-examined and attempts made to remove barriers to access in continuing education.

Extending Access

It has long been recognized that those people involved in existing adult education tend to be already well-educated; a situation that has given rise to the claim that post-school education reinforces inequality 'by allocating the greater share of resources to those who gained the highest attainments at school and least to those with the greatest educational and social needs' (TUC, 1978).

Meeting the needs of the non-participants, ie those adults who do not take advantage of current educational provision, is an almost universal concern for adult educators. It has been recognized that access to existing provision is often impeded by a number of obstacles. For example, the Advisory Council for Adult and Continuing Education recently documented three major barriers to access:

geography, finance and educational qualifications (ACACE, 1979). Whilst there is undoubtedly a need for the removal of such barriers to access, it may be even more important to consider how less tangible barriers can be overcome. It is the form and content of traditional education that deters many adults from participating in any kind of continuing education.

Social Effects of Schooling

The system of education in Britain (as in most other countries) makes each stage of schooling a preparation for a subsequent stage, rather than a self-contained preparation for the everyday experiences of life. It caters primarily for the minority who will pass on to the next stage, with normative rather than absolute criteria being employed to ensure that only a certain proportion proceed. The majority are left with feelings of failure and inferiority, despite the fact that, to a large extent, no amount of drive and effort is sufficient to penetrate the filtering mechanism that determines 'success'.

Cultural Values in the Content of Education

Of the subjects taught in schools, cognitive or intellectual subjects are afforded greater esteem than are practical or vocational subjects. This prestige derives from current or past associations with high status positions. Thus, whilst low status is attributed to practical or technical subjects, abstract or theoretical subjects often prove to be 'vocational' in that they offer access to occupations with prestige, and are perceived to fulfil this function. It is suggested that high status is accorded to academic curricula that 'tend to be abstract, highly literate, individualistic and unrelated to non-school knowledge' (Young, 1971) and that the stratification of knowledge is related to the stratification of society.

Thus, the form and content of schooling create barriers to continuing education, both in terms of contributing to the negative attitudes engendered, and the degree to which the values of schooling reflect what are considered to be the only legitimate concerns of education after school.

Conclusion

Very many of those who do not currently participate in continuing education are the ones who were designated 'failures' by a system in which the majority must be so categorized. The greatest barriers to access for many adults are the negative perceptions and expectations of the educative process created by their experience of formal schooling. The fact that much continuing education is currently organized in a similar manner to formal schooling, and often in premises that are primarily devoted to compulsory education, cannot serve to dispel negative attitudes derived from recollections of the past. Schooling has contributed to the establishment of a clear distinction between 'education' and 'training', between 'mental' and 'manual'.

If continuing education for the majority is to become a reality by the year 2000 it is important that educators and administrators stop thinking solely in terms of 'courses' that can be provided for 'students'.

The role of adult educators would necessarily be redefined; rather than designing courses that they feel will cater for people's needs, they should become more involved with those people for whom they claim to be providing a service.

When educators' interests in extending provision give way to a concern that people should have a greater opportunity to determine what and how they learn, a major step will be taken towards changing the negative attitudes of many adults towards continuing education. If continuing education is to become a reality, it is not sufficient that professional educators reconsider the goals of learning after school; a great deal will depend upon whether 'educational institutions are seen by people as powerful colonizing agencies or as potential resource systems which may be used to acquire and develop knowledge and skills' (Fordham *et al*, 1979).

References

Advisory Council for Adult and Continuing Education (ACACE) (1979) *Towards Continuing Education*. Leicester.
Fordham, P, Poulton, G and Randle, L (1979) *Learning Networks in Adult Education*. Routledge and Kegan Paul, London.
Trades Union Congress (TUC) (1978) *Priorities in Continuing Education*. Trades Union Congress, London.
Young, M F D (ed) (1971) *Knowledge and Control*. Collier-Macmillan, London.

7.5 Eductional Technology Applied to Retirement Education

W D Clarke and M Devine
BLAT Centre for Health and Medical Education

Abstract: This paper describes the planning, production, implementation and evaluation of a learning package designed to influence the way in which industrial, health and educational organizations prepare people to meet their new careers of being retired.

This presentation is about an educational package on retirement which was put together by the BLAT Centre for Health and Medical Education.

To understand why BLAT carried out a retirement education project, it is necessary to know a little about both the retirement scene in the UK and BLAT. BLAT is an educational charity that applies well-known principles of educational technology to the promotion of new ways of learning and teaching health and medical education. Retirement is not quite so easily dealt with. For example, although most people can correctly estimate the population of the UK at about 55,000,000 they fail to realize that we are an ageing population. Most people are unaware that about one-fifth of that population, that is 10,000,000, is within 10 years of retirement, or that 500,000 people retire each year – that is nearly 2,000 people *every day*. If the fact that there are already more than 8,000,000 people over the age of 65, that life expectancy at 65 is 12 years for a man and 16 for a woman, and that the birthrate is about static, is added to the statistics already stated, then a formidable picture of the future population structure emerges – an inverted triangle. It must be remembered, too, that there will be several more millions *approaching* retirement. It does not matter whether the picture is considered from the health point of view of the individual member of society, or from the economic viewpoint of society, as in both instances it is painfully obvious that some sort of education for retirement is needed.

Unfortunately, our understanding of retirement is not complete if only the statistics are known because, although the need for education may be accepted, acceptance is not synonymous with provision. Adult education has always been one of the Cinderellas of the system, which makes retirement education not so much the Cinders but almost the crematorium ashes! The following list of constraints represent some of the coffin nails for the educational technologist who thinks that providing retirement education is easy. Firstly, most individuals do not recognize that they need to prepare for retirement. Secondly, of those who do recognize the need, most no longer possess the academic skills of reading and listening for information, and resent any attempt to put them back into a school-learning situation of which they have unfavourable memories. Thirdly, society, in the guise of either employers or state, does not universally recognize the need to provide such education. The delivery system that does exist contains few professionally qualified educationalists and is often at the stage of development where the blackboard is something of an innovation.

It has been estimated, or rather guessed, that only about one in 10 people approaching retirement have the chance to undergo some form of education, or a series of half-days, of non-illustrated talks or lectures with little opportunity for questions and even less for detailed discussion. (In fairness, there are a few notable exceptions and even a few with a reasonable allocation of funds.) Our preliminary research, during which we talked to many interested parties, described the aims of our project. They were, obviously, to provide people with an opportunity for learning about the problems they are likely to meet in retirement and to equip them with the necessary skills to deal with such problems (the problems being categorized, but clearly overlapping, into health, wealth and social). It would have been relatively easy to follow educational technology procedure and devise behavioural objectives, but it would have been a futile exercise as the constraints or obstacles already mentioned would have made them unattainable. Instead, four more realistic aims were made: firstly, to foster a positive attitude towards retirement; secondly, to make people aware in advance of the issues they will have to face; thirdly, to draw attention to the kinds of decision they will have to make, and finally, to encourage them to find out for themselves the information needed.

Again, working within the constraints of limited teaching time of about one hour for each of eight topics, the reluctance and inability of the students to take in large amounts of information, and the lack of expertise of the tutors, six objectives were drawn up for each topic. They were stated in terms intelligible to the tutors rather than in behavioural terms. For example, the objectives for the health topic were:

1. to know the four major rules for being in health;
2. to know how to put the rules into practice;
3. to have an attitude of wanting to follow the rules;
4. to appreciate the importance of prevention;
5. to be informed, without being frightened, about major health hazards in old age; and
6. to know where and how to seek advice.

The overall strategy was to design a package that was easy to use and which was not too different in content from existing practice in education for retirement. It was thought that such a strategy would encourage existing tutors to adopt the package and make it easy for newcomers to enter the field.

A multi-media package, which we called 'The Next 20 Years', was produced and tested. Cassette tape and 35mm slides were chosen because of their ease of use coupled with the low cost of the equipment. One particular advantage was that it was easy to update the package by introducing new slides if, for example, the income tax rules changed, and more important still it enabled a tutor to substitute his own locally more relevant material and to add, subtract and modify in the way that he should. The tape had two tracks. Track one was a talk containing the six or so points that the subject expert considered to be the most important, but to give it authority a TV newscaster was asked to read it. The other side of the tape was not accompanied by slides but was a short dramatized episode (a sort of poor man's *Archers*!) in the lives of six fictional pensioners. To accompany the tape and slides a set of booklets for the students, a recording script for the tutor, and a tutor's handbook was provided. The student booklets recapped the points of the talk and listed follow-up activities or books to read or organizations to contact, but they were kept thin to encourage the students to resume their book-reading lives. Great care was exercised over the actual packaging, so that it would appeal to industrial trainers who tend to take more notice of appearance than do medical teachers, and to make the materials accessible, and therefore usable. Eight titles were produced:

The Next Step	*Making the Most of your Money*
Your Health	*Taxation in Retirement*
Your Home	*Leisure Activities*
Eating in Retirement	*Working for Money or Love*

It was decided to sell the package, albeit at a subsidized price; otherwise industry might think it had no value. All too often, well-designed educational innovations have failed because the development of an implementation strategy was neglected, so great care was taken on this point. However, it proved to be the most formidable of tasks for a somewhat esoteric academic body, and moreover a health education problem to attract the attention and win the respect of cost-conscious, no-nonsense, industrial trainers. Teachers and lecturers tend to have captive audiences, so learning to sell one's ideas was a salutary, but on reflection, worthwhile experience.

Unfortunately, BLAT was in the position of a publisher rather than a teacher, in that it had no direct access to any students and so our evaluation of the materials had to rely on feedback from others. What evidence there is suggests that the aims and objectives have been achieved.

The first evidence is the hard data of the market place in that, in the first two-and-a-half years, over 200 organizations have adopted the package. These organizations fall into roughly three equal categories: the industrial sector, including big national concerns like Unilever and the Post Office; the health authorities, such as Devon AHA and the Argyll and Clyde Health Board; and the educational sector, consisting mainly of further education colleges or adult education centres. One surprise was the interest shown by other countries which resulted in seven packages being exported and used as a model for the development of local materials. Most organizations are known to have used the package three or four times already and some are on their tenth use; a fact which gives even harder data as no less than 22,000 booklets have been re-ordered. Use does not necessarily indicate effectiveness but it is hard to believe that the repeat orders would be so frequent if good results were not being attained.

The first 100 purchasers of the package were asked to complete a detailed questionnaire. The questionnaire asked for the percentage achievement by the group of the detailed objectives for each topic, and for an opinion of the usefulness of the three major components of tape, slides and booklets (see Figures 1 and 2).

Although we must remember that these figures reflect the opinions of the course organizers, it is reasonable to draw the conclusion that the materials are successful. Every course organizer believed the programmes to be either helpful or very helpful as an aid to achieving our four major aims. Nobody found them unhelpful.

Did the programme help in	Very Helpful %	Helpful %	Not Helpful %
bringing about an attitude of confidence and optimism?	56	44	0
fostering a positive attitude?	60	40	0
encouraging a 'want to know more' attitude?	56	44	0
developing self-responsibility?	60	40	0

Did the COMMENTARY . . .	Definitely Yes %	Yes %	No %	Definitely No %
help in learning the facts?	93	7	0	0
stimulate valuable discussion?	64	32	4	0
help the development of sound attitudes?	57	43	0	0
entertain?	64	36	0	0

Figure 1. *Reactions to (a) the programmes and (b) the tapes.*

Did the SLIDES . . .	Definitely Yes %	Yes %	No %	Definitely No %
help in learning the facts?	82	18	0	0
stimulate valuable discussion?	75	11	14	0
help the development of sound attitudes?	75	18	7	0
entertain?	50	46	4	0

Did the BOOKLETS . . .	Definitely Yes %	Yes %	No %	Definitely No %
help in learning the facts?	48	52	0	0
stimulate valuable discussion?	30	51	19	0
help the development of sound attitudes?	31	65	4	0
entertain?	4	19	77	0

Figure 2. *Reactions to (a) the slides and (b) the booklets.*

A similar response was made to questions about the three major components. In each case we asked the same four questions.

The booklets were the only category that brought significant negative response, right at the bottom there in the entertainment section, but I suppose that's show business! Spontaneous comment from tutors also indicate a high degree of acceptability but almost predictably some were delighted and other horrified by the style of humour. It was possible to observe three groups of students and, whilst they all voted it a success, the degree of success reflected, again predictably, the skill of the tutor in running small-group discussions. Some 20 letters indicate that tutors are modifying the materials to meet local requirements. This is a disappointing figure but there may be others doing so unknown.

As far as it is known, this was the first time a systems or educational technology approach had been applied to retirement education. It clearly demonstrates the need for others to enter this tough field, because not only is the target audience growing rapidly and is a deserving one, but the existing teaching standards, at least in the areas of group work and attitude change, are dreadfully low. The success of our materials probably owes much to the fact that something is usually better than nothing. As MacLeod said of Macmillan, 'He's the best Prime Minister we've got. He's the only one we've got!'.

7.6 Does Adult Education Need Specifically Designed Textbooks, Teaching Strategies and Materials?

Martin Kirchmayer
University of Maryland (European Division)

To the year 2000 and beyond, there will be a continuous increase in the number of adult students (Ansello, 1979). To cope with this number of adult students (who differ from traditional adolescent students) it may be necessary to change many of the traditional teaching materials used, which were originally designed for traditional adolescent student classes.

The results of a survey of students taking evening classes in Earth Sciences (Kirchmayer, 1978-80) differentiated adult students as follows:

1. Degree-seeking adult students, comprising:
   (a) recurrent education adult students, who switch between job and education several times in their lives, mainly to stay up-to-date with their job; and
   (b) non-traditional adult students, who start further or higher education after a gap between compulsory and subsequent education, and who do not plan to continue a significant voluntary educational effort after finishing the compulsory one.
2. Non degree-seeking adult students.

At the time of the survey, the evening classes in Earth Sciences at the University of Maryland University College had the following students:

48.65 per cent (non-traditional adult students)
26.25 per cent (traditional adolescents)
15.75 per cent (recurrent education students)
 8.05 per cent (non degree-seeking adult students)
 1.30 per cent (undefined categories).

Some of the opinions of these students were as follows: 63.8 per cent of class members thought there were both similarities and differences between traditional students and adult-recurrent and/or non-traditional adult students; the same percentage felt the need for personal development in areas other than those being studied; 37.3 per cent believed there would be social discrimination advantageous to them as a result of gaining a degree; 42.5 per cent of the non-traditional adult students felt a need for education in areas other than those being studied, in order to rectify earlier deficiencies in their education; and 31 per cent of this group felt that there were no areas common to themselves and to the traditional adolescent students with regard to, eg environment.

These results led to the conclusion that appropriate teaching materials, strategies, methodologies, textbooks, etc should be introduced as soon as possible in order to serve adult students better and to ensure that the nation as a whole gets a better and more modern lifelong education.

References

Ansello, E F (1979) Older students in higher education: access and progress. *IUT Improving University Teaching*. 5th International Congress. University of Maryland, College Park.

Kirchmayer, M (1978-80) *SOCRATES — Student Opinion Course Results and Teaching Effectiveness Survey*. University of Maryland, University College; Academic Years 1978-79 and 1979-80. Unpublished results.

Section 8:
Distance Learning Systems

8.1 Flexistudy: from Pilot Scheme to National Network

Brian Green
Barnet College

Abstract: This college-linked distance learning system has led to an unfreezing of traditional attitudes to the professionalization of the teacher's role. The existence of a national network of Flexistudy centres creates the possibility of a truly national 'open college' in the further education sector.

Constraints on Open Learning

Flexistudy started out as an open learning system in the administrative sense, seeking to overcome the constraints that can effectively close educational opportunity to so many people. Coffey (1977) has identified three of these:

(a) The student must attend in a specified place, at definite times, and over a named period of time.
(b) He will join a group of minimum size. In order to keep a class in being, the group must not fall below the minimum size.
(c) He must pay a certain amount towards the cost of the course.

Flexistudy overcomes two of these and goes some way towards relieving the third.

Saturday Conferences Leading to Linked Courses

Barnet College had, since 1971, held Saturday conferences for corrrespondence students of the National Extension College, to spend a day working on and discussing their chosen subject area, or study problems, in small seminar groups. These conferences were well attended, with students coming to benefit from the face-to-face contact offered both with fellow students and with subject specialists. The frequent articulation of the need for such contact by students was an important influence on the development of Flexistudy.

These Saturday conferences also provided an opportunity for Barnet College lecturers acting as subject tutors to familiarize themselves with National Extension College correspondence course materials.

The consequence of this encounter, and the next step towards Flexistudy were National Extension College linked courses, operating as regular part-time courses within the college.

For these linked courses, students were supplied with NEC correspondence texts at cost. Students attended the college weekly where possible, but studied the course text at home. In this way the student was no longer totally dependent on a weekly class. If he missed a few weeks he could catch up at home, using the course books. Furthermore, the tutor was able to spend more time dealing with specific student problems, having been relieved of part of the burden of expository teaching.

This was clearly only a partial move towards relieving demands on attendance at definite times. The class still proceeded at a limited pace and required the minimum attendance to be maintained. However, Saturday conferences and linked courses did provide first-hand information about the problems and needs of students unable to attend normal classes and familiarity with correspondence course materials.

Flexistudy

It was with this experience and confidence in the course materials that, in September 1977, Barnet College launched Flexistudy — a mode of study combining the traditional correspondence course with face-to-face tutorials. By December 1977 there were 90 enrolments on 22 courses, and at the time of writing (April 1980), there are 340 Flexistudy students at Barnet and 140 more have completed their courses.

This system gives the student the opportunity to study independently and at his own pace and provides him with direct access to all the resources he might require: course book, tutorials, study skills, counselling, media resources, library, examination boards, social contact, etc. The student can enrol at any time, after talking to a Flexistudy adviser about the suitability of courses. After enrolment the student is contacted by his course tutor and an appointment is made. At this first meeting, course materials are handed over and a preliminary study timetable agreed. Tutorials are arranged at the mutual convenience of tutor and students.

The relatively frequent face-to-face tutorials (about one every three weeks) fulfilled the expected functions of:

☐ establishing a personal relationship between tutors and students;
☐ aiding learning through discussion with tutors and fellow students;
☐ allowing the practise of laboratory skills in natural science subjects and oral skills in language courses;
☐ encouraging the completion of written assignments by mutually agreed deadlines.

The latter function was most important in maintaining the students' momentum of study and reducing the predicted drop-out rate. The current drop-out rate of 29 per cent is considerably lower than both normal correspondence courses and regular part-time courses, although it still gives no grounds for complacency.

At this stage in the development of Flexistudy, tutors were paid per assignment marked and per tutorial held. Courses were mostly priced at £20 which included course material, 10-15 assignments marked by the tutor, and 10 tutorials. This was calculated as an economic fee to make the scheme largely self-financing.

It should be noted that all prospective Flexistudy students were encouraged to study on a regular part-time basis if possible, and that no part-time courses suffered as a result of Flexistudy. Students included shift workers, mobile workers, single parents and housewives unable to attend classes on a regular basis.

Further Developments

During 1978, four other colleges started their own Flexistudy schemes, using the same NEC materials and providing a similar formula of distance learning and face-to-face tutorials, and by March 1980 there were 16 Flexistudy centres.

At Barnet, the scheme was undergoing continuous evaluation. Changes were being made and resources reviewed. One change was to provide students with their material in stages, rather than all at once.

A resources centre was set up in the college during 1978 but experience showed that Flexistudy students were only really prepared to come in to view materials central to their course, such as video-tapes of television series linked to NEC courses.

Students felt that study skills should be incorporated into all Flexistudy courses at no extra cost to the student, and to this effect a few units, providing advice on organization, motivation, learning, memory, reading, etc have been prepared and will be presented to all Flexistudy students. Assignments will be based on the students' main subject course, and study skills counsellors will be available to provide additional back-up.

Since Flexistudy was not an integral part of the college programme, the normal conditions of student payment did not apply. It was realized that many of the target students who would benefit most from Flexistudy (eg single parents, the elderly, the physically handicapped) were finding it impossible to pay the course fee. An educational charity became interested in the scheme and provided some degree of help to those in need.

Nonetheless, it was felt that the original constraints had been largely overcome. Course work was done at home, students could attend by mutual appointment, if necessary outside the college campus. The student could take the course at his own pace. There was no minimum group size, and some degree of help was available for those unable to meet the cost of a course.

Remaining Administrative Constraints

However, many problems, both educational and administrative, remained and were sufficient to stifle, if not strangle the further development of Flexistudy.

The main administrative constraints lay in the self-financing mode described. There was an urgent need to integrate Flexistudy into the college programme, rather than treat it as an economic extra-mural activity. Among the reasons for this were:

1. THE COST OF FLEXISTUDY COURSES TO THE STUDENT
The amount of charitable help available is limited and the procedures involved are cumbersome. If Flexistudy became an accepted part of the college's part-time provision, however, reduced rates and exemption from payment would become available for Flexistudy students as for regular part-time students.

2. TUTORS' CONDITIONS OF SERVICE
Payment on the basis described was acceptable for a limited pilot project, but in the longer term the tutors, their union and the college were anxious to integrate Flexistudy work into the regular teaching timetable.

3. THE NEED TO CALCULATE STUDENT HOURS
Until a formula could be devised for calculating student hours — which would clearly have to be more than simply tutorial hours — Flexistudy would remain an appendage of educational value, but not of accounting value for the running of the college.

4. THE NEED TO PROVIDE MORE ACCESS FOR STUDENTS
Although the Flexistudy student had easy access to his tutor through telephone or

post, his tutorial time was somewhat limited. Some arrangement that enabled him to attend 'surgery' as often as he liked, albeit at fixed times, was required.

A Proposal

At Barnet College a possible solution to this problem has been proposed. A GCE class, consisting of 15 students meeting for two-and-a-half hours per week, covers the same material as a Flexistudy group of equivalent size. Using this fact as a basis for calculations, we suggest that two-and-a-half hours per week for a case load of 15 students, and *pro rata*, would be a fair timetable allowance for Flexistudy tutors. Since the average length of an A-level Flexistudy course is 30 units, a notional figure of six hours' support time per unit would yield a figure of 180 hours, exactly equivalent to the study time of a part-time A-level student over a period of two years.

At the same time, the concept of surgery time has been introduced. This operates on the basis that 60 per cent of the total remission allowed for Flexistudy teaching should be timetabled at a fixed time each week, during which time tutors would be available to take telephone calls and see students who could come without prior appointment. The remaining 40 per cent of the tutors' time would be available for arranging tutorials as before. The students are welcome to attend surgery as frequently as they wish. In this way, the confident student and the student with problems no longer find themselves with the same fixed number of tutorial hours.

Remaining Educational Constraints

Educational constraints can close opportunities just as effectively as administrative ones. If we are to provide an educational service for the whole community, we must examine and break down the remaining educational constraints on our system, eg:

1. LIMITED SELECTION OF COURSES
In the first phase of Flexistudy, courses offered were based entirely on the NEC output. NALGO and Barnet College are now offering Flexistudy courses designed by the NALGO Correspondence Institute including preparation for Institute of Personnel Management and Institute of Chartered Secretaries and Administrators Part 1 exams.

Programmed materials produced both by commercial and funded bodies are being examined with a view to expanding the range of courses offered on the one hand into the non-vocational crafts fields, and on the other into highly vocational technical fields.

A future system is envisaged that would enable colleges to collaborate in producing their own material, specifically for Flexistudy. In the present economic climate with the experience and expertise of the National Extension College and college educational technology staff available, existing materials could perhaps be adapted for use as Flexistudy courses and made available on a royalty payment basis.

2. LACK OF STUDENT CONTROL OVER SELECTION OF OBJECTIVES
This is not perceived as a problem by existing Flexistudy students, most of whom are working towards a rigid external assessment (Associated Examination Board, GCE, etc); nonetheless, it is recognized that, if we are to continue the trend towards learner-centred education and increased educational opportunity, we must offer the student increased control over the content of his course and methods of study.

To this effect, Flexistudy tutors are already editing courses, altering assignments, recommending additional material and producing their own print and audio-visual materials in order to tailor their courses more to the needs of individual students.

With a growing bank of material to draw upon, and the possibility of more flexible NEC courses, bound in smaller units, Flexistudy students will soon be offered more flexible courses to be 'compiled' in consultation with their tutors. This may, however, pose problems of assessment.

3. TRADITIONAL FIXED ASSESSMENT

Most Flexistudy students require a nationally recognized qualification and are content to sit GCE exams. This method of assessment, however, is quite inappropriate to the type of work that the majority of mature students will be doing when they finish their courses, and in some cases, such as with shift workers, the inflexibility of exam dates and times excludes prospective candidates from entering. A nationally recognized form of assessment, based upon course work and the attainment of mutually agreed objectives would, we feel, be more appropriate in most cases.

Educational innovations are all too often limited to peripheral activities, but the increased educational and administrative flexibility, crucial to the success of Flexistudy, together with the increased professionalization of the teacher's role will provide a precedent that must be applied to the full-time college curriculum if individualized learning is to be implemented successfully.

A National Network

In the meantime we now have the basis of a national framework for an open college. When the administrative problems are overcome, there are few institutions concerned with further education that will not wish to operate some form of Flexistudy. A network of Flexistudy centres, operating independently but sharing information and certain resources, now exists. Colleagues from existing and prospective Flexistudy centres meet to discuss problems and future possibilities, under the auspices of the Council for Educational Technology, Garnett College of Education and Barnet College of Further Education. There is, without doubt, a case for closer ties leading to a confederation of Flexistudy centres and closer co-operation between subject specialists, administrators and educational technologists operating the system, and to the establishment of a national referral centre for students. However, none of the present participants would wish for a structure imposed from outside by a government agency. It is one of the great strengths of the system that it has grown out of a genuine need to overcome the constraints of existing further education provision and is based on local centres, aware of the problems specific to local communities.

Such a confederation of Flexistudy centres would appear to meet most of the recommendations for an Open College, proposed in the Russell Report on Adult Education (1973).

> It is not likely, and not necessarily desirable, that a permanent institution or a range of institutions like the Open University should be created for adult education below degree level. What is desirable is not a super-organization but an organizational framework. Within such a framework, learning systems could be established involving different media and agencies, despite the logistical and organizational problems known to be associated with this kind of enterprise, despite the difficulties that can arise from matters of contract and copyright and from attempts to combine publicly-funded institutions with commercial organizations. Even more than this would be possible and necessary; diagnosis of need could be made; curriculum studies carried out of a kind at present undertaken for adult education only by the Open University at degree course level; and separate institutions brought together for the equivalents of the Open University's course team work.

References

Coffey, J (1977) Open learning opportunities for mature students. *Open Learning Systems for Mature Students.* Council for Educational Technology.

Russell, Sir L (1973) *Adult Education: A Plan for Development.* HMSO

8.2 Emerging Communications Technology in Canada: the Challenge to Conventional Educational Systems

Dennis Dicks and Gary Coldevin
Concordia University

Abstract: An outline is given of present trends in non-formal education resulting from recent technical advances; projecting into the future, conventional education is regarded as not being greatly influenced by emerging technologies, but non-formal education will keep in close step with developing technologies and function as the primary educational backdrop for an information society.

Introduction

As we write, a number of intriguing communications experiments are under way in Canada. Overhead, the Anik II satellite, while shuffling television, radio and telephone signals about the country, enables northern Eskimo people to generate for the first time their own news, entertainment and educational programmes. In Winnipeg and Toronto, fibre optic telecommunications channels are in operation, and videotex terminals are being installed in ordinary homes. In Ottawa, cable system operators and telephone companies jockey to get out of the gate with pay-TV and other new commercial services. In Hamilton, a TV 'superstation' lines up customers for programme delivery via satellite. And in Montreal, two of the world's largest producers of word processing equipment strive to create the last word in technology while the Department of Education allocates $40 million for the installation of minicomputers in schools and colleges.

These developments reflect Canadian expertise in many facets of communications technology while, to the south, the pace of innovation is such that it is impossible to keep abreast of the new services, new networks, or new corporate strategems. The American regulatory bodies are about to drop their reins, probably not just for policy reasons but because things are moving out of control anyway. And the Americans, with their immense domestic market for communications hardware and software, largely influence what the rest of us do.

Where is it all leading? Any attempt to predict the precise nature of machines or services available in the year 2000 would be foolhardy. We will instead try to discern the forces behind current developments, and speculate on the directions that these forces might lead us during the next two decades.

Emerging Technologies

In our opinion there are two key forces at work within the telecommunications field: first, technical innovation and second, regulatory change. Technological innovation is a rather obvious force for change. However, the important question is: what avenues of innovation will have lasting effects in the coming decades?

One avenue, perhaps approaching its zenith, is semi-conductor technology, permitting even smaller 'chips' to handle increasingly sophisticated computer operations. A second avenue of innovation is the expansion of transmission capacity, steadily accelerating reductions in the cost of sending messages (eg satellites and fibre optics). A third departure stems from the junction of the first two: as transmission systems increasingly rely on digital processing to improve reliability, switching speed, and capacity while reducing costs, the distinction between the transmission function and the computing function is fast fading.

Technological innovation tends to create pressures for regulatory change, as new types of action become possible. Regulatory change, in turn, acelerates technological innovation as new faces are allowed into the marketplace. The impetus for regulatory change has been strongest in the US. Over a decade ago, the 'Carterphone decision' began to erode the monopoly of telephone companies in providing telephone-based services. Now the Canadian and American Bell systems seem ready to accept the challenge of complete de-regulation in the telephone industry.

Similar 'de-regulations' have allowed cable TV to enter and rapidly consume the US market. In this case, the demand for alternatives to the ABC-CBS-NBC cartel has rushed the marriage of the transmission capacity and flexibility of satellites to the switch-and-feedback capabilities of cable converters, creating pay-TV systems that provide new opportunities for independent producers.

In North America, the regulatory question to be face in the near future is: 'How will potentially lucrative pay-TV/information services be divided among telephone companies, cable operators, broadcasters and entertainment distributors?'. The answer will have far-reaching effects.

Manifestations

The forces discussed above will show several manifestations in the next two decades. There will be new distribution systems, new display systems and new services. In the first case, we expect satellites to provide flexible distance-independent routeing for all forms of telecommunications. Satellites will supply cable networks in town and cities with a mix of broad and narrow-band services; isolated households will have their own receiving dishes. Given these distribution options and the demand for information displays, the ordinary TV set will become a generalized telecommunications monitor, with at least a modicum of computer intelligence built into it. It will thus be able to display TV programmes, programmed games, instructional packages, or on-line computer communications.

The range of information/entertainment services available will greatly increase in the coming decades. In the relatively mature Canadian cable business, there are already systems offering 35 or more TV channels (comprising regular Canadian and American networks, local originations, and specialized channels). Community TV and radio will probably become firmly established in Canadian cities by 1985, but will not grow much beyond that.

It is also likely that some form of pay-TV, for sports, movies and concerts, and some form of videotex will be introduced in the next few years. The special promise of the Canadian entry in the videotex field — 'Telidon' — is that it would not only permit retrieval of information from data-banks, but could encourage the

ordinary subscriber to create information for himself, for other subscribers, or
public data-banks.

The proliferation of high-capacity information networks is well under way in
the American business community. Large corporations have found that they can
fulfil their communications needs with systems tailor-made by the telephone
companies' competitors. The coming thrust will be towards 'value added' systems
which offer a mix of communications and information-processing capabilities.

One should not overlook the information processors that do not necessarily
form part of a structured service — stand-alone games, mini-computers, word
processors, and industrial robots, for example. As these become cheaper and more
flexible, as their memories, displays and interactive abilities increase, they will
subtly creep into everyday use.

The Software Dilemma

Underlying most telecommunications forecasts is a severe case of 'technological
push', a common affliction in which technical possibility is confused with economic
practicability and social utility. The technical barriers to information services of
enormous scope seem relatively facile in the face of other questions: 'Does anyone
want them?', 'Who will produce the information?' and 'What will the social and
economic costs be?'.

In its most general form, the software dilemma is as follows: the high cost of
producing 'professional standard' information requires that a mass audience be
enlisted to pay for it; at the same time, since uniqueness is a major selling point for
information, diversity demands that the audience be fragmented into small special-
interest groups. We believe that a battle to achieve equilibrium between these
opposing pressures has been unleashed by technological change and de-regulation.
The battle will last for some years, and the outcome will shape the
telecommunications scene for decades thereafter.

Visions of the Information Society

There has been considerable speculation on the nature of the touted 'information
society', a society dominated by the production and consumption of information
rather than things. As an overview, three scenarios have been proposed (Valaskakis,
1979).

1. THE 'TÉLÉMATIQUE' OR 'WIRED CITY' SCENARIO:

   ☐ characterized by the 'electronic highway' linking offices, schools and
      homes;
   ☐ micro-computers ubiquitous in production, consumption, and personal
      life styles;
   ☐ human interaction maximally mediated by teleconference, electronic
      mail and teleshopping;
   ☐ information sector economically dominant, automation causing
      increases in leisure time and unemployment.

2. THE 'PRIVATIQUE' OR 'WIRED MIND' SCENARIO:

   ☐ characterized by the small-scale personal computer, with minimal
      telecommunications features;
   ☐ micro-computers as extensions of human intellectual processes;

☐ organization at the level of primary groups, community groups, or non-territorial affinity groups reinforced by the personal computer.

3. THE 'REJECTION' SCENARIO:

☐ characterized by rejection of mediated communication in favour of a return to traditional forms;
☐ preponderance of low-scale, ecologically appropriate technology;
☐ labour-intensive information industries favoured over automation (eg opera versus computer games).

Unfortunately, while speculations proliferate, there have been few studies of the realities, sampling public reaction to the purported capabilities of new technologies, weighting costs and benefits. Our own work in this area (Dicks *et al*, 1979) suggests that the large systems typical of the 'wired city' scenario are not on the horizon. Rather, some features of the wired city — electronic mail is the best example — will arise not as coherent public utilities but as conglomerations of largely private services, interconnecting branch offices to one another.

We do not see information technologies adding significantly to unemployment, as typically forecast in 'wired city' scenarios. There is evidence (eg Whistler, 1970) that the introduction of information technologies does lead to redundancies in clerical staff. But this is a narrow perspective. If we broaden our view from the bottom clerical level to the whole enterprise, we should find that the new technologies create new opportunities in higher-level information-related positions (DePauw and Dicks, 1980). If we take a still broader view, we will find that the manufacture of these technologies — hard and soft components — requires skilled workers: engineers, technicians, programmers, machinists and so on. And all these new jobs are producing more disposable income than those lopped off at the lowest clerical level.

Educational Implications

Formal Education

1. INSTITUTION-BASED
Although we anticipate an increase in total demand for education and training, it seems likely that the formal educational institutions — primary, secondary, and post-secondary — will remain largely immune from the direct thrust of the information society, as far as utilizing advanced hardware and software is concerned. Entrenchment in the face of smaller peaks and valleys in enrolment and the 'return to basics' precludes the emergence of the 'wired school' as envisaged in the early 1970s. It is not the technical or financial difficulties in constructing networks but availability and quality of software that will thwart any master plan. Content may change to reflect new knowledge and skills, but the methods of conveying content will not be altered greatly by the burgeoning information services in offices and homes. In the face of much 'real' education for an information society occurring in the home, a logical reorientation for the conventional school would involve a 'brokering' role between formal instruction and out-of-school experience. Current and future university teacher training programmes bear direct responsibility in meeting this challenge. Inadequacies in providing a flexible curriculum directed toward rapidly evolving societal needs may signal a diminshed role for the conventional school with the bulk of useful educational experience occurring under alternate systems.

2. HOME-BASED
Similarly, we do not expect to see formal study at home expand simply because of the availability of new information services. Developments like the Open University

system, for example, are hindered by a 'reluctance on the part of manufacturers to take risks in investment in production and the lack of appropriate and sufficient hardware' (Bates, 1978). Few, if any, of the emerging technologies such as video-discs and videotex seem practical because of related problems. Print and broadcast media are likely to remain the primary vehicles for home-based formal education within the foreseeable future.

Informal Education

There are other forces which we believe will begin to constrain the role of the university. English-speaking societies have characteristically cherished a university degree as the ultimate educational goal. They are now discovering the price of this monomania: broadening the university clientele has been very expensive, the utility of university research and the quality of its graduates have been questioned, graduates have complained or being 'under-employed' while myriad jobs for skilled workers cannot be filled. This malaise and the increasing demand for continuing education both indicate that there is more to education than a strict adherence to the university model can offer.

The search for alternatives to formal post-secondary education and the thrust towards new information technologies are particularly synergistic forces. We see the development of videotex, word processing and electronic mail services abetting current trends to on-the-job training in industry and self-development at home. There will be considerable demand for algorithmic instructional programmes that can be drawn from libraries to local processors, as required. The more interactive the system, the greater will be the opportunity for local authors to contribute to the software pool.

The real crucible of informal education will continue to be the mass media. Newspapers, radio and TV unobtrusively shape the values and thence the knowledge of their audiences. Consequently, the impact of new technologies on the ways in which these institutions organize and disseminate information could profoundly affect the Western intellect. Some newspaper chains, for example, feel that the printed page is so threatened by teletext/videotex services that they have set up subsidiaries to supply these new media with information. Electronic newspapers may well change both the way news is created (concentration into short items is favoured [Logue, 1979]), and the way it is received (browsing becomes almost impossible). In the case of teletext/videotex and television, the software dilemma may be increasingly solved by renting time to advertisers. The question of how commercialization of information services affects the way in which content is structured has attracted some attention (eg Williams, 1974) but deserves much more. Here again, technology will present the alternatives, but there is a large possibility that economic considerations will not favour those that maximize freedom of access for both information producers and consumers.

Conclusion

In summary, changes in educational systems as a result of emerging technologies are expected to occur in converse relation to their degree of 'formalness'. Conventional schools are expected to remain immune to the utilization of advanced hard- and software components, but their continued survival may depend upon an ability to act as brokers between formal study and informal information sources. Higher education establishments are also expected to successfully resist emerging technologies, with home-based formal study relying on conventional media. Non-formal education, however, will remain in close step with developing technologies and function as the primary educational back-drop for an information society. In doing so, technology may thus provide both the challenge and salvation for the educational community.

References

Bates, A W (1978) New technology for home-based learning: the challenge to campus-based institutions. *Journal of Educational Television*, 4, p 2.
DePauw, K and Dicks, D J (1980) *Information Technology: The Impact on Organizational Women*. Concordia University, Montreal.
Dicks, D J, Malkin, M and Croteau, P (1979) The wired city: probable impacts on transportation and education in a suburban community. *Proceedings of the International Conference on Communications*. IEEE.
Logue, T (1979) Teletext: towards an information utility. *Journal of Communication*, 29, p 4.
Valaskakis, K (1979) *The Information Society: The Issue and the Choices;* University of Montreal.
Whistler, T (1970) *The Impact of Computers on Organizations.* Praeger, New York.
Williams, R (1974) *Television: Technology and Cultural Form.* Fontana, New York.

8.3 Distance Learning Within a Large Organization

D T Wynne and R M Adamson
Civil Service College, Ascot

Abstract: This paper deals with the theory, and common features, of existing distance learning systems. The features and practicalities are examined with respect to the organizational needs of a large fictitious organization, and whether distance learning is a viable solution to some of the training problems.

Introduction

The authors of this paper posed the question: 'Could a distance learning system help to meet the training needs of a large organization having both centralized and 'remote' training?'.

There was no timetable for an answer to be produced by; the impetus for the enquiry arose from themselves. The thoughts expressed within this paper are those of the authors as individuals rather than as representatives of their organization.

It is important to understand that their purposes were to define what a distance learning system is, to consider existing models, and to try to define from their experience what might or might not work in their own situation. As their enquiry developed it became clear that at the present stage they could only draw up a set of questions which should be answered before any distance learning system could be contemplated. This paper tries to summarize the current educational philosophy of distance learning and to identify the criteria by which a policy decision should be made whenever an organization considers embarking upon setting up a distance learning system.

Definition

We choose to term distance learning a 'system' rather than a 'strategy' or 'technique'.
We believe that a distance learning system incorporates a wide range of strategies for
learning adapted to a coherent philosophy. There are five features that define the
system. Students are situated at a distance from the creators of the training; they
work on materials pre-prepared in the self-instructional mode; they perform
assignments; the upshot of their effort is a two-way didactic conversation'. This
didactic conversation, which may also be said to be in two parts, is defined below.
The fifth feature, which provides the coherence of the system is that of 'guidance'.
Guidance is provided both to students and tutors of the system. The goals of such
guidance will be amplified in this paper. Thus, a definition of learning at a distance,
that is, the activity engaged upon by the student, rather than the system, is:

> a guided didactic conversation, conducted at a distance, initiated by pre-prepared
> self-instructional materials and sustained through the medium of tutor-assessed
> assignments.

Additionally the following features may be present in some systems:

- [ ] materials written in a self-instructional mode;
- [ ] the use of existing channels of communication and 'infrastructure' of
  the client, organization or society;
- [ ] a flexible curriculum that may be modular in structure and constructed
  on a credit system;
- [ ] 'capture' of new target populations;
- [ ] the coming together of learners and skilled people at local centres and
  situations.

The system that supports the distance learning activity must be designed to fit the
organization or society where the learning is required to take place. Since this paper
examines what must be decided by a large organization preparing to establish a
distance learning system, the criteria of design selected for scrutiny will be
appropriate to such a target field. These criteria may therefore not be all that are
relevant to a distance learning system.

The goals of a distance learning system may be those of the client society or
may be self-actualized goals generated by the students. Initially, the authors thought
to consider the goals only of the client organization. But they came to be aware
that the students taken up by any system they might design for their own
organization might soon be self-actualizing, might take responsibility for their
own learning and could then seek guidance from the central facilitators of the
distance learning system as to how they might pursue their own goals. This is an
aspect of discovery learning which would have significant implications and to
which much thought would have to be given within the client organization. The
client organization's goals may be vocational or educational. We set about
examining whether different systems were necessary for meeting either or both
goals, and identified criteria by which this question could be discussed.

Educational Philosophy of Distance Learning

Traditional distance learning has been the correspondence course conducted from
a postal tuition college. Educational technology entered the field to examine:

- [ ] the theory of learning under a distance learning system
- [ ] the production of learning materials
- [ ] profiles of the target population and their method of learning
- [ ] strategies for communication between tutors and learners
- [ ] systems of guidance to those involved.

Educational technology has also tried to construct a taxonomy for matching methods of teaching and guidance with various elements such as the cost, the subject matter and profiles of individual students' learning traits. The eventual project, for which this study has been a preparation, could help to construct the taxonomy, since the use of distance learning for 'vocational' purposes within a large organization is a new one, but perhaps more measurable in terms of how objectives have been achieved.

In surveying the results of educational technology's enquiries into distance learning, the authors perceived that it is universally accepted that a didactic conversation is essential to the learning process. Distance learning follows this precept, which states that the learning process occurs, irrespective of the medium used, as a sort of didactic conversation. This is in two parts. Partly the student holds an internalized conversation with himself: he considers the information he has absorbed, searches for further information and practical applications, performs exercises and articulates, perhaps verbally, what he has learnt. He also holds communication partly with the teaching organization in the form of tutorials, group sessions and so on. The two parts interact and it is useful to relate this model to Kolb's learning cycle, wherein there are continually recurring components of concrete experience observation and reflection, the forming of concepts and generalizations and testing their implications in new situations (Kolb, 1974).

Distance learning's strategies are expected to meet objectives in the cognitive domain and in the psychomotor domain where the conditions under which those objectives are measured can be set up at the remote learning point.

Thus a policy decision has to be taken by the authors of a distance learning system on what shall be the character of the guided didactic conversation and what learning model this didactic conversation is part of. Upon this decision choices can be based, for the selection of media, and for the aim and frequency of face-to-face tuition; for a control system: how curricula are publicized and student needs taken up; for a guidance system: how counselling on choice of study may be arranged and what advice is offered to the student on actual study techniques.

Media

The media for learning materials and assignment work are the outward evidence of a distance learning system in operation. Traditionally, the medium for distance learning was the printed word. Non-print materials have been tried; audio- and video-tapes, broadcasts and hybrid material. For assignment work, print and audio cassettes seem manageable and computer-assisted systems are also developing for assignment work. The more complex the material in audio-visual realization, the more difficult for use at a distance for assignments. Where self-instruction techniques are to be incorporated, the selection of appropriate self-instructional methods is bound up with the decision taken on the nature of the guided didactic conversation that is to take place.

'Face-to-face' or quasi 'face-to-face' strategies can be incorporated into some systems. They include one-to-one tutorials with either a central or local tutor; telephone contact with a tutor, either by individualized students or in groups, through the medium of the conference telephone; group meetings with or without a tutor to view films, conduct discussion, workshops, and soon face-to-face strategies may form part of the guidance procedure.

Guidance System

Each distance learning system creates a guided didactic conversation. There must be a guidance system, having the following facets, built into the structure:

- [ ] guidance to students on choice of study;
- [ ] guidance to students on study technique;
- [ ] guidance to the tutor (central or local);
- [ ] (where appropriate) guidance to the student's sponsors, ie line or training managers in a business organization, about choice of study.

Guidance systems adopt the approach of being prescriptive, student-directed, cybernetic, or (theoretically) student-autonomous — ie where guidance ceases to exist and the student assumes full responsibility for his own learning. Media for guidance range over a similar spectrum to those for learning materials.

The Nature of the Problem for a Large Organization

There would first of all be the actual size — if dealing with a group of companies there would be staff in many big cities in the country, with smaller offices spread throughout the country, and possibly overseas offices as well. Some of the subsidiaries are too small to run viable courses, so HQ organizes centralized training . . . but it is expensive to gather people together for a course.

The emphasis to be placed on particular knowledge and skills may well vary between different firms within the group, and by the time people can attend a course appropriate to their needs they may well have been doing the job for which they are awaiting training for six months or a year. The training cannot always be immediate. So, on the face of it, distance learning has many attractions: common-core tasks could be sent to all regions, thus helping to standardize training. Expensive courses would be limited to subjects such as management training. Local managers would accept a greater responsibility for training, but would have the back-up of the distance learning system to make this viable.

But where do you find the money to establish the system? After all, there is likely to be a fairly long overlap period when money is being spent on the production of resources but existing courses are still having to be run. The question of who pays for the administration of the scheme also has to be resolved. Also, how will students react? Will they feel sufficiently motivated to work on self-instructional materials, or will they prefer the old system which got them out of the office for a while? And will managers really accept their new role as tutors and mentors? If they belong to the subsidiaries in the large mythical company we are considering, they may well have had considerable autonomy, and might feel threatened by the introduction, or even the proposal, of a distance learning scheme.

So, what should happen? Is distance learning a viable answer to some of the training problems in a large, widespread and diverse organization?

Conclusion

The authors think that an organization should consider the following criteria when deciding whether to establish a distance learning system:

- [ ] that the proposed system incorporates the features already listed;
- [ ] that the system should only be introduced after full consultation with all who have a legitimate interest in the outcome, for example central and local management, existing trainers, trade unions;
- [ ] that a realistic assessment of short-term and long-term financial implications be made;
- [ ] that the essential tutorial role of managers be built into managers' job descriptions if a distance learning system were established.

It is hoped that this paper will act as a lens to focus attention on the concept of distance learning systems within organizations.

Reference

Kolb, D A (1974) On management and the learning process. *Organizational Pschyology; A Book of Readings,* second edition. Prentice Hall, New Jersey.

8.4 Distance Learning for Technicians

John Twining and Christine Ward
Guildford Educational Services Ltd

Abstract: This paper considers the background to, and the interim conclusions of, a project dealing with distance learning as a method of training technicians.

The Context of Distance Learning for Technicians

This can best start with a quotation from *The FE System in England and Wales,* published by The Further Education Staff College, Coombe Lodge:

> We tend to define all 14+ education as a course of study leading to this or that certificate issued by a national examining body.

The Haslegrave Report in 1969 led to the establishment of the Technician Education Council (TEC) in 1973. TEC's certificates, diplomas, higher certificates and higher diplomas are replacing the previous technician certificates of City and Guilds and the ONCs, HNCs, ONDs and HNDs of the Joint Committee. To appreciate the problems relating to distance learning it is necessary to compare (admittedly very superficially and without a fine degree of precision) TEC's requirements with those previously provided.

Table 1 compares course characteristics, Table 2 compares assessment characteristics, while Table 3 compares the various student requirements, of award-giving bodies.

The 'Yes but' at the bottom right of Figure 3 is 'shorthand' for the following extract from TEC's 1974 Policy Statement:

> There will no doubt continue to be many potential students seeking technician education who cannot attend a college regularly, and the Council intends to provide adequately for their needs. The Council believes that personal contact between student and teacher and the opportunity of studying in a college environment with access to specialist accommodation and facilities such as the library, will be a necessary part of the process leading to a TEC award. It therefore feels that a programme undertaken wholly by private study will not meet its requirements.
>
> It will be exploring the possibilities of combining studies undertaken by correspondence, or other forms of study which do not involve regular attendance at a college, with a system of occasional personal contact between the student and a college.

	City and Guilds	Joint Committees	TEC
Structure	Mostly grouped	Grouped	Unit/credit
Syllabus	Mostly central	Central guide	Central and college
Validation (1)	Specialisms only	All courses	All courses
Validation (2)	Content only	Resources > content	Content > resources

Table 1. *Course characteristics*

	City and Guilds	Joint Committees	TEC
End exam	Yes	Yes	No
In-course assessment	Projects only	Yes	Yes
Setting/marking	Mostly external	Internal + external assessment (detailed)	Internal + moderation (system)
Result determination	External (statistical analysis)	External (formula)	Internal

Table 2. *Assessment characteristics*

	City and Guilds	Joint Committees	TEC
Entry	Open	Rigidly controlled	Almost open
Registration	Exam entry only	Variable	Start of course
Attendance	Guide only	Rigid requirement	Flexible
External students	Few restrictions	Not permitted	'Yes but'

Table 3. *Student requirements*

TEC External Student Developments

Although TEC's main efforts have been focused on getting its main provision moving, a working party was able to develop some concepts of distance learning from its policy. The important step was the identification of 'exporting centres' and 'importing colleges' defined as follows:

Exporting Centre

The term *exporting centre* is defined as an establishment which has received approval for a TEC programme of units. If the exporting centre is a college, it is likely that it will be operating the programme/units internally by one of the conventional modes. If the exporting centre is not a college and is, perhaps, lacking in the experience and resources to guarantee the necessary standards, it is likely that it will be operating the programme/units in collaboration with a college. The function of the exporting centre is to devise learning material or purchase it and provide assessment in the form of phase tests and/or end-of-unit examinations. It will also need the administration and resources to keep the material up-to-date.

Importing College

The term *importing college* is defined as one which would acquire the learning material and the assessment plan from an exporting centre. It is not likely that an importing college would have approval to run the relevant programme by any of the conventional modes, but students would register there and receive tutorial support, or at least counselling. It is expected that most exporting centres will act through importing colleges.

In 1974, TEC worked with the Post Office Telecommunications Branch on a pilot scheme to replace the Post Office's correspondence courses which for 75 years had prepared personnel for the City and Guilds telecommunications technicians examinations. The impending withdrawal of these examinations was serious, as the right to obtain promotion from unskilled to skilled grades through examination success was enshrined in industrial relations agreements.

Another important TEC development was the acceptance that any individual unit could be studied separately. It seems likely that short modules like TEC units (nominal in-college time is 60 hours) will be more popular with potential distance learning students that complete programmes.

There have also been pressures within the TEC system for distance learning to help solve such problems of individual students as 'bridging', whether from old provision to a TEC programme, or from one TEC programme to another; and for remedial action when, say, one unit out of a group of five is not successfully completed. And while TEC has been developing, there have also been movements and pressure groups in education generally, in relation to adult education, open learning and retraining.

Distance Learning Technicians' Project

In order to bring together all these developments into a working system, my company (Guildford Educational Services) was commissioned to undertake a two-and-a-half-year investigation starting in April 1979. This project has close relationships with a major project under the auspices of the Council for Educational Technology on open learning systems.

After a year's work, the interim conclusions of the project are:

☐ That the concepts of 'importing college' and 'exporting centre' lead to the further concept of a network system — that is, one in which a

number of establishments and organizations are linked together to provide
a comprehensive service in which any student (who satisfied any eligibility
requirements, which could include a minimum age) could study for the
award of his or her choice without the need for regular attendance at a
local college;

☐ That such a network system is feasible in the context of UK further
education.

Unresolved problems include:

☐ assessment
☐ pacing
☐ financial arrangements
☐ the need for a central body

In our workshop, a report of which follows, we examined the problems of
assessment and pacing.

Workshop Report

8.5 Distance Learning for TEC: Pacing and Assessment Aspects

Christine Ward and John Twining
Guildford Educational Services Ltd

Organizers' Account

The workshop opened with a guide to some of the differences between the TEC
system and the City and Guilds and Joint Committee systems which it was replacing.
TEC has flexible attendance and entry requirements and a cautious acceptance of
external students. TEC advocates course work assessment or in-course tests
('phase tests') in place of a single external end-of-unit examination. The college sets
and marks the assessments and determines the results, subject to moderation by
TEC.

The opportunity for students to pace and time their own study is determined
by the degree of flexibility of the distance learning scheme. At one end of the
spectrum is the 'modified convoy' (as in Open University courses) where students
begin and end at fixed times, working to fixed examination and assignment
completion dates. At the other is the 'roll-on, roll-off' system, which students may
start and finish at any time. The latter clearly benefits students if the amount of
time available for study varies from month to month (eg because of the seasonal
requirements of their occupation). Ideally, students should be able to plan their
study timetable with their tutors in the light of their individual situations, but be
permitted to renegotiate it if circumstances change.

Problems of assessment for distance learning courses were then introduced.
Assessment is of concern to the students (as a means to an award) and to employers,
the public and the education sector (tutors, course designers, etc). Amongst other

concerns, the interested parties may wish to assess the effectiveness of distance learning as a mode of study. This is difficult to do in the TEC system because there is no uniform external examination, and therefore no yardstick by which to judge the results of the two modes of study. If they prove to have different pass rates one does not know whether this results from differences in the students' attainment or in the standard of the assessment.

The qualities required of the assessment scheme for distance learning, as for any other assessment scheme, are validity, reliability, efficiency and beneficial side-effects.

Validity is the appropriateness of the assessment, which should be related both to the course content and to the students' occupations. Particular problems in ensuring validity in the TEC/distance learning context may be:

(a) The need to assess practical course objectives by practical means.
(b) The requirement for a valid means of assessing the higher cognitive abilities (application and synthesis). Could the use of projects or assignments for distance learning students mean that their assessment was *more* valid than that taken by college students?
(c) The TEC requirement that the assessment should not be based on performance on a single occasion at the end of the course or unit.
(d) The desirability of relating the assessment for the award to the standard attained by the end of the unit, not the process by which the student reached that standard (this could conflict with (c)).

Reliability relates to the consistency of measurement. Will the student get the same result as he would have had if he had taken a different paper or assessment, on a different day, marked by another marker, at another college, or the assessment taken by a conventional college student? Particular problems for TEC may be:

(a) Questions must be objective or have a tight marking scheme, if they are to be taken on different occasions; otherwise the marker has time to forget the criteria he has used.
(b) Setting tests at different times poses security problems.
(c) Question banking seems to be required, but there may be insufficient distant students for pre-testing.
(d) Consistency of standards between colleges is desirable.
(e) Consistency of standards between distant and conventional modes of study is desirable.

The assessment should be *efficient* in terms of time, effort and resources required of tutors, examiners, moderators and students. Students can pace their study more effectively if they do not have to work to fixed test dates; their time should not be taken up unnecessarily by travelling to college for frequent tests; over-assessment should be avoided.

The *side-effects* of the assessment scheme on the course should be beneficial; it should not restrict the flexibility of distant study or encourage 'drop out' because of early poor test results.

The workshop then divided into three small working groups and reconvened later to share results.

Conclusions

1. The distance learning scheme must include provision for some face-to-face sessions for tutorials and/or practical and laboratory work.
2. The package would include self-monitoring tests and questions. These

would help the student assess his progress and would also be seen by the tutor, but would not form part of the assessment for the award.

3. Since some practical instruction would be needed in appropriate units, there should be no difficulty in combining the assessment with the instruction. Assessment would be in-course, based on a checklist of objectives which must be attained. Occasionally it might be necessary for instruction and assessment to be undertaken by the employer, although monitored by the tutor.

4. The higher abilities of application and synthesis (or invention) could best be assessed by means of projects or assignments done in the student's own time. Although this allows the possibility of collusion between students, it should be possible to check during tutorials that the student had indeed mastered the relevant material.

5. Recall, comprehension and perhaps some application could best be assessed by means of objective or short-answer/structured questions with tight marking schemes. It was envisaged that there would be co-operation between colleges in setting up a bank of questions, either nationally or for each area of the country.

6. The pre-testing for these questions should be undertaken using students on conventional courses, partly to ensure that there were sufficient students taking the pre-test, and partly to enable the standards of the two study modes to be related.

7. In the long term it was envisaged that a fresh test for each occasion could be compiled by computer from a central bank and transmitted to a VDU at which the student would work. Results for objective questions would be available immediately; constructed-answer questions would be sent to an examiner for marking.

8. The system used in the short term should be designed to be compatible with the long-term plans. Banks of suitable questions should be established and tests compiled from them. Tests might be available on demand or at fixed intervals (say, once a month). In either case, the test would be invigilated and the question papers returned afterwards to ensure security.

9. Considerable resources would be needed to set up the banks.

Section 9:
The Evaluation of Teaching, Training and Learning

9.1 Technology and Evaluation in the Year 2000

N D C Harris and J G Bailey
University of Bath

Abstract: The development of networks for the storage and access of information will put considerable pressure on evaluators to provide more immediate reporting. The use of such systems raises a range of issues: the paper looks at some of the questions involved and attempts some predictions based on present trends.

Introduction

In this paper we shall look at the impact of developing networks for the storage and access of information. We shall use these potential developments as a basis for looking at the possible impacts on educational evaluation and educational evaluators. It is our premise that evaluation has been the strength of some aspects of educational technology (Rowntree, 1976) and that *information about evaluation* will become increasingly important in the future.

The paper will be divided into three main sections. In the first section we shall outline the four paradigms that we consider to be in current use. In the second we shall suggest possible impacts of new communication systems on evaluation and evaluators. This second section will be presented as a series of arguments and counter-arguments along the lines of the adversary model (Kourilsky, 1973) of evaluation. In the third section we shall endeavour to draw conclusions of our view of the future in relation to evaluation. Others may draw different conclusions, and only time will tell how far off the target we were.

Four Paradigms in Evaluation Strategy

1. CONTROLLED INQUIRY

This approach is based on the classic concept of the scientific experiment. This style of inquiry assumes that it is possible to have a disinterested unbiased approach based on classical logic. The evaluator maintains distance between himself and what is to be studied. This style of carrying out evaluation usually involves large numbers of learners. The reporting of this style of inquiry is usually statistical, often involving complex analysis of data.

2. CONCEPTUAL INQUIRY

This approach accepts that other bases than the scientific approach exist and consciously attempts to use these other approaches. It acknowledges that the norm is an opinion based on theoretical perspective. Research programmes with an evaluation component are derived from the continual attempt to develop new conceptual frameworks, to try out innovations and to view these innovations from a variety of perspectives. Associated with this style are curriculum development, educational technology, innovation strategies, and the use of techniques from other disciplines. The reporting of this style of evaluation usually involves persuasion based on a preferred basis (eg discovery learning), use of examples showing the effectiveness of the new idea and often psychological or other evidence. The examples are seldom of a statistical basis.

3. ACTIVE GENERAL INQUIRY

This is based on the assumption that it is not possible for an evaluator to have a disinterested unbiased approach. The other main assumption is that education is a human activity and that educational evaluation is to promote human development on the widest possible scale. The evaluator deliberately makes contact with and interacts personally with the learning environment. The basis of such work may include observation, interviews and informal discussions in order to get a picture of the environment. The development of illuminative evaluation is in this category. The evaluator may choose co-operation or conflict as his basis for collecting data. The reporting style is still that of an outsider judging.

4. ACTIVE SPECIFIC INQUIRY

The evaluator acts as an enabler to the teacher or teacher-learner situation to enable the participants to improve understanding. The basic assumption is different from the other three styles because the evaluator is not aiming to report to other people what he finds.

The evaluators' reports are aimed at the participants to enable them to understand themselves and the situation better.

New Communication Strategies

In the section that follows, a number of points have been raised relating to the development of information networks. I am not sure that these information storage systems will be related very closely to the activities of evaluators. The whole approach outlined puts far too much emphasis on written reports, rather than on the use of reports to aid decision-making or on the use of the information as a basis for negotiation between people involved with an educational activity. My underlying doubts focus on whether there will be a parallel development in personal skills to enable the various audiences to make use of such information. Large networks (with few administrators) have the danger of being concerned with only autocratic and bureaucratic evaluations rather than democratic evaluations (McDonald, 1976). I would now like to take the points one by one.

Microelectronics and Academic Publishing

A major problem is to obtain evaluation reports. Often evaluation data are not made available to the innovator or sponsor until, at best, a few months after the completion of the evaluation (and not generally published for another few years). During that time potential users of the course lack key information.

Information systems are undergoing great changes. The intermediate state is the using of microfiche. Microfiche has enabled a much wider circulation of reports which had limited circulation (eg ERIC). The use of microelectronic storage systems, and rapid high-capacity data transmission systems will have dramatic effects on academic publishing over the next 20 years (Willis, 1979). Present evaluation reports mainly come into this category of academic publishing. At present such reports are often only available in college and university libraries. Access to evaluation reports will become not only possible but also easy for teachers, parents and learners.

Although academic publishing may become dominated by a new data system and reports of large-scale evaluations may be published via such a system, evaluation is not a self-contained activity (Schools Council, 1979). *It is, or should be, an organized activity within any educational process and not an activity to provide a report. I cannot see that the evaluation process can be improved by storage of reports in a viewdata system. Many educational courses are idiosyncratic and without a broad knowledge of the context of these courses, the use of selected information can be dangerous.*

Microfiche may have allowed quicker access to the academic/technical community but has had little effect on lay audiences.

Is it not rather naive to think that the storage of material in a microelectronic system will lead to the information being made more accessible? Pressing the correct button does not mean that the public necessarily have real access to the information. If the research community cannot translate its findings into simple language on paper, why should it be able to on viewdata?

Viewdata and the Use of Such a System

It seems likely that an index system would be used similar to PRESTEL (the Post Office viewdata system), CEEFAX or ORACLE (the BBC and IBA viewdata systems). So an evaluation report in the future will have to be written to fit the system.

You say the report must fit the viewdata system. Is this a straight-jacket comparable with the problems of teaching machines and programmed learning? I think you have identified a major worry concerning the loss of evaluation independence. Although you discuss the points more thoroughly later, I cannot believe that, firstly, any important negative information relating to schools (or any other educational activity) would ever be published on a public access system (Brighouse, 1979) *(it definitely is not the best way to solve problems — in fact, often the reverse); secondly, complex aspects would be simplified due to space restrictions.*

Publishing: Who Controls the Information

This all looks fine as an information system, but how does this evaluation information get into storage? At present, evaluators publish through books, journals and reports. These publications are vetted (usually using referees) to be acceptable for journals abstracted by ERIC. The new style publisher acts as intermediary between the author and the storage system. Your evaluation report (even an interim or initial report) can be typed in on your word processor and transferred to the new publisher. He may sell your report to the system which, in turn, charges the user.

You seem to be assuming that evaluation material will only be provided by the academic community. In that situation refereeing might be appropriate; however, like Independent Schools Handbooks the publishers might allow the institution to write its information for inclusion at a fee.

Who Actually Controls the Information?

Who controls the information? The evaluator, the sponsor, or the college? It is clear that the evaluator is put in a position of considerable responsibility. If Boxo Drinks or Corringhon College refuse to allow information into the system, then the potential course user will only have factual course data.

What about confidential information? Obviously, this presents a considerable problem. However, confidential information could be coded to prevent access to this other than for, say, *bona fide* research workers or other authorized persons.

I still cannot believe that negative reports will be allowed onto a public system. Therefore, this so-called evaluation information will amount to a list of non-controversial information. I think this is rather 'weak' evaluation data (Hamilton, 1977). *We seem to agree that overall 'control' of the system will create problems of confidentiality if more than low-level information is to be stored. For any evaluation activity depends on honest co-operation between many people who trust the evaluator.*

Financing and Controlling of Information

Who is going to pay for all this information and evaluation? If access is in public libraries or similar institutions, some cost will have to be carried by local authorities. If domestic access does become common, a domestic user would probably pay on the basis of usage like electricity. The distributors and storers (let us call them suppliers) would have considerable income. If these suppliers find that most parents check on details of schools and their effectiveness prior to sending their children, investment in further information would be in the suppliers' interest. Here is a new potential source of funding for evaluation and research.

Taking the school example a step further, information may be provided on:

(a) Employment of past pupils (as already occurs for universities and polytechnics in the UK).
(b) Political/context information.
(c) Opinions about the curriculum.

The last two come nearer to the illuminative model and enable parents, politicians and society in general to bring pressure to bear on education, perhaps helping to break down the institutionalization of education. There is also an element of Big Brother watching, which is inevitable when information is more easily accessible.

Libraries at present carry prospectuses and they are free. A new system placed in a library is likely to be available at a price to the user. Alternatively, if the system does result in terminals in the home the costs again will be borne by the consumer. The worry is that in both cases cost (however low) may act as a barrier to certain people.

You point out that the suppliers would have considerable income; in our society this often leads to control. We have a complex system of publishing that allows a wide range of views to be expressed in professional journals. I wonder how errors of judgement and perception will be handled with a new data system?

Perhaps only 'popular' materials could afford to be put into the system. Big Brother certainly lurks in the shadows! A few people controlling a few large systems are possibly much more likely than the democratic access to even more information.

The Role of the Evaluator in the Future

What of the pressures on the evaluator? The evaluator's role will be more public. Pressure will be to provide information quickly, in the format of the system access relevant to the main potential audiences.

A key decision for the supplier will be the identification of potential audiences, eg:

(a) individuals selecting courses
(b) politicians and pressure groups
(c) professional educators
(d) professional administrators
(e) professional evaluators

On the face of it, the biggest potential users will be category (a). Parents and other students may be willing to use such information, even at a price, if it assists in decision-making. Unfortunately the information which is easiest to read (the third paradigm, active general inquiry) is often also open to most abuse by insensitive evaluators and pressure groups. The more generalizable quantitative information is often indigestible to any but professional audiences (such as (c) and (e)) who may have to pay more for access because of less use.

The pressure would appear to be on evaluators using the first and second paradigms for improved communication. Groups (b) to (e) will probably want regular cost comparisons of curricula, methods and institutions — especially in times of financial stringency.

The necessity for speed of access and continual updating puts another pressure on evaluators. Quick reporting will become necessary.

The workers using the fourth paradigm would appear to lose out, apart from providing information on techniques to other professionals. However, with more pressure on institutions, the workers of the fourth paradigm may have more than enough to do to maintain sanity amongst teachers.

The evaluator of the future must be very sensitive to his potential audience; able to make quick decisions and able to report those decisions in the required format. He will no longer be able to take a leisurely background place; it will be a pressure calling!

The other interesting feature is that parents and learners may all be evaluators, if they can meet the requirements. Is that not where evaluation started?

Considering a school's entry into a viewdata system, for a long time the length of entries will be restricted. This will mean that the entries will be stylized and contain only information under what categories are regarded as important by certain evaluators and/or decision-makers. The evaluator's role may easily become that of an anonymous technician. Certainly more information will be available, possibly more accessible, but will it be more useful?

This will lead to another type of 'evaluator' (if he may be called so), trained or untrained, leading to a stereotyped 'evaluation'. The need for reflection as part of an evaluation is understood but quicker reporting could easily lead to conveyor-belt evaluation. The various audiences certainly need a different style of reporting but the less quantitative styles of evaluation, if edited, can too easily lead to abuse. Although you had already made this point I would take it further because the qualifying sentences and paragraphs make the reader aware of the real situation.

Although one form of report may again shift evaluation to the first two paradigms I would hope a self-balancing system would emerge. The information in the system is a useful data-base for an evaluator of the fourth paradigm. trying to enable change from within an institution (and this surely is the real focal point of educational evaluation). He will have access to information that will (if your arguments are realized) enable them to back up their attempts to bring about an improvement in an institution by showing others good or bad examples.

In such a transmission system there is no reason why television recordings of actual practice could not be included. This enables more use of the fourth paradigm although opening it to public scrutiny rather than private discussion. However, the control of this is even harder than alphanumeric displays.

Conclusion

If data transmission systems do develop as suggested there will be considerable constraints on the style of reporting. In addition, the problem of who controls the information is very important. The possibility of uncritical neutral information may become the pattern, because negative comment may be precluded by the innovators and teachers in the institutions or systems being evaluated.

The possibility of evaluation editors who become journalists for data display systems also raises the spectre of changes towards dramatization and distortion.

References

Brighouse, T R P (1979) *The Four-Yearly School Report* Note 1. Mimeograph. Oxford County Council Education Department.

Hamilton, D (1977) Illuminations and ruminations. *BERA Research Intelligence*, **3**, 1.

Kourlisky, M (1973) An adversary model for educational evaluation. *Evaluation Comments*, **14**, 2, pp 3-6.

McDonald, B (1976) Evaluation and the control of education. In Tawney, D (ed) *Curriculum Evaluation Today: Trends and Implications.* Schools Council Research Studies. Macmillan Education, London.

Rowntree, D (1976) Evaluation: the critical ingredient of educational technology. *Programmed Learning and Educational Technology,* **13**, 4, pp 7-9.

Schools Council (1979) *An Introduction to Evaluation — Some Notes for Schools Council Evaluators.* Schools Council, London.

Willis, N (1979) Microprocessors and microelectronics and their effects on publishing. In Harris, N D C (ed) *Educational Implications of Microprocessors and Microelectronics.* Conference Report. STEC. University of Bath, Bath.

Acknowledgement

We would like to thank the Council for Educational Technology who funded an associated project during the preparation of this paper and gave us access to PRESTEL.

Workshop Report
9.2 Technology and Evaluation in the Year 2000

N D C Harris and J G Bailey
University of Bath

Organizers' Account

The aims of the workshop were (i) to allow participants to explore the issues raised in the paper in more depth, (ii) to allow participants to contribute further areas for consideration, and (iii) to give a practical example of one of the constraints, ie the problem of viewdata format when writing reports.

The workshop began with the practical activity: an illustration of the problem of summarizing two pages of an illuminative evaluation report onto one page of a viewdata system. Participants were given a grid with spaces for 40 characters horizontally and 24 characters vertically to help with layout. The resulting viewdata pages could be divided into two types: (i) those which attempted to select (edit) and display the material in a balanced PRESTEL-type layout, and (ii) those who attempted to use prose. The latter came closer to the illuminative style report, but omitted all quotations. This exercise enabled participants to experience the constraints of a viewdata system and the important role an evaluation 'editor' would have.

The group then discussed the issues raised in the paper, focusing mainly on the issue of control. The consensus seemed to be that the chances of information, useful to a critical public, being put on a public system was very small. This was not just because of bureaucratic control but also because of the problem of libel, ie institutions or individuals not agreeing with a viewdata report would sue for its removal and/or damages.

It was suggested that a useful style of report could be the type that is used in *Which?* magazine, but again it was thought that libel was a problem.

The problem of less sophisticated audiences accepting the information on viewdata pages as irrefutable facts was also discussed. The displayed statements being considered separate from the environmental context of the institution would be a nonsense.

In general we felt the workshop met its aims.

Participant's Comments

A Ashman *University of Durham*

The workshop centred on the problems of preparing a 1,000-character PRESTEL input of a recent illuminative evaluation. The example chosen was of an evaluation of a secondary school project on technology, which so far has not been published and is inaccessible to the general public and those interested in its findings. The practical exercise highlighted many problems which kept the discussion moving along well until long after its scheduled finishing time. The areas of discussion were:

1. Who shall do the editing of the evaluation? The original author, an educationalist, or a professional writer?
2. Who are the intended target audience? Is it possible to write the input to cover the variety of potential users, ie parents, teachers, pupils, academic researchers, people named in the report, etc? The reduction of unit costs by increasing the generality of the information conflicts with the differing needs of the target audience.
3. What information is required? At what level of generality and sophistication?
4. Political implications of the information — if the information is to be on public access, is it possible to make it libel-free, to prevent possible legal action from teachers' unions, Schools Council and other professional bodies that would be named in the report? Would the Schools Council permit publication of a report that contained serious criticism of its mode of operation?
5. How can reports on the recently announced programme of Schools Council research projects be disseminated? The programme would seem to require some form of computerized dissemination of the results of these mini-development projects to extend their influence outside the boundaries of the small initiating group.

9.3 The Development of Educational Technology: Alternative Perspectives on Evaluation

Alistair R Morgan, Graham Gibbs and Elizabeth Taylor
The Open University

Abstract: This paper examines approaches to educational evaluation and research in student learning and describes the trend towards using qualitative methodologies to increase the relevance of research findings.

Introduction

At the most general level, educational technology is concerned with the improving of student learning. At the Open University, educational technologists perform this role by (i) transferring information on students' reactions to teaching materials back to course team authors, and (ii) by attempting to incorporate general principles or more pragmatic guidelines about student learning into the design of the courses.

Many of the criticisms of educational technology have been directed towards the second activity, namely attempts to prescribe course design from general principles of learning. Fleming (1978) describes how, by taking a technological approach to education, what is to count as valid educational experience is determined by the system rather than the individual learner. At the Open University, Harris (1976) and Northedge (1976) are critical that some of the teaching strategies used imply a rather mechanistic conception of the learner.

Rowntree (1976) described how he saw that the emphasis of educational technology had changed away from a prescriptive approach to course development and identified *evaluation* as the critical ingredient of educational technology.

This paper will discuss developments in evaluation and in particular how a qualitative or illuminative approach is being used by the Study Methods Group at the Open University and will examine the assumptions this approach makes about teaching and learning.

Traditional Approaches to Evaluation

The traditional approach to curriculum evaluation is derived from the systematic objectives-based model of educational technology, which can be described in four stages: (i) identify the objectives, (ii) design the learning activities, (iii) evaluate the effectiveness of the learning activities in achieving the objectives, (iv) improve the learning activities in the light of the evaluation. The task of evaluation is to identify the objectives or goals of an educational programme and to design techniques to determine the achievement of them.

As the Open University is based on a distance-teaching system, where immediate feedback from students as in face-to-face teaching is not available, educational technologists have put considerable effort into evaluation, particularly of courses in their first year of presentation, so that the course teams can get some impression of students' reactions to the learning materials.

Henderson and Nathenson (1976) have done some of the most comprehensive work on evaluation in the Open University in the context of developmental testing. They used feedback questions inserted in the teaching text to gain students' reaction to the material, and performance tests to look at learning outcomes. On the basis of this feedback and performance data, modifications were made to the teaching materials.

Although this work is not entirely a goal-orientated approach, this conception of evaluation is based on the teacher's or evaluator's terms and takes no account of what is to count as an educational experience or achievement in the learner's terms. This evaluation contains the implicit assumption of producing one ideal teaching treatment, which does not recognize the wide range of students' abilities and learning styles.

Alternative Approaches to Evaluation

The emphasis on pre-specified goals or on objectives for the evaluation of *any* educational activity is problematic. Firstly this is because it ignores the *process* of the learning experience, which may be of equal or greater importance than the goal or product (as, for example, in open-ended project work) and secondly it is because in some subject areas, particularly the humanities, outcomes cannot necessarily be anticipated in advance.

As a response to the excesses of goal-orientated evaluation, Scriven (1976) advocated goal-free evaluation. This approach stressed the need to go beyond the intended goals of an educational programme, and to look for the unintended side-effects. It was claimed that familiarity with the goals would influence the evaluation in the direction of the intended outcomes, so external evaluators are needed who are unfamiliar with the educational programme in question.

This approach of goal-free evaluation has been developed and modified by Parlett and Hamilton (Hamilton *et al*, 1977). Their approach, termed 'illuminative evaluation', aimed to describe and interpret all aspects of an educational programme. It is 'methodologically eclectic, using interviews, questionnaires, participant observation and the analysis of documents'.

The insights that illuminative evaluation can provide are demonstrated clearly by Miller and Parlett (1974) in a study of assessment. This is illustrated in analysis of interview transcriptions with final year undergraduates on how they were preparing for their examinations.

One group of students talked of the need to be perceptive of the 'cues' given by staff and to pick up hints about examinations topics. A much smaller group, besides being aware of the cues, were actively seeking information on the examination. A third group — the largest — were not perceptive of cues and considered that sheer hard work was the secret of success. These three groups were labelled: cue-conscious, cue-seeking and cue-deaf, respectively.

The interesting feature of this study is that the concept of 'cue-consciousness' was identified, which had *not* been predicted in advance. A survey approach using a closed-ended questionnaire, designed from the perspective of the teaching staff or the evaluations, would have almost certainly failed to identify this key issue. Quantitative and goal-orientated research has to assume that the relevant variables have already been identified and can only examine the relationship between these pre-specified variables.

Research into Student Learning — Using Qualitative Methodologies

Although this paper has concentrated on activities termed *evaluation,* a considerable amount of work in the general area of 'research into student learning' seems very relevant to developing evaluation and educational technology for the future.

The research group of Ference Marton at the University of Göteborg, in Sweden, has been influential in developing qualitative methodologies, and their work has been reviewed elsewhere (Gibbs, Morgan and Taylor, 1980). In one study, Marton and Säljö (1976) asked students to study an article relevant to their course of study. They were then asked, in individual interviews, *what* the article was about, ie what the author was attempting to convey, and *how* they had approached studying this text.

Analysis of the interview transcriptions revealed two very different approaches to study: a reliance on memory, or an analysis for the principal ideas of the article. These qualitatively different approaches to studying were labelled as 'surface-level' and 'deep-level' processing respectively.

The different approaches to study were directly linked to the quality of learning outcomes. Students who had adopted a deep-level approach had a better understanding of what the article was about.

The main feature of the Swedish work is that learning experiences are described from students' perspectives rather than those of the researcher or teacher. Marton and Svensson (1979) draw the distinction between first-order and second-order perspectives as follows:

> One is observational, 'from the outside and noumenal, and the other is experiential 'from the inside' and phenomenal.

This second-order perspective is similar methodologically to the illuminative-evaluation of Miller and Parlett. We believe that this research work on student learning is essential for gaining students' reactions to learning materials and to develop a framework for understanding how students tackle learning.

The Approach of the Study Methods Group

The Study Methods Group in the Institute of Educational Technology has initiated a programme of research to investigate *how* students approach studying from our correspondence training materials and *why* they adopt a particular approach.

The Study Methods Group was formed because, despite eight years of evaluation, based primarily on survey research, the Open University understood little about how its students go about their studying. At the same time, *outside* the Open University there has been a trend in research into student learning which has been towards qualitative methodologies (Elton and Laurillard, 1979).

This work is methodologically very similar to that of Ference Marton's group at Göteborg, but attempts to link together aspects of student learning which have until now been studied separately. The four aspects which we are studying are students' overall orientation, their conception of learning, their detailed approach to specific tasks, and their learning outcomes.

Students' overall orientation (ie their aims and aspirations for studying) has been shown to be related to their approach to study but without precise specification of the nature of this relationship (Beaty, 1978; Mathias, 1980). Students have been shown to have different conceptions of learning (Säljö, 1979) and it has been *inferred* that these conceptions are closely related to the *approach* students take to tasks, but this link has not been directly explored. The approach students take has been shown to be closely related to the learning outcome (Marton and Säljö, 1976), but outcome has *not* been directly linked to students' conception of learning or their orientation. In the present study all these aspects are explicitly linked together.

The students are being interviewed about their overall orientation, their conception of learning, and their understanding of key social science concepts *before* they start the course. They are being interviewed during the course about the details of the approach they are adopting towards the course material in which the key concepts are taught. And they are being interviewed after their exam about their understanding of the same concepts, and about any changes which have taken place in their orientation or conception of learning as a consequence of having studied the course.

The crucial evaluation of the *outcome* of the course is in terms of the qualitative changes in understanding of key concepts which we will find. The categories of understanding against which student learning will be judged will be derived from examination of the variation which is found to exist, and *not*, as with conventional evaluation, from the course authors' pre-specified goals. For example, we have asked students: 'Is Britain capitalist?' Analysis of the variation of students' answers will lead to our defining categories of conceptions of capitalism which students actually hold. The benefit to the students of the course will be indicated by how students' conceptions of capitalism at the end of the course are categorized, and *not* by whether they have met the course team's criteria (in course work and exams).

It is anticipated that certain *orientations* and *approaches* to study will be associated with significant changes in conceptions of the subject, while others are associated with little significant change in conceptions. It is also anticipated that these changes in conceptions will not be as clearly related to performance on the assessment of the course (ie some students will pass the course, but will still hold simplistic conceptions of the social sciences).

The second interviews, half-way through the course, are designed to find out *how* students approach the OU learning materials and tackle the associated assignments. We have done preliminary studies on the Technology Foundation Course. These have shown that surface level and deep level approaches to study, identified by Marton and Säljö (1976), are also evident in Open University students.

We anticipate that similar differences in approaches to studying social science will be directly linked to learning outcomes as shown by changes in conceptions of the key social science concepts.

The Implications for the Development of Educational Technology

We have outlined developments in evaluation and how we are using qualitative methodologies to gain information on students' learning experiences. What are the implications for developing educational technology for the future and assumptions about teaching and learning implied by this approach to evaluative research?

By using qualitative methodologies to focus on students' perspective of learning, this approach recognizes the *complexity* of the individual student and his ability to reflect upon his experience and autonomously choose personally-relevant approaches to study. In contrast, traditional models of evaluation and behaviourist models of man ignore this consciousness of the learner, and instead adopt a somewhat manipulative stance towards the learner.

In designing learning materials, educational technologists must come to understand *how* students actually study in their subject area, and *what* influences the way they use learning materials. We have shown how *qualitative approaches to evaluation* can provide these insights.

References

Beaty, E (1978) The student study contract. Presented at the 4th International Conference on Higher Education, University of Lancaster.

Elton, L R B and Laurillard, D M (1979) Trends in research in student learning. *Studies in Higher Education*, **4**, 1, pp 87-102.

Fleming, W G (1978) The shared understanding of human action: a more appropriate goal
    for educational technology. In Brook, D and Race, P (eds) *Aspects of Educational
    Technology* **XII**, pp 361-6.
Gibbs, G, Morgan, A R and Taylor, E (1980) *A Review of the Research of Ference Marton
    and the Göteborg Group.* Study Methods Group, Paper 2. Institute of Educational
    Technology, Open University, Milton Keynes.
Hamilton, D, Jenkins, D, King, C, Macdonald, B and Parlett, M (1977) *Beyond the Numbers
    Game.* Macmillan, London.
Harris, D (1976) Educational technology at the Open University: a short history of
    achievement and cancellation. *British Journal of Educational Technology,* 7, 1, pp 43-53.
Henderson, E and Nathenson, M B (1976) Developmental testing: an empirical approach to
    course improvement. *Programmed Learning and Educational Technology,* 13, 4, pp 31-42.
Marton, F and Säljö, R (1976) On qualitative differences in learning, outcome and process
    I and II. *British Journal of Educational Psychology,* **46**, pp 4-11 and 115-27.
Marton, F and Svensson, L (1979) Conceptions of research in student learning. *Higher
    Education,* 8, 4, pp 471-86.
Mathias, H (1980) Science students' approaches to learning. *Higher Education,* 9, 1, pp 39-51.
Miller, C M L and Parlett, M (1974) *Up to the Mark: A Study of the Examination Game.*
    Society for Research into Higher Education, London.
Northedge, A (1976) Examining our implicit analogies for learning processes. *Programmed
    Learning and Educational Technology,* 13, 4, pp 67-78.
Rowntree, D (1976) Evaluation: the critical ingredient of educational technology. *Programmed
    Learning and Educational Technology,* 13, 4, pp 7-9.
Säljö, R (1979) Learning about learning. *Higher Education,* 8, 4, pp 443-51.
Scriven, M (1976) The pros and cons of goal-free evaluation: evaluation comment. *Journal
    of Educational Evaluation,* 3, 4.

9.4 Learning at a Distance: Evaluation at a Distance

R M Harden and C Stoane *University of Dundee*
W R Dunn and T S Murray *University of Glasgow*

Abstract: A new approach to in-service training involving distance learning, which has been
developed and implemented, is reported. This approach to distance learning is applicable to
other in-service situations; for example, the in-service training of teachers.

Learning at a Distance
A new approach to continuing medical education has been developed at the Centre
for Medical Education in Dundee. A series of six patient-management problems
was sent by post to 20,000 doctors throughout the UK.

Each doctor has to make decisions about the diagnosis, investigations and
treatment of the patients described in the problem. The problems cover topics
which are considered to be important to general practitioners, and ranged from
management of a diabetic patient who collapses to the management of a
bereaved family.

A unique feature of the design of the problems was the opportunity to obtain
immediate feedback about the decision a doctor made and to compare his own

decisions with those of a specialist and with those of a group of his colleagues. So that these decisions were not immediately visible, they were printed in invisible ink, using a latent image process. Supplied with the problem was a special pen which revealed the information as the doctor required it (Rogers, 1979). It was this opportunity to obtain feedback which gave the series its title — 'Instant Feedback' or 'IF'.

Professor Holmberg (1977) has said that organized non-contiguous two-way communication is a constituent element of distance study. It would seem that the use of the latent image technique provides immediate feedback and thus two-way communication is established. By requiring doctors to assess themselves by comparison between their own ratings, those of a specialist and those of their peers, a focus for speculation is provided for the doctor and the 'guided didactic conversation', of which Holmberg speaks, is set up.

Doctors who received the problems were invited to return to Dundee a postcard on which they had recorded their decisions about the management of the patient. Additional information was available to doctors in printed form or by telephone. With a reply-paid card a doctor could send to Dundee for a printed review written by the authors. The review discusses and compares the specialist's management of each patient with that of the general practitioner, and adds further reading and references. For a two-to-three-minute resumé of the case, a doctor could telephone Dundee to listen to a message on a telephone-answering machine and, if he wished, leave a comment or a question.

Evaluation at a Distance

The following were used to provide evaluation data:

1. Doctors' rating cards.
2. Comments.
3. Use of additional information.
4. Telephone interviews.

Twenty per cent of doctors returned these ratings cards, recording their decisions. Doctors could also add on the cards comments about the design and content of the series. A large number of helpful and constructive comments has been listed and classified. Preliminary results of this study have been reported (Harden *et al*, 1979). Some doctors commented that they had learned from the series; most stated that they had enjoyed using the materials; and a number admitted to deficiencies in their knowledge in certain areas.

It was found that almost 20 per cent of the total number of doctors who had received the materials made use of the additional information services. This figure, approximately the same as the number of doctors returning ratings cards was, however, no indication of the number of doctors who were actually using the problems although not sending for additional information nor sending comments. An attempt was made, therefore, to estimate this number. The method adopted was telephone interviewing and the remainder of the paper describes this technique of evaluation.

A random sample of names was taken from the medical directory and these doctors were telephoned. A total of 167 calls was made and of these 67 did not receive the journal (*Medicine*) which had been used to distribute the problems. This left 100 who received *Medicine* and had therefore received IF. Of the 100, 45 had used the series and 55 had not used the series at all.

Doctors were also asked to state whether or not they had returned any of the reply cards to Dundee. As the resultant figures from the sample were similar to the actual return figures it could be said fairly that the sample was valid.

It seemed reasonable to estimate that 45 per cent of the doctors who had received the problems had used them. This percentage represents 9,000 doctors in the UK.

Putting this figure in perspective, it has been stated (Matchett, 1978) by the Division of Continuing Education at Kansas University, that a five per cent return of answers is considered to be a favourable response for mailed materials.

In addition to providing us with useful statistical evidence it was found that the telephone interview was useful in explaining how and why doctors used the materials.

Doctors who responded favourably (to be called Responders for the remainder of this paper) were asked to comment about the way in which they had used the materials, and those who had not used the materials (Non-Responders) were asked to say why they had found the approach or the materials unsuitable.

The 100 doctors interviewed were located throughout the UK. Twenty came from Scotland, 76 from England, four from Wales and none from Ireland.

The Technique of Telephone Interviewing

An interview schedule was constructed, structured and yet flexible enough to allow freedom of ideas.

Interviews were conducted during the period January to February 1979. Each interview lasted for at least five minutes and at most 40 minutes. Doctors' willingness to talk in this way was impressive. Persistence was, however, needed in some cases to get beyond the efficient secretary who guarded her doctor very very loyally!

The 45 Responders were asked to state which Challenges they had used and what form of back-up material they had favoured, if any. The time taken for distribution of the materials and the fact that interviews were conducted over the period of distribution of several Challenges, obviously affected results, certainly of the later materials. It was found that even at the stage of interviewing, a number of doctors had forgotten which Challenge they had done, whilst others had put some aside to be completed at a later date.

It was found that doctors were willing and eager to discuss use of the materials by telephone. Not only was it possible, therefore, to obtain the required statistical information by telephone but it was also found that better quality data could be collected than by using the more traditional postal questionnaire.

Background on Responders

LOCATION
Looking first at the 45 Responders, 12 came from Scotland, 13 from the midlands and north of England, 18 from the south of England and two from Wales.

AGE AND SEX
Fifteen were aged in their 30s, 10 in their 40s, 15 in their 50s and five in their 60s. Thirty-seven doctors were male and eight were female.

Topics Relating to the Materials

A number of different topics relating to the materials was discussed.

CONTENT AND FORMAT
Doctors were asked about the content and format of the materials. Twenty-nine (64 per cent) found the materials attractive, 34 (75 per cent) found the series

easy to use and 36 (80 per cent) found the content relevant to general practice. Two doctors (both MRCGP) stated that the content was too easy and a third felt that the series was 'rather low key, not especially helpful, but quite good'.

USE OF BACK-UP MATERIALS
Twenty-one of the 45 doctors had used back-up reviews and five had used the telephone-answering service. These figures suggest that use of these materials by the sample was slightly above the actual return figures. Sixteen (76 per cent) doctors stated that they had found these services useful. Those who had used the reviews in preference to the telephone said they did so for the following reasons:

1. They did not like receiving information by telephone; or
2. Telephoning is too expensive.

Several put in a plea for a more local service. One doctor said that he had taped the telephone message so that he could listen to it again at his leisure.

HOW USED
Doctors were asked how the materials had been used. Forty-three doctors had used the materials individually as self-assessment exercises, one had used them in a group situation in his practice, and one had used both methods. Six of the 45 doctors had either used or planned to use the Challenges with their trainees. Thirty doctors (66 per cent) had used the materials immediately, 11 (24 per cent) after some delay, and four could not remember how soon they had used the materials. The majority had used them at home rather than in the practice.

EFFECT ON LEARNING
Of the 45 who had used the materials, 19 doctors (42 per cent) were able to comment about the effect on learning. Sixteen (35 per cent) said that they had learned from using the materials, whilst three (seven per cent) said that the approach provided only interest and fun. Those who could not answer this question felt either that it was too early to comment or that they needed longer to decide.

CONTRIBUTION TO CONTINUING EDUCATION
Of the 15 doctors (33 per cent) who were able to comment about this question, all stated that the series provided an answer to a need and therefore contributed in a useful way.

EFFECT ON ATTITUDE
Twelve doctors were able to comment on certainty about use of the series affecting their attitudes as general practitioners. Four (eight per cent) felt sure that attitude had been affected, five (11 per cent) said that it had not, and three (six per cent) did not know. The rest felt unable to comment but said that they liked to think that attitudes had been affected.

COLLABORATION WITH DRUG COMPANY
Doctors were asked to discuss their opinions about our collaboration with a drug company. Five approved wholeheartedly, none felt disapproval, but the majority had no particular opinion.

GENERAL COMMENTS
General comments about the materials, production quality, methods of use and usefulness were complimentary. 'Interesting', 'fun', 'super — helpful for my MRCGP exam', 'more than just fun', 'learned something, particularly about deficiencies in my knowledge'. 'amazed at results in feedback — enjoyed speculation',

'best in years', 'extraordinarily good idea', 'makes you think', 'learned and felt refreshed' were some of the comments given by the 45 Responders.

Two of the Responders were critical in their comments. A 60-year-old doctor who had used three of the problems said that he found the method of presentation and the type of question irritating and so stopped using the materials. He did, however, find the subject-matter relevant. A second doctor (aged 55) tried the first problem but was 'not impressed'.

Seven doctors claimed that the telephone call had reminded them to continue doing the problems. In every case those who were followed up with a second call had, in fact, done so. In nearly all cases, doctors who had stopped using the series did so because of lack of time.

Non-Responders

What information was gained from the 55 Non-Responders from the sample — doctors who received the IF materials but chose not to do them?

The 55 doctors were asked to comment about their opinions about the IF series, their feelings about its usefulness and contribution to continuing medical education and their reasons for not participating in the project by using the materials.

Shortage of time was stressed in the majority of cases. Typical comments from those short of time were 'shortage of time, not content of series at fault. Series looks interesting and could be illuminating'; 'lack of time because my partner has been ill, but I may have a look'; 'a good idea but I have no time'; 'I'm a bit tardy about finding time for new things but perhaps I will do it'; 'I spend more time writing than reading'; 'I put it aside meaning to do — will do it now'; 'I am busy but interested — will do now'.

A number of doctors had put the materials aside to do at a later date and were inspired by the telephone call to use the materials. They were asked if they objected to further contact to discuss the use of the materials and opinions about the series after use. None objected, and in every case they had indeed used the materials enthusiastically.

From this information it is clear that the majority of Non-Responders give apathy or lack of time as their reasons for not using the materials. It is clear that these doctors find it equally difficult to use materials which are more demanding of their time and generally do not find the time to attend courses and lectures.

The personal contact which can be made by telephone and used to remind or inspire doctors to use materials is seen to be a useful part of the strategy both for Responders and Non-Responders.

Discussion

The approach was initially evaluated by recording the number of doctors who returned cards with their decisions and analyzing the decisions made and by an analysis of comments sent to us in a number of ways by doctors. This data proved to be misleading, as results suggested that only 20 per cent had used the materials and gave little information about why and how doctors had used the materials. The results of the 167 telephone interviews, conducted to discover the number of doctors using the materials, how the doctors had used the materials and their feelings about the effectiveness of the approach, added considerably to the evaluation and enabled us to revise our conclusions about the project.

Forty-five per cent had, in fact, used the materials, and useful information had been gathered about doctors' attitudes to learning and to practice. Contact made with doctors who had not used the materials showed that these doctors did not find fault with the approach but complained about the shortage of time. Telephone contact, however, acted as a reminder in many cases.

Does the technique of telephone interviewing have any advantages over other means of data collection? The technique has been shown to be effective in other fields (Wood and Byrne, 1979). We have certainly found that the method has a number of advantages:

1. Telephone interviews allow a greater response rate.
2. They are more individualized than postal questionnaires.
3. They are more economical than face-to-face interviews.
4. Immediate and ongoing contact can be made.
5. Visual distraction is eliminated (Williams, 1974).
6. Interviews are relaxed.

We have found that there are a few disadvantages to telephone interviewing:

1. The method is more expensive than postal questionnaires.
2. Making contact with a doctor at a convenient time can be difficult.

Is it an efficient and economical method of data collection? In 70 per cent of cases contact was made with the doctor at the first or second attempt, and a small percentage required more than three attempts.

It has been stated (Evered and Williams, 1980) that not only is there little opportunity offered in continuing medical education to develop the intellectual attitudes necessary for continuing self-education, but also that appropriate evaluation of existing systems is rarely carried out.

We have made the following conclusions about the method of continuing education and the approach to evaluation described.

Conclusions

The distance learning approach enabled us to reach a large number of doctors who have been able to use the materials at the time, place and pace most suitable to them.

The approach to evaluation using the telephone interview technique was particularly useful in explaining why and how doctors used the materials and their attitudes to the approach to learning.

This approach to in-service training for doctors is applicable, we feel sure, to other in-service situations, for example the training of teachers, psychologists and social workers.

References

Evered, D C and Williams, H D (1980) Postgraduate education and the doctor. *British Medical Journal*, 1 March.

Harden, R M *et al* (1978) Medical education in the British Isles: trends identified in the GMC survey of basic medical education. *Medical Education*, 12, Supplement 25.

Harden, R M *et al* (1979) Doctors accept a challenge: self-assessment exercises in medical education. *British Medical Journal*, 2, pp 652-3.

Holmberg, B (1977) *Distance Education: A Survey and Bibliography*. Kogan Page, London.

Matchett, J A (1978) Continuing education via the packaged program. *American Journal of Pharmaceutical Education*, 42, pp 383-5.

Rogers, J *et al* (1979) The use of latent image printing in problem-solving and self-assessment exercises. *Journal of Audiovisual Media in Medicine*, 2, pp 27-9.

Williams, E (1974) The effects of telecommunications media upon interaction. Paper read to the 18th International Congress of Applied Psychology, Montreal.

Wood, J and Byrne, P S (1979) Lecturing to general practitioners — findings of a telephone
interview survey. *Journal of the RCGP,* pp 241-5. April.

Acknowledgements

The authors are grateful to Searle Pharmaceuticals for financial support and to *Medicine* for
distribution of materials. They thank the specialists and general practitioners throughout
Britain who contributed to the development of the materials and those doctors who so
willingly took part in the telephone interviews.

9.5 Evaluation of Educational Development Projects: Before, During and After!

David Williams and John Pearce
Brighton Polytechnic

Abstract: The authors draw on Stake's framework for educational evaluation to help define and
explore some of the subject's major issues, and then apply the model to some of the projects
carried out at Brighton Polytechnic in the past five years (Stake, 1967).

Introduction

The old army maxim 'If it moves — salute it; if it doesn't — paint it!' seems to have
a parallel in educational establishments, where innovation and evaluation have
tended to become the order of the day and are thought of as fashionable and a
'good thing', irrespective of their particular relevance or importance. But the
processes of educational innovation and evaluation need to be most carefully
considered, supported and followed through. Firmly believing this view, Brighton
Polytechnic's Learning Resources set up a mechanism for lecturers to undertake
innovative projects, and the Educational Development Unit (EDU) release scheme
has become a successful strategy for educational development. The evolution and
operation of this scheme is discussed in the paper 'Time Off for Innovation'
(Adderley *et al*, 1979). In essence, the scheme enables lecturers to have a reduction
in class contact hours in order to develop teaching and learning projects usually
concerned with an identified aspect of a particular course. To carry out these
projects or 'releases', lecturers are seconded to the EDU for periods ranging from
a half to two days per week for up to one year; and because the EDU is a part of
Learning Resources, which integrates library, media and educational development
services in the Polytechnic, they can draw on a wide range of expertise to support
their projects. Over 30 releases are now being pursued annually, ranging from the
evaluation of teaching and learning materials to the design and production of
specialized learning packages and video-tapes.

Evaluation of the Project

Now that the EDU release scheme is firmly established in the Polytechnic, attention is shifting from the specification and implementation of the projects to their evaluation. The apparently simple question 'Of what value are these projects, and to whom?' is being asked more frequently. Provision is made in the setting up and development of projects to obtain information and data which go a long way towards answering that question — but the focus is on the rather formal procedure of comparing the results of a project with its initial objectives as detailed in the EDU release specification. It is becoming increasingly evident to the Educational Development Assistants (EDAs) who operate the release scheme, and to other interested parties, that this is too simplistic and restrictive an interpretation of the evaluation process, and that it actually ignores some valuable aspects of certain projects.

What is needed is a more flexible and less constricting model of evaluation which can take account of changing circumstances, incorporate unexpected or additional outcomes and ask wider-ranging questions. This paper describes and explores such a model, comparing it to existing polytechnic practice, and applies it to a particular EDU release project which had other outcomes and developments than those initially specified as objectives.

Aspects of Evaluation

It may be useful, at this point, to distinguish between formal and informal evaluation processes as referred to in the context of this paper. Two aspects of formal evaluation are important here — one being the assessment of a project's success by the extent to which its results match its objectives and the other the monitoring procedures resulting from the institutionalization of the EDU release scheme within the Polytechnic's Board and Committee structure.

Recent discussions on monitoring EDU release projects in the various faculties have focused on:

(a) the assessment of the success of the project;
(b) the dissemination of the results of the project among colleagues;
(c) the initiation of further projects.

Implicit in these discussions was an emphasis on the 'objectives approach' to evaluation. Indeed, it is current practice to spell out an EDU release specification in terms of its target population, aims, application of materials, deadlines, and so on, and then assess the project's success by their achievement. In contrast, informal evaluation is recognized by its dependence on comparatively 'casual observation, implicit goals, intuitive norms and subjective judgements' (Stake, 1967).

This too-restrictive approach is identified in what has become a common problem — that of trying to use a scientific method of evaluation in an educational context. It has received a great deal of attention and criticism over the last decade, and alternative approaches which draw more on an anthropological rather than a scientific approach have widened the scope of evaluation (see Parlett and Hamilton, 1972; Hamilton *et al*, 1977).

Stake's Model for Evaluation

One of the earliest and most useful of these models for evaluating educational innovations was proposed by Stake. Instead of restricting evaluation to a consideration of outcomes, he identifies a much wider concept which enables different sorts of questions to be asked.

A simplified diagram of Stake's evaluation scheme is shown in Figure 1.

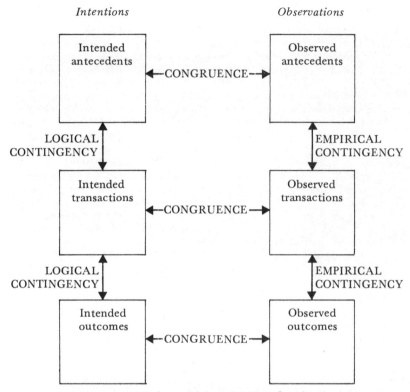

Figure 1. *Stake's model for educational evaluation*

This model quickly eliminates the view that evaluation is only concerned with the final product, and suggests that it should embrace the background and circumstances (Antecedents), the strategies and methods (Transactions), as well as the products (Outcomes) of any educational project. Stake also distinguishes between the logical and empirical contingency within a project, and the correlation of intentions with observations (Congruence).

Contingency is concerned with the inter-relationships of the antecedents, transactions and outcomes, whether intended (Logical Contingency) or observed (Empirical Contingency). For example, if a particular tutor, with specific teaching and research commitments, is allocated half a day per week to undertake an EDU release project, then are the proposed strategy for the project and its outcome reasonable?

Congruence examines the match or mis-match between the intended and observed antecedents, the intended and observed transactions, and the intended and observed outcomes, ie the horizontal connections in the diagram.

Formal evaluation focuses almost exclusively on the congruence between the intended and actual outcomes. Stake's model provides an evaluation framework which allows the consideration of a variety of perspectives of a project's value, and the posing of other and wider sorts of questions than 'Do the results match the objectives?'. The remainder of the paper is concerned with the application of this model to a selected EDU release project.

Case Studies in Applied Physics — a Semester I Course

The initial 15 weeks of the first year of the BSc Combined Sciences, Semester I, is a period during which students can sample four different subjects before committing themselves to a firm choice of 'core courses' which they will study thereafter. The physics tutors who were responsible for the Semester I Course in Applied Physics wished to change the concept and presentation of their course from a series of lectures and laboratory sessions to a number of case studies, at the same time making the course more student-centred. They obtained the support of the course leader, and an EDU release equivalent to 0.6 FTE (full-time equivalent) staff was negotiated and approved by the Boards of Study in combined sciences and physics.

The aims of the release — intended outcomes, summarized from the formal release specification — were to plan and prepare the methods and materials for teaching the Semester I Case Studies Course. However, in reality the case study element was a casualty of the validation process, the specially developed materials were not used and Semester I physics became a more or less conventionally taught introductory course. In terms of formal evaluation the project would seem to have been unsuccessful, and certainly the tutors were disappointed. We can see that there was a lack of congruence between the intended and observed outcomes — but should this be the sum total of the evaluation? With Stake's model in mind we can make some interesting and pertinent observations which illuminate other values of this project.

The Value of the Project

Firstly, the ways in which the release group worked were exactly as intended. The four physics tutors concerned, the EDA and the Course Resources Officer (CRO) — a term used at Brighton Polytechnic to describe a subject librarian who also contributes to educational development work — worked as a development group, meeting frequently to discuss and agree the structure of the course, with the EDA contributing general ideas and keeping detailed notes of the discussions and the CRO identifying appropriate resource materials. The physics tutors each developed the content of one case study and reported back to the group for comment and co-ordination. The group also kept in touch with the views of other teaching colleagues and the Boards of Study.

Secondly, and largely arising from the consultations just mentioned, it became apparent that there were a number of shifts in antecedent conditions, which resulted in quite major modifications to some of the bases from which the released group was working. There were, for example, comments from teaching colleagues, alterations in the hours timetabled for the course and extra restrictions on the availability of teaching staff. The comments were along the lines of 'What we really need is a course to teach the students some basic physics!', and there was a strong body of opinion urging the inclusion in the course of a number of prescribed physics topics which would lead into the physics 'core course'. Although this could be seen to be useful to those students committed to physics from the start, it would not be so beneficial to students using Semester I for one of its declared intentions — to sample a number of subjects before making a firm choice, because a course based on the prescribed topics could not offer the desired broad and attractive view of the scope of physics.

The alterations in teaching hours and restrictions on the availability of tutors both resulted from timetabling constraints which the release group could not foresee as it had no involvement in the timetabling for the BSc Combined Sciences. However, the impact of these constraints was considerable. One of the four tutors would not be free to teach the Semester I course and, instead of the expected two blocks of time in a laboratory, there would be three separate one-hour 'lectures' and a two-hour 'practical'. Added to this there would be two separate groups of students for practical work — meeting on different days of the week — but only one combined group for the three 'lectures'. The flexible use of time and grouping of students was basic to the original strategy, and the effect of these constraints was to impose severe limitations on the degree of integration and amount of student-centredness which could be built into the case studies — indeed it was debatable whether the course could honestly be described as a number of case studies. The changes just described were neither intended nor anticipated.

Thirdly, to use the general example outlined earlier in the paper, given the particular circumstances of this project, the tutors, the release time, etc, then the intended strategy and its results were certainly reasonable. However, there were many modifications — particularly in the antecedents — during the project, resulting in what could be described as a series of feedback loops where the changed antecedents led to slightly different observed outcomes which, in turn, affected the antecedents . . . and so on. For those involved it seemed that Catch 22 had struck again!

Outcomes

Although a formal evaluation indicated that the project had failed, one very valuable outcome in practice was the development of fruitful and constructive working relationships between the tutors, the EDA and the CRO. The exchange of ideas and the appreciation of each person's expertise has continued, for example, through the CRO's skill in making computer-aided searches on topics related to the course. Similarly, although the case study materials are at present 'on ice', it is recognized that they will probably make a valuable contribution to another component of the combined sciences course, that of Project-Based Studies in the third year.

Summary

The formal evaluation of educational development projects is most important in terms of accountability, but there is a danger that many valuable aspects of such projects will not be included in this process.

Stake's model of evaluation, on the other hand, provides a framework within which broader issues and concerns can be illuminated and different perspectives, including a formal evaluation, can be gained.

The terminology of 'Antecedents', 'Transactions', 'Outcomes', 'Congruence' and 'Contingency' may appear at first sight as unnecessary jargon, but these terms are merely a shorthand summary of many disparate situations and conditions, and behind them lies a most useful model which can help practitioners to clarify what type of evaluation is most appropriate to their own situation and to ensure that any comparisons made are also appropriate.

The message of this paper is simple but, we think, important. In evaluating, do not be content with only matching the outcome of a project with its original objectives, but consider also the wider insights and outcomes. In other words, 'evaluate the informal within the formal'.

References

Adderley, K, Pearce, J, Tait, J and Williams, D (1979) Time off for innovation. In Page, G T and Whitlock, Q (eds) *Aspects of Educational Technology* **XIII**. Kogan Page, London.

Hamilton, D, Jenkins, D, King, C, MacDonald, B and Parlett, M (1977) *Beyond the Numbers Game*. Macmillan, London.
Parlett, M and Hamilton, D (1972) Evaluation as illumination: a new approach to the study of innovatory programmes. *Occasional Paper 9*. Centre for Research in the Educational Sciences, University of Edinburgh.
Stake, R E (1967) The countenance of educational development. *Teachers College Record*, 68, 7, pp 523-40.

Acknowledgement

We wish to thank our polytechnic colleagues, in the departments of Applied Physics, and in Learning Resources, who took part in the EDU release project used as an example in this paper.

Workshop Report
9.6   Evaluation of Educational Development Projects: Before, During and After!

David Williams and Ken Adderley
Brighton Polytechnic

Organizers' Account

The workshop was based on the ideas and suggestions for a broad and flexible evaluation scheme discussed in the paper of the above title which immediately precedes this report. The object was to explore the applicability of the evaluation scheme — essentially a simplified version of Stake's model — to the sort of educational development projects undertaken within Brighton Polytechnic's EDU Release Scheme, with particular reference to the more limited 'achievement of stated objectives' approach currently being used.

In outlining this object to the participants, the organizers explained that the general issue of evaluation was a current major concern within the polytechnic, especially where there were implications for staff development. The organizers then summarized the essential points of the proposed evaluation scheme and the EDU release scheme, distributed copies of the workshop documents and divided the participants into two groups. The documents, it was explained, consisted of a formal release specification with its formal release report — both based on actual Brighton Polytechnic projects, and an informal diary of events that had occurred during the project, affecting its progress to a greater or lesser extent. Ten minutes were allowed for reading these, followed by a brief period to answer any points requiring clarification. The two groups were then asked to explore the extent to which the evaluation model could be applied to the release project and consider whether it was capable of extending and illuminating the evaluation of the project. Approximately 40 minutes were allowed for this, leaving some 20 minutes for the groups to report back in a concluding 'plenary' session.

From the group reports, the organizers noted the general feeling that Stake's model provided a useful framework for the evaluation of educational development projects, but that the release specification and report in their present format were clearly oriented to the evaluation of materials rather than the project itself. In particular it was stated that staff development aspects of the project could not readily be identified or evaluated. The groups commented that Stake's ideas provided an effective means of directing the mind towards the many components of evaluation, but that a strict application of Stake's model would be like 'using a sledgehammer to crack a nut'. However, it was encouraging to the organizers to see that the application of the proposed model had indeed extended and illuminated the evaluation of the given project, and to note the additional (though not entirely unexpected) outcome that the release specification and report were inappropriate in their present form.

The organizers wish to record their thanks to the participants for the useful comments and suggestions they produced. Most of them are being incorporated into the next programme of EDU release projects at Brighton Polytechnic.

Participant's Comments

H S Mathias *University of Southampton*

This workshop provided an interesting opportunity to apply Robert Stake's evaluation scheme to a number of documented educational development projects. The workshop leaders were involved in Brighton Polytechnic's Educational Development Unit (EDU) Release Scheme which enables lecturers to have a reduction in class contact hours in order to develop teaching and learning projects. They expressed some dissatisfaction with the traditional input-output model used in evaluating these projects and wishes the group to consider whether the broader and more flexible scheme advocated by Stake might be a feasible alternative.

Dividing participants into two small groups of about four, they set them the task of applying a reduced version of the Stake model to three documented cases of such projects. Each group was given documents representing formal project proposals and formal project reports which had been used as a basis for a formal input-output evaluation. In addition, there was a document outlining the informal development and activities of the projects which the groups were asked to take into account in their evaluations.

The workshop did not reach the stage where considered and consolidated judgements could be made about the value of the Stake model in the exercise. There was probably too much to do in the time available. Nevertheless, certain useful outcomes did emerge. Participants were made aware of the problems of sorting information unambiguously into the evaluation model's categories which, in part, related to the way the information was organized in the documentation, ie there were different category emphases between the model and the documentation. It also became apparent that there was some confusion as to what was the central focus of the evaluation. The workshop leaders expressed an interest in the evaluation of the actual projects as specific pieces of educational development, as well as in the evaluation of the EDU release scheme and the extent to which its intentions, as they related to staff development, had materialized. Quite by chance, one group took the former focus and the other the latter, although in retrospect it became apparent that the workshop leaders were interested primarily in the former for the purposes of the exercise.

This unanticipated outcome did have some benefits. In terms of the educational development projects, the Stake evaluation model did indicate a number of gaps and weaknesses in the way in which the projects were proposed and reported upon, as well as accommodating informal observations about their development. In terms of evaluating the staff development outcomes embodied in the intentions of the scheme, greater gaps emerged which implied that if one was concerned to justify the scheme to some institutional committee to which it was accountable, then such outcomes needed to be built rather more explicitly into the project proposals, accounts and reports for this particular audience.

9.7 Evaluating Industrial Training

Edward E Green
Brigham Young University

Abstract: A long-term evaluation of a marketing training programme is described. The paper deals with the model on which this evaluation was based, and the initiation, methodology and results of the evaluation.

Introduction

To company executives, the writing on the wall has become increasingly clear — employee training programmes must be cost-effective. Thus, a need for evaluation programmes has been created to help pinpoint weaknesses which prevent them from being as cost-effective as thought allowable by the company.

Unfortunately, however, evaluation of industrial training programmes has been less than ideal. For various reasons the evaluations may be spotty or conclude prematurely. As a rule the final evaluation report is politely accepted, paid for, and shelved, without effecting any change in the programme or the competence of the employees.

Interact Corporation, a Los Angeles-based development firm, recently carried out a long-term evaluation of Ford Motor Company marketing training programme, which comes very close to the ideal. This evaluation effort began with an analysis of the training courses, moved to a lengthy debriefing session with Ford personnel, and ended with the actual development of courses based on evaluation data. Thus both evaluation and development personnel worked in tandem and were able to effect change.

This paper will describe the model upon which this evaluation was based. It will first discuss the initiation of the evaluation study by the Ford Marketing Institute, and second, examine the methodology of the evaluation. Finally, the results for the evaluation will be discussed.

The Initiation of the Study: Ford Marketing Institute

The Ford Marketing Institute (FMI) is one of the major training arms of the Ford Motor Company, located in Detroit, Michigan. The central office of the Institute is responsible for curriculum planning and development for Ford dealerships throughout the United States. In addition to the central office it has four major training centres which oversee the implementation of seminars aimed at various management levels and automobile salespeople.

In 1978 the Institute asked Interact to conduct a major evaluation regarding the effectiveness and efficiency with which major courses were being conducted.

The evaluation was to be a part of an overall plan, which included needs assessments, research, content planning, evaluation, implementation and revision; a very traditional model now being used by FMI. The evaluation effort was to develop responses to the following major questions relating to specific courses:

1. What is the effect of the basic sales and service management courses upon the behaviour of trainees?
2. What model for training development should be used which will maintain the integrity and autonomy of individual units within the firm and at the same time allow for exchanges of experience from unit to unit? (This type of question is usually asked of those companies which decentralized their profit centres into individual units rather than into a central corporate office.)
3. What specific techniques might be used for each phase within the existing instructional development and evaluation model used at FMI?
4. What return on training investment should be realized and how should it be reported?
5. What do participants and management want from training?
6. How might evaluation results best be implemented within the development function?
7. What are the most effective instructional components which should be included in trainer and trainee guides?

Methodology: The Evaluation Plan

Many evaluations, though clear to the evaluators, are seen by the client as vague and difficult to act upon. Interact's plan was therefore intended to be very thorough and specific in its suggestions for improvement because most suggestions were based upon previous experience and evaluation research. The evaluation plan continued through three phases: on-site visits by Interact, analysis of data collected by FMI and Interact, and an extensive debrief with curriculum planners and developers at FMI headquarters in Detroit. In discussing each of these, the emphasis will be on methods and instruments, rather than on the recommendations.

Phase One: On-Site Visits

During the first phase an Interact evaluator attended several basic sales and management-level courses, most of which lasted three to four days. This first-hand view provided many valuable insights, not available by merely reading the materials.

During the seminar the evaluator took informal notes. These were in a two-column format, the left-hand column describing course content and activities and the right-hand column listing the developer's reactions. The report submitted to FMI adopted that format, the notes being followed by a conclusion synthesizing those reactions and recommending improvements.

Phase Two: Analysis of Participant Responses

The second phase was to analyze the responses of participants to the class, mainly those collected on questionnaires administered by FMI over the past several years. FMI had looked at small samples of these but had never examined the responses as a whole and hence had not seen important trends or the total picture. Interact collected and analyzed these questionnaires as a part of their evaluation procedure.

An example of the specific kind of work done in the first two phases might be useful here. A representative course studied was the Sales Manager's Course, which was evaluated from May 1979 to late August of that year. A review was made of the stated course objectives, materials and content; the stated objectives were revised and redefined into more realistic, measurable terms; evaluation instruments developed in co-ordination with the FMI research department; a representative service management course attended; data drawn from one FMI staff member's attendance and observations of another presentation of the course; 'in-class' and follow-up surveys administered and collected; and telephone interviews conducted.

The final report was based primarily on data from a mail survey of 466 course participants and in-class evaluations provided to Interact by FMI research. The recommendations for this course (and most others) usually included suggestions such as:

1. Slow down the presentation.
2. Pare the course down to a smaller number of topics.
3. Allow more in-class practice.
4. Modify participant manuals to make information more accessible on the job.
5. Revise and add to some of the instructor audio-visual materials.
6. Eliminate several of the presentations now being used.

Besides specific recommendations for course improvement, other recommendations for total programme improvement were included in appendices.

Phase Three: The FMI Course Developer 'Debriefing' Sessions

This phase represents a real departure from conventional evaluation procedures. Generally speaking, the evaluation effort would have come to an end with the submission of the report containing data collected in the first two phases. However, our evaluation model went a step further: Interact evaluators had the unusual opportunity of meeting with FMI curriculum developers for three days to explain the results of the evaluations and suggest improvements and alternatives.

To accomplish this, a development team was organized to explain major problems pointed out in the reports, and prepare examples showing ways in which these weaknesses could be improved. For example, one of the main problems was often the absence of a satisfactory introduction to a course or unit. To show how to remedy the problem, the development team prepared examples of good introductions adapted from FMI materials.

In addition, the team presented an overview of the elements of good instructional design. These included:

(a) Preparation of introductions.
(b) Explanation of presentation forms.
(c) Considerations for message design.
(d) The selection of teaching methods.
(e) Devices for training trainers.
(f) Development of built-in evaluation devices.

Thus the debriefing session became not only an analysis of the evaluation results but also a training session in the basic process of instructional development.

Results: Follow-up Development Work

The outcome of the three-phased evaluation was the opportunity to assist FMI developers in restructuring some of their courses and incorporating the recommended changes. Interact is now in the process of completing a revision of Ford's basic selling course for new sales people.

Conclusion

The evaluation model described in this paper has been very satisfying to all concerned. From the FMI point of view, the evaluations have been clear and useful in actually upgrading employee training packages. From the Interact point of view, it has been refreshing to see a long-term evaluation accepted and used, instead of being filed away on some dusty shelf.

It is true that this model takes time and considerable expense. It also requires considerable work in preparing revisions of materials and organizing a development plan for a company. It is much easier for consultants to state criteria and general reactions than to actually try to make changes.

It seems, however, that there is a way to streamline this model so that the major development, as well as evaluation benefits, might be retained. In any event we need to see ourselves not as evaluators only, but as instigators of change.

9.8   Education for a Working Life: an Evaluation of City and Guilds Foundation Courses

Jane Pearson
City and Guilds of London Institute

Abstract: This paper presents the results of an evaluation which was done in order to check whether the designed intentions of Foundation Courses were being realized.

Introduction

> The Foundation Course curriculum has been designed to motivate young people to improve their basic educational skills, to introduce them to the responsibilities and attitudes of the world of work, and to help them reach an informed choice of career. It should also greatly ease their introduction into industry and provide a basis for subsequent development of specific skills.

This paragraph appears in the introduction to the Foundation Course syllabus pamphlet. In March 1978, 18 months after the first of these courses was offered, a two-year evaluation study commenced (the first nine months in the form of a pilot study).

The aim of the evaluation was to check whether the designed intentions of foundation courses (specified in the opening paragraph above) were succeeding. This involved collecting information by questionnaire, from students and tutors on the student's academic progress, their approach to the job market, their success in achieving their various job or further education ambitions, and the use made of work experience and careers information during the course. Four hundred and ninety students completed the first questionnaire (in January 1979), representing a sample of 34 centres drawn according to four course variables. These variables were:

(a) The vocational area of the course (engineering, construction, community

      care and commercial studies).
(b) The age at enrolment of the students (15-plus and 16-plus).
(c) The site of the course (school-based, college-based and school-college link).
(d) The geographical location of the course; each region named by the Department of Employment in its monthly unemployment-by-region statistics was represented in the sample.

The 490 students were 10 per cent of the total foundation course candidates for the examinations in June 1979.

Providing Motivation to Improve Basic Educational Skills

What happened to these students' basic educational skills and qualifications during their year on a foundation course? When they began they had among them a minimum of 119 O-levels and 666 CSEs (ie O-level ABC plus CSE 1 = 0; O-level DE plus CSE 2-6 = CSE). (114 others were omitted for lack of information on grades.) The average per student, then, was 0.2 O-levels and 1.4 CSEs.

All but six of the 34 centres intended to encourage the students to add to their qualifications during the year. The intention was to add, on average, 0.5) O-levels and 1.9 CSEs per student. In fact, the 259 students who were followed up fell only marginally short of this target, managing to double their original qualifications by achieving an additional 0.3 O-levels and 1.4 CSEs apiece on average. As for basic educational skills, eight subjects were selected from the syllabus and students were asked to estimate their level of improvement in these areas. The majority of engineering and construction students felt moderately or greatly improved in three areas — addition, subtraction and measurement. The majority of community care students felt moderately or greatly improved in essays and comprehension. Commercial studies students felt the widest improvement, the majority claiming a moderate or great improvement in spelling, essays, comprehension, punctuation, addition, subtraction and handling money.

An Introduction to the Responsibilities and Attitudes of the World of Work

Forty-nine per cent of these students had already experienced part-time jobs, and 10 per cent had been in full-time jobs, so the course was not an initiation into work for more than a minority. Full-time was defined as a job lasting for more than two weeks of full days. Fifty-six per cent of the students had been exposed to 'work experience' as part of the course by the time they had completed the questionnaire. The vocational groups with the most and the least wide experience were respectively the most and the least certain that their choice of job lay within that vocational area. The group with the most work experience also enjoyed it more than the group with the least. Students aged 16-plus, as a group, were more enthusiastic than students aged 15-plus about work experience.

    What reasons did the students give for valuing work experience? Thirty per cent appreciated the chance to practise and prepare some work skills (including confidence); 20 per cent the opportunity to find out what to expect of work; 15 per cent the help it gave them in choosing the job they might like. The community care students were much less concerned with what work in their vocational area would be like, but they were conversely more anxious to learn skills in advance of the real test. Both these students and the engineering students expressed more pleasure in the work they did on their days and weeks out of college and school. Many clearly found it challenging and interesting, quite apart from its relevance to their future life.

The provision of work experience calls for dedicated work from the course tutors. It involved an average of 15 employer contacts per course and seven follow-up employer visits in addition to an occasional visit when the students were on location.

Helping an Informed Choice of Career

When the foundation courses began (September 1978), 60 per cent of the students knew that they wanted a job in the particular vocational area of the course, and their decision had not changed by the time they had completed the questionnaire (January 1979). Thirty-two per cent had changed their minds about the job that would suit them since beginning the course. Of these, 35 per cent changed their choice of job but the choice remained within the vocational area; 64 per cent changed their choice of vocational area — 35 per cent entering the course vocational area and 29 per cent opting out of it. More of the 15-plus students had changed their minds (36 per cent compared with 26 per cent of the 16-plus groups). The community care students had remained more faithful to their original vocational area than had the others.

Twenty-one per cent of the students stated that the course had changed their idea of the job that would suit them. Their answers as to why the course might have had this effect were almost all to do with an increase in their knowledge of which jobs were available and what each entailed. Twenty-six per cent of those who changed their minds discovered a more interesting alternative; 21 per cent realized that their first choice was unsuitable; and 19 per cent considered they now had a wider area of choice.

Careers guidance should be an integral part of foundation courses. Eighty per cent of the tutors in the sample provided formal careers interviews, and 52 per cent held careers lessons. All gave their students access to careers literature and informal careers discussions. Careers lessons were more usual at school-based foundation courses and for 15-plus students.

Easing the Students' Introduction into Industry

The tutors were asked whether they felt foundation course students were better prepared for employment than they might otherwise have been. Eighty-eight per cent answered 'yes' and gave the following reasons: the students' self-confidence, maturity and social skills had improved (30 per cent); their attitude towards, and knowledge of, work was more realistic (23 per cent); their practical and academic ability had improved (19 per cent); they were better prepared to choose and find a suitable job (18 per cent); and their motivation was improved (nine per cent). Eight per cent of the students left the course before the end to take up employment, and eight per cent left for other reasons.

Assessors reporting on all the foundation courses in the four vocational areas (ie, 2,171 students) reported that 33 per cent of the students who stayed to take the examinations had found a job, and 24 per cent had decided to proceed to a full-time further education course (these reports were made in June 1979).

In November 1979, five months after the end of the course, 86 per cent of the students who had completed the original questionnaires were contacted again and asked to supply information on their current occupation. Two hundred and fifty-nine students returned this information (a response rate of 61 per cent). Seventy-two per cent were in employment, 22 per cent were in full-time further education, and five per cent were unemployed.

The unemployed percentage merits closer examination. The (mostly female) community care and commercial studies students were far less successful in finding jobs than were their (mostly male) peers on engineering and construction courses. Students aged 16-plus were slightly more successful (five per cent unemployed compared with six per cent of students aged 15-plus), and were also much more interested in further education.

Of those who replied, 72 per cent were in employment. Of that number, a small percentage (about eight per cent) were on a government work experience programme. None of the construction students was unemployed, but less than half the commercial studies students were in employment. (These were the students who had expressed least interest in a job in commerce, and who had had least work experience and disliked this part of the course.)

Foundation courses 'are designed for students of about average ability . . . who have expressed a general interest in an occupational area, yet without having committed themselves to a specific job!' Thus, the students are not aiming at any job, but to one that suits their abilities and provides prospects for advancement and the learning of skills. To what extent had the students found jobs with some kind of prospect? Seventy per cent of the jobs obtained included either apprenticeship or training. Engineering and construction students fared particularly well in this respect. Fifty-two per cent of the students had found jobs in their vocational area and several others had found temporary jobs to fill in the time until they joined the services or started nursing training.

With the exception of commercial studies students (who were in any case less keen to find a job in their vocational area), about half the students had achieved the job they had originally said they wanted (in January 1979). Students aged 16-plus were slightly more successful in this respect.

When the student 'follow-up' information was compared with the regional Department of Employment statistics on school leavers, the discrepancies were very marked. It was decided to write to the Careers Service in the regions to ask for relevant school-leaver employment statistics for the areas surrounding the schools and colleges within the sample. Of those contacted, 64 per cent replied. The picture they gave was of 'pockets' of high or low unemployment figures influenced by factors such as the proximity of county towns, the efforts made by colleges to find work for their students, the lack of certain types of employment, etc. Thus, where the Department of Employment figure was four per cent of school leavers unemployed in their North West region on November 8th 1979, the local Principal Careers Officer gave a 'crude estimate' of a figure reducing from 55 per cent in the summer to 35 per cent in February.

The letter from the Principal Careers Officer went on to say: 'this clearly shows that the achievements of these students are gained against a background of extremely serious youth unemployment. However . . . similar figures could be produced for all clerical schemes and courses attracting reasonably well-motivated young people'. Might this also be true for construction and engineering courses? In the Welsh region, for instance (the Department of Employment gave figures of five per cent of school leavers unemployed on 8 November 1979) all the students followed up had found jobs — 67 per cent apprenticed to the engineering or construction industry, 19 per cent on government work-finding schemes and 14 per cent in non-apprenticed employment. The local careers officer, quoting a current level of youth unemployment of 9.1 per cent, wrote that: 'the districts of Aberdare and Merthyr offer very limited prospects of employment in most types of work . . . 570 engineering and building apprenticeship applications each year for approximately 268 local opportunities . . . the majority of school leavers obtain their first experience of work/training via the Youth Opportunities Programme'.

The most that can be said at this stage is that in some areas the sampled foundation course students defied the job market statistics. Some of the contributory factors have been outlined in this paper. The influence of regional (rather than course) factors requires further study.

9.9 Reliable Short Answer Questions

Paul Ellis
Hotel and Catering Industry Training Board

Abstract: Although short-answer questions are generally classified as an objective testing technique, reservations have been expressed about the reliability with which such questions can be marked. This paper reports a City and Guilds of London Institute study which produced recommendations for increasing the reliability of short-answer questions.

Introduction

The short-answer question is generally found classified as an objective testing technique. It requires the student to write a short response to a question. The length of the answer may be from one or two words to a few sentences, and may include calculations and graphs.

Example 1 — A short-answer question

What is the correct source of information on the procedure for applying paint to a given surface?

Amongst the various types of objective testing techniques, short-answer is unique in requiring the student to supply or construct the answer. For this reason it may be the most valid technique for measuring achievement of course objectives which specify the recall of information and where supplying the answer is a necessary part of the performance.

The very uniqueness that makes short-answer questions so valuable is also the source of their greatest weakness; since answers are not pre-determined, marking may be highly subjective for an 'objective testing technique'. (Argent (1974) writes: '[short-answer questions] are deceptively easy to set and usually difficult to mark with any degree of speed and consistency'. Other authors express similar views (eg Gronlund, 1968; Hudson, 1973).

Example 2 — A question and marking scheme

Q. What is the correct source of information on the procedure for applying paint to a given surface?

Marking scheme:

British Standards Code of Practice   —   2 marks

These problems have led some authors to suggest the use of alternative question types in preference to short-answer. Gronlund (1968) states: '. . . the short-answer item should be reserved for those special situations where supplying the answer is a necessary part of the learning outcome to be measured'.

Argent (1974) argues: 'there is very little in terms of subject-matter or objectives which can be tested by short-answer questions that cannot also be tested by objective items'. The above authors do see a role for the short-answer question, but not necessarily in the context of a national examining body, eg 'Nevertheless, short-answer questions are useful in classroom progress testing.' (Duckworth and Hoste, 1976). Hudson and Argent comment similarly.

The Study

As a large national examining body, the City and Guilds of London Institute uses a range of examining techniques, including short-answer, as considered appropriate to the competencies to be tested. With all examination techniques used, considerable safeguards are built into the system to ensure the quality of the examinations (CGLI, 1973; 1975).

In view of the previous reservations, however, it was decided that the Research and Development Department should undertake an investigation to determine how far the above criticisms held true in the level of examination provided by the Institute and within the particular system in operation, and to recommend any action which might be necessary.

A sample of 200 marked scripts, representative of colleges entering candidates and of examiners' marking scripts, was analyzed. Normal examination procedures had been followed in the processing of these scripts and the short-answer questions covered one of the Institute's advanced craft areas. The marking scheme used was typical of those resulting from a scheme under which a draft question paper is submitted accompanied by a marking scheme, both being subsequently moderated.

The following findings emerged from the study:

☐ Where a student gave the exact wording which appeared in the marking scheme, credit was consistently given.

☐ Students who gave answers other than those which appeared in the marking scheme were not consistently marked wrong.

☐ Some variant answers were consistently awarded credit and some others were consistently not awarded credit.

☐ Other variant answers were sometimes awarded credit and sometimes not.

	Credit given	No credit given	Total	%
Marking scheme answer	54	—	54	11.7
Other answers	134	274	408	88.3
Total	188	274	462	
%	40.7	59.3		100

Table 1. *Analysis of marking*

Table 1 shows a summary of the answers given and marking (combined for three questions), which highlights the weakness of the type of marking scheme shown above. Less than 12 per cent of the students' answers directly corresponded with the marking scheme answers. In giving credit to any answers other than these, examiners' judgement would be involved thus allowing the possibility of variations, both between examiners and with the same examiner from occasion to occasion, to creep in. Fortunately, as noted above, the system coped with many of the answers given by students, awarding or not awarding credit consistently, but the instances of answers which led to inconsistent marking are a cause for concern.

It can be estimated that inconsistency in marking affected, at most, 10-15 per fifteen per cent of all responses made, but the fact that only 12 per cent of student responses corresponded to the anticipated answers provided by examiners is one area for attention. Even the most experienced examiner is unable to anticipate the full range of alternative answers that students will provide, and further problems are created by the differences in language used by examiners in the marking scheme and students in their answers. This leads to the suggestion that actual student responses should be used in the construction of marking schemes. This has some support in the literature; eg Massey (1977) states: 'in preparing mark schemes, the information generated by students is of inestimable value'.

Massey also offers some assistance on the detailed structure of the marking scheme:

> The simplest mark allocation is where each question is scored 1 (correct) and 0 (incorrect). It is often true that this is the best as well as the simplest method . . . If, however, it is decided to allocate more than one mark to some questions and part marks are to be allowed, a mark scheme should be prepared which either lists every point for which marks can be allocated or gives the clearest possible description of the criteria by which the marker must make judgements. It is probably not desirable to give more than about three points within a question for which the marks can be allocated in order to keep the scoring consistent.

Conclusions on Marking Schemes

The guidelines for development of short-answer marking schemes which emerged from the study are outlined below. These often confirm and reinforce established practices within the Institute, and sometimes extend them.

1. At the stage where the question paper and marking scheme are agreed, the marking scheme should detail the marks to be awarded and the correct answer envisaged by the examiners. Where there are sections to the question this information should be specified for each section. Thus, for a multi-part question the marking scheme might be as shown in Example 3.

Example 3 — Initial marking scheme

1. (a) B S Code of Practice   — 2 marks

   (b) National Working Rule Agreement   — 1 mark

   (c) British Standards Institution *or* Building Research
        Establishment, accept either   — 1 mark

   Total for Q.1 = 4 marks

---

2. Once examination scripts are available a study should be made of the answers actually given by the students. The information derived should be used to develop a marking scheme which takes account of the answers typically found, and goes into considerable detail in order to provide clear guidelines for marking. In its simplest form a marking scheme of the type shown in Example 4 might result. Examiners marking scripts should be instructed to obtain the chief examiner's consent if they wish to award marks for an answer not appearing on the scheme.

3. The study revealed that 80-90 per cent of the responses made by students could be summarized in about 10 categories. Any responses falling outside these categories were almost always incorrect anyway. This opens the opportunity to give more precise guidance to the examiner, detailing incorrect as well as correct responses, as illustrated in Example 5.

Example 4 — A simple detailed marking scheme

1. (a) *2 marks* for the following answers:

   British Standard Code of Practice
   Code of Practice
   British Standards Code
   Manufacturers
   Manufacturers Specification, Manual (or similar)

   0 marks for any other answer

Example 5 — A more tightly-specified marking scheme

2 marks	0 marks
British Standards Code of Practice	Side of tin
Code of Practice	Bill of Quantities
British Standards Code	Clerk of works, architect
Manufacturers	British Standards
Manufacturers' specification, manual (or similar)	British Standards (+ erroneous material
	Manual, specification, reference book (or similar)
	Any other answer

4. If it is decided that part-marks are to be awarded, this approach can be extended to provide the necessary guidance on award of part-marks, as illustrated in Example 6.

Example 6 — Specifying the award of part-marks

2 marks	1 mark	0 marks
British Standards Code of Practice	Code of Practice	Side of tin
British Standards Code	Manufacturers	Bill of quantities
	Manufacturers' specification, manual (or similar)	Clerk of works, architect
		British Standards
		British Standards (+ erroneous material)
		Manual, specification, reference book (or similar)
		Any other answer

Organizational Considerations

Recommendations such as those which have been made cannot be divorced from the system in which they are intended to operate. In the context of a national examining body, the introduction of a procedure which involves the finalization of the marking scheme in sufficient detail to ensure the highest feasible reliability in marking only after examination scripts are received, and therefore student responses are available, is likely to produce additional problems at a time when there is considerable pressure to 'get the results out'.

Possible courses of action to minimize these difficulties might include:

(a) using multiple-choice questions in preference to short-answer wherever validity and economy permit;

(b) where short-answer questions continue to be used, the same kind of banking procedure as is in common use for multiple-choice items could be introduced. Included in the bank would be (i) the question, (ii) its detailed marking scheme, and (iii) the examiner's report for each time the question is used.

The first use of the question might be in a real examination or in a specially arranged pre-test. In either case the bulk of the work in producing an effective marking scheme could be done in advance.

The emphasis of this discussion has been on improving the marking schemes for short-answer questions. It is worth noting, however, that where a system of pre-testing and item banking is adopted, opportunity exists for improving the quality of the question itself. On receiving the students' responses to a question the examiners may, for instance, decide from the range of responses that the question is ambiguous and set out to frame it more clearly. In this way it is possible to improve reliability through better questions, as well as better marking schemes.

References

Argent, B B (1974) Short answer questions and objective items. In Macintosh, H G (ed) *Techniques and Problems of Assessment.* Edward Arnold, London.

CGLI (1973) *Setting and Moderating Written Question Papers.*

CGLI (1975) *Instructions and Guidance to Examiners on the Marking of Examination Scripts.*

Duckworth, D and Hoste, R (1976) Question banking: an approach through biology. *Schools Council Examinations Bulletin 35.*

Gronlund, N E (1968) *Constructing Achievement Tests.* Prentice Hall, New York.

Hudson, B (ed) (1973) *Assessment Techniques — an Introduction.* Methuen, London.

Massey, A J (1977) *Restricted Response Tests.* Test Development and Research Unit, Cambridge.

Acknowledgements

I would like to thank my colleagues in the City and Guilds at the time of this study for their invaluable help, and most especially Len Bill for the support and advice he gave as Head of Research and Development.

Section 10:
Applications of Audio-Visual Techniques

10.1 Educational Experiments with the Videodisc

J J Andriessen, D J Kroon and K H J Robers
Philips Research Laboratories, The Netherlands

Abstract: The results are presented from a computer-controlled videodisc individualized teaching system which was available for use throughout the conference.

The VLP-Videodisc will certainly become an important instrument in education. It provides facilities for displaying moving and still pictures, as well as for fast forward, slow motion and very fast access to any part of the programme. Due to the optical read-out there is no wear. Each TV frame carries its number on the disc. This number can be used as input to a computer control system for rapid and reproducible selection of parts of the film or specific pictures. To study the possibilities and difficulties of a computer-controlled VLP system for individualized teaching, two systems were built and tried out on students.

1. A special fast random access VLP player controlled by a minicomputer was constructed. A special disc was made on the basis of an educational film. On the same disc about 100 still pictures were recorded with explanations, glossary of terms, selection menus, questions and answers pertaining to the course material. In the computer a program was stored allowing the student, by making choices in selection menus, to generate sequences of text pictures and film fragments. A dozen students took part in this course.
2. A consumer VLP player was interfaced with a consumer home computer. A consumer disc was used. All text pictures were stored in the computer and displayed on a separate screen. This made additional comments possible during the running of the film and it facilitated adaptation of the program during the experiment.

The results of both experiments indicate that the following options have to be present:

(a) *Interrupt.* The student may stop the program and continue easily at any point.
(b) *Return.* A multi-level return facility has to be provided to permit the student to recap on the material.
(c) *Still VLP picture.* To study details, make notes, drawings, consult books but also as an illustration to clarify computer instructions.

(d) *Repeat.* Part of the film, comments and questions should be repeated if asked for by the student.

A demonstration micro-computer controlled VLP-videodisc system was available on open access throughout the conference; an analysis of the usage is given in the following tables:

	Tests	Time		Keys
Total	101	15h16m35s	Pressed	1520
Stopped in introduction	4	6m54s	Errors	98
Net	97	15h07m41s	Correct keys	1422
Time/test		9m21s	Keys/test	14.7

Table 1. *Number of tests and keys pressed, and duration*

Items	Per test chosen %	Film finished per choice %	Questions finished/choice %
1 Tomato sauce	35	44	29
2 Meat balls	18	41	35
3 Courgettes	14	38	38
4 Spaghetti	17	13	13
5 Wine	47	80	42
6 Cheese	41	56	33

Table 2. *Choices made and completed*

	Total			Followed by		
	stops	go on film	go on quest	repeat	new choice	end lesson
Stops in film %	95	9	15	34	9	23
Stops in question %	5	33	0	11	11	33

Total number of stops 167; stops/test 1.7

Table 3. *Analysis of stops made*

Subject	Questions/ choice	Answer asked per question %	Film asked per question %	Film + answer per question %
Tomato sauce	0.7	68	44	44
Meat balls	1.4	54	41	33
Courgettes	2.0	48	37	19
Spaghetti	1.2	31	10	5
Wine	0.9	55	42	25
Cheese	0.8	56	59	40
For all subjects		53	41	30

Table 4. *Analysis of questions per choice and responses made*

Some testees completed a questionnaire; their opinions are listed below and in Table 5:

Number of questionnaires returned   23

Q1   — Did you like this system?   Yes   90%

Q2   — Did you have problems in controlling the system?   Yes   4%

Q3   — Did you like two displays? during film   Yes   79%
                     during questions   Yes   79%

Q4   — Would you like the system to have a 'search' facility?   Yes   48%

	Value for teaching	Value for home education
VLP	4.1	4.3
Class	3.4	1.9
VCR	3.4	2.6
TV	3.0	3.1
Book	2.7	2.8
Radio	2.2	2.6
Written course	2.2	2.8

Table 5. *Ratings of merits of various teaching/learning systems, on a scale from 5 (high) to 1 (low)*

10.2 Visual Design in a Technical Subject: a personal view

Mike Tyrrell
The Institute of Chartered Accountants in England and Wales

Abstract: Many subjects taught at a professional level appear not to be easily converted into visual material. Using experience gained in accountancy and its related business subjects, this paper shows how visual design is essential to the effectiveness of a technical presentation, and how the design material can be well-integrated with the rest of the subject matter, comprising both participants' notes and accompanying lecture.

Background

Modern training theory regards the visual element of a presentation as at least as important as the aural part. More information appears to be received through our eyes than the other four senses. Therefore, without effective visuals, a presenter's listeners will be distracted by any non-relevant visual information, from the colour of the ceiling to the trailing laces of the presenter.

This much is conventional educational technology wisdom. But I find that most technical presentations in business, law and accountancy appear to ignore this advice. Even those who accept the importance of visual support in a presentation are tempted to agree with the Post Office who argued, 'Accountancy is not a visual subject' when deciding not to issue stamps commemorating my employer's 1980 centenary. When 'visuals' are provided they are often lists of headings, indicating where the lecturer is, or detailed tables or entire pages of accounts. A presenter will put up a very detailed calculation or form. 'I am just letting them know what I am talking about'; even though viewers need binoculars to read the fine print!

Why Visuals?

Visual support for a technical presentation is not only a matter of technical accuracy but aesthetic judgement. Therefore, if one is to criticize the effectiveness of existing designs it is important to establish their exact purpose. I have therefore developed the following rationale for myself.

Presentations are about the communication of information essentially between the presenter and the listener. Using a computer analogy the listener has a number of information channels, the two most important of which are the eyes and ears. The listener needs, like a computer, to focus on the item of information being given, identify what to do with it, and then relate it appropriately to what has gone before whether in the presentation or earlier in life.

In focusing the listener's attention on the material, the presenter need not use all the information channels. But he must be sure that the unused channels are not to be used for distracting information. Research (Patterson, 1962) indicates that 83 per cent of information is received through sight and that 50 per cent of information both seen and heard is remembered, in contrast to 20 per cent of information heard only. Certainly, common sense observation seems to back up these figures and it would seem incredulous to think that much technical information can be conveyed by the presenter's gesticulations. Therefore, a presenter needs exceptional abilities if he is to focus his listener's attention on the material for a long time without using the visual channel.

The listener then has to identify the context within which the information should be placed. Clearly, naming of concepts and syntax within a sentence are an important part of this process (although not visual and may in fact distract from the visual information). But, with care, a visual design can complement aural information. The picture and the speech are not, perhaps, completely comprehensible on their own. In this case, both information channels are used and focused on the same point. Using an optical anology, astigmatism has been avoided.

The information then has to be related to what has gone before. Traditionally, many subjects are seen sequentially, that is, each item of information relates to its immediate predecessor but not elsewhere. The development, however, of sophisticated concepts and systems means that the interrelationships between information items are as important, or even more so, than each information item itself. Visual support material can show interrelationships in a way that the spoken word, which is sequential, cannot.

Identifying relationships is not solely done by diagrams. Visual images can be used to evoke a particular context much more effectively than words. For instance, a 'think balloon' out of someone's head can be used to stress conscious thought about the items in the bubble.

In business subjects a picture of Big Ben can evoke the idea of statute law or a slatted roof building evoke the concept of an operating company. Similarly, colour can be used as a further method of identifying relationships although the incidence of colour blindness in the population limits the use that can be made of this approach.

Present Design — Good or Bad?

My concern with the visual design of support materials for accountancy presentations was a result of difficulties experienced in designing effective overhead slides for use by inexperienced presenters. I became convinced that, with a few notable exceptions, the overall standards of visual design were very low despite the often high standards of production by professional graphic artists. My consequent crusade and the involvement in the design for presentations for my employer make it impossible for me to evaluate current design in my own field.

However, some indication of current design standards can be obtained from a catalogue of overhead slides produced by a regional management centre (Cawthray, 1978). This identifies in business studies some 360 overhead slides. How does it compare with the criteria suggested above? Each slide illustration was subjectively evaluated against these criteria and the results expressed as a percentage of the total.

Would listeners' attention be focused on the material? Only some 28 per cent of the designs drew attention to one or two major elements on the slide. Other designs had no obvious foci of attention and encouraged sequential reading of the material like a printed page.

In fact, only three per cent had writing greater than 1/30th of the width of the slide. This makes it extremely difficult for listeners to read any detail. The thought that they might be missing something may tempt them to focus on what is difficult to read rather than on the main point.

Would listeners be able to identify the context? Yes, in the sense that all the slides are self-explanatory if the detail is read. However, these are intended to be presented as slides complemented by aural input. The fact that all the information is available means that listeners will concentrate on one channel, usually the visual, in preference to the other.

Would listeners find the visual effective in relating the information to what had gone before? This would be where words are clumsy or where non-sequential interrelationships are important. Only some 33 per cent of slides used pictures or non-sequential interrelationships. Twenty-four per cent of all slides were just lists, quotes, or detailed calculations. Forty-one per cent were lists with borders or other devices to enliven the presentation but which still presented material sequentially.

Why Poor Visual Design?

I feel there are two reasons why the majority of present designs are ineffective. First, the traditional presentation approach inhibits it, and second the equipment manufacturers focus users' attention on the materials used and not the design.

A 'traditional' presentation emphasizes three things: material is usually presented sequentially; precise calculations are stressed, often through worked examples which themselves contain detailed workings; and the legal emphasis on the meanings of specific words focuses attention on the words themselves rather than the underlying ideas. All these points inhibit effective presentation according to the model outlined above. All these emphases encourage highly detailed wordy design with little or no visual impact.

Manufacturers and graphic designers have traditionally concentrated on the range of equipment and materials available rather than the design within those materials. Lettering systems and coloured masks, for instance, have stressed the use of words and colours on the acetate rather than the visual make-up of the acetate. Graphic designers' publicity orientation may result in visual impact, but the ideas and pictures used are inappropriate or even distracting.

I myself cannot see how a 'tabloid page three' picture can be used to illustrate tax-free uplift. I suspect that the listeners will always remember the picture but never the presentation!

The designer's problem is a very real one. He has been taught to produce visual impact without considering the technical nuances behind the material. He is unlikely to have the confidence in the subject to discuss alternatives with the presenter. Those likely to suggest the least effective visuals are likely to be least prepared to consider suggestions from a non-technical source.

An Approach to Visual Design

The disease might be identifiable but what of the cure? In the ideal world, good visual design for technical presentations involves teamwork between the presenter and designer with each having an appreciation of the other's skill. Individual presenters will develop designs to suit their style, but I believe it is possible, using simple criteria, to develop approaches to particular subjects. I have an approach which I use when giving advice and lecturing on visual design to presenters of accountancy subjects.

I start with three criteria as the basis of developing further ideas. Designs have to be clear, visual and relevant. Clarity focuses the listener's attention on the key ideas. Visual effectiveness enables the listener to place the information in context and relate it to material learnt earlier. Relevance is important if the presenter is to avoid the mistake of having visual information that actually interferes with the information carried by other channels to the listener.

Clarity

Clarity is the first hurdle to be overcome. Technical presenters are acutely aware of the complexities and nuances in their subject. The argument runs: 'If the fine detail is not on the design then the listeners will miss it'. That is just what *should* happen!

The design should focus on one, or possibly two, key elements. With care, it is possible to crystallize complex technical ideas into a key diagram as, for example, with the deceptively simple sequence of slides intended to show the difficulties of defining 'profit' in a period of rising prices (Figures 1(a) and 1(b)).

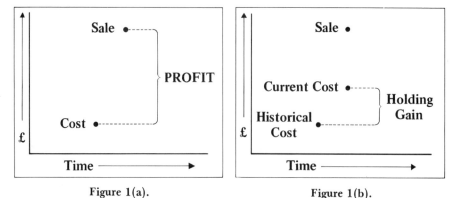

Figure 1(a).   Figure 1(b).

The designer has to ask: 'What is the key idea you wish to show? Is it that? Or is it this?' This discipline of analysis not only improves the design but also the whole presentation.

Visual Effectiveness

The listener needs to be able to get the message in context and relate it to earlier learnt information. The visual element of the design is potentially very effective in showing the interrelationships of ideas in an easily remembered way. Take, for example, the slide designed to illustrate year end administration of the PAYE system (Figure 2):

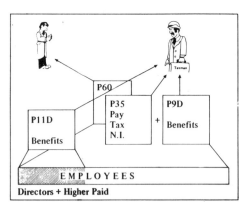

Figure 2. *Slide designed to illustrate year end administration of PAYE (the 'Directors and Higher Paid', the shaded area and P11D are illustrated in red)*

Small pictures can be used to great effect to evoke a context such as in Figure 3 where traditional book-keeping terms are compared with the equivalent terms in computer jargon. The same idea is used to highlight the key elements of a current cost-adjusted Profit and Loss account of a manufacturing company (Figure 4).

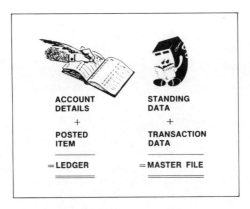

Figure 3. *Comparing equivalent terms in traditional book-keeping and in computing*

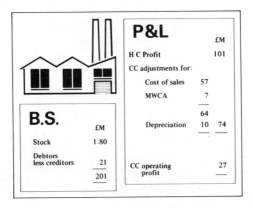

Figure 4. *Current cost-adjusted Profit and Loss account* (Colour is used for the adjustments)

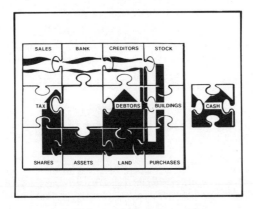

Figure 5. *A problem in auditing*

In some instances it is possible to use visual incongruities to make a point in a very memorable way. The problems of fitting together the evidence when auditing the accounts of a small business are illustrated in Figure 5.

It is correct; the 'cash' piece does not fit properly! The presenter can use this incongruity to discuss the difficulties of reconciling the cash balance or the auditor's job to look for areas where the evidence does not fit together.

Relevance

Relevance brings the designer back full circle to ask 'What is the purpose of a visual or a lack of it at each point in the presentation?' There are occasions in a presentation when it is inappropriate to use the visual information channel for technical information. It is a matter of judgement just when.

Conclusion

I have called this 'a personal view' because an approach to design is essentially personal. I hope, however, that my experience will be helpful to others. Technical presentations will increase, the complexity of the material involved will increase, and the associated costs of mounting such presentations will increase. It is possible that, with good visual support material, their effectiveness will improve dramatically. No more money is needed — just ideas!

References

Cawthray, B (ed) (1978) *The Business Studies and Management Teacher's Handbook and Catalogue of Overhead Projector Transparencies,* 1. Management Teacher Development Unit, South West Regional Management Centre, Bristol Polytechnic.

Patterson, O E (1962) *Special Tools for Communication.* Industrial Audio-Visual Association, PO Box 676, Old Post Office Annexe, Chicago.

Acknowledgement

Thanks are due to the Institute of Chartered Accountants in England and Wales for permission to use the illustrations.

10.3 A Use of Audio-Visual Methods in Anatomical Instruction

Vladimir Sistek and John Harrison
University of Ottawa

Abstract: Reductions in course teaching hours place more burden on the efficiency of teaching methods and the competence of the teacher, and lead logically to an increasing demand for high quality visual aids. The development of a pilot series of conceptual multi-media modules in anatomy is described.

The Curriculum

Since the 1960s, widespread changes in the curricula of schools of medicine, particularly in the basic sciences, have cut into the hours allotted to the teaching of basic morphological sciences with a particular impact on the courses in human anatomy. In some cases the reduction of hours has been by 30 per cent, and in the case of our department by more than 24 per cent.

Since 1969, the Department of Anatomy of the University of Ottawa has offered a clinically oriented course in topographical and living anatomy, within the limitations of an allotted 280 hours with content which, we firmly believe, gives the future MD a solidly based and balanced knowledge of the structures of the human body (Sistek and Harrison, 1978).

In our course, approximately one-half of the hours allotted are used for a mode of classroom teaching, using a wide variety of carefully selected and painstakingly timed audio-visual aids, supplemented by additional activities.

A typical three-dimensional morphological science, anatomy relies heavily on the visualization of its content. In our discipline, students must be offered all possible help to achieve and maintain the identified desired level of conceptual anatomical, mentally illustrated spatial knowledge. It is not surprising that, in the past, many more teachers of anatomy than of any other medical subject have been (and in rapidly decreasing numbers still are) excellent anatomical illustrators, frequently using a set of coloured chalks and a blackboard.

The ultimate answer in the illustration of the structures of the human body is the cadaver in the dissection laboratory, and a surgically-opened living human being in the operating theatre. Should the medical student dissect a cadaver? In our opinion, ideally, yes. But this is very time-consuming, and to learn anatomy during vivisection is rather too late.

We believe that we have found a solution (Sistek, 1973) in professionally dissected, carefully prepared and checked-out specimens covering the entire body, with which small groups of students are given scheduled and organized demonstrations.

However, thorough preparation for work in the dissection room is essential. Should the students enter the dissection room without any previous theoretical and conceptual visual foundation, they would soon be lost. Their precious time would be largely wasted, and after a while, not knowing what to look for, where, how and why, they would become discouraged, unenthusiastic, and even hostile to the subject, with disastrous educational results.

Therefore, every effort must be made by faculty to bridge the gap between their classroom discourse and the complicated three-dimensional morphological puzzle in the dissection room. This gap represents a pedagogical space which, we believe, can only logically be filled by a series of carefully selected, prepared and aimed two-dimensional audio-visual programmes.

A Use of Audio-Visual Aids

An unselected confused mess of audio-visual aids thrown at a student by a teacher without a basic knowledge of the technique, its limitations, aims and impacts, does considerably more harm than good.

Audio-visual aids in anatomy must be aimed at an exactly identified series of targets in order to reach the principal educational objective. The most effective aids will invariably present their carefully selected facts in a relatively easy, simple and attractive way, without going into an ever-increasing chain of minutiae but with enough crucial details to give positive support to the proper combination of all other means used in the teaching and learning process.

With the exception of three-dimensional models and of (ultimately) a cadaver, all other audio-visual aids in anatomy are two-dimensional. This is their crucial limitation. Used wisely, they represent an excellent aid within their dimensional framework.

SLIDES
35mm slides are currently the most widely used aid in anatomy, usually as a supplement to the teacher's discourse in the classroom, or by students for self-instruction or for summary-review repetition.

CLOSED-CIRCUIT TELEVISION (CCTV)
Use of CCTV in medical education has been assessed by several authors, particularly by Olsen (1970). We are in agreement with his basic conclusion: within its limitations, CCTV may give proper educational results only if used properly and selectively.

FILMS
8mm, Super 8mm and 16mm Mobius loop cartridges are valuable for help in general orientation, self-instructive reviews and summaries, but of those commercially available we would classify only a fairly limited number as being useful. For our purposes, they tend to present too many details or concentrate too much on techniques with consequently diminished impact in terms of concepts. In addition, they frequently use obsolete terminology. Visualization of the structures and angles of view used are frequently less than ideal.

BLACKBOARD DRAWINGS
Though this traditional aid perhaps might be considered to belong to the past, it still has its special place and is used by probably a handful of anatomy teachers in an elaborate way, in dynamic, exactly-to-the-point illustration (usually conceptual) of the topic under discussion.

The Implementation of Audio-Visual Aids in Anatomical Instruction

We are firmly of the opinion that there is a definite gap between the symbolism of the words used in classroom teaching and reality met in the dissection and operating theatres. We have, over the years, felt increasingly the lack of a proper series of audio-visual aids in anatomy which would be able to fill this pedagogical lacuna. We have been engaged since early 1975 in a project to produce such a series, and have been able to produce to this date 10 modules.

Aimed at first-year medical students, the modules are intended both for pedagogical support and autodidactic purposes. A sufficiency of detail has been provided to assure complete conceptualization; yet the treatment is of a basic nature in order to ensure a sound inculcation of fundamental principles.

The modules are designed as a supplement to our classroom teaching and most definitely not as a replacement. It is for this reason that the modules have been prepared in such a way as to make it possible to complement exactly the material treated in the lecture series, and in the same order of presentation.

After careful analysis of the educational objectives and of the media available, the slide-tape presentation was selected as being at present best adapted to our needs for the following reasons.

The slide-tape medium chosen for these modules imposes a strict discipline. It requires a particularly clear conceptualization and careful control of the visual elements selected. In like manner, a certain asceticism is required in the aural element in order to maintain artistic integrity and therefore communicative unity.

The discipline of the medium indeed promotes the elimination of redundant matter and thereby permits a certain reduction of what is often described as 'noise in the communications system'.

This choice of communications medium offers the following benefits:

1. International acceptability for presentation purposes. Only the 16mm motion picture format offers a similar degree of compatibility, but at a considerably increased cost.
2. The technical costs of production are relatively low (Baggott *et al*, 1977).
3. The technical quality of a colour slide can be very high.
4. The system offers ease of random access to visuals, making possible the individual use of a specific image. In addition, updating is relatively simple and inexpensive.
5. The medium offers ease of conversion to other distribution media.
6. The medium readily lends itself to use in an autotutorial mode.
7. Distribution costs for both the visual and aural elements are potentially low.
8. Relatively low production costs make the entire project economically attractive as a pedagogical investment.

Conclusion

The following comments represent a synthesis of our current concerns:

A pedagogical space exists between the symbolism of words used in classroom teaching and the three-dimensional visualization of reality.

The basis for conceptual understanding and knowledge of anatomy should be in building up a proper 'mental library' of illustrations of the structures of the human body.

In order to help in building the 'mental library' of anatomical illustrations, and to bridge effectively the pedagogical space between classroom and dissection room teaching, a series of audio-visual aids, carefully selected or developed and properly timed in their application are helpful.

The proper use of the tools of instructional technology, and intimate familiarity with principles governing their use, is a prerequisite for professionalism and competence in the execution of the educational process.

We have the tools, the technology and the administrative systems that make the rational management of learning resources a practical possibility. Can we reasonably hope for a widespread movement towards advanced pedagogic techniques? As realists, we presume that both external and internal pressures will impose change (Sistek and Harrison, 1977a).

Generally the diminshed time allotted to the production of a graduate, either absolutely or relatively, has placed a continually increasing burden on academic leaders in developing proper curricula and pedagogical methods, and on the competency, teaching professionalism and time of academicians in classrooms, laboratories and hospital wards (Sistek and Harrison, 1977b).

Negative incentives have traditionally been provided in medical schools for improving individual teaching competency: most likely an academician devoting most of his time to teaching has had to, and still has to, fight hard to maintain his pedagogical integrity and position. Opportunities for teachers to improve their pedagogical skills and to learn about and to use the currently available means of instructional technology are not encouraged; indeed in respect of the technological support facilities we detect a somewhat Luddite mentality.

We believe that the new technological means and aids are very useful in medical education, but there remains one inescapable fact: audio-visual or other aids, no matter how advanced, cannot replace the teacher. They can, at times, help make a difference between 'good' and 'bad' teaching. If we were to sum up our ideas in one sentence, we would have to say that they cannot save a bad teacher, but properly used they can help make a good teacher better.

References

Baggott, J, Lawrence, D M, Shaw, F, Galley, M and Devlin, T M (1977) Efficiency of do-it-yourself slide-tape programs as an alternative to the lecture in medical biochemistry. *Journal of Medical Education,* 2, p 157.

Olsen, I A (1970) Advantages and disadvantages of CCTV. *British Journal of Medical Education,* 4, p 312.

Sistek, V (1973) Dissection or prosected specimen? *Gross Anatomy Workshop, National Symposium on Instructional and Audio-Visual Teaching in Medicine,* 16 June. Memorial University of Newfoundland, St John's.

Sistek, V and Harrison, J (1977a) Improving teaching efficiency and the role of the audio-visual aid. Paper presented at the *International Conference on University Teaching,* 7 June. McMaster University, Hamilton, Canada.

Sistek, V and Harrison, J (1977b) Medical education — new initiatives? *CMA Journal,* 117, p 1362.

Sistek, V and Harrison, J (1978) Anatomical instruction: curriculum development and the efficient use of audio-visual aids. *British Journal of Educational Technology,* 9, 1, p 17.

10.4 The Arts: Interdisciplinary Design, Multi-media Format

Moylan C Mills
The Pennsylvania State University

Abstract: Describes a new course which uses an interdisciplinary approach to teach a basic introduction to the arts. Because the course is predicated on the student actually seeing and hearing illustrations of the material under discussion, it could only be possible with the development and reasonably-priced availability of media technology.

One of the most exciting developments in education in recent years is the impact of technology on the teaching of arts and culture-related courses. Not long ago, schools would have found it almost impossible to create and offer an interdisciplinary arts-type course that featured numerous in-class examples of the works under discussion. Now, with the availability of sophisticated media technology, such as video-cassettes and disc players, and with the fairly reasonable prices of both hardware and software, we are in a good position to expand the cultural awareness of our students.

A course in the arts developed at the Pennsylvania State University uses an interdisciplinary approach to provide a basic introduction to the arts. The subject matter, though flexible, ordinarily encompasses film, theatre, painting, print-making, photography, sculpture, music, opera, dance, and architecture.

The focus of the course is on the cognitive elements of the arts areas under study. In other words, students are discouraged from concentrating on whether or not they *like* a particular work of art, but are expected to understand the elements in the work that create its effect, ie counterpoint in a musical composition, focal area in a painting, subjective camera usage in a film.

Naturally, students enrolled in a course of this kind must be brought into a close confrontation with the works being studied. Although field trips are an integral component of the course, they are often too costly, inconvenient, or unavailable at the right time to provide all of the study examples needed. Thus, the use in the classroom of media and their concomitant technology has become the foundation on which the course is built. Obviously, because the course is predicated on students' actually seeing and hearing illustrations of the material under discussion, the course would not exist without the video-cassettes and tapes, the audio-cassettes, tapes, and records, the 35mm slides, and the 16mm films and their accompanying video, projection, and stereo equipment.

The course is designed to be taught by one instructor or by a team of instructors. The number of students in each class varies from 15 to several hundred. Each session is a lecture-demonstration format, with students encouraged to question and comment.

Although there is a basic syllabus that is expected to be followed by each instructor who teaches the course, individual instructors may vary the emphasis placed on a given area.

Since one of the goals of the course is to show students how certain concepts are common to a number of the arts, often two of the arts areas may be examined at one time. For instance, instructors might play several musical selections and project several paintings on a screen. The students will be asked to connect the musical selections with the paintings and to explain why they made certain choices.

Comparison is an important element of the course. For instance, the two examinations, a mid-term and a final, are objective and focus on a comparison of one painting with another, one film with another, etc. The students will often find themselves comparing a work of art that they are familiar with through class examination with a work that they may not have experienced before. Thus, students learn that we do not explore fresh works of art in a vacuum, but in context with other works with which we are familiar.

Another important component of the arts course is the field trips. These trips are set up in order to force students to apply the information and knowledge gained in class to arts experiences outside class. Students are expected to attend three events during the term and to write a detailed report that analyzes, in cognitive terms, one of the experiences.

The Arts I course has been designed to introduce students to the various elements that artists use to create their works. The objective of the course is to make students more aware of, and sensitive to, the arts so that they will become more discriminating partakers of the arts. It is hoped, therefore, that they will become more perceptive and attain more insight, and that their lives will be enriched.

This object is a tall order, and the course is too new to determine if, in fact, these goals are being reached. It is true, however, that the course is immensely popular and that students appear to be very satisfied with the results. There is already a clamour for additional courses of this nature at Penn State.

The course has been scheduled successfully for regularly matriculated undergraduate students, as well as for adult students in the continuing education area. One of the advantages of the course is that, even with all of the media equipment used, it can be easily exported for special interest groups off-campus. A number of retirement homes in the Penn State area are currently very interested in scheduling the course as part of an enrichment programme for their clients. The course appears to appeal to all ages and to traditional and non-traditional students.

As mentioned at the beginning of this paper, without the availability of reasonably-priced equipment and materials a course of this kind would be impossible to set up. However, with the technology and arts resources, faculty and administrators have the chance to bring many people into a confrontation with the arts that has every possibility of adding immeasurable satisfaction to their lives. And, after all, is that not what education is all about?

10.5 Media Applications at an Illinois Community College

David Kozlowski and Lia Brillhart
Triton College

Abstract: The paper deals with the several distinctive applications of educational technology at Triton College, in areas such as cultural enrichment, career planning, individualized instruction, classroom enrichment, continuing education, and community outreach.

The community college, because of its comprehensive missions, needs to provide students with a variety of paths to a successful learning experience. The use of multi-media is one essential avenue for meeting this objective. A full range of media services is available at Triton for use in the classrooms, by individual students and by the entire community. Triton's commitment to media has led to such diverse programmes as a space centre used by all ages, from elementary school children to senior citizens' groups, to an allied health resource centre used for continuing education by professionals.

The State of Illinois is centrally located in the United States, and has been divided into 39 community college districts. These community colleges serve the population within their respective districts by providing:

1. The first two years of study towards a traditional four-year baccalaureate degree.
2. Vocational training.
3. General studies for self-interest.
4. Continuing education for professional refreshment.
5. Hobby, leisure and recreation courses.

One of 52 community college campuses in Illinois, Triton is the largest single-campus community college in the state and is located in the suburbs just west of Chicago. A brief statistical description of the college includes:

District population   388,200
Composed of 24 towns and villages covering 63 sq miles; 164 sq km

Enrolment (Fall, 1979)
    Full-time   4,595
    Part-time   17,755
    Total   22,350

Operating budget (1978-79)	$19,271,193 or £8,489,512
Sources of revenue	
Local taxes	37 per cent
State of Illinois	32 per cent
Tuition and fees	26 per cent
Other	5 per cent

The Learning Resources Centre (LRC) at Triton is divided into five service components. They are:

1. Library.
2. Audio-visual Services.
3. Media Production.
4. Independent Learning Laboratory.
5. Cernan Earth and Space Theatre.

The Library houses a basic collection of books, periodicals, microfilm and recordings. An automated circulation system is used and a materials security system has been installed.

Audio-visual Services distributes and maintains all audio-visual equipment on campus and the film and video-cassette collections. Materials are delivered and retrieved from classrooms via telephone requests.

The Media Production component has three service units; television, radio and graphics. The television area has two production studios (one colour and one black/white) and peripheral support equipment. The radio station serves as a training facility while giving the College additional access to the community through its broadcasts. Graphics provides the faculty with a wide variety of instructional aids such as original artwork, photography and computer graphics.

The Independent Learning Laboratory provides many instructional materials and equipment which supplement classroom activities through individualized instruction. For example, students may improve their foreign language skills by using language tapes, they may practise shorthand from dictation tapes, or watch assigned films, video-tapes or slide-tape productions. In addition, mini-computers are available, as well as terminals connected to a mainframe computer. These may be used for classroom assignments or personal use.

The Eugene Cernan Earth and Space Theatre, which is located in a separate building, contains an exhibit area of displays, illustrating the earth and space sciences. The exhibit area also serves as a waiting room for the more than 90,000 visitors per year who come to view one the multi-media sky theatre productions. About half of the visitors are school-age children brought by their teachers to view a particular programme explaining some astronomical phenomenon or geographic locale. The remainder are the general public who come on evenings and weekends to view the current show. The sky theatre contains a fully automated planetarium projector system, a 180-degree, 35mm 'all-sky' motion picture projector, a sophisticated wrap-around sound system and control panel and many auxiliary projection devices. The theatre seats 60 people. A musically synchronous laser light projector is at present being added to the facility. Available productions include:

Night and Day	Stars and Constellations
The Sun	Reasons for the Seasons
Planets and their Orbits	Man to the Moon
Universe	The Grand Canyon
The Christmas Star	Wings for Man
Exploring the Sky	UFOs: Fact or Fantasy
Down the Mississippi	The Chicago Experience
The Last Question	Hawaii
This England (in production)	Mexico: Land of Many Colours (in production)

As a further service to the community, Triton began its District Film Library. This service provides for advance booking of 500 16mm educational films which are delivered on a weekly basis to the 14 secondary schools within the district. This service has been provided free for the past two years. Films are also available to elementary schools who must provide their own pick-up and return. Beginning next fall, a rental fee is being added to provide revenue to increase the holdings within the collection.

To provide programmes for the continuing education of the staffs of the seven hospitals and nine nursing homes within the district, the Allied Health Learning Resource Centre produces programmes which explain new processes, techniques and equipment for the medical professional. These are usually produced in either a video-tape or sound/slide format. The college also offers a continuous schedule of seminars designed to update the backgrounds of many of the medical professions. Triton thus helps medical professions in the community to remain current in their fields and update their skills.

As a community college, Triton has felt a commitment to disadvantaged students in the district. During the last two summers, Triton has co-operated with the counsellors at the College to provide training for job interviews for these students. They are counselled, tutored and video-taped in mock interview situations and view their own performances. The objective of the programme is to impart positive interview mannerisms which enhance their opportunity for employment.

The description of functions of the Learning Resource Centre (LRC) has, so far, dealt with specific single system uses. In addition to this, the Learning Resource Centre also provides multiple services for a single curriculum. For instance, in engineering, video-tapes, slide-tapes, sound pages, and computers are used to provide students with various paths to successful learning experiences. Video-tapes are made of talks by well-known engineers to acquaint students with job opportunities and inform them of professional skills required by engineers. In addition, students produce video-tapes, both to improve their technical speaking skills and to clarify subject matter.

All lectures in statics and dynamics, two required engineering courses, are presented as slide-tape modules. Students may access them at any time for review purposes or for clarification of difficult subject matter. These same two courses have 250 problems per course recorded on a medium called the sound page. This system is useful in engineering, where one side of the page accommodates diagrams and script while the other side contains recorded instruction. Each sound page is 8″ x 12″ x .012″; hence they are easily stored, inexpensive ($.15/sheet) and virtually indestructible. They have proved to be very effective in courses where problem-solving skills are important.

Computers are used for student testing. Large data-bases are randomly accessed to produce individualized versions of tests. This allows for a secure, readily available testing system for self-paced instruction. In addition, interactive modules, have been placed into the computer primarily for remedial purposes for engineering students enrolled in the graphics and statics/dynamics courses.

The multi-media services described illustrate some of the methods which are at present being used to meet the needs of our district. Looking from the present towards the future, the advances being made in computers, video-tape and video-disc technology hold promise for being able to provide the ability to access and deliver instructional information economically, and in quantities previously unattainable. If the trend of domestic acceptance of consumer applications of these technologies continues throughout the 1980s, one could expect equal acceptance in the educational market as well, thus providing students, faculty, trainers and media professionals with exciting prospects to enhance learning opportunities.

10.6 A Technique for OHP/Tape Lesson Packages

John S Stoane
Kingsway Technical College, Dundee

Abstract: Tape/OHP transparency programmes would appear to be an advance on the well-known tape/slide technique. However, programming the teacher/presenter in the complex manipulations of the transparencies during the course of the taped lesson can present problems. The paper describes the development of a system which overcomes such difficulties. The system involves recording the lesson and the presenter's instructions on the left and right channels of a stereo tape.

What is to Be Gained by Combining Tape with OHP Transparencies Rather Than With Slides?

A well-designed interactive tape/slide has been shown to be a very powerful teaching method which is well-liked by pupils.

The OHP is an alternative way of showing diagrams and other illustrations. In many ways it is much more versatile with diagrams than the slides.

It can achieve four main things that slides cannot:

1. *Building up diagrams.* The model or diagram can be built up step by step, either by adding overlays or removing covers without having to remove the image from the screen as is necessary when using a succession of slides. If the screen is blank, even for a moment, the continuity of the argument is lost — the pupil cannot look back at the previous information.
2. *Altering diagrams.* A diagram can be altered while on the screen by, for example, changing overlays.
3. *Highlighting.* Attention can be drawn to a particular part of the information on the screen by use of a coloured overlay mask to outline the required part.
4. *Adding movement.* Using the 'Opasym' method, the appearance of movement can be created to emphasize the direction of flow of gases and liquids in diagrams.

It would seem, then, that a tape/OHP transparency system would in many ways be an advance from tape/slide.

It is worthy of note, however, that although it is widely assumed that the OHP techniques of build-up of diagrams, selective revealing, etc are an important help to understanding, research evidence to support this is very small. Maddox and Loughran (1977) carried out an experiment at the University of Newcastle, Australia involving 54 senior undergraduate geography students to compare recall of information presented by means of *complete* diagrams with recall from diagrams built up progressively in the best educational technology manner.

They could find no significant difference between results using the two types of diagram. However, 67 per cent of the students said they preferred the build-up method and 15 per cent said they preferred a mixture of both types.

While Maddox and Loughran's research compared the effect of complete diagrams on *slide* with built-up diagrams on OHT, it seems reasonable to assume that the complete diagrams could equally well have been presented on OHT without affecting the results.

How Could a Tape/OHP Transparency System be Operated?

Changing a slide can either be a simple matter of pressing a button or it can be done automatically by the bleep on the tape, whereas manipulating OHP transparencies calls for several more complex actions. How can the presenter be cued to: change the transparency; add an overlay; remove an overlay; remove a cover; replace an overlay; switch on the opasym; switch off the opasym; switch off the tape?

The simple audible bleep of the tape/slide system would need to be extended to seven bleeps to cover all these instructions. This is obviously impracticable. The number of bleeps could be reduced by using three different sounds (eg buzz, bleep, bell).

Either of these two methods would reduce the whole scheme to farce, be very distracting for the pupil, and be very difficult for the presenter to remember the code. Nor does it seem that there would be any possibility of an automated system analogous to inaudible pulsed synchronized slide-change systems.

The first attempt to solve this problem was to give the presenter a copy of the tape script which had the instructions for the manipulation of the OHTs written in as shown in Figure 1.

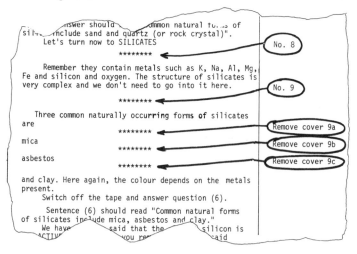

Figure 1.

The instructions were placed well before the place in the script where the action is required. This works fairly well but requires a fair degree of concentration and rehearsal on the part of the presenter, especially when the actions required become more rapid.

The next idea was to record the instructions on tape verbally so that the presenter could hear them on headphones without the pupils hearing them. It was decided therefore to play the programme and the instructions on two separate tape recorders. It would obviously be important to get the two tapes synchronized so that the instructions arrived at the correct time. In order to achieve this, a bleep was put onto each tape at the beginning. Before starting the lesson, each tape would be run on until the bleep was heard and then stopped immediately. This made sure that the two recorders started at the same place.

In order to allow pupils to write responses it was essential to switch the two tape recorders off and on absolutely simultaneously to keep them in step. This was achieved by interrupting the power supply to the two recorders which were fed through a two-way extension board.

Recording the Programmes

The method of recording is shown in the two diagrams in Figure 2.

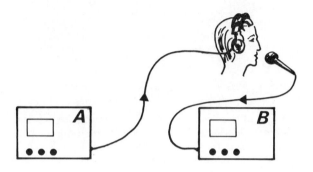

Figure 2.

The lesson was recorded in mono on tape recorder A. It was then played back to the commentator through headphones. As he listened to the lesson he recorded the presenter's instructions onto a separate tape in recorder B. Headphones had to be used instead of a loudspeaker; otherwise the lesson would have been recorded on recorder B along with the instructions.

When the recordings were tried out immediately afterwards, the two tapes seemed to keep in perfect step and the instructions arrived at the correct time. When this was tried in the classroom, using the same two tape recorders, the two tapes kept getting slightly out of step. The faster tape had to be held back momentarily every so often by putting down the pause button for half-a-second to allow the slower one to catch up. It was even worse when using tape recorders other than those on which the recordings were made.

However, one thing had been proved. The presenter could follow the instructions perfectly and had no difficulty in carrying them out. Also, the programme worked well as far as the pupils receiving it were concerned.

The obvious answer to the problem of keeping the lesson and presenter's instructions in step was to record them on the *same* tape by using the left and right channels of a stereo recording. That way, the two could not get out of step. Figure 3 shows how the stereo recording was made.

The mono recording of the lesson was played on the mono tape recorder A into the left channel line in of a stereo tape recorder. At the same time it was played to the commentator through headphones connected to the monitor outlet on the stereo recorder. As he heard the lesson, he recorded the presenter's instructions through a microphone connected to the right channel input of the stereo recorder. Four important points of technique emerged as a result of the experimentation that went into producing the final programme:

1. The presenter's instructions were given a little ahead of the point where he was required to act.

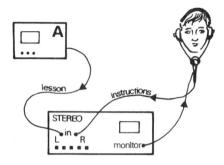

Figure 3.

2. Plenty of time was allowed for the presenter to change the overlay, remove covers etc by leaving adequate pauses in the lesson.
3. So that it would be easier for the presenter to go to the correct overlay quickly, the overlays were numbered in a clockwise sequence round the transparency, starting on the left-hand side. The covers were arranged in a similar way but labelled with the letters A, B, C, etc.
4. A 1,000Hz bleep was used as a signal to switch off the tape to allow responses to be made.

Administration of the Programme in the Classroom

The method of using the system is shown in Figure 4.

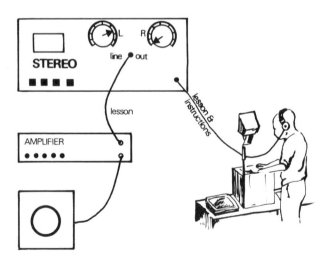

Figure 4.

The line out controls are set as shown: the left channel carrying the lesson is set high while the right channel carrying the instructions is set at zero. Thus, the lead from the line out socket carries only the lesson and not the presenter's instructions. This is amplified and played to the class through a loudpseaker.

The presenter listens to both channels on stereo headphones connected to the monitor socket. (The line out level controls do not affect the monitor outlet.) The presenter in fact hears the lesson in his left ear and the instructions in his right ear.

Experience in Use

A slight degree of cross-talk was noticed in that the presenter's instructions could sometimes be heard faintly by the class. This was really noticeable only when there was a moment's silence in the lesson. The bleep to switch off the tape could be heard more readily, although no pupils commented on it.

An essential preliminary is to get the transparencies stacked up in the correct order, with all the overlays and covers in their initial state, ready to go straight onto the projector. The initial states are listed in the written instructions that go with the package.

The presenter had no problems in hearing both the programme and the instructions and distinguishing between them, although it was sometimes helpful to be able to turn down the volume of the programme in the presenter's left ear by adjusting the volume control on the left earpiece of the headphones. Neither did the presenter have any difficulty hearing, understanding and carrying out the instructions in the pauses allowed. The length allowed depended on the complexity of the operation. Even people who were completely unfamiliar with the technique, programme or subject matter managed to manipulate the transparencies successfully after a little preliminary experimentation.

Conclusion

A viable method of combining OHP transparencies with a taped lesson has been achieved. The technique is undoubtedly more complicated to produce and use than tape/slide and is therefore unlikely to be as widely used. However, for particular topics which demand the versatility of the OHP, the extra effort needed can be justified.

Reference

Maddox, H and Loughran, R J (1977) Illustrating the lecture: prepared diagrams vs built-up diagrams. *Audio-Visual Communication Review*, Spring, 25, 1, pp 87-90.

10.7 Coming to Terms with Educational Technology in the Arab World

Salah A El-Araby
The American University in Cairo

Abstract: Assimilating instructional technology within the educational system in the Arab World requires more than imported media and equipment. A survey of some of the problems and their causes for Arab educators leads on to possible solutions. These are not presented as revolutionary measures, but would rearrange the pieces of the puzzle of the educational system quite differently, while the central pieces would remain the same.

Introduction

The learning environment in some Arab countries is suffering from student flood, scarcity of expertise, money and learning resources, and occasional administrative inertia and inefficiency. The most serious problem of all is that the type of output of the educational system, namely the university graduate, is not well prepared to cope with the nagging demands of a developing society.

Rising national expectations and the rapid increase in population are largely to blame for the over-eagerness of students to acquire public and higher education. The present system of education does not cope with the explosion of knowledge which has shifted the emphasis away from the rigid prescribed text and the inadequately qualified teacher as the only sources of information.

Striving hard to catch up with modern trends in education and to satisfy the needs for national development, Arab educators are caught in a difficult conflict between a die-hard traditional way of teaching and the demands of new educational trends that cannot be easily grafted onto the existing system. Education is still largely regarded as an institutional affair between teacher and taught, verbal and textual in style, paternal and disciplined in orientation. It over-emphasizes the importance of retaining information about different subject-matter disciplines. The learner is expected to remember many minute details about various topics, which he can easily look up in many of the available references. A specified body of knowledge has to be memorized, although such knowledge may soon become outdated. The student is evaluated according to what he knows, verbally and theoretically, rather than what he can do, apply and transfer to real-life situations. The result is a mammoth number of graduates all looking for desk jobs, unable actively to participate in crucial areas of national development.

Using Instructional Technology

As educational media are playing a key role in the instructional process, many schools and universities in the Arab World have recruited media specialists, purchased instructional equipment and sought to modernize their teaching procedures. Educational media can be simply defined as any materials, machines or activities used to reinforce and complement verbal communication. Films, filmstrips, TV programmes, slides and transparencies, as well as equipment used to show them, are educational media. Pictures, the recorded voice, and models are also instructional aids. In fact any material, programme or machine used to help the teacher explain his lesson in a better way than just talk can be included under teaching aids.

It is a sad fact of life that many Arab teachers avoid using teaching aids because they are not willing to learn new ways and skills. They are afraid that something might go wrong with the machines they are using. They do not realize that the advantages of instructional media far outweigh their shortcomings. Media are designed to help the teacher save time and effort. Many of them can be effectively used in large classes relieving the teacher from many routine tasks. All of them make the class more lively and interesting for the teacher and the taught.

Modern trends in education depend on learner-oriented, resource-based learning, self-instructional techniques, problem-solving approaches and individualized instruction. The main objective is not to impart a body of knowledge to a passive listener, but to use instructional technology amongst learner-based techniques to help the student *learn how to learn on his own*. Once the learner has perfected the learning strategies that are in keeping with his abilities and interests, he is ready to tackle many of the problems in our changing world. Such skills will never be outdated and can always be called upon to gain fresh knowledge and data to help solve new challenges.

Just as the human body would reject a transplanted organ if the tissues do not match, so would the Arab educational system resist or at least ignore Western technology if the way has not been paved for its utilization. Educators and decision-makers in the Arab World have realized that introduction of new trends should be well co-ordinated to blend easily with the existing educational structure.

Pioneer efforts started in February 1967 when the Standing Committee for Cultural Affairs in the League of Arab States issued a recommendation that a conference of specialists survey different educational media used in all Arab countries. One year later, the Conference of Arab Ministers of Education, in its third meeting, recommended forming a committee of experts to research the feasibility of establishing an Arab States Educational Media Centre to consolidate, co-ordinate and develop educational technology resources among Arab States. In May 1970, the cultural section of the League of Arab States sponsored a conference on audio-visual aids and educational technology in Amman, Jordan.

On 25 July 1970, the Arab League Educational, Cultural and Scientific Organization (ALECSO) was established as a specialized agency of the League of Arab States. Among its educational responsibilities was the development of awareness of the importance of educational media among Arab educators. In 1974, a questionnaire was sent to all Arab States eliciting information about educational media facilities including human and material resources . This data-gathering tool was validated by field visits and structured interviews. On the basis of the results of this survey, the fourth general assembly of ALECSO decided in 1975 that an Arab States Educational Media Centre was to be established in 1976 in Kuwait.

Establishing a regional media centre does not of necessity guarantee a comprehensive solution to all educational technology problems in the area. Supported by the financing and expertise available in Arab countries, it is a step in the right direction to explore common needs and obstacles and to recommend measures conducive to improving the use of media in the educational process. Furthermore, it is a concrete proof of the awareness of Arab States of the contribution of media in upgrading the quality of instruction.

Adopting Western Technology

Perhaps it is necessary to review our thinking about importing unadulterated versions of Western media, although in the majority of cases instructional technology equipment and media have worked well, especially in the hands of younger professors who have kept their knowledge and expertise well up-to-date. What is distressingly lacking is an overall plan that would modify Western technology so that it might be assimilated comfortably into the Arab system of higher education without cultural or social after-effects.

In order to develop this comprehensive plan a committee of at least three people should be involved: a media specialist, a sociologist/anthropologist and the subject-matter expert. Starting with the learner as the core of the learning process they have to define his attitudes, motivation, age and maturity level, past experiences, present interests and learning strategies. The last property refers to the communication media and techniques which the learner can easily respond to and understand. Second, the committee should determine the precise objectives of the teaching unit: what they want the learner to know, which skills they want him to be able to perform, and finally what theoretical knowledge they want him to apply in practical situations, relevant to the needs of a developing nation.

Once learners' characteristics and objectives have been clarified, the three specialists should define the learning environment in physical and human terms, ie the kind of lecture halls they use, the available equipment, the number of students in each class, the teaching style of the professors, library and AV resources. Then the committee should consider the most appropriate communication strategies and techniques that are in keeping with the above factors, with special emphasis on local culture and traditions. These strategies include individual and group discussion, independent learning, student-oriented research techniques, problem-solving approaches, face-to-face verbal communication and other means of imparting and assimilating information. In this area, the contribution of the sociologist/ anthropologist should be significant.

The media specialist can then recommend software and hardware that can best realize the instructional objectives of the learning unit, in the light of all the above. He may recommend importing ready-made media from abroad if they meet the cultural, psychological and academic requirements. On the other hand, he may prefer to have some aids developed locally or specially made abroad to fit the specific needs of the learners.

Figure 1 is meant to emphasize the importance of the learner as the consumer of the learning process and the major factor in controlling all other aspects of the situation. The final phase in the schematic drawing, ie evaluation, will be discussed under a separate heading. Although this overall plan may seem time-consuming and expensive to carry out, the contribution of instructional technology to solving some of the problems in Arab institutions should justify the effort and time spent.

Evaluation

Introduction of expensive techniques and equipment is always met with resistance from educational authorities, especially if they consider them lower in priority to more pressing needs. Some would even go as far as believing that instructional media are more suitable for entertainment than for serious study. Adherents of instructional technology have to prove it is cost-effective in that the educational benefits can justify the financial investment. Criteria based on learners' and teachers' gains should be devised to assess the impact of the contribution of instructional technology in higher education. The results of such evaluation may necessitate re-considering the instructional objectives.

Research studies in Europe, the UK and the USA on the effectiveness of media in higher education have promising results, but most of them have ended up with the cliché: 'no significant difference between groups using media and those who do not use them, other things being equal'. Perhaps the last phrase is the reason for such non-conclusive findings. Other things are never equal when experiments involve difficult-to-control variables such as human beings, teachers, students and learning

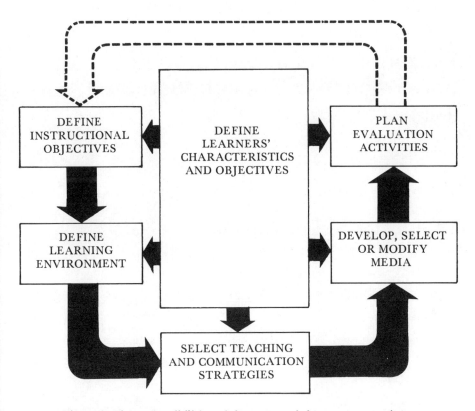

Figure 1. *The responsibilities of the suggested three-man committee*

gains! The product of instruction cannot be easily measurable or quantifiable. Structured observation and in-depth interviews, however, have proven beyond a doubt that groups using instructional technology have enjoyed the learning process and have felt more relaxed and better motivated to learn more. Professors also are reported to have realized how such techniques facilitate teaching, clarify concepts and take most of the drudgery out of routine instruction. More controlled research and in-depth studies are needed to reach more definitive results.

Industrialized countries suffer from an overload of culture-bound media. What the Arab World lacks is original resources about its social and economic development that reaches learners in either the first or third worlds. To remedy the situation, more should be done about creating media departments in universities, establishing media-producing companies and adapting and selecting suitable Western AV resources.

Enlightened use of instructional technology in the Arab World is bound to change the conventional roles of professors, students, textbooks and examination systems. Arab educators should try their best to adjust their usual teaching/learning activities accordingly to produce the kind of university graduate that can cope with the needs of developing nations.

Section 11:
Developments in the Theory and Practice of Educational Technology

11.1 A New Look at the Analysis of Knowledge and Skills

Alexander J Romiszowski

Abstract: This paper outlines a new attempt at a classification of learning, based on a clear and precisely defined distinction between knowledge and skill. The approach is not a rigid procedure but is rather a flexible, conceptual scheme for organizing one's thoughts about a given learning problem.

Introduction

Practical approaches to job analysis or task analysis for training purposes have traditionally tended to list the 'knowledge and skills requirements' for each of the tasks or sub-tasks that require to be learnt, often laying out this information in columns on a standardized analysis form. Modifications include a three-column format for 'knowledge/skills/attitudes', or sometimes a subdivision of the skills category into skill-types (eg physical/intellectual/social). However, few of these early approaches defined with any precision exactly what the column headings meant, nor was much effort made to ensure that analysts interpreted the categories in a consistent manner.

Approaches that have attempted to be more precise and consistent (eg the taxonomies of Bloom (1956) and Krathwohl (1964), the learning categories of Gagné (1974) and similar models) have tended to be behaviouristically oriented, classifying the different types of behaviour changes that may be observed and measured as a result of instruction. These approaches seem to have abandoned (or lost involuntarily) the basic distinction between *knowledge* and *skill*.

An analysis of the well-known classification systems reveals much inconsistency and some gaps. For example, the three domains of learning (cognitive, psychomotor and affective) are not at all synonymous with the three practical categories of knowledge, skills and attitudes, although some authors would have us think that they are. Also, there are several categories of learning that do not fit into the existing models, for example interactive, or social skills.

This paper presents a fresh attempt at a classification of learning, based on a clear, precisely defined distinction between knowledge and skill that enables the instructional designer to approach a learning problem from two distinct viewpoints — the information inputs required (and the structure of this information) and the performance outputs required (and the deficiencies possible in this performance).

This two-pronged approach has been found to be practically effective and conceptually more satisfactory than other models for the design of instruction.

The Learner as a System

The following approach to knowledge and skills analysis is based firmly on systems thinking. Therefore, we start with our learner represented as a 'black box' receiving *information* as input, and outputting certain *performances* which are indicators that learning has taken place.

The two tangible elements that we can analyze are:

(a) The information we feed the learner.
(b) The performance he emits.

Now we should define 'knowledge' and 'skill'.

Knowledge will be used to refer to information stored in the learner's mind. This is akin to the normal use of the word when we say that we 'know' something.

Skill will be used to refer to actions (intellectual or physical), and indeed 'reactions' (to ideas, things or people) which a person performs in a competent way in order to achieve a goal. In practising a skill, one uses certain items of knowledge that are stored in the mind. One uses perception (of the situation/problem/object) to gain new information which is combined with the knowledge, and one acts on the basis of planning decisions. Any skilled action may have four component activities: (i) perception, (ii) recall of prerequisite knowledge, (iii) planning, and (iv) the execution, or performance, of the action.

Knowledge is a 'go — no go' quantity. Either you have it or you do not. Either it is stored or it is not. If you 'know' part of a subject, it means that you know certain elements of information and you do not know others.

Skill, on the other hand, is something which develops with experience and practice. You can be highly skilled, or not so highly skilled in *using* information to achieve a certain purpose.

The Four Categories of Knowledge

We have four categories into which we can classify knowledge:

1. Facts
2. Procedures
3. Concepts
4. Principles

These are the four categories of information used by Williams (1977) in his suggested improvements to the taxonomies of Bloom and Gagné. They are also not so different from the categories of information used by Horn (1969) as the basis of information mapping.

The Four Categories of Skills

Skills are divided into a wide variety of categories by various writers and are given various names. We will adopt a basic division into four categories:

1. Thinking, or cognitive skills. (I will avoid using 'intellectual skills' so as not to create confusion with Gagné's terminology.)
2. Acting — physical or motor skill (psychomotor to be exact).
3. Reacting — to things, situations or people, in terms of values, emotions, feelings. (This is largely synonymous with attitudes.)

4. Interacting — with people in order to achieve some goal, such as communication, education, acceptance, persuasion, etc.

The 'Knowledge Schema'

Let us now expand the basic concepts presented above into a more comprehensive schema which can act as the basis for our system of classifying types of learning. First, let us consider the 'knowledge' domain.

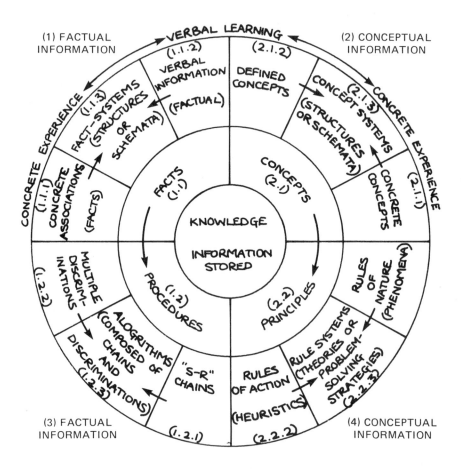

Figure 1. *The Knowledge Schema*

The schema presented here subdivides our four basic types of knowledge (facts, procedures, concepts and principles) in order to illustrate several aspects of knowledge.

(a) That the information stored (the knowledge) may have been gained directly through concrete experience ('observation' of the outside world by any one of our senses) or it may have been gained through 'vicarious' experience, usually by means of the spoken or written word but also through the use of other symbolic languages (this implies the previous mastery of the language in question).

(b) That the information may be stored as discrete items (individual facts, concepts, rules, etc) or it may be combined into information systems (or schemata) which relate the discrete items to each other in particular ways. (Note that the form of these systems or schemata may have been received 'from outside' as part of the way in which the information was communicated in the first instance or else they may have been constructed 'internally' by the student himself when he tries to relate new information received to information previously stored — the processes of assimilation and adaptation described by Piaget.)

(c) That knowledge of a particular topic is seldom of one type but is usually a combination of several types of factual and conceptual knowledge, both concrete and verbal, some stored as coherent schemata and some as discrete unrelated items. Hence the circular nature of our diagram is intended to emphasize the non-exclusive, non-hierarchical nature of the categories.

The 'Skills' Schema

A second schema was developed for the skills area. This postulates four domains of skilled activity, rather than the commonly accepted three domains (of Bloom *et al*, 1956). The reasons for subdividing the 'affective' domain into reactive and interactive skills domains were outlined above. Within each of the four domains, one sees a continuum of skills, from the fully automated 'reflexive' actions that make up sensory-motor skills, attitudes, habits and the following of algorithms, to the more complex types of skilled activity based on a high level of planning and decision-making.

The 'Skills' Cycle

A further schema was developed for the skills area, identifying the factors which influence the successful execution of skilled activity. This schema was based on the idea of a 'skill-cycle', involving *perception* of the relevant stimuli, recall of necessary *prerequisite* knowledge, *planning* what to do, and actually doing it *(performing)*. Four types of 'essential' sub-systems are therefore involved: (i) the 'receptors', (ii) the memory 'store', (iii) the 'processor' of higher mental activity and (iv) the 'effectors'. The development of a skilled capability may involve different degrees of attention to each of these four sub-systems. Analysis of these led to the identification of 12 factors to consider when analyzing a skilled activity, whatever its basic category.

THE 12 FACTORS IN SKILLED PERFORMANCE

Combining the factors, it is possible to conceptualize an 'expanded' version of our skill cycle, as shown in Figure 3. This shows the 12 types of ability which *may* have to be present for the efficient performance of a skilled activity. I stress the word 'may', as I am not implying that all skills depend in equal measure on all 12 of these factors. We have already seen, for example, that reproductive skills require very little planning and thus rely little on the presence of analytical, synthetical or evaluative abilities.

	Reproductive skills	Productive skills
Cognitive skills	Long division Writing a grammatically correct sentence	Proving theorem Writing creatively
Psychomotor skills	Typewriting Changing gear Running fast	Page design layout Driving with 'road sense' Playing football
Reactive skills	Attending, responding, valuing Approach/avoid behaviours (Mager)	Devaluing a value system Self-actualization (Rogers)
Interactive skills	Good manners Pleasant tone Verbal habits Etiquette	Leadership Persuasion Discussion Salesmanship

Figure 2. *The Skills Schema*

The expanded skill cycle is a conceptual tool to aid the analysis of any given activity in order to identify the causes of poor performance. It is a language for analyzing skills — a taxonomy if you like. But no hierarchical dependencies are implied. Any given skilled activity may require any combination of the 12 factors in varying degrees. Any trainee may come to the learning situation with any combination of any of them in different degrees. The function of skills analysis is to identify the 'gap' between performance requirements (the 'what should be') and existing trainee abilities (the 'what is'). The analyst must identify for the particular case in hand, the exact combination of factors that make up the 'what should be' and, through target population analysis, compare this with 'what is'.

The Interface Between Knowledge and Skills

This 'expanded skills cycle' illustrates clearly the 'interface' between knowledge and skill. Any activity can be considered (as a whole) a skilled activity, in that inevitably some people 'learn to do it better than others', due to differences in the development of some of the 12 factors. However, three of these factors (interpretation, procedures and schemata) are, in fact, the relevant knowledge. Thus, the knowledge schema and the skills schema interlink.

If one is in the business of transmitting *information,* then one would use the knowledge schema by itself as a tool to assist in the analysis of the information to be transmitted, the selection of suitable transmission methods and the design of the message itself.

If, on the other hand, one is in the business of developing *performance,* then

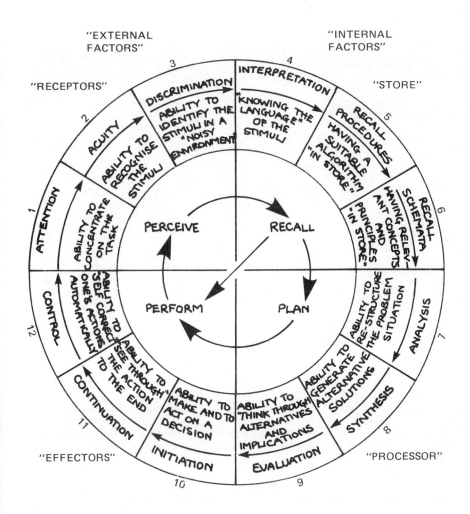

Figure 3. *The 'Expanded' Skill Cycle*

one would start by using the general skills schema to identify the type (or combination of types) of skilled activity to be developed, together with an idea of how far along the 'productive-reproductive' continuum they lie. The more 'productive' the skill, the more will knowledge play a part in its efficient execution. Passing to a more detailed level of analysis of each skill involved, one would use the 'expanded skills cycle' as a conceptual tool to search for the sources of difficulty in execution. One should consider the perceptual factors involved and the psychological/ physiological factors governing performance. But also (and especially in the productive skills area), one should consider the exact knowledge requirements.

References

Bloom, B S *et al* (1956) *Taxonomy of Educational Objectives. Handbook 1: The Cognitive Domain.* McKay, New York.

Gagné, R M and Briggs, I J (1974) *Principles of Instructional Design.* Holt, Rinehart and Winston, New York.

Horn, R E *et al* (1969) *Information Mapping for Learning and Reference.* Information Resources Inc, Cambridge, USA.

Krathwohl, D F *et al* (1964) *Taxonomy of Educational Objectives; Handbook 2: The Affective Domain.* McKay, New York.

Romiszowski, A J (1980) *Designing Instructional Systems.* Kogan Page, London. (In press.)

Williams, R G (1977) A behavioural typology of educational objectives for the cognitive domain. *Educational Technology,* 17, 6.

Workshop Report

11.2 The Use of Conceptual Schemata as Aids to Instructional Design

Alexander J Romiszowski

Description

The idea of conceptual schemata as job aids to instructional design has been developed by the author over several years, in workshops, courses and instructional design projects of various types. Several papers have already appeared outlining the approach. A schema for 'front end analysis' and training needs identification was presented at ETIC-79 and a schema for knowledge and skills analysis is presented at ETIC-80. (See the paper immediately preceding this report.)

The workshop gave practice in the use of schemata as job aids in instructional design and concentrated particularly on the schemata presented in the second of the above-mentioned papers. This approach is an alternative to most of the widely-diffused and used models (eg Bloom, Gagné, Mager, etc).

In developing the rationale for the approach suggested, one must necessarily highlight the gaps or the limitations of other models. A further aspect of this workshop was, therefore, an analysis of different approaches to the design of instruction and an opportunity for the workshop participants to voice their criticisms both of the model presented and of other well-known models.

After a brief summary of the relevant paper, presented earlier in the conference, the workshop participants were presented with copies of the three schemata suggested as job aids for knowledge and skills analysis. These are the three diagrams which are reproduced in 11.1 of this volume.

One or two examples were presented of the use of these schemata in analyzing skills such as typing, and mathematical problem-solving.

The workshop participants then formed interest-groups concerned with: knowledge, psychomotor skills, cognitive skills and interactive skills. Each group appointed a leader and selected one or more topics for analysis. The job aids were applied to the analysis of the selected topics. Discussion was encouraged on two main questions:

(a) Are the job aids conceptually useful? — ie are the categories of learning suggested in the schemata useful in the particular context chosen by the group?

(b) Are the job aids practically useful? — ie do they facilitate the search for possible learning difficulties in the topic? Are they easy to use and would they be easy to communicate to relative novices to instructional design?

At the end of the session, the group leaders summarized the deliberations of each group. This was followed by a general discussion, when various suggestions for the use or the improvement of the job aids were made. The general findings were that it takes a bit of practice to get started — the meanings of each of the categories must be most carefully defined and illustrated by clear examples — but that, once mastered, the job aids would be useful conceptual tools assisting the 'trouble-shooting' of learning difficulties and the matching of instructional methods to those difficulties.

11.3 The Concept of Individualized Instruction in the Microelectronics Era

P David Mitchell
Concordia University

Abstract: The possibility of truly individualized instruction has increased greatly with the availability of cheap logic control systems, but new theoretical foundations for individualized education are needed. Some current ideas in educational technology are challenged, and a model presented for a cheap student-centred-self-instructional system.

Introduction

We have been asked to share ideas on the way in which educational technology may develop during the next two decades in various learning environments and for various learning purposes. Enormous problems must be solved if mankind as a whole is to share in the potential for human comfort, achievement and eudaemonia now restricted to a tiny minority. To refurbish our ideas about how to implement man's educational aspirations we need more than new equipment and empirically validated instructional materials. We need to develop the requisite theory and practice of educational technology — or educational engineering (my preferred term). Moreover, we need to place much more emphasis on the learner and his idiosyncratic capability and less on packaging standard instructional sequences for him. We need to ask how educational technology can help *each* person to maximize his learning potential, despite wide variations in individual capability.

Telecommunications and Information Systems

The emergence of interactive video-computer systems, cheap microprocessors programmed for a specific instructional procedure, and increasing interest in distance education schemes presage a radical shift to home- and job-based education. Ideally the learner might consult a terminal to determine what printed materials, TV programmes, chip-based games, or computer-aided learning lessons are scheduled or available to meet his educational needs.

A cable distribution system in Montreal now offers 13 English and French television stations but provides an additional 20 channels for other services, including six channels for television on demand (from a large library). One of these is reserved for children's programmes, another for science, etc. Moreover, there are two channels for computer-based games (using the telephone as an input device) where one can play the computer or another subscriber (there are even clubs with tournaments). Additional channels provide community news, programme announcements, etc. It takes little imagination to see the educational potential of such a system — especially when we realize that children or adults who watch, eg the science channel, may learn far more about certain aspects of science than in school. Yet this is largely a non-responsive information display system whereas individualized instruction demands responsiveness.

Current and Forthcoming Technology of Education

Educational technology is nothing if not eclectic. Anything that may help to understand, design or operate a macro- or micro-educational system is part of our purview. School provides only a special case of a more general phenomena (Mitchell, 1975). Education is a lifelong process over which the person has much control (except in special circumstances in school or training). Academic entrepreneurs may choose to produce learning centres that exploit opportunities for learning overlooked by school. By incorporating cost-effective, self-instructional systems, such alternative institutions may begin by contracting services to industry or parents of children with learning difficulties. However, it should be noted that some American corporations already are accredited degree-granting institutions (through to doctoral level). With inexpensive individualized instruction a possibility, might they compete with regular schools and universities? Will education become a competitive enterprise? Already rumoured is a franchise for local learning centres reminiscent of hamburger restaurants.

Predictions of decentralized workplaces, very cheap computers and radio-distributed computer programmes for home computers will permit distributed education not only for job-related learning but also for formal and informal education. School truant officers will encounter children whose knowledge is greater than if they attended school.

Here is an attempt to portray some current technology of education; against each point is a prediction of forthcoming knowledge or systems which will supplement or replace it (see Table 1).

The Idea of Individualized Instruction

Not De-Synchronized but Adapting to Individuality

The possibility of truly individualized instruction, long anticipated in several forms of de-synchronized instruction that permit different learning rates and in a few schemes that offer choices, may become a reality with the ubiquitous chip. Chip-based didactic games permit an intellectual revolution.

Unlike mass instruction, or self-pacing through common software, individualized instruction implies adaptation of instruction to individual differences in learning style, preferences, attitudes and intention. Here we confront the most vexing aspect of instructional technology.

To ignore the characteristics of the learning system when we design an instructional system is to guarantee a mis-match much of the time. Gordon Pask's research shows that synchronization of only two teaching/learning styles reveals a tenfold increase in learning rate for matched over mis-matched styles. Equally important, we ignore most of the research on learning that shows the futility of hoping to invent scientifically-based instructional methods and materials which routinely produce intended instructional outcomes in students. So, can individualized instruction be realized? What is needed?

Current technology	Forthcoming technology
Expensive TV and computer systems	Inexpensive video-discs Cheap micro-computers Micro-processor-based instructional games and teaching machines Talking books (chip-based)
School's monopoly on education	School's use of open learning systems and school's accreditation of out-of-school learning Competition from educational service corporations
Synchronized instruction in class	Choice of content, media, time Group discussion — centred learning
Instructional design to package information	Avoiding instructional design (job aids, study aids) Selecting available resources Designing many learning activities
Model of learner as information receptacle and behaviour system	Model of learner as active, self-determining information processor
Instructional design to control learner's progress	Instructional design for learner's internal locus of control
Institution-centred self-instructional system	Student-centred self-instructional system
Emphasis on task analysis and behavioural objectives	Emphasis on conceptual analysis and cognitive objectives, fuzzy objectives and activity objectives
Relatively fixed hierarchical sequence of topics	Richly inter-connected network of topics with choice of sequence and content
Testing for achievement of instructor's objectives	Self ratings Observation of success with CAL, simulations, games, etc
Little emphasis on increasing learning rate	Research, development and training in speed learning techniques
Non-individualized instruction	Individualized instruction

Table 1. *Current and forthcoming technology of education*

Organization and Representation of Knowledge

Most computer-based systems involve pre-stored presentations of knowledge and pre-stored teaching strategies which either are fixed or essentially non-individualized with respect to learning style. Adaptive systems can be prepared but these are very costly if we seek truly individualized instruction. The most that we can anticipate without fundamental *theoretical* change is de-synchronized instruction where the student works at his own pace through essentially the same material as his fellows. A major theoretical breakthrough is in progress (Pask, 1976; Mitchell, 1979).

Individualized instruction requires a new approach to curriculum analysis, one similar to task analysis but stressing the structure of the subject matter. Such conceptual analysis clarifies important ideas as well as skills, and most importantly, shows their inter-relationships.

The inter-connectedness of ideas is immediately obvious if we stop to think about any subject or topic with which we are familiar. In order to understand that topic we must understand other topics which, in turn, entail our understanding of further topics.

Thus, one might begin to understand a selected topic in one module but not develop further understanding without understanding related topics. This integration, in which principles, operations and groups of fact coalesce into a higher order of knowledge, is characterized by the absence of predetermined objectives (though predictions may be made of the outcome if a coalescent transformation occurs). And it is critical if we wish to personalize instruction by *building upon the learner's existing knowledge.* Today's, and especially tomorrow's students should be able to build complex cognitive associations with new academic information and learn faster than their counterparts of a few decades ago.

Representation of Knowledge for Personalized Teaching and Learning

Any teacher or instructional designer who plans to individualize instruction must have and use a model or representation of the subject matter. The structure of knowledge includes facts and concepts as well as the various operations and processes which are required to understand the subject. Equally important, but often neglected, is the need for the *instructional system* (eg computer) to incorporate a *knowledge representation of the subject matter.* This may be trivial (eg a network of topics) or represent organic structure; it may as complex as Pask's (1976) conceptual entailment structures for conversational teaching systems. Despite the popularity of behavioural objectives, a representation of *knowledge* is more important for curriculum development than a list of behaviours. Knowledge cannot be represented best by a list structure but by a complex network of related topics (*cf* research on human memory).

Similarly, for personalized instruction the instructional system must have a *representation of each student's inferred knowledge state* and representations of his capability for carrying out the required operations to acquire new knowledge or skills. At its simplest, this may entail only a network of topics with an indication of which have been mastered, but more complex probabilistic representations can be made which indicate the likelihood that the student will acquire (or has already mastered) a new topic.

Finally, the teaching system must have a knowledge *representation of the teaching process.* This enables the selection, organization and implementation of teaching strategies and tactics to be matched to the learning style and capability of each student. Teaching algorithms form the basis of this knowledge representation. Chip-based devices and micro-computers are well suited to this. Advances in micro-electronics present many opportunities but we need basic research first.

Avoiding Instructional Design and Instruction

Limited Success

The received wisdom in the instructional design movement is, if not wrong, incomplete. In part this is because conflicting approaches appear to be equally useful. The recommended decomposition and instructional design process succeeds in a simple situation, but in a more complex subject or when a student does not master a topic, it is essential that the instructional designer should plan the next lesson or sequence of lessons using feedback from the student's capability state, the lesson plan and knowledge of the student's learning style. This requires feedback-controlled selection of instructional materials (eg using computer-aided learning or a human controller), not a rigid design (Mitchell, 1979).

I do not wish to imply that instructional design advocates are deliberately misleading the rest of us when they imply that we can find a unique instructional plan suitable for virtually all learners. The problem is that they happen to be wrong. The process works because students adapt to it (as they seem to for virtually any other instructional procedure).

What is really annoying about many suggestions, especially those that focus on tasks, task analysis and behavioural objectives, is that the writers imply that theirs is the only proper way to design a course and its component learning activities. Though there may actually be only one way to perform some tasks it is inconceivable that there is only one best way to come to an understanding of such subjects as, eg, research methodology, psychology of learning or mediaeval literature.

The Myth of Task Analysis and Behavioural Objectives

The idea of conducting a task analysis; specifying behavioural objectives; identifying possible instructional strategies, media and materials; and selecting appropriate learning resources is ubiquitous. I do not believe that most real planning is anything like the recipes commonly presented. Why? Quite simply because this sort of decision-taking process requires a tremendous investment of time, far more than is available to the ordinary educational technologist. Only if the return on investment is potentially very great will resources be available for this sort of exercise.

The Limiting Dogma of Behavioural Objectives

Current instructional technology methods are well-suited to inculcate skills, including some intellectual skills (eg performing a T-test) by placing them under the systematic control of instructional materials and control procedures. They are less well-suited to education than to training because there is no philosophical or empirical justification for the dogma that terminal criteria of instruction should be decomposed and expressed in terms of a set of observable behaviours and that these behaviours are all that we need to 'know' in order to understand that subject. I may perform a T-test without understanding it; so can my computer. Behaving and knowing are not synonymous.

Knowing is Not Doing

It is impossible to state what may be known in terms of what may be done. Not all states of knowing are induced by correct performance of behaviour segments, and it is necessary to consider what changes occur from reading or using AV materials (where attending is not a behavioural objective). I am sure that you have experienced growth of knowledge without any external observation of behavioural change and have altered your behaviour without increasing knowledge.

Behavioural Objectives or Behavioural Observations

The key to the educational objectives paradox lies in the problem of detecting changes in the learner's capability, not in specifying intended outcomes of learning. A behavioural objective is essentially a criterion test to operationalize a fuzzy objective. Instead of rejecting fuzzy objectives dealing with, for example, expertise, understanding or creativity, we should try to improve our inferential judgements about a student's capability. And we should help the learner to monitor and rate his own developing knowledge, attitudes and skills. Thus individualized instruction becomes a meaningful proposition.

Complementarity of Conflicting Views

I see two approaches to the development of personal knowledge. One is concerned with teaching; the other focuses on the student's characteristics and the facilitation of learning. The two schools of thought ask different questions: How can we prepare an optimal instructional sequence which virtually guarantees that a student will achieve mastery? versus how 'to free curiosity; to permit individuals to go charging off in new directions dictated by their own interests; to open everything to questioning and exploration; to recognize that everything is in process of change? . . . Out of such a context arise true students, true learners, creative scientists and scholars and practitioners' (Rogers, 1967). Surely the latter is the aim of individualized instruction?

Interpersonal Technology

The literature of group dynamics and group-centred education is replete with examples of sharing knowledge, perspectives and feelings amongst several persons who interact in an existential situation. In most group discussions the medium involved is air but in principle it can be an interactive computer system. Such sharing on the part of communicants may alter the capability of the others but this is not tantamount to saying that specified changes were intended by the instructional designer. Thus, group-centred education may promote learning and be responsive to individuality but other instructional activities (eg reading) are also required.

Student-Centred Self-Instruction

One advantage of a tutor (or fellow-student) is that often he may suggest a particular book or learning activity to the student as a result of his understanding of the student's abilities and desires. Why not adapt this flexible approach to the development of a student-centred self-instructional module where intended learning outcomes may be met in any of a variety of ways? Though not fully individualized, the student-centred self-instruction system may be a reasonable facsimile (Mitchell, 1979).

The simplest approach is to identify a variety of alternative self-instructional activities and materials which, singly or in some combination, can help the learner to meet one or more curriculum objectives. Note that one course of action (eg a chapter in a programmed text) might be specific to one objective, whereas another (eg viewing a film) might contribute to several and a third (eg engaging in research) might contribute to many.

The Learning Tableau

A student-centred self-instructional module could begin with a learning tableau that identifies various forms of printed and instrument-assisted learning materials and other learning activities considered to be pertinent to the intended learning outcomes of the module. For each alternative course of action open to the student — listed in rows of the learning tableau — the likelihood that it will lead him to the intended capability state is indicated in the cell where that row intersects the column corresponding to the learning outcome. Because not all activities need be chosen and they are not equally effective in producing mastery of the curriculum, the student may choose any combination which he deems effective, including the possibility of selecting all of them and encountering great redundancy (and therefore greater opportunity for learning).

In an advanced form, it should be possible for the student to identify a topic or objective which he wishes to pursue and would then receive a visually represented curriculum and instruction network which allows him to designate alternative modules and instructional paths that permit him to link up his present with his intended capability. *Unique* routeing through a curriculum is thus extended to the content and not merely the selection of modules.

A Systems Approach Implies a Humanistic Instructional System

A teaching system for individualized instruction can be an assembly of people, materials, media and knowledge (including a control procedure) which is responsible for providing learning opportunities for a specified population of students. Attendance on campus is a design decision. The educational technologist's focus, therefore, is the optimal allocation of human, material and financial resources available to produce desired educational outcomes, subject to constraints implicit in the consultative or planning situation. An example of one such constraint would be the need to develop a distant study system which could provide *no* direct human contact with the student except via the post. However, in most self-instructional schemes some human contact is possible, either with the instructor or his proxy, or with other students.

Conclusion

Instructional systems design for individualized instruction is concerned with organizing a variety of human nad material resources to produce educational outcomes. Applications of system analysis to education usually stress analysis into micro-components whereas the systemic nature of a course is likely to become more important.

The learning tableau was introduced as an expedient solution to the complementarity of conflicting views. The learning tableau approach to instructional design permits empirically produced and validated lessons, those based on theoretical models and a variety of audio-visual presentations, CAL, microprocessor -based lessons, recommended readings, assignments, projects, examinations or human contact with other students or proctors.

The emergence of micro-electronic devices is not necessary for implementation of this approach to individualized instruction but as instructional toys, games and lessons become available they can be incorporated as resources to be used. At the same time, we recognize that the learner may already have encountered the new device, or otherwise have acquired the pertinent knowledge. Thus it becomes possible now to introduce a form of individualized instruction, one that increasingly will be handled by computer programs. The era of individualized instruction for the masses is at hand. Educational technology has come of age. All we need now is a massive research effort to fulfil our promises.

References

Mitchell, P D (1975) A system for *Education Permanente. Programmed Learning and Educational Technology,* 12, pp 241-54.

Mitchell, P D (1979) Can CAL link the theory and practice of instruction? *Computers and Education,* 3, pp 295-307.

Pask, G (1976) *Conversation Theory.* Elsevier, Amsterdam.

Rogers, C R (1967) *Freedom to Learn: A View of What Education Might Become.* Charles Merrill, Columbus.

11.4 A Language for the Design of Teaching/Learning Situations

E M Buter
University of Amsterdam

Abstract: There seems to be a need for a language in which designers can express their thoughts, in an objective way, about the construction of teaching-learning situations. This paper offers suggestions for solutions to the problem.

Designers of Teaching-Learning Situations (TLS) Observed in Action

Put people, who are in the business of developing situations for optimal learning, together round a table. Have them think aloud, let them discuss the TLS they want to develop. Listen carefully to what they say.

That is exactly what the author did, over a period of about 10 years. A long time observing lifelike situations is tiring and time-consuming, but it is necessary in order to get the material on which to base analyses and deductions.

This is the first presentation of some of the results of these observations, together with the reasoning behind them. I hope that this account will encourage others to think about the same problem.

Problems Perceived — Criteria Evolved

As a specialist in educational matters, I thought I knew all about the designing of TLS. That was in the 1960s, when we thought that behavioural approaches gave us the key to all design problems. But systematic observation of designers in action made me intensely aware of the complexity of designing, and how troublesome and time-consuming it could be. And, at the start of my observations, how unruly and chaotic it often seemed. Let me list some general observations:

- ☐ Designers often want some kind of prescription, but they also need enough freedom to be creative.
- ☐ Designers know that they have nothing more practical than a theory, but very often they do not use theories, or theories do not work with designers.
- ☐ Designers often do not like to have structuring influences on the students, yet they cannot escape from the fact that they (re)structure learning environments all the time.
- ☐ Designers do a lot of talking in order to define criteria for TLS, but meanings often change when 'converted' into practice.
- ☐ Designers are often very much influenced by the materials they are used to, or the general taxonomies they have in their tool kit. But taxonomies of objectives, of learning, of motivation, of media — all may be cleverly made, but taxonomies are only to choose from. They serve no other purpose.
- ☐ What controls or influences the designers' choices?

These are some of the more general problems. How, then, can we solve the tension between structuring and freedom? Is it possible to evolve a theory that is meaningful to designers? Can we develop strategies to deal with taxonomies?

I have noted that a large proportion of the wording of design proposals refers to the interaction between student and environment. In fact, it seems that the more operational the instructions for TLS become, the more strongly some of the wording used indicates interaction.

In this paper I will direct my attention particularly to this area of interaction.

INFORMER	INTERFACE ☆	LEARNER
keywords: code, coding, codability, etc	keywords: interact, interactions	keywords: strategies and tactics of learning

Figure 1. *In this paper attention is focused on the interface*

This seems a very considerable condensation, knowing that in designing everything hangs together with everything. Systematic and scientific approaches, however, tend to encourage reducing things — there are too many publications that try to solve, in 15 pages, the entire design problem. In this text we will deal specifically with the interface between informer and learner, where informers can be teachers, peers, all types of media, books, etc. The informer and the learner are both outside the scope of this paper. It is the area in between which is of major concern here, mainly because it has brought to light criteria that seem relevant for the generation of a useful design language.

Some Criteria for a Language for Designers of TLS

1.1 *Generally, terminology as used in the educational disciplines cannot be used in design terminology. Terminology from other disciplines must therefore be adapted, or maybe new terminology will be necessary.* Existing terminology is generally descriptive, but we need prescriptive language. For designing, a certain limitation in the meaning of the terms used is necessary, in order to make them more operational. It seems appropriate to propose terminology that cannot be identified with specific disciplines or subdisciplines.

1.2 *A proposed terminology must be unequivocal.* It is amazing how long a time it sometimes takes designers to discover that they are talking about the same thing. One of the reasons is that words, language and terminology used often have so many different (shades of) meaning. So it seems very desirable to try to develop a language wherein pertinent elements are denoting the same thing to both speaker and listener.

1.3 *The design language must aid the designer to think at the appropriate level of abstraction.* We often find that those engaged in teaching express their ideas in wording that is 'way up high', so that it is very difficult to relate it to the practice of teaching. The user of a design language must, as far as this paper is concerned, be able to relate this language directly to the interactions between student and environment. According to Buter (1977a) and Leedham and Berruer (1979), the organization of teaching institutes can be roughly divided into three levels. The micro-level deals with actual teaching, the macro-level with formulating general trends and policy. In between is the meso-level.

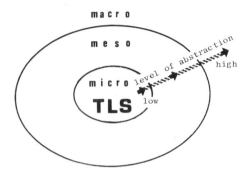

Figure 2. *It is convenient to conceptualize educational organizations as roughly divided into three levels*

The levels of abstraction of language about teaching roughly correspond to these levels. Typical macro-expressions deal with words or sentences like personality-development, freedom for the student, more differentiation, structuring, preparing for, etc. Typical micro-expressions deal with words like 'Take book 1'; 'Let us use the blackboard'; 'I have still 10 minutes'; 'Would you please behave, John'; 'Next question', etc.

The meso-level seems empty, devoid of any specific language. It is here that educational technology should have its own domain and its own identity.

1.4 *Expressions that denote actual materials must be deleted from the design language.* Specific names and indications of software and hardware, eg projector, television, lecture, should not be part of the language used. In the final analysis, hardware could function in very different roles: taxonomies about media (etc) have not even a small indicative value regarding learning results and types of learning. The design language must therefore have a facilitating character: it must enable (eg) the media specialist to choose from alternative options within the domain indicated by the designers.

1.5 *The language shall have an interface character.* The word 'interface' is no longer unnecessary jargon. It indicates the area between two or more interacting objects, material, institutes, and generally (sub-) systems. It so happens that in many cases it is necessary to develop specific language and mathematics to deal with problems of the interface. In our case, we need a language to accommodate very different inputs. Psychologists, media specialists, administrators, theoreticians and practitioners must all be able to recognize and express their task and task criteria in the language as it relates to their own discipline. The interface has a certain redundancy with the internal language and structure of the systems it connects. But, at the same time, an interface develops its own language, its own structure, and with that, often its own specialism.

1.6 *Design languages must be productive or generative.* This may be an even more important point to make than 1.5. Taxonomies are systematic inventories at their best. They in no way provide the kind of selection, of argument, of decisions that must be taken to *yield* a TLS.

What is needed is something quite different. We need a vehicle for reasoning that, without prescribing specifics with a high semantic load, is able to bring balance and consistency to the elements put together to 'make' a TLS. This means that such language must *not* lead to eclecticism in the sense that we choose randomly, from available sources. It means, too, that, as in any language, the structure must be recursive. It is thus generalizable in time, eg you can use it over and over again in very different situations.

1.7 *The language shall be primarily based on the conceptualization of the interaction between student and environment.* This is put in here not only because we are dealing with the interface area, but also because of the intensified attention being given by the educational community in general to interaction in the classroom, and to related disciplines such as socio-linguistics.

The main reason, however, is that as 'my' designers in experiments indicated, the interactive area can be operationalized. From a purely rational point of view, we can safely say that the interaction of a person with his environment is the first indicator in any analysis of behaviour.

1.8 *The language must be operational and, if possible, quantifiable.* One of the main difficulties in the design of TLS is the indication of degree: the question 'How much shall we (re)structure a TLS?' has been, up to now, nearly unanswerable. (Is a criterion degreeable? And to what degree?). Note that when I am referring to a language, this is to be interpreted as a vehicle of communication for designers of TLS. Such language will be a mixture of natural language and specific, formal elements, coined for the purpose of designing. Such elements will have great value in prescribing TLS, and hence we will call such specific elements prescriptors.

From Analysis to Example

Using the word prescriptor, we can make some pertinent observations:

2.1 *A prescriptor must be semantically neutral to various inputs but the reverse should not be the case. The same prescriptor can thus follow from various inputs.* A prescriptor is *not* semantically neutral to the TLS. From the prescriptor we can derive basic constraints for the interactive aspects of the TLS. With the use of prescriptors we can thus construct (parts of) the blueprint or design of the TLS.

In this paper I will give one or two exemplifying prescriptors, and use them for indicating TLS. The reader will see that I try to adhere as closely as possible to already existing terminology; slight alterations, however, are necessary in order to conform to the previously given criteria.

Semantic demarcation has been striven for, and I hope achieved, as the following example shows.

2.2 *Let* response-range (R_r) *be defined as the variety of (discrete) responses (as expected by the designer) following upon a given stimulus (in a unit audience).* It will be clear that R_r should be subdivided into categories, eg expected R_r and realized R_r. We are dealing here with variation in *content.* Intuitively, it seems that R_r will be small when learners receive stimuli that asks for knowledge of mastered facts or for simple solutions to standard problems. Wide R_r's will be generated when content deals with complex problems, or areas where normative participation of the learner plays an important part. The R_r will also be influenced by the amount of information handed to the learner in a unit of time, and by the content of the learner's repertoire.

Yet, and this is the most important aspect, R_r is a prescriptor for only one aspect of a future TLS. As we can see from this example, there is no indication of hardware or other implementation in this R_r, nor can one easily link it with a specific discipline.

In Figure 3, an example of the linking concept of response range is given in relation to the continuum of domains of objectives and the continuum of TLS.

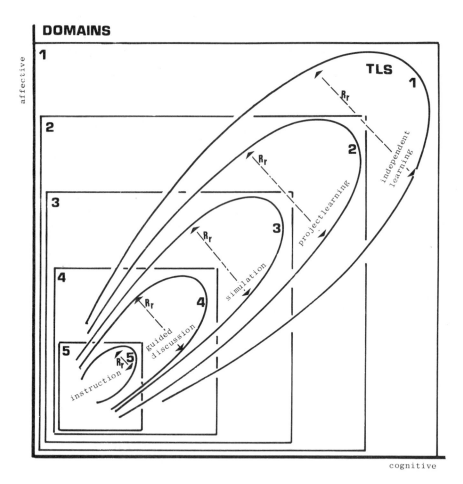

Figure 3. *The continua of objectives and of TLS linked by R_r*

The R_r is growing along the continua, and I have found that even a very crude grading of the R_r is very efficient when designing TLS (the grading being: very small/small/mean/wide/very wide).

Elsewhere I have argued that there is in fact a good correspondence with the domains of cognitive and affective learning (Buter, 1977a and 1977b).

2.3 *Let* response-quality (R_q) *be defined as the outward or visible or physical form of the response (as projected by the designer) following a given stimulus.* Thus we separate form from content. This is an entirely legitimate approach on this level of abstraction. While R_r is gradeable, R_q is not. (The response quality consists of a range of separate elements.)

2.4 *Let us define* response-frequency (R_f) *as the number of (discrete) responses a student has to give (in a unit of time). R_f is related to content complexity, to state of mind of the learner, group size, etc.* Designers who want to 'blueprint' TLS will find these three prescriptors give a good idea of the consequences of implementation when organizing and restructuring TLS. We will not consider the more detailed prescriptors such as R_r variations per period, R_f variation in time and R-clustering.

In passing, we must mention that we are *not* neglecting the value of the stimulus component here. For our discussion this component is not necessary.

Perhaps I should say here that the word 'designer' alludes to a *role*. The role can be performed by very different persons, but the level at which such designing is mainly done in any educational organization is totally lacking in professionalism.

Let us now look at some other prescriptors. These are secondary in the sense that, without the R-descriptors defined, they are not operational.

3.1 *Let us define control as the development of stimuli to influence the interaction within a TLS.*

3.2 External control (C_{ext}) *is defined as all influences of control exercised by the environment (of the learner).*

3.3 Internal control (C_{int}) *is defined as all influences of control exercised by the learner.*

Again, I have deliberately reduced the definition here to the interface area earlier called interaction. Intuitively it will be clear that C_{ext} and C_{int} form the ends of a continuum. In fact, 100 per cent C_{ext} or 100 per cent C_{int} never exists.

In this paper we will link control with the previously given prescriptor response range (R_r). We can make the following statements:

3.4 *There is an inverse relationship between R_r and the* possibility *of exercising* C_{ext}.

3.5 *There is a direct relationship between R_r and the* possibility *of exercising* C_{int}.

Let us analyze these expressions somewhat more closely. In 3.3 it is said that, as the range of responses grows there is less external control; thus, freely interpreted, the learner has more autonomy. In the same imprecise way, we can translate 3.4; the student gets more chance to exercise influence on the TLS.

The Use of Prescriptors

As an exercise, let us apply this approach to two TLS which are often very loosely described. Typically, linear programmed learning is characterized by a small R_r, little variation in R_q, a high R_f, realization of a high degree of C_{ext}; and no formal reliance on C_{int}.

Typically, project teaching is often characterized by the inclusion of a high incidence of wide R_r, great variation in R_q, a great variation in R_f, a low degree of C_{ext}, and formal reliance on a high degree of C_{int}.

Two things can be seen in these examples: it seems possible to define TLS operationally with this approach; and the descriptors have been phrased very carefully, because in fact we need more prescriptors in order more fully to define the possible continuum of TLS.

Thus it seems possible for designers to relate a great variety of inputs to interactional definitions via the prescriptors, and to arrive at the appropriate 'blueprints' for TLS (Buter, 1969).

It is then, and only then, that the introduction of the most suitable implementation or instrumentation can be selected and, where necessary, adapted. Afterwards, the different alternatives can be costed. Thus we have the ideal at which a designer should aim . . . !

If this article is only of very limited usefulness, and the writer thinks it is much more than that, it seems wise to explore along these lines the possibilities of developing an operational language for design of TLS. Media specialists, trainers of teachers, and teachers themselves, seem to be in great need of such a language, a language in which very different inputs can be translated or expressed, but which nevertheless has a high degree of objectivity.

References

Buter, E M (1969) Educational technology in Holland. In *Educational Technology,* **IX,** 11, p 22. New Jersey, USA.

Buter, E M (1977a) *Thoughts about Productive Models.* Council of Europe, CCC/TE 2.

Buter, E M (1977b) The great shift. In Hills, P J and Gilbert, J (eds) *Aspects of Educational Technology* **XI.** Kogan Page, London.

Leedham, J and Berruer, A (1979) Status of Staff Employing Modern Educational Techniques. Unesco Report. ED WS/49.

11.5 New Chips but Old Problems . . .

Clive Lawless
The Open University

Abstract: The paper questions how learning experiences are to be designed, by whom and on what principles, in the future. Four interrelated issues are dealt with, and the conclusion drawn is that educational technology must come to terms with variety and abandon the idea of a single set of procedures for all instructional situations.

Introduction

By the year 2000, extremely sophisticated micro-electronic equipment, based on the silicon chip, will be available for education and training, providing the facility for adaptive, individualized instruction far beyond anything available at present. We must not, however, be dazzled by this prospect because the problems of designing instruction and of providing learning experiences will remain. Though these developments will offer the prospect of more effective learning, they will not make teaching, or preparing the instruction for them, any easier; quite the reverse will be the case. Indeed, the danger will be that the supply of instructional materials will fall behind the availability of equipment, as is already happening in contemporary computer-assisted instruction (Shaw, 1979). The result of this will be that equipment will be unused, underused, or be used to convey existing models of teaching, unsuited to the new devices. Although the problems will be made more acute by the complexity of the hardware and the scale of resources needed to use them, the basic issues that will have to be faced in providing effective learning are the same as those which have to be faced today. Hence the title, 'New chips but old problems . . .'.

Four interrelated issues need to be faced, each of which goes beyond what have usually been considered the boundaries of educational technology. The first of these issues concerns the content or subject matter of instruction, its selection and nature. This is in contrast with the traditional approach of educational technology (though one must beware of setting up 'straw men' to knock down) which left selection of content to others.

Decisions about the subject matter to be taught must be considered because of their influence on learning and teaching. Hence the importance of grounded decisions, whose basis is clear and implications fully understood. Whether the criteria for choosing particular subject matter is based on student needs, on the needs of society, on the structure of a discipline or merely reflect a teacher's preference, will influence the nature of instruction. To avoid confusion between ends and means is an important task in the design of instruction. Although this issue may appear abstract, even philosophical, if it is ignored in the design of instruction it means that vital questions are left to others. Essentially it involves an analytic approach, asking 'What is being chosen?', 'Why?', 'By whom?'.

Linked to the selection of content is concern for its nature. This assumes the existence of knowledge as an abstract entity apart from the behaviour which demonstrates that an individual knows. It involves looking at the ideas and the concepts which make up subject matter and of recognizing that knowledge involves procedures as well as facts. Indeed, the skills required to carry out these procedures can be seen as the long-term purpose of education, though skills cannot be taught in a vacuum without content on which to be practised.

The Teaching of Science as Enquiry

Lack of concern for content may well explain why educational technologists as such have had little or no influence on the design of the new curricula in science and mathematics. Analyzing the nature of subject matter enables decisions to be made on which parts should be included in a course of study, but its primary importance is for the nature of instruction. The nature of content, ie the structure of subject matter and its related procedures, should be an important influence on the type of instruction. In contrast to the idea of a set of 'neutral' procedures applicable to all instructional situations, this approach recognizes variety; different types of subject matter need different types of teaching; this is one aspect of instructional methods being 'contextual' (Mansfield and Nunan, 1979). Analysis of the nature of subject matter enables clarification of purpose, eg are students to be admirers or performers? Are they to think for themselves or state the thoughts of others? All this may seem to have little connection with problems of practical training, but unless a task is merely repetitive and mechanical ('putting the fourth chocolate in the third row . . .') the knowledge behind the performance of the task is important, since most tasks require discrimination between when they should and should not be carried out. Knowledge of principles behind performance 'is the surest (and most economical) safeguard against unforeseen occurrences' (Macdonald-Ross, 1973).

Closely linked to the consideration of the content of instruction is the question of values. Values cannot be avoided in education; even the very language used reflects values! The word 'instruction', for example, carries a sense of authority and of teacher direction (McKeachie, 1974). This contrasts with the idea of a set of procedures for the design of instruction which are value-free. Skinner (1971) claims that 'a behavioural technology is ethically neutral', while Bruner (1966) calls for: '. . .a prescriptive theory on how to proceed to achieve various results, a theory which is neutral with respect to ends but exhaustive with respect to means'.

The idea of value freedom or neutrality which seems to lie behind much of the writing on educational technology stems from the science-based concept of technology. It is doubtful whether this concept can be applied accurately to what we call educational technology (Atkin, 1967-68), and if it could it is arguable whether science itself is value-free. The idea of a neutral, value-free set of procedures for the design of instruction is both inadequate and invalid.

It is invalid because it does not provide for the selection of content, the subject matter and skills for instruction. The previous section illustrated the practical importance of decisions about content, but the criteria for its selection reflect values showing how both the subject matter and student are viewed. An example of this is the Open University's modular degree structure in which students have virtually a free choice of courses for their degree programme. This structure resulted from a recommendation by the Planning Committee (HMSO, 1969), which was aimed at providing a 'broadly based higher education'. It is not a question of whether this decision was 'right' or 'wrong' or whether it would be 'better' to have more specialized or professional courses. This decision was value-based and since it was, arguably, the decision which exerted most influence on the types of course developed, these values cannot be ignored in designing instruction. Whether students are expected simply to learn and reproduce factual material, or whether they are expected to share in the discipline by solving problems and criticizing authorities, reflects values held about both the subject matter and the student.

The value-free idea is invalid because it fails to recognize that the procedures and methods of instruction themselves represent values. Means do affect ends. The insistence, for example, on behavioural objectives represents a value position, that what cannot be observed or, indeed, measured is of little worth.

Evaluation seen simply in terms of a try-out-revision cycle related to pre-specified objectives represents different values from the wider framework of illuminative evaluation (Parlett and Hamilton, 1972). Side effects of educational developments can have value implications. Taking an example of particular relevance to future developments: 'The continually increasing people-costs involved in the production of good teaching material will far outweigh the savings due to the employment of micro-electronics, unless there can be very extensive communal use of materials. The problem is political and personal rather than technical.' (James, 1979.)

While such communal use might be achieved by voluntary co-operation, what would be the value implications if its use and its associated programmes were centrally enforced?

Essentially all decisions affecting teaching and learning are decisions of value which have to be faced. Rowntree (1979) stresses the importance of awareness of the problem and the necessity of those designing instruction coming to terms with their own value systems. While educational technology as such cannot prescribe values, educational technologists will have their own values. Selection of subject matter is clearly a value issue and so is the way students are regarded, and this is discussed in the next section. Should students help frame objectives or have free choice of courses? What respect is paid to their responses and arguments? Are they to take a critical view of 'authorities.? If they are to solve problems, whose problems? Although such questions appear practical they are basically value questions. A decision to exclude alternative views, for example, because they might confuse students is clearly a decision of value. Whether with chalk and talk or micro-electronics, there is a need to analyze and expose the values behind both content and method and to work out the implications of these values.

The view taken of the student is the third important issue to be faced. *How does the student learn? Why does he learn, or not learn?* are crucial questions to answer. No one approach to learning will provide all the answers. Rather than being seen as all-embracing theories of learning, different approaches to learning need to be seen as models which 'unify limited aspects of a particular reality' (Elton and Laurillard, 1979).

Through the influence of Skinner's work on programmed learning and the earlier work of Thorndike, educational technology has been strongly influenced by behaviourist stimulus-response views of learning, which provide a model of the learner as a *performer*. The behaviourist approach forms the basis of the systematic approach to designing instruction, task analysis, behavioural objectives, active learning, knowledge of results, try-out and revision evaluation. This approach persists in spite of considerable criticism, notably on the grounds that it cannot be applied to all fields of knowledge, though even its critics concede its utility where the object of instruction is a clearly defined task (Stenhouse, 1971). Since the model makes no allowance for, indeed does not recognize, mental states it is essentially a mechanistic view of the learner. It provides no explanation, for example, for the boredom experienced by many students studying Skinnerian-type programmes. More serious, it does not allow for individual differences in any deep sense; it ignores the fact that individuals react quite differently to the same teaching. Perhaps most serious of all, the model does not extend to those mental states which are the key to higher levels of learning. The model is useful with its stress on activity and the need to analyze it, but it provides no way to explain what lies behind that activity.

If the behaviourist model takes the learner as a *performer,* cognitive psychology provides a model of the learner as a *thinker* or, possibly more accurately, as a *processor.* This cognitive model is concerned with internal states, 'with the complicated processes which underlie the intellectual side of life' (Broadbent, 1975). Information is received through the senses, transformed, encoded and stored; when required it is retrieved and applied in the response (see Gagné, 1977; Bower, 1975, for a fuller description) by the student. The student is an *active* processor of the information, not a passive receiver of stimuli. Learning, therefore, depends not just on teaching, on the information presented, but on whether the learner has adequate processing skills and adequate existing knowledge to store the new information in such a way that it can be retrieved in usable form. This model of the learner has important implications for the design of instruction (Lawless, 1979), the close analysis of the subject matter (the information to be presented) and its relationship to the performance expected from students, enabling them to process information presented in various ways and to store it so that it can be retrieved and applied to new situations, to develop problem-solving skills, in other words. On the basis of the behaviourist model, when a student fails to learn it is the stimulus, the teaching material, which is changed. With the cognitive model it may be that it is the student who requires changing, in terms of developing his learning skills and remedying knowledge deficiency.

Learning in the cognitive model is not mechanical because the model contains a control aspect, 'control processes' (Atkinson and Shiffrin, 1971), 'executive strategy' (Gagné, 1977). The learner consciously decides whether to learn or not, whether particular educational material fits in with his purposes and what sort of strategy is required by a particular piece of material. This motivational or affective element provides a link with a third model, that of the learner as a *person.*

Considering the learner as a *person* leads into the area of humanistic psychology, into the work of Maslow (1968), Rogers (1969) and Kelly (1955), and into concern for the effects on learning of the student's personal valuing of what is to be learned. The influence of personal values on learning has been demonstrated by Perry (1970) in terms of stages from acceptance of authority to personal commitment, though Baron (1975) has criticized the hierarchical relationship he gives to these stages. Lack of congruence between the nature of a course and personal values can have two implications (Ford, 1979): ideas are stored for short-term retrieval only and the student's approach is dominated by the extrinsic constraints (usually assessment requirements) of a course. Laurillard (1979) has shown that students' perception of course requirements are a crucial factor in determining how they study. Hence the prevalence of study strategies variously described as 'surface level processing' (Marton and Säljö, 1976), 'operation learning' (Pask, 1976) and 'cue seeking' (Miller and Parlett, 1974), leading to a concentration on memorizing facts rather than getting to grips with depth meaning. The results of incongruence between personal valuing of course material and the aims of the course can seriously inhibit learning. Action is possible at two levels. Firstly, where student perceptions of the demands of a course are at variance with the actual requirements, explanation and, above all, discussion with students is a minimum first step (in itself showing appreciation of the student as a person). More difficult is the second level, of involving the student in the selection of course content and methods of study, so that it is in concert with the real purposes of the student.

The need to come to terms with variety and the use of different approaches is the fourth issue which has to be faced. The types of variety which have to be considered have been sketched out in earlier sections. In practical terms, two particular areas can be highlighted: the individualization of instruction and the evaluation of outcomes.

Although educational technology has, from the days of programmed learning, been concerned with individualizing instruction, this usually meant nothing more than allowing the student work at his own pace. Biggs (1978) has summarized the individual differences which affect learning in terms of values, motivation and strategy. Effective instruction must provide for such differences, providing coherence between student needs and characteristics and the demands of subject matter. In this area, micro-electronic developments offer the prospect of individualizing instruction in three ways. Adaptive tutorial sequences are already in use (Cooper and Lockwood, 1979), in which instruction is individualized according to students' responses. Secondly, it will be possible to study in a variety of places as Viewdata and similar devices become widely available in the home and office. Such developments will, thirdly, provide rapid access to an enormous range of knowledge and styles of presenting it. Such instruction need not chain the student to a flickering screen, learning can be computer co-ordinated and involve a variety of media, even books! Indeed, the most effective instruction will be 'when they are used thoughtfully in partnership with the teacher' (Howe and Du Boulay, 1979).

A second area of individualization is the development of students' learning skills. This involves not only enabling students to acquire and improve specific learning skills, important though this is. Laurillard (1979) has shown that the type of student learning style identified by Pask (1976) is not a fixed characteristic, but varies according to student perceptions of the demands of a specific task. Hence the importance of students learning how to select the appropriate learning style. Aiding students to develop their learning skills must be rooted in their experience; not simply teaching particular content and skills, but enabling students to learn more effectively as well. Students with apparently lower attainment are those most likely to need to improve their learning skills. Indeed, one of the aims of any course of instruction ought to enable the student to learn from the unstructured, unprepared materials of real life.

Concern with variety must lead to consideration of variety of outcomes, which may be unexpected or side-effects not directly connected to pre-specified objectives. The usual procedure has been to concentrate on how well students achieve the objectives and to revise the instruction until they do. A wider approach to evaluation variously called 'goal free' (Scriven, 1972) or 'illuminative' (Parlett and Hamilton, 1972), stresses the need to look at all the outcomes or results of learning, not just those which are considered relevant or desirable. Evaluating the whole process of instruction will inevitably focus attention on the issues discussed earlier: content, values and students. To fail to take this wider approach will be to consign the design of instruction to the periphery of the educational debate.

References

Atkin, J M (1967-68) Research styles in science education. *Journal of Research in Science Teaching*, 5, pp 338-45.

Atkinson, R C and Shiffrin, R M (1971) The control of short-term memory. *Scientific American*, 225, pp 82-90.

Baron, J (1975) Some theories of college instruction. *Higher Education*, 4, pp 149-72.

Biggs, J B (1978) Individual and group differences in study processes. *British Journal of Educational Psychology*, 48, pp 266-79.

Bower, G H (1975) Cognitive psychology: an introduction. In Estes, W K (ed) *Handbook of Learning and Cognitive Processes* 1, pp 25-80. Lawrence Erlbaum, Hillsdale, NJ.

Broadbent, D E (1975) Cognitive psychology and education. *British Journal of Educational Psychology*, 45, pp 162-76.

Bruner, J S (1966) *Toward a Theory of Instruction*, p 31. Belknap, Harvard, Cambridge, Mass.

Cooper, A and Lockwood, F (1979) The need, provision and use of a computer-assisted interactive tutorial system. In Page, G T and Whitlock, Q (eds) *Aspects of Educational Technology*, XIII. Kogan Page, London.

Elton, L R B and Laurillard, D M (1979) Trends in research on student learning. *Studies in Higher Education*, 4, 1, pp 87-102.

Ford, N (1979) Study strategies, orientations and 'personal meaningfulness' in higher education. *British Journal of Educational Technology*, 10, 2, pp 143-60.

Gagné, R M (1977) *The Conditions of Learning* (3rd edn). Holt, Rinehart and Winston, New York.

HMSO (1969) *Report of the Planning Committee for the Open University to the Secretary of State for Education and Science.* HMSO, London.

Howe, J A M and Du Boulay, B (1979) Microprocessor assisted learning: turning the clock back? *Programmed Learning and Educational Technology*, 16, 3, pp 240-6.

James, E (1979) Review of 'Microelectronics: their implications for education and training'. *Programmed Learning and Educational Technology*, 16, 2, 183-4.

Kelly, G A (1955) *The Psychology of Personal Constructs*, 1 and 2. Holt, New York.

Laurillard, D M (1979) The processes of student learning. *Higher Education*, 9, pp 395-409.

Lawless, C J (1979) Information processing: a model for educational technology. In Page, G T and Whitlock, Q (eds) *Aspects of Educational Technology*, XIII. Kogan Page, London.

Macdonald-Ross, M (1973) Behavioural objectives – a critical review. *Instructional Science*, 2, pp 1-52.

McKeachie, W J (1974) Instructional Psychology. *Annual Review of Psychology*, 25, pp 161-93.

Mansfield, R E and Nunan, E E (1979) Towards an alternative educational technology. *British Journal of Educational Technology*, 9, 3, pp 170-6.

Marton, F and Säljö, R (1976) On qualitative differences in learning. *British Journal of Educational Psychology*, 46, pp 4-11 and 115-27.

Maslow, A H (1968) Some educational implications of the humanistic psychologies. *Harvard Educational Review*, 38, 4, pp 685-96.

Miller, C M L and Parlett, M (1974) *Up to the Mark: A Study of the Examination Game.* (Monograph 21). Society for Research into Higher Education, London.

Parlett, M and Hamilton, D (1972) *Evaluation as Illumination: A New Approach to the Study of Innovatory Programmes.* Occasional Paper 9. Centre for Research in the Educational Sciences, University of Edinburgh.

Pask, G (1976) Styles and strategies of learning. *British Journal of Educational Psychology*, 46, pp 128-48.

Perry, W G (1970) *Forms of Intellectual and Ethical Development in the College Years: A Scheme.* Holt, Rinehart and Winston, New York.

Rogers, C R (1969) *Freedom to Learn.* Merrill, Columbus, Ohio.

Rowntree, D (1979) Educational technology to educational development – a bid for survival. In Page, G T and Whitlock, Q (eds) *Aspects of Educational Technology*, XIII. Kogan Page, London.

Scriven, M (1972) Prose and cons about goal-free evaluation. *Evaluation Comment: Journal of Evaluation*, 3, 4, pp 1-4.

Shaw, K (1979) Some educational uses of computers in UK schools. In Page, G T and Whitlock, Q (eds) *Aspects of Educational Technology*, XIII. Kogan Page, London.

Skinner, B F (1971) *Beyond Freedom and Dignity*, p 17. Knopf, New York.

Stenhouse, L (1971) Some limitations on the use of objectives in curriculum research and planning. *Paedagogica Europaea*, pp 73-83.

11.6 Towards a New Paradigm in Education

E A Soremekun
University of Ife

Abstract: This is a theoretical paper aimed at providing a new paradigm in education based upon a conceptual re-analysis of technology in education.

The paper is divided into two parts: Part 1 identifies the problems concerning educational technology as an innovation. The two problems identified include (i) the inadequate conceptualization of educational technology, and (ii) lack of understanding of the concept of technology. Given these problems, it is suggested that the present paradigm for applying technology to education is inadequate. Part 2 provides a model for paradigm change based upon T S Kuhn's structure of a scientific revolution. This new paradigm has implications for educators in general and educational technologists in particular.

Summary

This paper tries to show the importance of understanding change as a natural phenomenon. In this regard, man's place in nature must be re-assessed in order to see ourselves as part of the overall natural cycle. Just as we try to create change we are also a natural part of change.

Technology is man's attempt to create. Unless, however, he fully understands his proper relationship to nature (ie to cultivate it rather than control or dominate it), technology can only be a destructive rather than a constructive force. The thinking behind technology or creation must, therefore, be employed to live in harmony with nature.

Education is the vehicle towards ensuring the continued awareness and skills necessary to live in harmony with nature. It is a shared responsibility by every adult with overlapping activities primarily in the home, school and church. Education does not occur in a defined place necessarily, but in a defined atmosphere. We as educators are stimulators of the inherent learning process. The objective as educators is to produce future 'creators' or 'creative' people.

A circle has no end. Likewise, the cycle of life goes on and on — changing, and modifying existence into what we perceive as new. Unless we grasp the fundamental conception of life as cyclical, it will continue to elude us.

Section 12:
Developments in the Use
of Equipment for Educational
Technology

12.1 The Impact of Technology
on Higher Education

Ray McAleese
University of Aberdeen

Abstract: This paper examines the demand for and the impact of 'heavy' technology on teaching, learning and administration in higher education. Two frameworks are presented indicating the demand for and the impact of heavy technology over three time periods — the immediate future, the near future and the distant future.

The Nature of Technology in Higher Education

Early man used to communicate with his colleagues, friends, children, etc, using a stick to draw ideograms in the sand. The micro-electronics industry based on the silicon chip has at least a claim to be the descendant of this early form of communication, based as it is on silica; sand to sand. The wheel turns full circle (see, for example, Gosling, 1978).

During the time that it has taken man to progress from ideograms in the sand to electronic chips, we have seen the growing impact of technology and technological artefacts on communication and teaching. During the last two decades, education at all levels has had to respond to the stealthy attack by instructional technology and the full frontal assault by audio-visual aids. In education, some have suggested that we are experiencing the most recent wave of attacks that may eventually test our assumptions about teaching and learning in education. Early revolutions were: the movable type of Gutenburg; early audio-visual technology related to film in the early part of this century; computer-based technology of the 1960s; and now the microchip. Four waves of attack — or so it might seem. Other 'technologies' have made their impact on education. The concept of *educational or instructional technology* is now becoming central to the design and evaluation of instruction: for example, the work done by educational technologists in tertiary education research and development units (a critique of this position is found in Hall, 1978). However, such technology is systems-oriented and not based on hardware or component technology to any extent. Mitchell, in an analysis of the concept 'technology', observes: 'it is clear that the influence of technology, in shaping our lives, is unsurpassed even if it is not clear what meaning is ascribed to the word' (Mitchell, 1978). He goes on to develop a wide view of educational technology and concludes that educational technology is: 'concerned with all aspects of the organization of educational systems and processes.

[Educational technology] is a hybrid of education and technology . . . rather than a simple grafting onto education of technological products' (Mitchell, 1978).

While it is more logical to take a systems view of technology rather than the somewhat restricted view that sees technology being only technical artefacts, this paper restricts itself to the narrow definition. The technical artefacts that have had, or may have, an impact on higher education are: computers, television, satellites, laser-holograms, telephone technology including optical fibre transmission, word processors and micrographics (microfiche, etc).

The Future of Higher Education

As this paper is concerned with the future, it is therefore necessary to indicate the general nature of higher education that will, or may, exist some time in the future. Assumptions are limited, but a back-cloth is necessary which will help determine the extent to which universities and colleges will need to be, or will want to be, dependent on technology. Assumptions made can best be summarized in a series of statements that reflect what is thought will, or should, happen by the year 2001.

1. There will be considerable collaboration and sharing of technical resources (eg computers) between institutions, both in the same sector (university with university), and between sectors (universities and polytechnics, colleges of education).

2. Institutions will find a significant part of their funds from outside the present funding arrangements. This may well mean more contract research in universities with a drift towards more specialization between research staff and teaching staff. In universities and other institutions, teaching 'non-graduating' students will significantly increase (ie in-service courses).

3. Institutions will be run on management principles with less departmental authority and responsibility for funds and purchasing. Central bulk purchasing of equipment and materials will be further co-ordinated between institutions.

4. Higher education will be much more 'open', in two ways:
   (a) There will be an increased representation of mature students (ie aged more than 23). This will happen to such an extent that institutions of higher education will become separated from the primary/secondary continuum. That is, there will be an increasing age gap between the normal and the mature entrants; up to, say, 10 years.
   (b) The second assumption is that many institutions will become involved with distance teaching or extension studies to such an extent that a significant proportion of their funds will be used for this purpose. It is this assumption that will have most effect on the take-up technology (see Table 1 and below for further details). It is unlikely that such openness will occur in less than 20 years. Existing educational assumptions are still firmly held to, and established and significant 're-tooling' of higher education will be a slow business.

These assumptions may well seem normative as opposed to deterministic. This is recognized and it is unlikely that higher education will evolve towards such a scenario *without* the help of positive or affirmative policies. Whether these come from without or within higher education, only the institutions themselves can determine.

Available to all

Open to all

At any time during lifetime

Consisting of short courses

Unitized teaching

Open to scrutiny

Open to government intervention

Open to innovative educational methods

A heavy user of communication technology

Table 1. *Open educational philosophy*

The General Position with Regard to Technology

In general, technology has had little across-the-board impact on existing academic practice. The present situation may be summarized as follows. Technology has had:

- ☐ Little impact on an academic's ability to communicate, although there is some evidence that learning patterns may have changed.
- ☐ Quite a lot of impact on a teacher's capacity to organize teaching, research and administration; students have experienced some impact on their allocation of time between tasks.
- ☐ An effect on the time to prepare instruction, both positively and negatively.
- ☐ An effect on the cost per unit of instruction and the cost per hour.
- ☐ Little effect on the overall effectiveness (measured in learning gains).
- ☐ Some effect on the nature and amount of social interaction between those in the learning milieu.

In the future, it is likely that technology will extend the capacity of teachers, researchers and administrators; mean more individualization of teaching/learning; alter further the work pattern for teachers and learners; but is unlikely to ease the workload for teachers and learners.

Little consideration has been given to date with regard to the social effects of technology. (However, see McAleese, 1980.) It is likely that by the year 2001, considerable dissonant effects will be apparent; for example, deskilling, segmentation, further man-machine ambivalence and structural unemployment. In general, higher education has *less* to fear from these quarters than other sections of society. Nevertheless, in particular areas, notably research and administration, deskilling and unemployment or underemployment may raise considerable problems.

The Impact of Technology on Higher Education

The impact that technology makes on higher education is a direct function of existing practice, that is, the usefulness of artefacts. Figure 1 is a schematic representation of the balancing forces that result in the impact or effect of the artefacts. The main positive forces are: present stock (the number of artefacts available) and this in turn is determined by what may best be called commercial push.

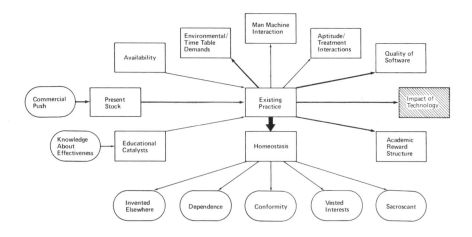

Figure 1. *Factors influencing the impact of technology*

Normal commercial practice is to exploit goods and services to other industrial units and the general consumer public. This practice is governed by market research. In recent years, the research and development sections of industrial concerns have been seen to *push* their own products directly to the public (through the host commercial concern). A prime example would be the silicon chip. To achieve economies of scale, a major push was made to sell direct to the educational and general market. This was achieved by marketing the pocket calculator — a device based on existing silicon chips and *not* designed for a particular market need (eg a device with alphanumeric input and non-volatile memory). This exploitation of new technologies (often ill-developed and seldom market researched as other products are) is commercial push.

Educational catalysts, that is, educational technologists and instructional designers, operating with what knowledge they have, make a positive contribution. The third factor that increases demand is the availability of component technology, ie, the fact that an institution has a TV studio will ensure that at least some of the time it will be used.

Operating against these forces are a cluster of powerful negative influences. Environmental and timetable demands limit the use of non-standard teaching aids. Rooms are not suitably designed for projection or recording; timetables are not sufficiently flexible to permit individualization of access to computers, calculators, etc. Bottle-necks occur, which require detailed queueing analysis, over the supply of components.

Little is known of the long-term effects of man-machine interactions. Problems exist which can be tackled by ergonomic experts, but the ambivalent relationship which exists between man and machines is a strong disincentive for extensive use of machines. An example of this is in the area of man-computer interface. VDU screens create eye strain; keyboards limit data input to those with the appropriate motor skills. What evidence there is suggests that strong aptitude-treatment interactions exist. The application of individual components technologies to different learners produces differential learning gains; for example, with regard to visual acuity and motor skills.

Software is most often criticized for its quality. Technical developments have far exceeded the conceptualization and production of good software. As a result, many artefacts are emasculated of their potential use by inappropriate software. Computer and television related technologies are most prone to this criticism.

The academic reward structure, particularly in universities, does not benefit the exploitation of hardware (or software) by academics. Traditional basic research, the stamp of academic approval, is reliant on technology, but in such a way that its demand is not direct, but through the process of research methodology. Little reward (in terms of tenure and promotion) is given for the exploitation of component technology (eg CCTV).

By far the most important factor is what McAleese (1978) has called institutional homeostasis. That is the natural, (and to some) proper, resistance to change by an organism. This can be seen as having five aspects:

1. *Not invented here.* Unless the artefact or software was produced in an institution, it is not used.
2. *Dependence.* A liking for one piece of favourite, but out-of-date, equipment.
3. *Conformity.* Claims that such a change would be against normal functioning, operating practice, etc.
4. *Vested interests.* A new technology challenges the social organization and alters the interests of users of 'old' technology.
5. *Sacrosanct.* Some things are so standard that a change is like altering a fundamental rule of nature. For example, the use of secretaries to take dictation.

Such forces, acting in a complex way, achieve an organic balance in such a way that determines the impact of any technology. In essence, commercial push can be seen as operating through the existing stock in opposition to institutional homeostasis.

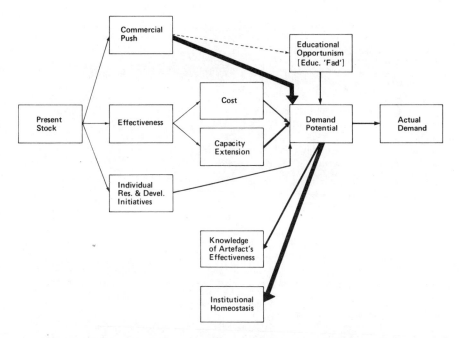

Figure 2. *Factors influencing the demand for technological artefacts*

The Demand for Technical Artefacts

In general, the main demand for technical artefacts has come as a result of commercial push. However, as with the impact of technology, the resultant demand is a balance between competing forces. Four factors positively influence the demand. Commercial push has been referred to above. The effectiveness of any artefact in achieving an end is a positive force. This has two components, one related to cost saving and the other to capacity extension.

Where a technical artefact can achieve a cost-saving result (eg a word processor), then its demand is positively affected. In some cases existing practice and capacity are extended (with or without cost-savings), for example with simulation and modelling procedures undertaken by computers. In general, technology can be thought of as extending four types of skills (see Table 2). Each skill or facility (eg storage) is affected by different technologies. Computer-related technologies extend more skills than other technologies.

Skills, facilities	Technology
Storage	Computer-related CCTV Laser holograms Micrographics
Manipulation	Computer-related CCTV
Retrieval	Computer-related Micrographics
Communication	Television-related Telecommunication-related

Table 2. *Skills extended by the use of technology*

Individual research and development projects have made positive effects with application of microprocessor technology; for example, the use of computer technology in machine control and in specific areas such as time-compressed speech.

Educational opportunism, while it has a positive effect, may not be entirely desirable. It is the demand for 'in' gadgets or artefacts. A particularly good example of what may be called 'riding the educational wave' was the demand for CCTV in the early 1970s.

Acting against these forces are two main forces: institutional homeostasis (referred to above), and knowledge about the effectiveness of artefacts. Little knowledge is open to operationalization or is available about the effectiveness of artefacts. Indeed, such knowledge is unlikely to accrue as it has to be related to use. Where such evidence exists, it is probabilistic and conditional.

The resultant demand for technical artefacts has meant a buoyant market in certain areas (eg computers) with a potential demand in others (communications).

The Impact of and Demand for Technology

Figures 3 and 4 summarize the qualitative assessment of the impact of technology and the likely demand for it. No attempt has been made to *quantify* either the impact or the demand. Although it is feasible that demand could be quantified,

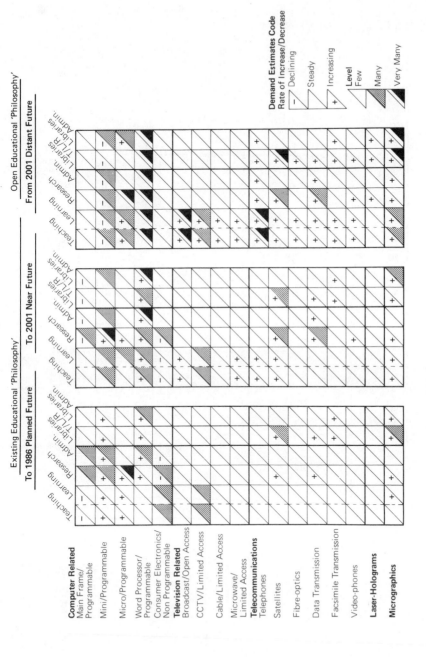

Figure 3. *Demand for technology*

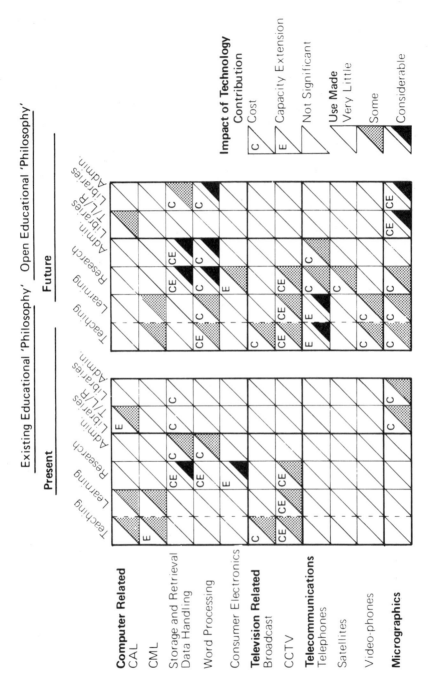

Figure 4. *The impact of technology*

given certain assumptions about stock and growth, this sensitivity analysis has not been possible in the time available. Each figure represents the processes or artefacts that are judged and the periods and categories for judgement. In each case, activities in higher education are broken down into six closely-related clusters. Teaching, learning (difficult to separate in most cases), research, and administration represent the usual classification. The library, standing as it does at the centre of the teaching-learning process, is taken separately and sub-divided into a teaching/learning/research function and an administrative function.

Figure 3 is the assessment of the contribution that technological artefacts have made with respect to cost-saving and capacity extension facilities, and the use made of the processes or artefacts tested. In this figure, existing education covers the period 1980-2001, and is under present educational philosophy. Future (open) education refers to a likely future, in which education could be defined as more open. Table 1 summarizes the assumptions made for open education (see above). This important scenario is both the result of, and dependent on, a take-off in communication-related technology in higher education (as well as the other factors mentioned).

Computer-related technology is divided into computer-assisted learning (CAL) and computer-managed learning (CML); data storage, handling and retrieval; processing and the use of consumer electronics (ie non-programmable hand or desk calculators and micro-computers).

Under existing educational assumptions, the most significant contributions have come in the area of fundamental research through data handling and word processing. Although some use is made of large computer-related systems (PLATO, SOCRATES, TICCIT), little further use will be made in these areas. With regard to CAL and CML, although some use will be made of these techniques, CML is foreseen only as extending the teachers' capacity, while in library appreciation there may be some use of CAL to extend the meagre resources of reader services division.

In the future, it is likely that the most significant impact will come from data handling and word processing in the areas of research and administration.

Figure 4 represents the assessment of the demand for various technical artefacts. Two assessments are made. Whether the demand is increasing, steady or decreasing, and the *level* of the demand. It is the latter that requires a little detail.

Attempts were made to derive demand functions for various items by using present expenditure. Mainly owing to the lack of precision in the demand equations, this exercise is not satisfactory.

(This paper is a revised and updated version of a submission the author made to the Myers' Committee of Enquiry into Technology for the Federal Government of Australia (1979). The original is published in *The Australian Society for Educational Technology Yearbook*, 1980 (edited by D Shearer).)

References

Berstecher, D et al (1974) A University of the Future. Martinus Nijhoff, The Hague.

Carnegie Commission (1976) Sponsored Research. McGraw-Hill, New York.

Coates, V T and Coates, J F (1976) Technology Assessment and Education.

Computer Education (1978) The computer in the year 2000. Computer Education, February, pp 6-8.

Fabun, D (1974) Australia 2000. Carrel.

Gosling, W (1978) Microcircuits, Society and Education. CET Occasional Paper 8. Council for Educational Technology, London.

Hall, W (1978) Tertiary Education. In Unwin, D and McAleese, R (eds) Encyclopaedia of Educational Media Communications and Technology. Macmillan, London.

Henchley, S P and Yates, J R (eds) (1976) Futurism in Education. McCutchan, Berkeley, California.

Hiffle, T W (1975) (ed) The Future of Education 1975-2000. Goodyear, New York.

Hore, T et al (1978) *The Future of Higher Education in Australia.* Macmillan, London.

Kahan, H (1973) *The Next 200 Years.*

McAleese, R (1980) Technology in higher education. In Shearer, D (ed) *ASET Yearbook,* 1980.

Medows, D H et al (1972) *The Limits to Growth.* Earth Island, London.

Mitchell, P D (1978) Educational technology. In Unwin, D and McAleese, R (eds)
    Encyclopaedia of Educational Media Communications and Technology. Macmillan, London.

O'Brien, P W (1976) Future research in education. *Australian Journal of Education,*
    20, pp 46-58.

Toffler, A (ed) (1974) *Learning for Tomorrow: the Role of the Future in Education.* Vintage,
    New York.

Toffler, A (1975) What is anticipating democracy? *The Futurist,* 9, pp 224-9.

Toffler, A (1970) *Future Shock.* Pan, London.

Wearing, A J et al (1976) *Computers and Teaching in Australia.* Australian Government
    Publishing Service, Canberra.

12.2 Training Technology in the Army in the 1980s

P J Phillips
RAEC

Abstract: The author highlights some of the recent developments in Army training and gives a personal view of where he believes future development will take place.

I should like to highlight some of the recent developments in Army training and suggest where I believe future development will take place. I would emphasize that this is a personal view, not an official one, and it is based on some intensive 'crystal ball gazing'.

Thinking of changes in Army training in the 1980s may cause some of you to wonder if it has changed at all since National Service, since the Second World War or, if being particularly unkind, since the 1880s. We are still very much concerned with what has been called 'the poor bloody Infantry'. Of course, today a man in the Infantry has to be trained to do much more than simply fire a rifle. He is required to operate a wide range of sophisticated weapons and equipment, including wire guided missiles, anti-tank rockets and advanced radio communication equipment. He may be trained as a driver of heavy vehicles, tracked armoured personnel carriers or even the Scorpion light tank. In addition, he must be physically fit, able to read a map, carry out first-aid, have a knowledge of basic tactics and, most important with that range of weapons at his disposal, he must be trained to recognize enemy vehicles, tanks and aircraft. The RAF are understandably quite keen on that aspect! It is a daunting list and one that is becoming longer all the time.

Despite changes in warfare, there continues to be a vital role for the infantry soldier, usually working in a small group and provided with an increasingly wide range of weapons and equipment. His training has become more complex, and to cope with his needs the training has been subjected to the analysis and design of the systems approach to training. The particular model adopted, the Mellor Loop, will be familiar to most educational technologists.

In the 1980s, the Army will be moving more towards the position where we man equipment like the RN and RAF rather than simply equipping men as has been our custom for centuries. The training implications of new equipment are now considered at the early stage of design. When the Army receives its new tank or fighting vehicle in the 1980s, you may rest assured that the training technologists will in some measures have been involved in its design.

The major problem faced in Army training is that we are training people for an employment which we cannot practise, for which, we may say, thank God! We must remember that we are training men ultimately for employment in war. This presents a number of rather special problems.

First of all, because most of the time we do not have a real enemy, we have to simulate the enemy. We call this exercising. Secondly, there is the lack of opportunity to do the actual job. Although, of course, this is very welcome in terms of World peace it does produce real training problems of motivation, maintenance of skills and design of effective simulation of battle conditions.

For many military jobs, the presence of war conditions, although significant, does not affect the job itself. Much of the maintenance and supply which the Army terms 'support' falls into this category. Here, the problems are associated with the increasing complexity of equipment and the limited availability of expensive equipment for training. This applies particularly with new equipment being introduced into service where the operational requirement must take priority. (The introduction of the Lynx helicopter was a good example of this problem.)

There are constant pressures to train more efficiently in terms of time and use of resources, but I recognize that this is a problem not unique to the military.

In all this, we can job-analyze, refine objectives, increase the effectiveness of tests, and validate and evaluate to ensure our training is both effective and efficient. To achieve this the systems approach is now generally accepted and it has been developed to meet specific needs in special areas. In particular, we are attempting to use it to assist our need to train groups of people in teams. These may be infantry sections, tank crews or the complete Command Headquarters staff. We refer to this as *collective training*.

In the future there will be continued development of these techniques. This will involve research and development and consultancy tasks throughout the Army for the specialists in the Army training organization. Apart from these developments, more effective training devices will be needed and we look for developments particularly in the field of simulation.

An area of interest is that of weapon-effects simulation. When a weapon is fired in an exercise, whether against a tank, vehicle or man, some indication of having hit the target is necessary. We already have in use a system called Simfire, which uses a sight-safe laser for this purpose.

That represents the present state of the art, but it is hoped that there will shortly be a whole range of weapon-effect simulators, including an indication for men on the exercise battlefield. It is likely to involve some form of harness with sensitive receptors — a sophisticated 'bang, you're dead' system. The American Army does have a system currently in operation and this highlights another problem, that of having a degree of standardization of equipment and training throughout NATO allies. It is to be hoped that the 1980s will see a greater degree of standardization between the NATO forces.

In many other ways simulators will play a part in making our training more effective. Some will replace expensive equipment, or equipment which is expensive to run. A tank does gallons-per-mile or litres-per-kilometre: that is bad news in whatever units you use.

We have already increased the use of driving simulators. This has been particularly successful with the training of the Chieftain tank drivers where a sophisticated computer-controlled simulator has been developed. A gunnery simulator has been developed for training the crew of the same tank. In both cases, total realism has been attempted, and the layout and controls of the simulator are an exact replication of those found in the battle tank.

The Royal Electrical and Mechanical Engineers (REME) and the Royal Signals are developing in black-box format a simulator for electronic equipment to train maintenance and repair engineers in fault-finding when the real equipment is not available. We see this as a major development for the 1980s and await with interest the results of a feasibility study at present under way.

So much for equipment simulators, but there is a need in some situations to simulate the whole environment; for instance, a complete urban training area in which small groups and/or patrols can be exercised while being monitored on closed-circuit television. This type of training area can be used by day and night. A very high degree of realism is achieved, particularly at night when simulated shots are being fired.

You may be glad to know that the art of war games is not dead. We still need to simulate battles to train commanders at all levels, and one of the most exciting developments is in the use of computers to provide real-time results of a commander's action. A very successful project providing this specialized training is the Battle Group Tactical Trainer. This system was developed to train battalion commanders or battle group commanders and their staffs in tactics. At the heart of the system is a map table on which movable symbols represent the enemy and friendly forces. The commander and his staff are located in a separate part of the building in a mock-up of their headquarters. They do not have sight of the main map, but must fight the battle through a radio net. The computer provides information on the outcome of engagements and assesses casualties and damage.

The Army has identified three areas for the use of ADP:

(a) Computer-managed learning (CML).
(b) Computer-assisted learning (CAL).
(c) Computers supporting simulation.

The first, CML, is the area where most of our effort to date has been concentrated. We have projects in test marking and analysis; in record-keeping and student profiling and routeing and in item banking of examination questions and subsequent production of test papers, their marking and analysis. In the 1980s we see an extension of such activities; indeed the projects we have mounted in the period 1976-80 were designed to provide us with the evidence on which such expansion of ADP could be based.

The introduction of CAL has been much slower, but with the advent of cheap micros we expect to increase our interest in those areas where appropriate training stuations exist. It may never have more than a limited role in Infantry training, but in gunnery, engineering and signals training there are obvious possibilities. We have taken an interest in the development of the PLATO and MENTOR systems, but it is the Royal Navy who have taken the lead in these areas and we look forward to receiving their reports in the near future. As with many other organizations, much of our training is unique and there is an enormous problem of producing the software to match our training; however, with the use of the high-level author languages, and with increasing awareness of the use of computers by our trainers, this problem may be overcome in the next few years.

As for computers in support of simulation, I have already mentioned our increasing interest and I can only re-emphasize the point that the computer can be an effective aid to more realistic simulation. This, of course, begs the question as to how realistic simulation should be in order to be effective.

We predict an increasing need for our trainers to be able to use computers and to produce courseware, but we recognize that this will not happen overnight and that there will be a considerable in-service training commitment involved.

I would not like to give the impression that the computer will be dominant in Army training in the 1980s. It will have an important, an increasingly important, part to play, but it will be another tool available to the trainer and its development must not be at the expense of other effective methods of learning, whether by lesson technique or the more common visual aids.

In the area of visual aids, I believe the use of CCTV will expand enormously in the 1980s. Already, over 140 military units use TV for training purposes and I would anticipate that in the next five to ten years all units will have video facilities available. The cost of distributing 16mm film to the whole Army will make a switch to video financially more attractive, the slight cloud on the horizon being the multiplicity of formats. However, in the next few years this may be partly resolved and the introduction of digital recorders in five to ten years will give an opportunity for standardization and will overcome many of the problems currently associated with multi-generation copies. The Army is well-prepared to develop the use of CCTV, as it has its own studios, while the SKC operate a mobile studio for us.

Another significant area of development is that concerned with affective training. Training technology could play an important part in this area of training, not only by providing the means (TV?) whereby affective (leadership/management) training can be assisted and enlivened, but also in providing the backing in terms of analysis and design. Considerable study, linked to experience, will be needed to examine and further develop this aspect of training.

Finally, and really bringing together all I have mentioned so far in the nature of training design and technology, the 1980s should see an extension of the use of what we call packages in the Army; packages to support instructors with viewfoils, notes, slides, video-tapes, exercises, etc using the best of audio-visual presentation methods and carefully structured learning material. There will be other packages, just as carefully designed, but in this case aimed at individual self-paced learning. Such packaged learning, derived from the programmed learning stable but perhaps having few of the PL features, will be found in learning resource centres where the instructor officers' skills will be needed in counselling and giving guidance over a wide spectrum of subject material. ADP help to keep records and aid information retrieval will be in evidence and there will be magnetic and microfiche store materials as well as high quality visual material.

Nevertheless, training in the Army of the 1980s will have a familiar look. There will still be a need to get wet, cold and tired in simulated battle conditions, and imagination will be required to maintain enthusiasm. Army training will continue to need the support of training technologists who will be seeking ways to improve effectiveness and efficiency, and you will still find us at ETIC asking about what's new in the world of training and education.

12.3 Technological Developments and Domestic Applications of Computer-Based Education

John F Huntington
Miami University

Abstract: A projection of advances likely in the development of computer hardware during the next two decades and the effect of these on learning environments.

Introduction

During the next two decades, dramatic advances in the development of computer hardware will significantly affect the learning environments of millions of learners. The development of novel learning environments will be the result of a hierarchy of technological developments progressing through improvements in microprocessors, input/output peripherals, communication networks, lesson development and learning management systems. Educational experiences that do not require group learning environments will become portable and most likely domestically centred. This paper will explore the impact of potential technological developments on computer-based education (CBE) and the prediction that domestic CBE will develop to a significant extent before the end of this century.

Technological developments in microprocessor technology suggest two major thrusts from design perspectives. Reduction in size through efforts to uniquely combine electronic and physical interactions of circuitry is progressing rapidly. Size reduction from the 1950s to the 1970s is of the magnitude of a factor of more than 100x. During the past few years, the reduction factor approximates 10x. Microprocessor size is a critical determinant of computer cost and portability. CPUs with addressable memories of tens of thousands of bytes can now be held in the palm of a hand. Processing speed will also be considerably reduced. Powerful microprocessors with large memories and fast processing speeds will be available in the near future at relatively low cost for home use.

Simultaneously, developmental break-throughs will occur with input/output (I/O) devices. An ideal design goal would be the capability to directly link a computer to the human mind. I/O development will progress towards this ideal by simulating as many human perceptive and performance characteristics as possible. I/O devices will become more sensitive and will sense and produce information with ever greater fidelity and flexibility. Visual, auditory, kinesthetic and tactile channels of human I/O will be coupled to computer peripherals for information exchanges between the computer and the person. I/O requirements for information exchange will permit naive users easier access to computer/person dialogues.

Communications technology development will also occur at an accelerating pace. Links of persons with computers will be possible at ever-decreasing costs through increasing varieties of I/O devices. Computer accessibility will be increased to encompass more people at lower cost and through more easily used I/O devices. These hardware developments have significant implications for CBE.

CBE is a system co-ordinating lesson development and instructional management with general educational objectives. Some (Hicks and Hunka, 1972) have previously proposed the concept of community-based educational systems to describe a more holistic perspective of the integration of CBE with traditional education. The important considerations which must be faced by the end of the century are that: (i) learning sites do not have to be fixed, (ii) teacher/student interactions can occur through the medium of CBE rather than through direct contact, (iii) control of learning may be transferred to an interactive trialogue between teacher, student and CBE system and (iv) the variety of teaching/learning formats available for CBE will increase dramatically and will tax the resources of educational institutions to provide adequate CBE software.

The analysis presented in this paper will be based on CBE developments from the 1960s to the present. It will progress along a functional hierarchy from developments anticipated in hardware, communication networks and learning systems software and management systems. Essentially, the analysis will focus on the simultaneous, interactive aspects of these developments and their potential for providing information of value toward constructing a set of predictions for future CBE uses.

Hardware

During the 1960s, two systems represented state-of-the-art developments of hardware available to a limited number of computer users. The IBM 1500 instructional system consisted of an 1100 series computer coupled to a DOS, card reader/punch, video display terminals (VDT) with light pens, a film projector, and other peripheral devices capable of being coupled to the system. The DOS and VDT were devices not generally available at a cost favourable to a majority of users. The I/O times for these devices considerably decreased interactive time requirements and permitted efficient as well as effective student/computer dialogues. The PLATO instructional system was based on a large CDC computer coupled to VDTs, an optical/video/microform reader/writer, as well as to other devices. Both systems initially were restricted to local use because of coaxial transmission limitations.

In the 1970s, the IBM system was enhanced by the addition of audio/tape units. The PLATO system added an improved image generating sub-system developed in conjunction with the plasma panel display. Audio units became computer driven and time sharing applications via telephone lines were added. Each system evolved into capable and relatively expensive collections of specialized hardware. A new system based on currently available hardware was developed and named TICCIT. It employed time-sharing functions for remote users possessing standard terminals connected to home colour television receivers (Alderman, 1978).

The main breakthrough during the late 1970s has been the development of low cost microcomputers. Increasingly, schools are purchasing these devices for tutorial and data processing uses. The use of microcomputers avoids telecommunication's costs but places the burden of systems maintenance with the local user. Hardware configurations usually include a combined Keset/CPU, video monitor, DOS or audio-tape I/O and printers, light pens, voice translator input, audio output translator and communication modems. These systems, which are available at relatively low cost, compare quite favourably with the state-of-the-art systems developed by IBM and at the University of Illinois during the past two decades.

The trends in hardware development will progress toward larger and faster CPUs with smaller physical size, more sophisticated video/audio displays and substantially more capable I/O devices and more efficient communications equipment. Voice recognition, graphic, analytical processing of written symbols and effective couplings to analogic input will characterize the most significant developments in hardware. The ultimate foreseeable goal for I/O operations is direct interfacing with the human neurological system. Hardware developments will permit enhanced CBE applications in homes as costs and complexities of operating systems decrease. Domestic study via a CBE system will become common by the turn of the century. Educational institutions will experience incredible pressures to reconfigure their structures and organizations to permit responsive reactions to developments in CBE.

Communications

Computer communications systems evolved from direct, hardwired configurations to coaxial extensions with time-sharing and then to telecommunications using phone and/or microwave transmissions. Currently, satellite communications systems permit extensive broadcasting but limited receive/send operations. Electronic specialists found that it became increasingly difficult to push increasing numbers of signals rapidly through wire and coaxial cables. The limitations of these signal carrying materials will become increasingly problematic as more and more people generate signals to be transmitted and received. Multiplexing on a large scale using wireless carriers and satellite relays will become more common in the next few decades. Cable television communication hardware and regional computer mediated communication networks will permit I/O operations between domestic locations and CBE systems on a scale believed unattainable 10 years ago. Signal carriers and multiplexing will evolve to greater levels of sophistication through the applications of fibre optic, high frequency radio and other, as yet unknown, technologies applied toward the development of highly capable communication networks. Viable CBE systems with potentials for great impact on masses of people will require elaborate communication networks. Networks permitting millions of time-shared dialogues between CBE systems and users will be on line by the turn of the century.

Software and Management Systems

The IBM and PLATO systems used rather elaborate instruction building languages and management systems when compared to others available during the 1960s. Coursewriter, TUTOR, NCR-CAI and other high-level author languages (Coursewriter; Fernstermaker and Huntington 1972; Huntington, 1978) were developed to permit easy lesson-building and student record generation. These languages are system dependent and as a result are not usable on other systems. The availability of general purpose microcomputers and time-sharing systems has made these special purpose languages and management systems unavailable for general use. Yet, they have great utility for building complex, extensive CBE systems. Their greatest limitation, besides that mentioned previously, is that each reflects a set of ideas about managing instruction which might not be acceptable to all users. Coding instructional algorithms in these special purpose languages, however, requires much less attention to systems management than that required when a general purpose language like BASIC is used.

The development of higher level general purpose, as well as special purpose, languages and management systems is anticipated during the next two decades. The most important developments, however, will be focused on creating translator/transforming algorithms which will permit modifying one language version of a computer program to another. This important capability will permit the use of instructional software written in one language to be used on systems supporting other languages. The logics involved in producing translator/transforming algorithms are complex (Landa, 1974). Undoubtedly, systems capable of employing facets of artificial intelligence to produce best matches between versions of languages and from one language to another will be required to permit authoring CBE materials in forms that are available to critical numbers of users possessing different computer systems. Many more instructional algorithms and record management operations will be available to more users. Packaged instructional systems will be tailored to users possessing different kinds and levels of computer system. The range of applications of computers in education will increase significantly. Barriers provided by inter-systems language incompatibilities will be significantly reduced during the next two decades. CBE systems will become available to tens of millions of people living on several continents. Traditional educational institutions will be required to adapt to changes in instruction, locations of instruction and monitoring of student activities if they are to remain viable.

References

Alderman, D L et al (1978) PLATO and TICCIT: an evaluation of CAI in the community college. Educational Technology, pp 40-5. Educational Technology Publications, Englewood Cliffs, NJ.

Coursewriter III – Version. IBM Corporation, White Cliffs, NJ. Student Text (5734-E13) (OS) 5736-E11(DOS)). (Consult Newsletter (GN20-0360) for latest version.)

Fernstermaker, C and Huntington, J F (1972) NCR-CAI Course Author's Guide. NCR Corporation, Dayton, Ohio.

Hicks, B and Hunka, S M (1972) The Teacher and the Computer. W B Saunders Co, Philadelphia, PA.

Huntington, J F (1978) Language limitations for CAI. Association for Educational Data Systems, Atlanta, GA.

Landa, L N (1974) Algorithmization in Hearing and Instruction. Educational Technology Publications, Englewood Cliffs, NJ.

12.4 Educational Television: the Present and the Future

Lawrie Lawler
University of Manchester

Abstract: The role of television as a tool or instrument for use in education is discussed in the light of the present revolutionary changes in communication technology. These rapid advances prevent any clear prognosis of the form which educational television will take by 2000 AD, but six of today's trends are extrapolated and their future is discussed.

Introduction

In this paper 'educational television' is taken to mean the widest possible use and application of the television medium for educational purposes. Much narrower definitions have been used. For instance, in British broadcasting, 'educational television' is only applied to certain programmes which can be used and restrictively copied. In the USA 'instructional television' was considered to be different from educational television, which was expanded to cover almost all serious programming. This is now largely re-named public broadcasting.

Some attempt is made in what follows to establish a base-line from which we can expect the educational television (ETV) to develop in the next decade or two. It is not intended to give more than a passing reference to the technical aspects involved. Obviously, in what Lord Briggs now calls the 'Communication Revolution' (Briggs, 1979) which has burst upon us so dramatically, some understanding of the implications of new technology must be taken into account.

It is important for any student of educational technology to apply to ETV the harsh analysis of educational effectiveness and to balance this against cost. However attractive, or useless, ETV might appear to different observers, it should be studied objectively for its own sake and as part of a rapidly changing society. A review of video in education from 1977 to 1982 by Henri Dieuzeide (1977), UNESCO Director of Methods, Materials and Techniques, makes salutory reading in this respect.

There have been few other innovations which have been studied so closely for cost-effectiveness as ETV, but until very recently it has been very difficult to make comparisons because other teaching techniques, especially those of the traditional teacher-class structure, have not been so carefully and critically examined. Let us hope that one outcome of the present financial cuts in education will be to apply more strictly the disciplines of educational technology and establish what changes must be made in our educational system to match the great changes in society which are now occurring. The Council for Educational Technology for the UK (1979) is particularly working to this end.

The Position of Educational Television Today

There have been tremendous changes since, for instance, Professor Himmelweit and her colleagues studied the effect of television on children in the 1950s (Himmelweit *et al*, 1959). The recent survey by Katz, Wedell, Pilsworth and Shinar (1978) of the role of television in the Third World shows that television is becoming the main means of international communication for the masses and that in urban societies, at least, a standard pattern of broadcasting is materializing. McLuhan's 'Global Village' is well on the way to becoming reality.

Broadcast ETV is, of course, fundamentally a one-way system and this has been the major obstacle. Even the Open University has found the effect of its broadcasts disappointing even though they have been so carefully tied in to course structure. The remoteness of educational broadcasting has been largely offset by the spread of closed-circuit television in education and it is in this area that the members of the Educational Television Association have been most active over more than a decade. Much of what is said in this paper stems from the activities, discussions and publications of Association colleagues, in particular in the Journal of Educational Television.

Two trends which affect us today and will do so in the future are, firstly, the production of teaching and learning aids on video-tape; the importance of high standards, both educational and technical, is now recognized as essential if the effort is to be worthwhile. The second trend is the wide range of useful techniques which have stemmed from the spread of modest and inexpensive television equipment, in particular those for modifying the behaviour of individuals or groups.

We now see three main categories of equipment involved in ETV systems. The most expensive and complex are broadcast-standard systems: at the cheap end is a plethora of items manufactured with the enormous domestic and commercial markets in mind; and in between are moderately priced but high standard and flexible systems suitable for institutions. Education is always the Cinderella of society and has to be satisfied with making the best of what is available. At the domestic level, the two curses are still incompatibility and instability. At the college level, there has been a great improvement technically and the modestly priced systems are serving needs very well.

But it is the recent technical improvement in the cut-price market of domestic and surveillance equipment which may prove to have the greatest influence on the use of ETV in the future. In 1968, Tony Gibson wrote: 'The greatest educational use of TV is not the showing of taped or live programmes to passive audiences but the actual making of a TV tape'. Today, we are only now on the threshold of video for everyman and we should be able to put Gibson's conclusion to the test on a large scale (Gibson, 1968).

Present and Future Technology

It would be rash to try to forecast in any detail the state communication technology will have reached by the year 2000. Today, we have a pocket-sized video-cassette capable of storing eight hours of programmes in colour, and a TV camera weighing just over a kilogram, based on a single charge-coupled device (CCD) with 210,000 picture elements. Few would have forecast those in 1960. On the other hand, we could have predicted that television would become commonplace and that it would be mainly in colour, in the industrial world at least; that telephones would still be our main person-to-person communication; and that satellites would be involved in a global communication network. We would have had a strong bet on the spread of what was then called the walkie-talkie and perhaps dial-access for information. I think we would have predicted that there would be no change in the TV frame format and that 3-D would not have been developed.

There does not seem to be any reason why technology should not still be pushing ahead as now (at least in those countries with an adequate source of trained engineers) and hence producing new wonders in telecommunications as the Broadcasters' Yearbooks cheerfully point out (BBC, 1980; IBA, 1980). But we can also be sure that its effect on social behaviour will be as sluggish as now, and its effect on human nature will be nil.

The most important technical developments will undoubtedly stem from micro-electronics, which today are based on the silicon chip. The chip will probably be surplanted by other more exotic technologies which will do the same kind of thing quicker, be smaller, and be even harder to understand. In television, the advantages of small size, cheapness, fantastic speed and flexibility which the chip brings will convert the TV screen into a terminal for displaying the computerization of many social activities including education. Digitalization of video will eventually mean programme storage in computer memories together with alphanumerical information on a gigantic scale. Professor Gosling has recently published a very clear account of these developments (Gosling, 1978).

The current major exhibitions and conferences concerned with television are demonstrating the application of *optical fibres* as vastly superior to other forms of transmission lines; *voice controllers* which respond to their master's voice and switch things to order; *optical long-play video-discs* based on the deflection of laser beams by microscopic indentations in the plastic disc (this promises to be a very cheap way of mass-producing video-copies); and, of course, chips with everything else, including colour TV cameras and recorders.

These are some of the innovations here today which will influence tomorrow. Others are just emerging over the horizon and are scheduled to be available for use in the next decade or so. For instance, *High Definition Television (HDTV)* based on scanning rasters with 1,000 to 2,000 lines; in the last Shoenberg Memorial Lecture of the Royal Television Society, Joseph Polonski (1980), late Technical Director of Thomson CSF, gave a masterly survey of the future of this development which will lead to large screen TV equivalent in definition to 16mm film projected in a small cinema. This is, of course, of great importance to teaching in higher education, especially as the screen shape can be changed to aspect ratios of 5 : 3 and 8 : 3.

Another such development is the network of *Broadcast Communication Satellites* which have sufficient power sources to enable them to re-broadcast from fixed earth orbits at strengths sufficient to be received on small, cheap aerials at a domestic level. The UK satellite is scheduled for 1986-87, but in southern England it will be possible to pick up the Franco-German 'Symphonie' satellite in three years' time. The influence on the world population of free access to a vast output over a large network of such satellites is of great significance. Shakespeare put it:

> ... the isle is full of noises
> Sounds, and sweet airs, that gives delight and hurt not,
> Sometimes a thousand twangling instruments
> Will hum about mine ears ...
>
> (*The Tempest,* Act III, Sc 2)

The engineers predict beautiful reception of sound and vision for all, and a vast output of music, entertainment, news and current affairs — perhaps even some education. But some politicians are frightened out of their wits!

Finally, *digital sound and video* is with us but will take a long time to work its way through the whole system. It will be interesting to see whether, by the year 2000, the domestic user will have equipment to display and replay both digitalized pictures and sound or whether the translation from digital to analogue video and sound recording will still be done before transmission. Certainly, digitalized sound recording now being introduced creates an amazing authenticity and can be transmitted with no distortion or interference. In particular, the use of optical long-play video-discs for sound reproduction promises beautiful and inexpensive recordings.

Digital video is still developing behind the scenes and is used by engineers to improve picture quality and create some marvellous video trickery. The hold-up is availability of computer capacity, but news of computerization based on optical phenomena promises increases of speeds a hundred-fold and with far greater storage capacity (Smith and Miller, 1980). So who knows — by the year 2000 all television may be handled in a digital fashion.

This links to the problem of how education will take advantage of the digital systems such as Teletext (CEEFAX from the BBC and ORACLE from the IBA) and Viewdata (PRESTEL from the Post Office). At the moment there is no doubt that in one way or another the home TV set will be used as a display of digital information for a very wide range of purposes. Let us hope that education can be one of them.

Extrapolation from Present Trends in ETV

From the rapidly expanding technology of telecommunications, six trends have been chosen. These are interlinked with each other and with the wider public use of TV. Whether these trends will be of significance in the year 2000 in the form envisaged now depends largely on whether strongly entrenched traditional educational patterns imposed in the nineteenth century are retained. If we can free ourselves from these shackles, ETV will have a great part to play; if not, Britain may be a banana republic by the end of the millenium. Here are six educational areas in which ETV can play an important role in the next two decades.

Self-tuition

Given access to a colour TV set and an interactive device linked to a national or commercial system, the control of the picture on the screen is, to some extent, put in the hands of the viewer. The device which would appear most likely to be available in the next few years is the video-cassette recorder. Video-tape material is already produced but the viewer can, at least, stop, start, view, run on, run back, repeat, absorb, discard at the touch of a button. If the viewer is motivated to learn, he will; if not, he can either change the cassette or leave it. Motivation is all important. The style of presentation must be right for a single viewer's needs.

The pace, composition, structure and programming must be directed towards self-instruction. Above all, the material must be attractive and to the point.

Some believe the video-cassette will not be the self-tuition television tool because of its complexity. The video-disc player might be the front runner. The snag here is that cheap video-discs are only likely to carry those subjects which will sell in large numbers; also flexibility will be lost and with it the ability to control the material because once recorded the material cannot be changed as with video-tape. There is another possibility and the television game may hold the key. Once a home computer becomes widely available, TV games will flow in and, with them, self-tuition programmes. In this case, the audio-cassette will be the medium for inserting educational programmes into the computer in a similar way to the Open University CYCLOPS device (Read, 1978), in which one channel of the stereo-cassette replays a sound commentary while the other puts diagrams on the TV screen. Tony Bates, of the Open University, has already given a comprehensive and thought-provoking report on the new technology for home-based learning (Bates, 1978) which includes this idea. Self-tuition will encourage individuals to learn skills, seek information and reinforce educational weak spots in a relatively easy way, via the home TV screen. And the library at the end of the digitalized link will supply further material, either directly into the home computer or on tape as a supplement to the generous communication flowing from a world-wide network of broadcast satellites.

Digital Video

With the extension of the present trend towards digitalization, the areas of particular interest to educational television are those of alphanumerical display and computer graphics. The former allows the display of writing, numbers and symbols; the latter can, via graphics, maps, diagrams, etc display movement not easily available in any other medium. At the moment, the frames of material are fixed by the producers, but with a home computer the material becomes interactive by means of a keyboard or a light-pen. Using the capacity of large computers linked via memory devices or by cable to the home television screen, a wide range of procedures in the field of computer-aided learning and instruction can be carried out.

The Eclipse of Paper

In the next decade or so it looks as if the book will price itself out of the market. Professor Gosling in his lecture at the Council for Educational Technology (Gosling, 1978) has vividly described the massive storage capacity of tomorrow's electronic libraries. Nearly half a million volumes can be stored in a memory the size of a TV set with an access time to any page of one second. It is probable that the TV display of tomorrow will appear more like the printed page today, ie without glare, with strong contrast and crisp characterization.

This radical change will not mean the end of paper as a print medium — far from it; a paper record of whatever is shown on the screen will undoubtedly be required by scholars. But it does mean that every village branch can, in effect, become a legal depository library with electronic access to any volume. The days of libraries which are mammoth book warehouses will be over, except perhaps as museums of past glories.

Access Television

For most people, personal access to television seems to arouse the greatest interest. In the next 20 years, in most communities, it will become commonplace for everyone to appear 'on the box'. With video recording equipment entering the home market more and more, the family will be able to replace the professional whenever they wish. This access will apply to the members of institutions, clubs, societies, schools, resource centres and so on, until the majority of the population will have as much access as they want.

As this happens, attitudes to television may become very different from those of today. Video-tape (or its equivalent) will be accepted in law, in sport, in education and in society as valid evidence of involvement. And 'professionalism' may take on a very different connotation as effective handling of video systems becomes a commonplace occurrence. With new formats and widespread electronic facilities, television will certainly become an art form. Then universal access will be a vital factor in the exploitation of the medium.

Global Communication

The proposed network of satellites intercommunicating and relaying broadcast output from across the world heralds just the situation Marshall McLuhan envisaged when he discussed the Global Village. Whether a global network, by which anyone anywhere can communicate at will with anyone else on earth, comes about by 2000 AD is unlikely, but it is probable that great strides towards this goal will be made. The capital cost will be enormous but maintenance and usage should cost very little. The educational significance, though interesting, is not great compared with political and social implications. If there is free access to the output of every contributing country, copyright control will cease to apply and this could have serious repercussions. Will, for instance, the Open University broadcast freely, knowing that anyone throughout the world might record, replay and even market their programmes without payment to them?

Video in Self-Analysis

This may prove to be the most far-reaching aspect of educational television in the future. With a camera and video-tape recorder we can see ourselves a few minutes later as through the eyes of a non-critical observer. This power to see and judge ourselves, as objectively as we wish, seems to have the effect of helping us to change our minds and our behaviour. Usually this change is deliberate and is connected with a skill such as is involved in teaching, sport, or arts and crafts, but it has also been shown to go much deeper. Psychiatric patients use self-viewing as therapy. Video-taping emotional situations, such as occur with parents of handicapped children, allows them to observe objectively, and a series of such video-tapes made at intervals allows a long-term improvement to be more easily appreciated.

But it is in the practical field of personal interaction, which includes interview techniques and assessment of abilities and aptitudes, that the use of ETV is showing such important results. As more and more experience is gained in this field, the real importance of this valuable tool for education will be realized.

Some Implications for the Future

The six trends which may have important repercussions in the next 20 years are only some of the ways of using television in education and ETV only covers a small part of what we now recognize as the Communication or Informational, or Technological Revolution. A new vogue word, TELEMATICS, has appeared to cover the whole field of telecommunications, microprocessors, data-banks, etc. In a recent report, the EEC Commissioner for Industrial Affairs, Viscount Etienne Davignon, pointed out that the Telematics Industry of the EEC was lagging behind that of the USA and Japan and he was quoted as saying:

> One key element we have identified is the training process, education in schools, the adaptation of the public to the science fiction era . . . We would like to see the new techniques playing a bigger role in educational programmes.

These, he felt, should cover both the understanding and the use of telematics (Davignon, 1980).

How is this to be done? At the moment, a few teachers are playing at 'Media Studies' with very little background experience in journalism and broadcasting. Although there has been this remarkable technological advance in the last few years, the economic squeeze has frightened many educational authorities from providing new facilities to meet the needs of the future. There is still an underlying fear of using new techniques, especially those involving electronics, at all levels of education. This fear sometimes has an almost Luddite intensity although it must be obvious to all that great changes are occurring in our society, which must be reflected in education.

Education must not lag behind the Communication Revolution. It must forge ahead anticipating the inevitable changes, understanding their potential and, through continuing education, influencing everyone to accept and make the best of the social changes as they arrive.

At the moment, this effort would seem impossible to achieve. Our educational system has drifted so far away from the needs of society that it appears to be an insurmountable task unless we, the educators, change ourselves and our system dramatically from within.

I believe that educational television has a vital role to play in this struggle and we should be given every encouragement to apply this most valuable instrument at every stage.

References

Bates, A (1978) New technology for home-based learning: the challenge to campus-based institutions. *Journal of Educational Television*, 4, 2, p4. The Educational Television Association, York.

Briggs, A (1979) The communication revolution. The University of Manchester, Ludwig Mond Lecture, 1979.

British Broadcasting Corporation (1980) *BBC Handbook 1980*, pp 191-9. BBC, Broadcasting House, London.

Council for Educational Technology for the UK (1979) *The Contribution of Educational Technology to Higher Education in the 1990s — A Statement*. CET, London.

Davignon, E (1980) Telematics. *Europa*, VII, 4. London.

Dieuzeide, H (1977) Video in education, the next five years. *Journal of Educational Television*, 3, 4, p 130. The Educational Television Association, York.

Gibson, A (1968) *Experiments with Television*. Educational Foundation for Visual Aids, London.

Gosling, W (1978) *Microcircuits, Society and Education*. CET, London.

Himmelweit, H T, Oppenheim, A N and Vince, P (1959) *Television and the Child*. Oxford. University Press, London.

Independent Broadcasting Authority (1980) Television and radio 1980. *Better Viewing and Listening*, pp 175-93. IBA, London.

Katz, E and Wedell, G (with Pilsworth, M and Shinar, D) (1978) *Broadcasting in the Third World: Promise and Performance*. Macmillan, London.

The Media Studies Association (1980) *The Media Reporter Quarterly*. Brennan Publications, Derby.

Polonski, J (1980) Over a thousand lines: the next engineering goal. *Television*, 18, 1, p13. The Royal Television Society, London.

Read, G A (1978) *CYCLOPS: An Audio Visual System — A Brief Description*. The Open University Press, Milton Keynes.

Smith, D and Miller, D (1980) Computing at the speed of light: report on work at Heriot-Watt University and elsewhere. *The New Scientist*, 85, 1195, p 554. London.

12.5 'Expert Systems' in Educational Technology?

P Lefrere, R H W Waller and P Whalley
The Open University

Abstract: Artificial intelligence techniques are increasingly being applied to the codifications, in automated 'expert systems', of the knowledge of 'domain experts'. The development of such knowledge-based information systems is now being proposed in some areas of educational technology. After reviewing the basic features of systems which already exist a brief resumé of possible educational applications is given, and an outline of what could be involved in designing and implementing one particular expert system.

The term 'expert system' is relatively new, having surfaced in the literature as recently as 1977. You may be more familiar with previous terms, current in the 1960s, and covering more or less the same idea, such as 'knowledge engineering', or 'general problem-solving programmes'. All these terms have been invented by workers in the field of artificial intelligence, which has been defined by one of them as 'the science of making machines do things that would require intelligence if done by men'. (Minsky, 1968.)

It is sometimes argued that the fact that conventional digital computer programmes require all steps in a procedure to be made explicit means that there will always be some things we do, which computers will never be able to do. This is argued because the process of making anything explicit requires some recourse to tacit knowledge, knowledge which is indeterminate in the sense that its content cannot itself be completely explicitly stated (Polanyi, 1966).

However, while there will always be areas of knowledge which are felt to be essentially intuitive (or at least have yet to be made explicit enough for 'computerization') there exist many areas of previously tacit knowledge, both in the 'hard' sciences and elsewhere, which have already been formalized to the extent necessary for incorporation in so-called 'expert systems'.

But what is an expert system? The definition we prefer says: 'an expert system is a computing system which embodies organized knowledge concerning some specific area of human expertise . . . sufficient to be able to do duty as a skilful and cost-effective consultant'. (Michie, 1979.)

Such systems already exist in areas as disparate as mineral exploration and medical diagnosis. For example, one programme (PROSPECTOR) developed at Stanford Research Institute, can advise users when and where to drill for ore. Each consultation with the machine costs only 10 dollars in machine resources, a remarkable achievement when it is realized that questions put to the machine are not in general answered by simple calculation, but require solution by 'reasoning, search, pattern-matching, acquisition of new concepts, judgements of likelihood and revisions of judgement in the light of new data'. (Michie, 1979.)

A similar picture emerges when we look at medical systems, such as MYCIN. This programme simulates a medical consultant specializing in infectious diseases, which provides antibiotic therapy counselling, in consultations typically lasting 20 minutes, with doctors needing specialist help. The machine contains a series of clinical rules, which allow it to provide advice on the identification of micro-organisms and the prescription of appropriate antibiotics.

What do these rules look like? Here is an example of an 'IF-THEN' MYCIN rule for blood infections:

Rule 85

IF:

1. The site of the culture is blood, and
2. The gram stain of the organism is gramneg, and
3. The morphology of the organism is rod, and
4. The patient is a compromised host

THEN:

There is suggestive evidence (.6) that the identity of the organism is pseudomonas aeruginosa.

(*Note:* each rule supplied by an expert has associated with it a number between 0 and 1 — here it is .6 — which represents the expert's 'degree of certainty' in the validity of that rule.)

Users receive a summary of the system's recommendations at the end of the consultation, and have the opportunity at any time to question MYCIN's line of reasoning. The user can ask why certain conclusions were ruled out, or how conclusions were reached, or —if the system asks the user for information — the user can ask why it wants the information. This facility, being able to justify the advice given or the demands made, is necessary so that the programme's advice may be better appreciated, or rationally rejected. In the latter case, it is possible for users who are already expert to make general improvements in its consultative ability, without their needing to know anything about programming. They would do this by teaching the machine — by telling it about specific cases which are inadequately covered by its existing clinical rules, so that it can formulate, or be taught, new rules, to be validated using further cases (Shortliffe, 1976).

What is the nature of the knowledge that an expert brings to a problem? The areas in which expert systems are now, and will increasingly be, used tend to be those lacking a complete (or even partial) mathematical base. Knowledge in such fields is largely heuristic knowledge, 'good guesses' and 'good practice', experiential and uncertain. The experience of many of those who have devised expert systems indicates that such private knowledge can be uncovered in several ways, if one has available a large number of examples of an expert's work. First, we have simple introspection by the expert; an alternative would be the careful, painstaking analysis of a second person. Often that person has a knowledge of programming, and works intensively with the expert on a systematic analysis of the various examples, trying to extract workable MYCIN-type rules. Another intriguing possibility, currently the subject of much research work, is that the system itself might be capable of adding to, or refining, its own rules in the light of examples and counter-examples — that is, discovering some of its rules by induction (Quinlan, 1979). (Since many curricula emphasize the importance of concept acquisition, we wonder whether some day their associated teaching material might be evaluated in terms of the ability of an expert system to learn from it!)

There are several topics in educational technology which seem *prima facie* susceptible to embodiment in expert systems, for example questionnaire preparation (eg selection of aspects to be asked about; actual form of feedback questions); producing adjunct material (eg self-assessment questions and other study aids, such as study guides, objectives, etc); and advising on the presentation of ideas (eg sequencing; use of graphics; use of house style). While any of these could form an interesting case study, we have chosen to examine how one might codify the use by designers, editors and others of the last of these — the 'house style', defined by the British Standards Institution in BS 5261 as 'a set of standard practices governing design and composition associated with particular printing or publishing houses'. This term would cover a relatively large set of rules in knowledge-engineering terms, since it governs the use of spatial and graphic devices to articulate the structure of the discourse; and the visual organization of peripheral components of the text such as footnotes, an index, etc.

The publisher's notion of house style is central to the effectiveness of those charged with responsibility for the presentation of texts, such as educational technologists, designers and editors. But what is the nature of editing expertise? How much of it can be systematized and augmented by expert systems? Editing job functions have never been very well-defined, and there is sometimes confusion between commissioning editors, some of whom rarely handle a manuscript, and copy-editors, who do process manuscripts, but to varying degrees of detail and responsibility. Editorial training has always been a haphazard, on-the-job affair, and the problem is compounded firstly by the fast-changing nature of the printing industry and, secondly, by new techniques of presentation and evaluation suggested by educational research. Technical knowledge about printing processes needs continual updating, and in technical and educational publishing the editor is also expected to act as educational technologist — to predict and possibly even to measure the instructional impact of the text. This expanded knowledge-base demands a new type of 'super-editor', for whom the term 'transformer' has been suggested (MacDonald-Ross and Waller, 1976).

At the same time, the de-mystifying (de-skilling?) of printing processes (through office-based text-composition systems and automated reprography) is making the role of editor accessible to more people on a transitory basis. Authors can now prepare their own material for printing — and the soaring costs of academic publishing mean that in the future they will often be required to do so. Expert systems for editors, then, will have to cater for a wide range of user sophistication and for a wide range of tasks; they will be expected not only to make the skilled editor's job easier, but also to augment the limited experience and knowledge of the new or occasional editor (Lefrere and Whalley, 1979).

Table 1 categorizes some aspects of the skilled editor's knowledge. We can distinguish between non-explicit, personal knowledge of the language and culture and between relatively well-articulated public information about printing processes, grammar and so on; in between lies task-specific information about the job in hand that can be explicated to some degree, but which more often than not is carried in the editor's head.

Table 1 also distinguishes between the editor's information-base and the practical tasks for which this information is relevant. A categorization of expertise along a personal-public dimension is useful because it illustrates those areas in which we can expect an expert system to operate in either a weak or a strong consultative mode. ('Strong' and 'weak' refer here to the extent to which the system initiates its advisory or consultative function.) Listed below are four possible levels of consultative function:

1. User requests information or procedure.
2. System uses continually-changing 'menu' to indicate information or procedures available.
3. System volunteers detailed information.
4. System operates automatic procedure.

At level 1, the initial availability of information is indicated on a general index or contents list prepared by the system from its data-base. The user is expected to perceive his own need for advice, and select the appropriate keywords, since the system is unable to cope otherwise with browsing. The information provided at this level will typically be in a generalized form — checklists, references to other authorities, and even the direct provision of training or education material.

Levels 2 and 3 cover those aspects of text-editing that can be monitored but not evaluated by the system. For example, it can alert the user when he has used one of a number of words that appears in the system's memory as commonly

Information-base	Task	Consultative mode
Personal knowledge		
General world knowledge	query facts	none
General literacy (sensitivity to language, argument etc)	query argumentation, style etc	checklists, training packages
Repertoire of heuristics, precedents etc	integration of complex text structures	checklists, training packages
Task-specific knowledge		
Knowledge of target audience	query vocabulary and syntax; prepare access structures	evaluation advice; readability indices
Overview of text structure	layout decisions; prepare access structure	formatting advice; figure/text juxtaposition checks
Overview of task structure	job planning and monitoring	recommended task sequences; critical decision reminders
Memory of task-specific precedents	proof correction; consistency checks	display previous decisions if inconsistency suspected
Technical knowledge		
Spelling, grammar, high-agreement word usage	copy-editing, consistency checks	display apparent errors
Printing constraints	manuscript preparation, typographic specification	alert user to specification error or inadequacy; elicit and enforce technical constraints
Copyright law	check permissions, prepare acknowledgements	query permission status; compile acknowledgements list

Table 1. *Some aspects of the skilled editor's knowledge*

misspelt or misused, but only the user will make the decision. As soon as a page has been edited, or before it is edited, if desired, the system may offer level 3 facilities not in conventional house-styles, such as a readability index; again, it is up to the user to decide how much attention to pay to the advice offered. At level 2 the system can also keep a 'diary' of the job progress: previous decisions can be recalled, to ensure consistency; various manuscript preparation tasks can be related to a pre-specified schedule; headings or summaries can be isolated from the text to enable the editor to overview the text structure; and the alternative recommendations of several users (co-authors, perhaps) can be recalled for comparison.

Level 4 operations involve the delegation of tasks to the machine; decisions are then initiated and automatically operated by the system. On entry, for instance, the system will elicit a task-environment specification from the user. This will enable the system to narrow down its field of search and only offer appropriate advice. It may also lead to further level 4 operations. If the specification indicates that the user is preparing a manuscript for a particular photocomposer, the machine may actually block wrongly-specified typographic decisions, or translate them in to the nearest available option.

The four levels of man-machine interaction are important, not only because they reflect a realistic view of the extent to which language can be handled automatically or because they represent a respect for the professional skills of the user. They are also essential if the expert system is to be a learning system — the request and take-up rate of its advice will enable the system designer to adapt the system and the advice it offers has to be more sensitive to the needs of its users. These needs may be monitored via a simple statistical record of consultations and take-ups, but might also involve a 'suggestion box' system. The user, perhaps prompted by the system, would be able to enter requests for modifications or additions into the suggestions file, for later analysis and response by the system designer.

While this case study could be treated in much greater detail, it should be clear that expert systems for house-style will offer aids for a far wider range of tasks than has been the case so far. In addition to offering traditional advice about punctuation, spelling and word usage, they can also be used as a job management aid and in a training programme. The range of topics included with the traditional house-style advice will be extended too.

Information will be included about aspects of instructional design, illustrations, typography, and evaluation techniques (eg Waller, 1980). This is not so much a direct result of the application of computers but a continuation of an existing publishers' trend towards the provision of increasingly detailed guidance for authors.

It seems that many of the 'standard practices' in a task as complex as editing can be converted into MYCIN-type rules, either by existing experts or by machine-based induction from examining actual decisions made. By extension, many other aspects of an educational technologist's work may be influenced by the availability of such systems, in the 1990s if not before. What is less clear is whether it is possible for a machine to discover 'meta-rules' representing an expert's knowledge of 'what to tackle first' — strategy knowledge, showing how the expert analyses a complex task. Such rules will probably always need to be added by the original designer of the system, at the same time as an explanation facility is incorporated.

'. . . there is a moral imperative to provide accurate explanations to end-users whose intuitions about our systems are almost nil.' (Shortliffe, 1976). This imperative will apply until the standards of computer 'literacy' among the populace rise, for only then will users recognize the subjectivity (programmer-dependence) of a programme's judgements, or will see through 'plausibility tricks' such as the stored messages (YOU'RE WELCOME!) currently used by programmers intent on making machines seem friendly. Such caveats must be taken as seriously as the effects of conventional automation on privacy, work patterns and leisure. Only if 'intelligent' expert systems are seen to be helping people rather than replacing them, and as under their control, doing what they want, will these systems counteract dehumanizing attitudes in our society, rather than foster them (Boden, 1977). In the interim, we should consider the connotations of the term 'expert system', since the name a type of programme is given may determine the style in which it is written. Perhaps some other, less elitist term might be a happier choice.

References

Boden, M (1977) *Artificial Intelligence and Natural Man.* Harvester, NY.

Lefrere, P and Whalley, P (1979) Computer-assistance in multi-media educational publishing. *Proceedings of the PIRA/RPS International Conference on Trends in Educational Publishing.* PIRA, Leatherhead.

MacDonald-Ross, M and Waller, R H W (1976) The transformer. *The Penrose Annual,* **69,** pp 141-52.

Michie, D (1979) Expert systems — the cost-effective consultants of computing. *University of Edinburgh Bulletin,* **15,** 11, p 24.

Minsky, M L (1968) *Semantic Information Processing,* p 5. MIT Press, Cambridge, Mass.

Polanyi, M (1966) The logic of tacit inference. *Philosophy,* **41,** pp 1-18.

Quinlan, J R (1979) Discovering rules by induction from large collections of examples. In Michie, D (ed) *Expert Systems in the Micro-Electronics Age,* pp 168-201. Edinburgh University Press.

Shortliffe, E (1976) *Computer-Based Medical Consultations: MYCIN.* Elsevier, NY.

Waller, R H W (1980) On the nature of expertise in text transforming. IET Text-processing Paper 3. The Open University, Milton Keynes.

(Further information on such topics can be found in a series of mimeographed documents on text processing, produced by the Open University's Textual Communication Research Group. These are available direct from the authors).

Closing Address

L F Evans
The City University

(Norman Willis of the Council for Educational Technology was due to give the closing address, but was indisposed. Leo Evans, in the dual capacity of chairman of AETT and of the 1980 Conference, substituted for him.)

I recall very well five years ago standing to close the 1975 ETIC Conference. That conference was on the theme of 'l'Education Permanente — Continuing and Continuous Education', and I find it intriguing that this conference, which has as its theme 'Educational Technology to the Year 2000', has so many interactions with the theme of the 1975 Conference which, in 1975 perhaps, were very little recognized and realized. If there is one thing which has come through this conference it is the need for people continuously to update their information, their knowledge, their abilities, and also to learn, to develop, to educate for life and for leisure as well as for work and for learning. The interaction of these two conferences was, to some extent, intentional since, when we were planning this conference, we tried to establish a matrix in which there were cells concerned with learning on the job, learning about the job, learning for life generally, and learning for leisure and the environments of learning — both *institutional* (school, college, university, industrial), and *commercial* (home); and the whole, if you like, unstructured social learning environment were aspects of the future of educational technology which we hoped would be considered. In the event, I feel that we have been very fortunate that the conference participants, the conference speakers, and the workshop presenters have responded so well to the theme.

A number of organizations which previously have had some, but perhaps rather a tenuous, contact with the Association have come forward and have made major and important contributions. Dr Ashworth, who similarly was standing in, giving the opening address, set a tone which, without his knowing it, was running like a thread and has been very important during the conference. This was the whole question of training and the association of training and education. You may recall that he constructed the aphorism that education is what we can afford to do if we get our training right, and it has been, I think, illustrative of a recognition of this that we have had such a very welcome effective input from people who are so concerned with training. The demonstration we have had, the examples we have had, have been, I think, some of the finest that we have ever seen at any conference. This has been a very salutary lesson to those who consider themselves rather more educationists than trainers.

It is perhaps significant that the City University is considered in terms of the provision of audio-visual equipment, media facilities generally, and technician services, to be in official terms a well-found University for the teaching of between 2,500 and 3,000 undergraduate students. Yet we have found that with about 250 educational technologists, the services, the media and the equipment have been at full-stretch, and operating at full-bat, to meet those requirements; this, I think, is in no small way due to the presence of so many people who are concerned in 'training' as distinct from 'education' and who have come to this conference from industry, from commerce, from the services and from Government service.

We have had, I think, an enjoyable and extremely inspiring conference. We did not realize, when the conference was being planned, that in addition to many of the learning environments, we would learn about 'learning by tram'. Someone was wondering whether this meant that the process was an extremely narrow directive and restrictive. But those who heard Mia's explanation, and who have seen what has been going on, will recognize that it is in fact a very welcome innovatory and revelatory experience. I would like to commend, in fact, the way in which our European friends and colleagues have made such a useful and important contribution to this conference and, in particular, Philips (Netherlands) who have made such a tremendous display and who have also been prepared to share with the conference members ideas which, to use the English phrase, might still be regarded almost as only twinkles in their father's eye, and which has made such a very useful contribution to the conference as a whole.

Another innovation which I would like to commend is that, for the first time, academics have recognized that their whole being depends on the active existence and productivity of industry, and that we had a very useful and effective (although perhaps too little recognized) industrial panel which was an innovation which I hope will be considered and continued in other conferences.

I was, in effect, twelfth man, substituting for Norman Willis. He did, however, manage to communicate in writing some of his thoughts which, to use the Americanism, I would like to share with you.

At the beginning, we said we should look in a very realistic way at the possibilities for the future of educational technology, and we heard from the opening speaker, and we have seen through the conference, that a whole number of possibilities which were spoken of but virtually not believed in the early 1970s are now practical and useful and, more importantly, quite cheap and readily available systems and devices. Many of our children have 'Little Professor' calculators. Many of us recognize that, if we want to, we can have recipes on ready access instead of thumbing through greasy cookery books; we can have the instructions displayed on television while we are setting light to the kitchen, and I think that this is an illustration of the way in which learning in the home and learning for leisure has interacted with technology and is producing a whole number of interesting developments.

However, we must recognize (and this is Norman's thought) that the present situation for many in education looks and appears to be extremely gloomy. Cuts are being mentioned not only in Britain but throughout the world; when one speaks to people in education they are feeling apprehensive about periods of contraction and recession. This is a common experience when one is entering a period of major change and it is that major change, the threshold of which we are entering rather than standing and gazing at, which should give us hope and courage for the future. If we are, as we claim to be, in educational technology, expert specialists and facilitators in the design of teaching/learning methods and teaching/learning systems, we must have the courage to think forward and to think clearly; the courage to say that this systematic approach can make an enormously constructive contribution during the next two decades, and if we can show and justify that confidence, then I feel that this conference, and perhaps our Association and all who call themselves educational technologists, can look to the future with courage and with confidence. That is, I feel, an extremely encouraging and inspiring note on which I would like to conclude this conference.

Papers Not Included

Owing to technical reasons, reports of the following authors' presentations at ETIC '80 have not been included in this volume.

B **Alloway** *(Huddersfield Polytechnic):* Ergonomic Factors in the Learning Environment — Their Appreciation and Sympathetic Control.

T **Baum and G Wilkinson** *(Ulster Polytechnic):* The Evolution to a Contemporary Technology of Education.

G **Burt** *(The Open University):* Educational Technology at the Open University — Why Some Problems Don't Get Solved.

W D **Clarke** *(British Life Assurance Trust for Health and Medical Education, London)* and **M C Dowling** *(Worth Health Organization, Geneva): Workshop —* The Role of Educational Technology as a Support to Primary Health Care.

K **Donovan** *(Council for Educational Technology, London): Workshop Report:* Learning Resources in Colleges: Their Management and Organization.

L F **Evans** *(The City University, London): Workshop Report:* An Objectives Approach to Gustatory Discrimination.

M **Finbow** *(University of Surrey): Workshop Report:* Computer-Assisted Learning.

D **Freeman** *(Canadian Armed Forces): Workshop Report:* Improving Behavioural Objectives.

J **Green** *(Middlesex Polytechnic): Workshop Report:* Constructing Training Profiles for Jobs in Educational Technology.

G **Hay** *(TEACH, London):* Science Fiction — Your Role in its Application.

M **Hope** *(Council for Educational Technology, London): Workshop Report:* The Printing Press Game.

C McC **Jones** *(City and Guilds of London Institute):* Examination Boards into the 1980s.

C **Lavy** *(Israel Institute of Productivity):* Attitudes towards Industrial Participation.

D **Lewis** *(Surrey County Council): Workshop Report:* The Preparation of Games for Less Able Children in Mathematics and Phonics.

J S **Stoane** *(Kingsway Technical College, Dundee):* The Educational Technologist in Schools.

A J **Trott** *(Bulmershe College, Reading):* Requirements for Persons Interested in Overseas Consultancy Work.

M S **Yadav** and **M Seshadvi** *(University of Baroda, India):* The Modernization of Mathematics Instruction at Secondary School — A Developmental Project.

Table Indicating Articles with Common Themes

SECTION / PAPER	INDUSTRY (1)	TEACHING–LEARNING STRATEGIES I (2)	TEACHING–LEARNING STRATEGIES II (3)	COMPUTER–AIDED LEARNING (4)	COMPUTERS – OTHERS (5)	TEACHER TRAINING & STAFF DEVELOPMENT (6)	INFORMAL LEARNING (7)	DISTANCE LEARNING (8)	EVALUATION (9)	USES OF A/V (10)	THEORY (11)	THE FUTURE (12)
1·1	X		/	/								/
1·2	X			/						/		
1·3	X							/				
1·4	X							/				
1·5	X											
1·6	X						/	/				
2·1		X					/		/	/		
2·2		X										
2·3		X										
2·4		X						/				
2·5		X										
2·6		X	/						/			
2·7		X							/			
2·8		X		/								
2·9		X		/					/			
3·1		/	X									
3·2			X									
3·3			X									
3·4			X									/
3·5			X	/								
3·6			X									
4·1		/	X									
4·2		/	X									
4·3		/	X									
4·4			X									
4·5	/		X						/			
4·6		/	X									
5·1					X							
5·2					X							
5·3					X							
5·4					X							
5·5					X							
5·6					X							
6·1		/				X				/		
6·2				/		X				/		
6·3						X				/		
6·4	/					X						
6·5						X			/			
6·6						X	/					

Table Indicating Articles with Common Themes *(continued)*

SECTION / PAPER	INDUSTRY (1)	TEACHING–LEARNING STRATEGIES I (2)	TEACHING–LEARNING STRATEGIES II (3)	COMPUTER-AIDED LEARNING (4)	COMPUTERS – OTHERS (5)	TEACHER TRAINING & STAFF DEVELOPMENT (6)	INFORMAL LEARNING (7)	DISTANCE LEARNING (8)	EVALUATION (9)	USES OF A/V (10)	THEORY (11)	THE FUTURE (12)
7·1							X	/				
7·2						/	X					
7·3			/				X	/	/			
7·4		/					X					
7·5		/					X	/				
7·6							X					
8·1		/						X				
8·2		/		/				X		/		/
8·3	/							X				
8·4		/						X				
8·5								X				
9·1				/					X			
9·2		/							X			
9·3								/	X			
9·4		/						/	X			
9·5						/			X			
9·6									X			
9·7	/								X			
9·8	/								X			
9·9									X			
10·1				/					/	X		/
10·2		/								X		
10·3		/								X		
10·4										X		
10·5		/								X		
10·6										X		
10·7										X		
11·1		/									X	
11·2		/									X	
11·3				/		/					X	
11·4		/									X	
11·5		/									X	
11·6											X	
12·1				/						/		X
12·2	/		/	/								X
12·3												X
12·4							/	/		/		X
12·5					/		/					X

Keyword Index

Author Index